# THE NEW
# Aerobics for Women

**Bantam Books by Kenneth H. Cooper, M.D.**

AEROBICS
AEROBICS FOR WOMEN (with Mildred Cooper)
THE AEROBICS WAY
THE NEW AEROBICS
THE AEROBICS PROGRAM FOR TOTAL WELL-BEING
RUNNING WITHOUT FEAR

Dr. Kenneth H. Cooper's Preventive Medicine Program

CONTROLLING CHOLESTEROL

# THE NEW
# Aerobics for Women

Kenneth H. Cooper, M.D., M.P.H.,
and
Mildred Cooper

BANTAM BOOKS
Toronto • New York • London • Sydney • Auckland

NOTE

The information contained in this book is intended to complement, not replace, the advice of your own physician, whom you should always consult about your individual needs. You should always consult with your own physician before starting any medical treatment, exercise regimen, or diet.

THE NEW AEROBICS FOR WOMEN

*A Bantam Book*

*PRINTING HISTORY*

*Evans edition published June 1972*
*Bantam paperback edition / January 1973*
*41 printings through January 1988*
*Revised Bantam trade edition / July 1988*


*Book design by Lurelle Cheverie.*
*Interior art by Chris Cunningham.*


LIBRARY OF CONGRESS
Library of Congress Cataloging-in-Publication Data

Cooper, Kenneth H.
The new aerobics for women / Kenneth H. Cooper and Mildred Cooper.
—Rev. Bantam trade ed.
p. cm.
Revision of: Aerobics for women / Mildred Cooper and Kenneth H. Cooper, 1972.
Includes index.
ISBN 0-553-34513-3
1. Aerobic exercises. 2. Exercise for women. I. Cooper, Mildred. II. Cooper, Mildred. Aerobics for women. III. Title.
RA781.15.C6625 1988
613.7'1'024042—dc19 88-966
CIP

*Published simultaneously in the United States and Canada*

*Bantam Books are published by Bantam Books, a division of Bantam Doubleday Dell Publishing Group, Inc. Its trademark, consisting of the words "Bantam Books" and the portrayal of a rooster, is Registered in U.S. Patent and Trademark Office and in other countries. Marca Registrada. Bantam Books, 666 Fifth Avenue, New York, New York 10103.*

PRINTED IN THE UNITED STATES OF AMERICA

FG 9 8 7 6 5 4 3 2 1

## Dedication

To those women who have been exercising for years because they know that it makes them feel good.

May this book add a scientific dimension to their feelings and help to explain that wonderful, symbiotic relationship between regular exercise and a heightened sense of well-being.

## Acknowledgments

Many people have contributed to this book. Unfortunately, to express adequately my appreciation would require most of its pages. Yet, a few deserve special recognition and personal thanks.

Jacqueline Thompson, a very talented writer, helped immensely in the research organization and final preparation of the book. Her recommendations and overall contributions were invaluable.

Amy Jones and Kay Mikesky, outstanding leaders of the women's programs at our Aerobics Activity Center in Dallas, Texas, helped with some of the new exercise programs and added their recommendations regarding safety, including proper warm-up and cool-down techniques. Both of these knowledgeable young women are held in high esteem by such prestigious organizations as the American Association for Fitness and Business (AFB) and the International Dance Education Association (IDEA).

Cindy Kleckner and Georgia Kostas, outstanding clinical nutritionists who direct all of the dietary programs at the Cooper Clinic, contributed the new information in the dietary sections.

Barbara Bartolomeo coordinated the typing of the manuscript. And, as always, my personal secretary, Harriet Guthrie, makes my life tolerable with schedule adjustments when I am working on a book.

Bruce Peschel, a multitalented artist and member of our Aerobics Center staff, was responsible for all of the drawings and charts. Bette Mulley helped in collecting and organizing the research papers and publications. Dr. Steven Blair, Director of Epidemiology for the Institute for Aerobics Research, reviewed the manuscript and made major contributions to the final book, particularly in the area of injury prevention.

My editorial adviser for over twenty years, Herbert Katz, helped in all aspects of this book from its inception to its publication. And my editor at Bantam Books, Coleen O'Shea, helped enormously regarding direction, content, and the underlying theme of the book.

To all these people—and many others far too numerous to list—I want to say again, "many, many thanks."

—Kenneth H. Cooper, M.D.

# Contents

# Preface

# Aerobics— It's Come a Long Way

Before 1968, the word *aerobic* was used as an adjective and was defined as "growing in air or in oxygen." A microscopic organism—such as a bacteria—which could live and grow in the presence of oxygen was called an "aerobe."

With the publication of my first book, *Aerobics,* in 1968, the word was used for the first time as a noun. I used it to refer to those exercises that were endurance in nature and required increased amounts of oxygen for prolonged periods. Examples were walking, running, stationary running, cycling, swimming, and competitive sports such as basketball, handball, and squash.

Aerobic dancing didn't exist back then. But by the early 1970s, aerobic dancing began gaining popularity based primarily on the work and the promotion of Jackie Sorensen. In fact, her first program was called *Jackie's Aerobic Dance.*

Later, many others—primarily women—started their own aerobic dance programs. But it wasn't until Jane Fonda came out with her videotapes that aerobic dancing literally exploded.

Despite the fact that my books on aerobics have now been translated into thirty-four languages, I'd venture that the majority of people today believe that "aerobics" implies only aerobic dancing. In *The Aerobics Program for Total Well-Being,* published in 1982, I classified thirty-one different exercises as aerobic, and aerobic dancing was only one. That's how popular aerobic dancing had become.

Ultimately, I see the pendulum shifting back to the original meaning of the word. For example, I am pleased to see that in the 1986 edition of the *Oxford English Dictionary,* the word *aerobics* is defined as: "a method of physical exercise for producing beneficial changes in the respiratory and circulatory systems by activities which require only a modest increase of oxygen intake and so can be maintained."

In 1968, I did not anticipate that many women would be interested in aerobics, so my first book was written primarily for young men. The interest in *Aerobics* and the acceptance of the program by older men necessitated the publication of the second book, *The New Aerobics,* in 1970. Still, the book was aimed at men, and many women expressed concern that nothing had been written for them.

That's when my wife, Millie, and I decided to collaborate on a book exclusively for women. And so *Aerobics for Women* was released in 1972. As many of my women readers will recall, the book was strictly a motivational work, filled with personal, anecdotal stories. It had very little scientific information. But as the enthusiasm for aerobics has continued over the years, so has the quest for knowledge. No longer is there a need for a "let's get started" book. There is, however, a great need for a book filled with information and facts.

I would compare this book with *The Aerobics Program for Total Well-Being*. The major difference—this one is strictly for women.

I have tried to touch on the subjects of concern to women who exercise. In many of these areas, there were only theories in 1972. Much research has been done since then, so what you are about to read are well-documented facts. For over twenty years I have been trying to bridge the gap between fadism and scientific legitimacy in using exercise in the practice of medicine. I believe this book takes us a step closer to that goal.

I hope that you will find this book both interesting *and* motivational. But, even more important, I hope you find it an invaluable addition to your exercise library. It's my aim to see you exercise safely, enjoyably, and effectively for the rest of a long, healthy, and active life.

—Kenneth H. Cooper, M.D., M.P.H.

# Introduction

# You've Liberated Your Mind; How about Your Body?

When Ken and I wrote *Aerobics for Women* in 1972 the world was a different place—especially for women.

The readers of that book were largely homemakers, and of those women who did have careers, only a minority had achieved the prominence in the business and professional worlds that so many women have today.

To most of the readers of that earlier book, *exercise* was almost a foreign word. Aerobics was an even stranger concept: it was something they knew a little about from magazine articles, and was something they associated with men. After all, it was the men they knew who had donned running shoes and taken to the streets for daily workouts. Aerobics didn't seem to apply to women.

I'm happy to report that *Aerobics for Women* convinced millions of women—of all ages and lifestyles—that aerobics is for everybody and represents a healthier lifestyle. It's a goal within any persevering person's grasp.

They also learned that the amount of time it takes to achieve cardiovascular fitness is minimal. A half-hour, four or five days a week, will suffice. For increasingly busy women, this is probably aerobics' biggest selling point.

I've always thought women the more remarkable sex. I look at my female friends and marvel at their ability to keep their heads above water in the whirlpools of activity that comprise their daily lives—career, husband, children, a house to maintain. The demands made on them are enormous. Yet they still seem to cope.

How?

Many of them tell me that aerobics is a large part of their secret. Of course, they don't have to tell me. It's been my secret, too, for some eighteen years now.

You may be asking yourself how you can do it all, how you can fulfill all the roles you have to play in life, meeting the needs of the people you love and still having time and energy left for yourself, for exercise.

A lot of women, including myself, share your pressure-cooker lifestyle. We've got incredible time problems—and often other kinds of problems too. But believe me when

I say aerobics is part of the solution to those problems. It's part of the solution for two big reasons and many smaller ones (all of which you'll learn about in this book).

*Reason 1:* Aerobics will keep you healthy and fit. Without good health, you can't meet your responsibilities. And if you can't meet your responsibilities, you really will be letting down those you love.

*Reason 2:* Regular aerobic exercise will release that daily tension buildup that threatens to undermine your emotional and physical well-being. Aerobics is one of nature's greatest natural tranquilizers. It's a way to clear your head and keep your composure in the worst situations imaginable.

For those of you who haven't yet discovered aerobics, I hope this book will introduce you to a new world of possibilities, not all of them purely physical. But I mustn't get ahead of myself. My story in chapter 1, I think, speaks for itself.

—MILLIE COOPER

# 1

# One Woman's Exercise Odyssey

You think you're leery of exercise. I doubt your skepticism could equal mine at the beginning of my marriage. For years I was convinced that my husband Ken's commitment to exercise was an eccentricity. It certainly was *not* something I wanted to emulate.

That was twenty-eight years ago, to be exact. And both my thinking and my body—because of exercise—have changed a lot since then.

I wish I could say that Ken's powers of persuasion and example made me into a runner early in our marriage, but I can't. In fact, when Ken was getting his master's degree at the Harvard School of Public Health in the early 1960s and training for the Boston Marathon, I still viewed his daily running as an embarrassment.

Running wasn't a popular sport then. I can remember how I felt when we'd go to dinner parties and people would say, "Isn't your husband that nut who runs all the time?"

They said it jokingly but it was no joke to me. I'd smile and nod my head, all the while wishing Ken would drop the idea of a career in preventive medicine and exercise physiology and take up something more normal. I'd look at Ken across the room and think, *Why can't you become a pediatrician or some other specialty that people understand?*

Little did I, or anyone, at those parties know that "the nut" would just a few years later become a pioneer in the preventive medicine field and write a book that would inspire millions of people to follow in his footsteps.

In truth, I didn't start running until everyone else in America did—after Ken's first book, *Aerobics,* was published in 1968. Ken was still in the service then and we were assigned to Lackland Air Force Base in San Antonio, Texas. The overwhelming response to *Aerobics* was a surprise to everyone, especially us.

For years I'd been ignoring Ken's entreaties to me about exercise. Playing on the girl's basketball team in high school had been the extent of my athletic endeavors. Exercise and sports were wonderful for schoolchildren and professional athletes, I thought, but not for a grown woman.

I continued to resist also because I felt that what Ken wanted was too radical. He didn't just want another runner in the family—he wanted me to adopt fitness as a total lifestyle. It would mean a commitment to daily exercise as well as a healthier diet.

Another thing held me back. I'd recently given birth to our daughter Berkley and I was about 15 pounds overweight. I thought, *Workout clothes are the last thing I want people to see me in. I'll look as dumpy as I feel.*

However, I began to pay more attention when Ken said that exercise, combined with a moderate diet, would help me lose weight. I was, and still am, very vain. But it wasn't that argument that finally struck home. It was something else Ken said—about my heart.

Ken made his point graphically. One evening as we were lying in bed, Ken took my pulse. My resting heart rate was 80 beats per minute. Ken's was 50. *A 30-beat difference!*

"Honey," Ken said, "do you realize that while we're sleeping tonight, your heart will beat ten thousand more times than mine? Even though our hearts are pumping the same amount of blood, it takes yours that much more work and effort to do the job because you're not in good physical condition. At the rate it's going, your heart will wear out much faster than mine."

I was stunned. Visions of Ken as a widower came into focus, followed by scenes of Ken at the altar with the next Mrs. Cooper. I finally fell asleep hours later, comforted by the thought that it was within my power to do something about my racing pulse.

Because I'd typed the manuscript for *Aerobics,* I knew a lot about exercise theory—including the fact that exercise, over time, reduces your resting heart rate. I was learning even more about the subject every day while working as Ken's correspondence secretary. With our daughter, Berkley, looking on from her playpen, I had been typing away for months, helping Ken answer the hundreds of letters he got from readers of *Aerobics.*

The letters had started as a trickle but soon had turned into an avalanche. Many were filled with questions; others were moving testimonials about how aerobics had changed a person's life. Those letters from real people all over the country—and later, the world—had a great impact on me.

If these strangers could follow my husband's advice, why didn't I?

When I finally capitulated, Ken was overjoyed and extremely supportive. We discussed the various aerobic exercise options—walking, swimming, cycling, stair climbing, rope skipping—but I chose jogging. Because of our baby, Berkley, I wasn't free to go to a gym or a pool every day, which was fine with me since I don't like water sports. Running appealed to me because of its efficiency: for the least expenditure of time and disruption of my daily routine, I could achieve the most aerobic benefits.

I'll never forget that first attempt. Ken took me by one hand and gripped Berkley's stroller with the other and steered us down the street, our blond cocker spaniel lumbering along behind. Ken could walk as fast as I could jog. Knowing I needed encouragement, Ken continued to accompany me for months, often pushing the stroller while I alternately jogged and walked alongside them.

The beginning of any exercise endeavor is hard. I'd be lying if I said I instantly fell in love with running. To this day, I'm not in love with running, but I am in love with the results—starting with the pride of my husband.

I've felt that pride for years now. I can't tell you how good it still makes me feel when I hear Ken tell people, "Millie is a remarkable woman. At age 51, she can stay on the treadmill for 23 minutes. That means, compared to other women we've tested at the Cooper Clinic, she's among the top 1 percentile in her age group."

While I admit that pleasing my husband and slimming my figure were my initial goals, it wasn't long before I began to see other virtues in regular exercise. Amazingly, all the physical changes I'd read about in Ken's book started to happen to me too. I felt better, for one thing. My body relaxed. I hadn't realized how constricted I'd been until the tension began to drain out of me through running.

In those early days, I always ran in the late afternoon. Because I was cooped up in the house, I often found myself getting headachy, irritable, and lethargic by four o'clock. My afternoon run dissipated those end-of-the-day blahs. It was a welcome change.

I also learned what a good night's rest meant for the first time in my life. I fell asleep easily and slept more soundly than ever before.

My resting heart rate did just what Ken predicted—dropped from 80 to 57 beats per minute. I noticed that I was breathing easier and I was seldom out of breath anymore.

But the thing that thrilled me most was my weight loss. *I shrunk two dress sizes!* I went from a size 12 to an 8. Hippiness, I'd always felt, was one of the burdens I had to bear in life. In the hip area alone, I took off 4 inches.

The best thing about shedding those pounds was that I hadn't felt the deprivation I'd experienced previously on restrictive diets. Sure, I did change my eating habits when I started running. I dropped my calorie intake to about 1,000 a day; it even dropped as low as 850 for a short time. But it wasn't hard to do, because, I discovered, running depresses my appetite.

Ken explained that it wasn't the running alone that was trimming my figure. It was the combination of eating fewer calories and expending more through exercise. Exercise contributes to weight loss in other ways too: it speeds up the metabolism, which makes the body burn fat faster. And it firms muscles, toning up those pockets of flab every woman hates to see.

Naturally, as I began to look better, I gained more self-confidence. But there were other psychological benefits as well.

Before Berkley was born, I'd held various positions in the field of social work and I knew the sense of achievement that comes from a job well done. Then I became a full-time homemaker and discovered, firsthand, why women express mixed feelings about this role. Suddenly, I was alone with a small child all day. I had no adults to talk to, and no one was patting me on the back or making me feel I was making a contribution to a team effort.

Running was something I was doing for myself. It was a reward of sorts. It was mine—*my* hobby, *my* way of releasing tension, *my* vehicle for staying fit and improving my looks. Nobody could take it away from me. Running also gave me a greater sense of self at a time in my life when every move I made seemed to revolve around my family.

My running ability increased slowly and steadily. During each workout, I'd set a goal for myself—running a little longer that day, getting three houses farther down the street without stopping, and so on. It took me about six months before I could jog a mile nonstop. It sounds like nothing now, but it seemed a milestone then. I'm sure I could have progressed more rapidly, but my motivation was still lacking at that time.

Our life changed drastically soon after I started my aerobics program. Ken left the Air Force and we moved to Dallas, where Ken hoped to set up an independent practice focusing on preventive medicine and exercise. It seemed a crazy step to take, since Ken had no prospects or contacts in this new, strange city and I was pregnant with our second child, Tyler.

It was a stressful time and running helped us both get through it. But we no longer exercised together because of our differing schedules.

I firmly believe that there are seasons of exercise. As women mature and their lives change, exercise takes on different connotations. Depending on their circumstances, women change their exercise goals, often switching the type of exercise in the process.

I've stuck to running, but it's meant different things to me at different times. In our early years in Dallas when I was housebound with two small children, it became more than a physical fitness program: it was my social outlet.

I found eight other women runners in our neighborhood. We'd gather every weekday morning at five-thirty in front of my house and walk to a nearby school, where we'd run 4 miles, chattering away the whole time. It's the only period in my life that I've ever run regularly with other people, and it was a great deal of fun.

As the decade wore on, that group slowly dispersed, and my life with Ken changed too. After the early years of struggle, Ken's practice was thriving. He had written several more books, including *Aerobics for Women,* on which I collaborated. They were all translated into other languages and circulated worldwide. That brought invitations from foreign governments asking Ken to spearhead drives to promote physical fitness in their countries.

Our globe-trotting promotional trips continue to this day. We both enjoy them very much. We appear on local radio and TV programs and speak at various meetings and banquets. We also participate in running events, all the while meeting the people and mingling with top government officials and the heads of major corporations.

Yes, today I too am a speaker. I speak about aerobics to major corporate and convention audiences. I always talk about my own running program, how it's changed over the years and what it's done for me.

In retrospect, I think running has actually done more for me on an emotional and spiritual level than it's done for me physically—not to belittle the fact that it's helped me reduce to a very slim size 6. Yes, you read that right. Aerobics has helped me, a

5-foot-5-inch 125-pound woman, move from a size 12 dress some eighteen years ago to a size 6 today.

Running has helped me become more self-confident. With that theme in mind, I could speak for hours about the I-can-do-it attitude that exercise fosters.

Let's face it. It takes a great deal of self-discipline to exercise regularly, especially in the beginning when it's uncomfortable and you've got lots of aches and pains in your body. It also takes perseverance.

If you've got those two traits, you've got what it takes not only to stay with an exercise program but to build a happier life for yourself. And I think that's a key benefit of exercise—it emphasizes the character traits that get you through life's ups and downs.

It's certainly done that for me. I feel more alive, more attractive, more in control of myself, and younger today, at age 51, than I felt at age 36. Running has taught me things about myself and brought me a quality of life I didn't know existed before.

I probably sound horribly self-righteous about all this. But I guarantee you'll feel virtuous and smug too if you can stick with an exercise regimen over the long haul, in all kinds of weather, no matter what obstacles are placed in your way. If you can do this, even if other areas of your life are haywire, you'll experience a marvelous sense of control. And you'll discover that the traits you bring to bear on your exercise program can be used in other areas of your life. You can gain control of virtually any problem in your life if you set your mind to it.

My running program today is a solo endeavor. It falls in the same category with brushing my teeth in the morning: it's a matter of personal hygiene. I would no more start a weekday without running than I would without brushing my teeth. Skipping either one, I'd feel "fuzzy."

My running routine works because I've made it an integral part of my life. I fall out of bed at six-thirty every weekday morning. I throw on some old clothes, don't bother with makeup or combing my hair, do a few warm-up stretches, and then set off down the street, never knowing what route I'll take that morning.

During my run, I rid my mind of any worries I woke up thinking about. Some people are midnight worriers. But to me, troubles always seem the most nettlesome when I first wake up.

As I wend my way around the neighborhood, I plan my day. I might think about what I'm going to fix for dinner that night, a forthcoming speaking engagement, or errands I must do that day. One thing I never think about, though, is the process of running itself. Nor do I divert myself with earphones hooked up to a radio or cassette player. Personally, I think it's dangerous to have your hearing out of commission when you're running on streets where cars, even if infrequent, pass by.

On most mornings I run 3 miles, but occasionally I get distracted by my thoughts and run even farther. On our promotional trips, for example, I participate in 10K races (6.2 miles) all the time. What I haven't run yet is a marathon (26 miles). It's one of those things on my mental to-do list.

While I haven't felt the enormous sense of accomplishment that must come from finishing a marathon, I still feel great satisfaction every morning as I round the bend in the road leading back to our house. I'm pleased with myself because I know I've already accomplished one thing and I'm eager to get on with my day.

I always cool down for 5 minutes before I go into the house. I may do a bit of yard work or leaf through the morning paper awaiting me on our front lawn.

My workout is officially over when I finally go inside and settle down with a cup of coffee and a piece of fresh fruit for a half-hour of Bible study. Then I hop in the shower and I'm dressed and ready to start the day by eight o'clock.

This morning ritual is simple enough, but to me it's golden. It gives me the inspiration and fortitude to tackle any event of the day, no matter how challenging. Everyone has coping devices. This is one of mine.

I've described my morning ritual to you to make a point: *You'll never have a successful exercise program until it fits into your lifestyle.*

At this point in my life, exercise is a rejuvenating experience, a way to recharge my batteries. Undoubtedly it will have different connotations for you. Just as I could no more put on makeup and make myself look presentable enough to exercise at a health club, you might be horrified at the idea of emulating my routine.

Ken and I have written this book to inspire you to take up aerobics. We've laid out all the sensible reasons for exercising. But we also want you to look into yourself and understand *why* you're exercising, beyond the mere goal of improving your physical fitness.

We think aerobics is a very personal experience. We also think that staying fit isn't enough motivation to keep the average healthy adult on the exercise track. But we also know that if you stay with an aerobics program long enough—at least beyond the crucial three-month start-up point—you'll discover values that you never dreamed possible. They'll surprise and delight you. And they aren't all physical.

But don't take our word for it. Try it yourself.

# 2
# Aerobic Exercise—It's as Natural as Breathing

Here you are, reading this book. Your mind is working but your muscles aren't.

It may surprise you to learn that you're in an aerobic state right now. You're breathing, after all. And breathing is what aerobics is all about.

Cut off your oxygen supply, even for a short period, and you die. That's because your body cannot stockpile oxygen. New supplies of this essential gas must be pumped throughout your system at all times. This means when you're sleeping; when you're awake and moving around; or when you're exerting yourself in the act of exercising.

## Aerobics Defined

Let's get down to basics. Just what is aerobics anyway, and why is it so good for you?

Aerobic exercises are endurance activities—which *don't* require excessive speed or strength but *do* require that you place demands on your cardiovascular system.

There are many forms of aerobic exercise. Brisk walking, running, swimming, dancing, and cycling are the most popular, but there are others too.

Here's the point. All these forms of exercise have one common objective: *to increase the maximum amount of oxygen that your body can process within a given time.* This is called your *aerobic capacity.* It involves your ability to rapidly take in large amounts of air; your ability to forcefully circulate large volumes of blood; and your ability to effectively deliver increased supplies of oxygen, via the blood, to all parts of your body.

For your body to do these things, you need healthy lungs, a powerful heart, and a well-developed vascular system. Because aerobic capacity is an accurate reflection of the health of these vital organs, it is one of the best indicators of your overall physical fitness.

## A Heaving Chest and Pounding Heart Are Good for You

Aerobic exercises force your body to consume a lot of oxygen. That's why they're termed "aerobic." In short, they make you huff and puff. Believe it or not, a heaving chest and the pounding heart that goes with it are good for you. In fact, "good for you" is too mild a phrase. It could extend your life. And it will surely make you feel better and look better too.

## Your Physiological Response to Aerobics

Aerobics keeps that marvelous machine called "the human body" running smoothly as this mini-tour will show.

• **Lungs.** The air you breathe is about 21 percent oxygen and 79 percent nitrogen. Your body accepts the oxygen and rejects the rest.

Your lungs do the filtering. They take in air, extract the vital oxygen, and move it on into your bloodstream. Think of oxygen as an igniting agent that can't do its appointed job until it reaches its final destination in tissue cells. There it helps to convert food into energy and new tissue.

When you breathe more deeply during aerobics, you're exercising the muscles surrounding your lungs—the muscles of your rib cage and diaphragm. As these muscles increase in strength and elasticity, two processes become more streamlined: you can inhale more air into your lungs and you can exhale more carbon dioxide out of your body. Over time, your lungs gradually open up more and more space for this process of oxygen extraction and removal of carbon dioxide. The better condition your lungs are in, the more efficient this intake-and-discard process becomes.

• **Bloodstream.** To visualize the positive effect that aerobics has on your body, try to think of it as one vast production system.

On a microscopic level, your body is made up of a multitude of individual cell "factories" that manufacture the end products of energy and new or replacement body tissue. To do this, these factories need raw materials. Your bloodstream is the transport operation that gets these crucial supplies to your cell factories and carts away useless byproducts.

Your bloodstream transports two types of substances—life-sustaining oxygen and foods and such gaseous waste products as carbon dioxide. These waste products, just like garbage in your house, must be disposed of. Otherwise they become health hazards that eventually will kill you.

• **Tissue.** Not all cells in your body are the same. On the contrary, your body is composed of many different types of cells. Each different type is known, collectively, as "tissue." There are bone, muscle, and nerve tissue, for instance. The cells of these different kinds of tissue are the ultimate destination of the foods you eat and the oxygen you inhale. But how to get them there?

If your bloodstream is the body's transport system, let's pretend that the red blood cells are individual ships. They circulate throughout your body twenty-four hours a day, carrying oxygen and carbon-dioxide cargo. From your lung tissue, for example, red blood cells take on oxygen. When they reach their tissue destinations, they dump their oxygen payload and refill with carbon-dioxide waste, immediately carrying this noxious gas back to your lungs for disposal during exhalation.

Aerobics has an important impact on the distribution process just described. Over time, aerobic exercise increases your blood volume, thus the number of red-blood-cell "ships" available to transport extra oxygen to your cell factories. The end result: you feel more energetic and alert. Why? Because more oxygen is on hand to produce energy, whether it's producing that energy from food you just ate or body fat you are burning. Either way, oxygen is the igniting agent that makes possible the food-and-fat–burning process.

• **Blood vessels.** There are many other physiological benefits you experience from aerobics. One has to do with your vascular system.

This time, picture your body's blood vessels as a complicated network of oceans and rivers and streams upon which those red-blood-cell ships travel. Here is what happens to this network when the volume of blood in your body increases:

Through a process called "vascularization," oxygen-enriched blood becomes an empire builder. It starts carving into tissue even more intricate and extensive blood-vessel supply routes. Naturally, as the number of blood vessels in your body grows, the distribution of oxygen to your tissues improves dramatically.

Vascularization is largely responsible for a phenomenon referred to by athletes as "plateaus of progress." When people begin a conditioning program, they often agonize for weeks. Then, practically overnight, the exercise routine becomes much more effortless. The obvious conclusion is that new blood vessels aren't created one by one, but one network at a time.

There's yet another merit of aerobic exercise—expect it to lower your blood pressure. It does this in several ways.

First, count on that greater quantity of blood coursing through your body to enlarge and tone up your vessels and make them more pliable to pressure.

Aerobics also helps your body develop a more favorable ratio of "good cholesterol" (high-density lipoprotein—HDL) to "bad cholesterol" (low-density lipoprotein—LDL). HDL cholesterol is believed to act as an arterial cleanser, scrubbing out clogged arteries. This lessens the possibility of arteriosclerosis, or hardening of the arteries, a precursor to strokes and heart attacks.

Additionally, superoxygenated blood helps the body metabolize fat faster. When a well-conditioned person eats a meal high in fat content, the fat doesn't circulate as long in the bloodstream, so it is less likely to collect and form a crust on the artery walls. Cleaner vessels offer less resistance to blood flow, hence the lower pressure.

There's one final point about metabolism in general:

To keep your cell factories running at maximum efficiency, you must stoke them with the right proportions of food and oxygen. Many people shovel in too much food and deliver too little oxygen to burn it. That's when food stacks up in cellular "storerooms" and people gain weight. Before long, they're obese, not realizing that lack of exercise was a key contributing factor to their plight.

• **Heart.** The heart muscle is the supreme ruler over your body's vast production system. This powerful pump keeps your blood circulating around the clock. More and faster circulating blood means your tiny cellular factories stay well supplied at all times with the food and oxygen they need to function optimally.

Aerobic exercise is just about the best thing you can do for your heart. Just as vascularization helps other tissues of the body, it does wonders for your heart's muscle tissue. Nowhere is this saturation coverage of large healthy blood supply routes more crucial than in the heart.

A heart made healthy through aerobics is a heart with a lightened workload. It's a more productive heart, which means it can do more work with less effort. It beats fewer times a day than a deconditioned heart but pumps more blood with each beat.

Less work but more output. What accounts for this apparent contradiction? Your heart likes to work. And the more it works, the stronger and larger and more efficient it becomes.

For example, an athlete's heart is usually slightly larger than that of a normal person, is far more resilient, and does its job with amazing ease. Of course, it would be a mistake to think that all enlarged hearts are healthy ones. Some grow that way to compensate for a deficiency in the cardiovascular system or a deformity of a heart valve. Such hearts are terribly *in*efficient pumps because, despite large exterior size, they've got small interior space, affording minimal room for blood to course in and out.

However, people with normal hearts who are merely out of shape are another matter. Their hearts are relatively small and weak because, like any other muscles that are not exercised properly, they atrophy somewhat.

The critical test comes when you measure an out-of-shape woman's *resting heart rate* with that of a woman who exercises aerobically. Likely the inactive woman has a heart rate of 80 or more. That translates to 80 beats per minute, times 60 minutes, which equals 4,800 beats per hour. Over a 24-hour period, that's an astounding 115,200 beats. Hard work for that poor heart!

Compare these figures with the average resting heart rate of an amateur female runner: approximately 60 beats per minute. Do the same arithmetic and the result is 86,400 beats per day. That's almost a 30,000-beat-a-day difference. Now you tell me whose heart is working harder.

Ahhh, you say. Forget about resting heart rate. What happens when these two women exert themselves? What happens to their respective heart rates then?

Here, we're talking about *maximum heart rate.* Sure, both conditioned and deconditioned women's hearts beat faster during strenuous activity, but that discrepancy in their resting heart rates is still there. Healthy hearts will peak out at 190 beats per minute or less—and there won't be any strain—while poorly conditioned hearts in young women may race as high as 220 beats or more per minute and the strain will be enormous, approaching the danger level.

We see this difference time and again when we put people on treadmills. Those with healthy, conditioned hearts can do literally twice as much work—by either running twice as fast or twice as long—with a lower heart rate than people with deconditioned hearts. Some women long-distance runners have even been able to run to exhaustion on our treadmills, yet their heart rates never exceeded 170 to 180 beats per minute.

What a lowered heart rate amounts to is this: at rest, your heart conserves energy, saving at least 15,000 beats per day. And during exhausting activity, it still avoids the strain induced by beating too fast.

However, if you're about to begin an aerobics program after a long period of inactivity, bear this in mind: during the first few weeks, maybe even months, of regular aerobics, you may tire every time. But, as your heart and body begin to adapt to your new regimen, this will change. Eventually, you will get all the exercise you need without feeling any discomfort at all.

• **Skeletal muscles.** Aerobics' key targets are the essential organs—the heart, lungs, and blood vessels. But this form of exercise will do plenty to improve the health of the skeletal muscles as well.

Skeletal muscles are the ones that show, the ones responsible for slimming waistlines and creating curves in the right places. Many women mistakenly think that the way to attain a properly proportioned body is through calisthenics, weight lifting, isometrics, and other exercises aimed directly at these muscles. We're sorry to disillusion you. While this is partially true, it's not the whole story.

Here's the rub: people who are aerobically fit are almost always muscularly fit too. But those who are muscularly fit are not necessarily aerobically fit. This goes back to the process of vascularization that aerobics fosters.

If muscle building is your only form of exercise, you'll build muscle—thicker, knottier muscle tissues with fewer, rather than more, blood vessels serving them. What you're actually building is bulkier muscles that have more difficulty getting enough oxygen and disposing of wastes. These overdeveloped muscles tire easily.

Aerobically conditioned muscles, in comparison, are longer and leaner and well nourished with blood vessels. They have more elasticity, certainly as much tone (or firmness), and sometimes even as much strength. We'd match the muscles developed in a marathon runner's legs or an Olympic swimmer's arms against those of a body builder any day. And we'd bet on the runner's or the swimmer's grace, speed, and agility over that of the body builder.

• **Bone tissue.** Bones, like muscles, get stronger the more they're used. Numerous studies have shown that exercising against gravity—or some form of resistance—increases the mineral content of bones. Such findings are especially important for women because as they grow older their bones demineralize, or lose calcium, much faster than do men's.

Weight-bearing aerobic exercise is the best kind for promoting denser, healthier bones. Thus, a program that includes the primary activities of walking and running with some calisthenics and weight training is ideal.

• **Digestive system.** Even though you may not feel relaxed when you're doing aerobic exercise, it does have a soothing effect on your body, in particular on your digestive system.

Your stomach will feel it when you begin aerobics. It's well documented that most conditioned people produce less stomach acid. For hypertense, driven people who have trouble relaxing, this is especially important. For them, aerobic exercise could spell the difference between a normal stomach and an ulcerated one.

Aerobics also acts as a natural cathartic. It helps the digestive tract muscles move waste material and it increases the activity of the bowels. Indeed, you could say that exercise and regularity go together. It's axiomatic that *women who exercise regularly are rarely irregular.* Elderly women, often the victims of chronic constipation, would do well to take note of this fact.

• **Hormonal system.** Most people feel euphoric after an aerobic workout. This sense of well-being has a biochemical cause: the pituitary gland orders the body to release powerful hormones called *endorphins.* They are natural opiates, similar to the painkiller morphine, but dose to dose they are actually two hundred times stronger.

Neurophysiologists say that endorphin levels in the blood can stay higher than normal for as long as 2 hours after exercise, giving a physiological lift. That's why we say that the hardest part of daily exercise is putting on your shoes. The best part is the shower after you finish, when you feel so good, so virtuous. In reality, all you have done is given yourself a physiological fix!

• **Nervous system.** The beneficial effect of aerobics extends to the neurological system as well. Exercise enhances blood flow to previously inadequately supplied corners of the brain and increases the speed with which nerve messages can travel through the brain. The result: greater alertness, response time, and even mental capacity.

Yes, researchers have demonstrated that aerobics can have a positive impact on reasoning ability. A Purdue University study focused on a group of sedentary middle-aged men. Half were put through a 4-month fitness program; they exercised about 1½ hours a day, three times a week. The other half remained inactive. The results on ten tests of mental ability revealed a marked improvement in the active men's mental processes controlled by their brain's left hemisphere, the part responsible for logical thinking and mathematical ability.

In today's competitive work world, this is a crucial plus. Suppose your job requires the utmost intellectual concentration and the absolute minimum physical movement. As our society makes the transition into the twenty-first-century age of information, where brainpower will be highly valued, jobs such as this will be more and more common.

To ease the tension you often feel at the end of a mentally exhausting workday, we recommend aerobic exercise instead of the usual cocktail or tranquilizer or other drug. We guarantee that, after the cool-down part of your workout, you'll begin to feel refreshed and relaxed—in *mind* as well as body.

No matter how intense your concentration has been all day, aerobic exercise will free your mind of your job-related concerns. Studies have proved that aerobics can even aid your problem-solving abilities. Wouldn't you like it if the solution to a particularly thorny work problem suddenly came to you, when thinking about it directly all day long did no good whatsoever? While we can't guarantee that a muse will whisper sweet solutions in your ear after every single workout, aerobics' adherents have reported to us far stranger benefits than this.

We can make one hard-and-fast prediction, though: overall, aerobics will make you feel less emotionally keyed up and better able to forget your cares and get a good night's sleep. (Yes, aerobics helps cure insomnia, too.)

## The Training Effect: A Cornucopia of Health Benefits

All the exercise-induced anatomic and biochemical changes just described are known, collectively, as the *training effect.* The training effect is real. It's been studied and documented time and again at the Aerobics Center and by some of the country's leading doctors and research scientists.

The training effect is what makes all the initial work of starting an aerobics program worth every bit of the effort. You'll feel better after exercising, and this feeling will enhance every aspect of your life.

Perhaps even more important, the training effect acts as preventive medicine. It strengthens your body's immune system so it becomes more impregnable to minor ailments as well as to major diseases.

The message here is that your body will deteriorate, slowly but surely, and become more susceptible to disease if you don't exercise it. If that concept doesn't disturb you, read on. Your ego—or your fear of not living to a ripe old age—may yet open up your ears to our aerobic arguments.

## Vanity Fair

Granted, fully functioning internal organs may seem too abstract to motivate you to start exercising. After all, no one can see clear lungs, clean blood vessels, or a pulsating heart. Nor will anyone shower you with compliments about them. But people can see the outer trappings of health—a firm body rounded in the right places, glowing skin, shining hair, and so forth.

If you're like most women, looking good is important to you. Here's a short true/false test. It will indicate how highly you value your looks and whether you think you deserve compliments based on your appearance right now.

### Fit Test: My Looks and Self-Esteem

| | True | False |
|---|---|---|
| I'm satisfied with my weight. | ______ | ______ |
| My weight doesn't fluctuate much. | ______ | ______ |
| I'm pleased with my body's contours. | ______ | ______ |
| I'm happy about my dress size. | ______ | ______ |
| My family and friends give me sincere compliments on my appearance. | ______ | ______ |
| I admire my figure clad in a swimsuit. | ______ | ______ |
| I haven't found flab or cellulite anywhere on my body. | ______ | ______ |
| Stress doesn't increase my appetite. | ______ | ______ |
| I don't have a strong desire to look like someone else. | ______ | ______ |
| I characterize myself nutrition-and-health conscious, moderate in all my habits. | ______ | ______ |

If you checked just one "false," you've got a more than sufficient reason to embark on the aerobics program outlined in this book.

Our aerobics program involves more than just exercise. It means eating right, too. Two chapters in this book are devoted to the subject of nutrition. One involves eating to maintain health; the other, eating—and exercising—to lose weight.

Looking better will bolster your self-esteem, the wellspring of confidence. To be sure, greater confidence could translate into all sorts of pluses—on the job, at home, and in your relationships with friends.

How will aerobics improve your looks? In two big ways and many little ones. Aerobic exercise will help control your appetite. You'll be amazed to discover that the amount you eat and what your taste buds crave will change after you've been exercising for a while. Even without dieting, aerobics will also change your fat/muscle ratio. Your body will become more firm; and likely your weight will redistribute itself.

The other cosmetic benefits are legion. Unfortunately, they haven't been documented in controlled studies. However, the thousands of women members of the Aerobics Center, as well as the faithful who write to us, have reported everything from clearer skin to brighter eyes (perhaps because aerobics makes you more alert). One woman even claimed that, several months into her aerobics program, her nails became harder and stopped breaking off for the first time in her life.

If improved appearance is your motivation, we think that's just fine because the end result is improved health and self-esteem.

## The Longevity Factor

To explain the impact aerobics can have on your old age, let's return to biology class for another moment.

Women reach physical maturity in their late teens. For the body, it's all downhill from there—that is, as long as you remain relatively inactive and do nothing to retard the aging process.

With each passing year, your heart's ability to pump blood declines by about 1 percent. The amount of air you can inhale continues to lessen as your chest wall stiffens. Your muscles lose strength, tone, and suppleness; nerve impulses travel more slowly; metabolism slows and food turns into fat more easily; and bones lose calcium, become brittle, and have a greater tendency to fracture.

Admittedly, none of this occurs overnight, but by middle age you'll notice the signs. For one thing, your blood vessels will be 29 percent narrower, placing an extra burden on your heart. And each decade after age 30, you'll have lost another 3 to 5 percent of all the muscle fibers in your body.

By age 60, the effects of time will be unmistakable. You'll have a 10 to 30 percent loss of muscle power and a marked gain in body fat. In addition, the blood flow from your arms to legs will be 30 to 60 percent slower than it was at age 25.

By age 70, you may feel "under the weather" most days. Your alertness will be waning because the speed with which your nerves transmit messages has dropped off sharply. Your body's flexibility will be reduced 20 to 30 percent and your bone mass 25 to 30 percent.

By age 75? The news keeps getting worse. The amount of oxygen your body circulates could be reduced by more than 29 percent.

By age 80, as you sit in that creaking rocking chair, barely able to propel it back and forth more than a couple of inches, it's no wonder that you have days when you feel you would welcome the Grim Reaper.

A morbid picture, isn't it?

We don't want to mislead you. Aerobics isn't a fountain of youth. But new research suggests that each hour you spend exercising aerobically can help add 2½ hours to your life span.

The most definitive research is that of Dr. Ralph S. Paffenbarger, Jr., using a sample of 17,000 Harvard alumni. His continuing studies reveal that expending as little as 2,000 calories a week through activities such as walking, jogging, stair climbing, or vigorous sports can reduce a person's risk of coronary heart disease by as much as one-third. This translates into a significant increase in life expectancy.

Clearly, a moderate exercise program can *retard* the aging process. But recent gerontology studies suggest it can even *reverse* the process to some degree.

Dr. Herbert A. deVries, a pioneer in the geriatrics field long associated with the Andrus Gerontology Center at the University of Southern California, studied the effects of a fitness program on more than 200 men and women, ranging in age from 56 to 87, who lived in a retirement community. Participants did a walk-jog routine, calisthenics, and stretching for one hour a day, three to five times a week. After just six weeks, the changes were marked: blood pressure dropped, percentages of body fat decreased, maximum oxygen capacity increased, arm strength improved, and signs of nervous tension in the musculature diminished. The average participant achieved peak fitness between week 18 and week 42 of the program; Dr. deVries claims the people who improved the most were the ones who were in the worst shape to begin with.

## Enjoying Your Sunset Years

Perhaps as important as the number of years you live is the *quality* of your later years. Study after study has shown that people who exercise tend to have fewer debilitating diseases in their senior years.

At the Aerobics Center, we work with some remarkable older women. Many of these women didn't accept responsibility for their biochemical fate until well into their sixties and seventies. But once they did, they all demonstrated a tenacious determination to do whatever was necessary to make their next years their best years.

Marilla Salisbury is a prime example. This retired San Diego math teacher never gave exercise a thought until well into her sixties. Finally, by age 70, her debilitating arthritis and the aches and pains of her contemporaries pushed her over the line. "Just listening to all that whining and watching people deteriorate got me depressed."

Her antidote was a brisk walking program that accelerated into a marathon-type running program. Since then, she's won more than two hundred national and international medals and garnered a flock of loyal fans who love cheering on "the granny in the bonnet." The bonnet—and her fantastic Betty Grable legs—is her trademark.

"It gives me such a lift to run," Marilla told one of the many reporters who've written of her septuagenarian exploits. "Sometimes I just float through my workout. Maybe it's the runner's high or maybe there's no name for what I'm experiencing. What's important is that I've never felt better. It's rare for me to have a sick day, and I haven't had a cold for years. I'm living proof that you can teach an old person new tricks."

She's also living proof that you can turn back the biological clock. When she first visited the Aerobics Center in August 1985, she was 77 years old. Granted, she wasn't a drinker or a smoker, she avoided caffeine, and she had always eaten sensibly. Still, as a medical specimen, she's in a class by herself. In one category after another, her results were that of a woman twenty to thirty years younger:

Marilla is 5 feet 5 inches tall and weighs 116 pounds; her waist measures 26 inches, her hips 36. Examination revealed a body fat of 20.28 percent when, for a woman in her sixties, 22.5 percent is considered perfect. Her blood pressure was 130/68, her pulse 70.

Her cholesterol level was 157. Even better, her cholesterol/HDL ratio was 2.3, while anything below 4.0 is considered superb. Her triglycerides were 80, while anything below 120 is terrific. Except for some mild Parkinsonism, which was well controlled with medication, she had none of the usual age-related symptoms of coronary disease, osteoporosis, or diabetes.

Her treadmill test was off-the-charts. She kept going on our machine, which we gradually elevated to give the effect of walking fast uphill, for 15 minutes. That places her among the top 5 percent of women almost thirty years her junior!

There's a moral here. Even if you're 50 or 60 or 70, like Marilla Salisbury, and have never exercised a day in your life, you can still take advantage of aerobics' benefits.

# 3

# You've Got It All Wrong—Misconceptions about Exercise

Even today, when more and more women are health-and-fitness conscious, it's surprising how much misinformation there is. Everybody—from medical doctors to sports equipment and clothing manufacturers—seems to have his own idea about *how* to achieve fitness. All sorts of elaborate theories are concocted, often based on the slimmest scientific evidence, to woo women into the fold.

We hear the following statements time and again from women who think exercise is important but don't understand exercise physiology enough to make informed choices about what will work best for them. In this chapter, we'll set the record straight about the various nonaerobic exercises and where they fit into a total program to boost women's health and well-being.

## "Muscular Fitness Is My Exercise Goal"

There's nothing wrong with muscular fitness. It just shouldn't be your primary or only exercise goal.

Why? The best explanation harks back to a recent experience at the Cooper Clinic. Three women came in for complete physical examinations. They represented extreme contrasts in every way.

One was a 28-year-old bodybuilding champion. Her waist was slim and her muscles bulged; she told us proudly that her exercise program consisted of many long hours of weight lifting every week.

The second was a successful New York City career woman, age 40. She was too busy with her job and family to bother with a formal exercise regimen. When she could carve out the time from her tight schedule, she and her husband played tennis and swam in the summer and in the winter competed against other couples in platform tennis. In passing, she mentioned that, no matter what the season, she did plenty of brisk pavement pounding in Manhattan as a sales representative for a major office-products company.

The third woman was a grandmother, 64 years old. The phrase "bundle of energy" certainly applied to her. Just being in her presence made you feel tired. She was quick about everything she did, from talking to gesturing. She'd been in and out of various exercise programs all her life. But she'd never stuck with any for very long, until two years earlier, when her cardiologist had prescribed walking to help her recuperate from a mild heart attack.

Who do you think had the best overall fitness, as measured by their endurance on our treadmill?

It wasn't the bodybuilder—not by a long shot: her performance on the treadmill was little better than that of the 64-year-old grandmother. The 40-year-old career woman gave lie to the notion that city folks are poor physical specimens. Without making a conscious effort to exercise aerobically, this woman racks up aerobic points by walking every workday, heavy sample case in tow.

Our message is this: a moderate weight lifting or bodybuilding program is fine. It can help strengthen not only your muscles but your bones, an important benefit for women. But a program aimed solely at muscle building is of limited health value because it does nothing to promote cardiovascular fitness. It's like sprucing up the outside of your house with flowering shrubs and new paint and shutters while the inside has antiquated plumbing, crumbling walls, and the boiler is about to blow up.

## " 'Instant Exercise' Is the Only Answer for the Busy Woman"

We know you're busy. Most people are, these days. While aerobics may take you 20 minutes longer each day than the so-called instant exercise of isometrics, the vast difference it will make in your health is worth every extra second.

Like bodybuilding, isometric exercises are aimed at the skeletal muscles. They involve tensing one set of muscles against another or against an immovable object. Place the palms of your hands together and push, or grip the sides of your chair and pull up. Hold these positions for several seconds, then relax. You've just completed an isometric exercise.

Both bodybuilding and isometrics involve the movement of muscles. But bodybuilding, at least, requires a little extra intake of oxygen. Isometrics require practically none.

Isometrics may be the most passive form of exercise; no sweat, no panting, no hard work. That's why isometric exercises to prevent muscular atrophy are great for people who are bedridden—provided, that is, they're not heart patients. At the Aerobics Center, we advise our cardiac patients specifically *not* to engage in any isometric-type exercise (lifting a heavy object, changing a tire) because it causes a brief increase in blood pressure that could be dangerous. For people with severe hypertensive problems, isometrics can trigger cardiac irregularity, a heart attack, or even a stroke.

Isometrics do have one other invaluable use. For astronauts on long space voyages, traveling in a weightless state, other types of exercise are difficult to perform. But for women whose feet are firmly planted on the ground, isometrics are to be used *in addition to, not in place of* aerobic physical activity.

## "Anaerobics Fulfills My Exercise Needs"

Anaerobic exercise is no shortcut to fitness.

Anaerobic means "without oxygen." Exercises of this type require a short, exhaustive burst of effort that depletes you of oxygen to the point where continuing could make you collapse—or, if you've got a heart condition, cause a serious problem.

Sprinting, for example, builds up an "oxygen debt" so quickly that the only way to pay it back is to stop dead in your tracks and breathe as hard as you can for a few moments. Indeed, the typical sprinter runs portions of a 50- or 100-yard dash in such high gear that she holds her breath. Thus, she is, as the term implies, exercising "without oxygen."

At the beginning of an aerobic workout, you're exercising anaerobically. You feel out of breath and uncomfortable. Just when you think you've had it, a so-called second wind comes to the rescue. This second-wind phenomenon is the point at which you make the transition to aerobic exercise. It's the point when your breathing finally settles down into a deep, steady, *aerobic* pattern and suddenly you feel as though you've got much more stamina and endurance.

Which type of exercise does you more good over the long run?

We answer that question with another tale about an Olympic-caliber sprinter tested at the Aerobics Center. Every medical test we put her through revealed a marvelous example of human machinery—until she stepped onto our treadmill to be tested for cardiovascular endurance. She reached a maximum heart rate of 196 and admitted defeat—that is, total exhaustion—after only 16 minutes. Like our bodybuilder mentioned earlier, she received a mediocre cardiovascular-fitness rating for a woman in her age group.

She's living proof that focusing exclusively on anaerobic or sprint-type exercise is short-sighted. Some nonaerobic exercise is fine. But, if you're the average woman, your objectives are to feel good, look better, and live longer—not to win medals for speed. That's why you should concentrate mainly on aerobic exercises that demand a steady supply of oxygen without creating an intolerable oxygen debt.

## "Isotonic (or Isophasic) Exercise Will Make Me Fit"

Grouped under these headings are such flexibility- and strength-oriented exercises as calisthenics and weight lifting. Like isometrics, they require contraction of a muscle. Unlike isometrics, they also require movement of a joint or limb. Some mild participant sports such as shuffleboard, archery, and horseshoes fall into this category.

We're advocates of isotonics because they toughen your body, increase your coordination and agility, and make you less prone to injuries during aerobic exercise. However, isotonics should *not* be on the top of your exercise agenda.

By this time, you can probably tell us why. Right—they don't make you breathe long and hard enough to trigger the training effect.

Weight lifters often argue this point. They say they can feel their hearts pounding harder as they struggle to hold up a barbell. True, their hearts are pounding harder and faster because they're under strain. But, unfortunately, that cardio-stress phenomenon is not accompanied by an increase in their blood flow or blood volume because of the static nature of weight lifting.

In fact, the stress that weight lifting places on the heart is a compelling reason why all bodybuilders *should* exercise aerobically. In short, aerobics helps ensure that their hearts can take the strain of weight lifting.

## "Team Sports Are My Way of Combining Fitness with Fun"

The fun part may be accurate, but the fitness part is exaggerated.

Many team sports—such as basketball, touch football, and doubles tennis—are a mixture of anaerobic and aerobic exercise. Like sprinting, they require spurts of energy that may deplete you of oxygen so fast that you have to stop for a moment to catch your breath. On the other hand, such sports also afford you the opportunity to move around continuously, even if only to run in place or shift your weight from one leg to the other. Therefore, they're quasi-aerobic.

While it's true that many team sports demand extra oxygen intake, few require it in steady enough doses over a long enough period of time to produce much training effect. That's why they can't be classed as primary aerobic activities.

Some team sports, such as baseball, have no aerobic aspect whatsoever. Baseball does have isometric, isotonic, and anaerobic components, however. You step up to the batter's box, grip the bat, and tense your arms awaiting the pitch (isometrics). Next, you swing at the ball, moving your arms, shoulders, and hips (isotonics). Once you connect with the ball, you break into a dead run around the bases (anaerobic).

Even if team sports have limited or no aerobic value, most offer both a physical and an intellectual challenge. They also exercise your social skills, so we don't discourage them.

But, as we said about isotonics: team sports are fine as long as they are done *in addition to* rather than *in place of* primary aerobic exercise.

## "Exercise Will Wear Out My Heart"

After everything we've explained about the heart and how it works, this statement may strike you as laughable. But for those who still believe the old wives' tale about hearts being genetically programmed to beat only X amount of times during a lifetime, it's a deadly serious matter.

According to this theory, it's unsafe to exercise because it raises the heart rate and ticks away the hours of your life that much faster. Even if the basic premise were true—and there is not one shred of scientific evidence that it is—the statement still makes no sense.

While your heart does beat faster while you're exercising aerobically, the healthier your heart gets, the slower it pulses during the other twenty-three or more hours of the day. The bottom line: an aerobically fit woman is one whose heart experiences a net drop in heartbeats over time, not a net gain.

## "I Must Get Enough Exercise Because I Feel Bone-Tired at the End of a Day"

Feeling bone-tired at the end of the day does not necessarily signify an adequate amount—or the right kind—of exercise. It could represent mental fatigue from the pressure and tedium of your workday.

It doesn't matter whether your workday consists of cleaning house and tending to your family sixteen hours a day, or shielding an aloof boss from the real world via the telephone for eight hours, or battling your company's bare-knuckled competitors in the marketplace every day and on into the night. Each of those situations could, understandably, create emotional and mental weariness. Exercise has nothing to do with it.

Rather than induce fatigue, aerobics erases it. It's a mistake to equate the momentary physical exhaustion you experience immediately after exercise with more long-lived fatigue. The tired feeling after exercise is soon replaced by a marvelous feeling of renewed energy and relaxation.

Bone-tiredness doesn't disappear so fast. A good night's sleep—or a major change in your life—may be its only antidote.

## "Running Will Make My Legs Unattractively Muscle-Bound"

Picture the most attractive legs you've ever seen. Maybe they're the legs of the chorus girls in 1950s' MGM musicals, or the legs of the Rockettes at Radio City Music Hall. Or, if you were around in the 1940s, the stunning legs of movie star Betty Grable, who built a career around hers.

All these women's legs could be a runner's legs because running, unlike bodybuilding, does not create bulging muscles. Most women who jog regularly develop firm, lean calf and thigh muscles and lose unwanted cellulite.

## "I Expend Less Energy Than a Man When I Exercise"

No you don't. For any given aerobic activity, the energy requirements are comparable for everyone—male and female—with some slight variation due to body size and physical condition. If this weren't true, the aerobic point system described in the next chapter could never have been invented.

# 4

# The Aerobic Point System—Quantifying Your Effort

By this time, you should have a clear picture of the type of exercise that fosters the training effect. It's the kind of exercise that forces you to breathe deeply and rhythmically over a period of time while your limbs move steadily through the air or water.

That's a good explanation, as far as it goes. What you don't know yet is the *amount* or *intensity* of aerobic exercise that triggers the training effect.

Here's the theory:

If your aerobic exercise is limited to 12 to 20 minutes per day of activity, the exercise must be vigorous enough to produce a sustained heart rate of 150 beats per minute or more. If your exercise doesn't do this, but still demands extra oxygen, you'll have to exercise longer than 20 minutes. In other words, your total exercise period depends on the amount of additional oxygen you consume and energy you expend.

Your next question might be: "How am I supposed to know how fast my heart is beating or how much oxygen I'm consuming?"

## A Lab in Your Pocket

You'll be pleased to learn that these measurements aren't your problem. The laboratory calculations have already been done. The result is the *aerobic point system.*

The figuring was done a long time ago when I was directing health and fitness programs for the United States Air Force and working with NASA in the 1960s. It took four years of trial and error to come up with the system. But being able to quantify aerobics has made a great deal of difference in its popularity.

This is how I, with the help of a dedicated research team, devised the aerobic point system that is now utilized by service personnel and the public all over the world:

During the research, we studied every exercise we could think of that demands oxygen aerobically. We excluded *an*aerobic exercise. We put our subjects through their paces—either in a laboratory or in a controlled outdoor environment—while studying their body's responses on delicately calibrated measuring equipment. We also studied the before-and-after effects of aerobics. We examined our subjects thoroughly before they embarked on a carefully detailed aerobics program and at regular intervals thereafter. We saw definite benchmarks of progress that spoke volumes about aerobics' effects on the body.

Our initial sample consisted of 5,000 people. I've since tested almost 30,000 others to make absolutely sure those initial conclusions were accurate—and universal.

## Turning Hypotheses into Conclusions

We discovered, to no one's surprise, that not all aerobic exercises are equal. Some demand more oxygen than others to produce the energy needed to keep going.

We eventually translated each exercise's oxygen quantity and energy cost into points. Naturally, those that required more oxygen and energy merited more points.

That's not all. We included a time and distance factor in the point system too. And that's where the accelerated heart rate comes in.

Let's say you choose to run, one of the very best aerobic activities. If you run slowly, it takes you longer to process the same amount of oxygen as someone who is running faster. Not only that, but jogging, as opposed to running, doesn't elevate your heart rate as much. Since more oxygen and a faster-pumping heart are your twin aerobic goals, you'll have to jog for a longer period of time and cover more ground than your counterpart, the runner, in order to merit the same number of aerobic points.

Now compare the exercise of running with a singles tennis game. The scenario is quite different. While tennis makes you dash about the court chasing the ball, you also stand around a lot. Someone serves, there are several moments of scurrying about, someone finally scores a point, and the action stops, albeit temporarily. Your heart rate may be elevated beyond the training-effect threshold level of 150 beats per minute, but it doesn't stay there long. So your *average elevated heart rate* during singles tennis is certainly lower than that during nonstop aerobic activities such as running, swimming, and cycling.

There's a definite aerobic benefit from tennis, but it falls somewhere between running and walking. You'll have to play singles tennis far longer to match the points earned from running or aerobic dance.

The points you earn, then, depend on three things: the type of aerobic exercise and the demands it makes on your heart and lungs; the duration of activity; and the intensity with which you do it.

## The F.I.T. Formula

To simplify the concept of the aerobic point system, we came up with the acronym *F.I.T.*, which stands for *F*requency, *I*ntensity, and *T*ime. These are the three factors upon which the point system is based.

Frequency refers to *how often* you should exercise. Three or four days a week is ideal, but we'll discuss more about that later.

Intensity refers to *how hard* you exert yourself, whether on the tennis court or the swimming pool or a bicycle. The rule of thumb is this: you should be moving at a brisk enough pace to notice a definite increase in your breathing and pulse rate, and you should eventually begin to perspire. But you should never be panting so hard that you can't talk. That's overdoing it.

Time refers to *how long* each aerobic session lasts. The time is related to the two earlier factors of frequency and intensity. For example, if you exercise at a relatively low intensity for 20 to 30 minutes three days per week, your fourth session should be either longer—say, 45 minutes—or more intense. Or you might want to limit your workouts to the minimum three days but exercise at a medium intensity for 40 minutes each time.

For healthy women, a weekly maintenance fitness goal is to attain 30 aerobic points per week. Here are three means to that end, although there are many, many other possibilities:

| Aerobic Activity | Frequency | Intensity | Time |
|---|---|---|---|
| Running 2 miles at a 10-minute-mile pace | 4 times a week | Heart rate 140+ | 20 minutes |
| Aerobic dancing for 30 minutes | 3 times a week | Heart rate 130+ | 30 minutes |
| Walking 3 miles at a 15-minute-mile pace | 4 times a week | Heart rate 110+ | 45 minutes |

## The Point System's Goal Orientation and Efficiency

Our point system was a success from the moment we introduced it, for an obvious reason: people like goals. Goals provide motivation, something to strive for. When people meet a goal, they experience an instant, wonderful sense of accomplishment. Nobody else has to give them this reward. They give it to themselves.

The aerobic point system is both concrete and explicit. It's a numerical standard against which all people everywhere can judge their exercise effort.

We guarantee that you'll have more pride in your aerobic achievements if they're written in *tangible* numbers on a chart after each workout than if they're given in the form of an *intangible* biochemical lecture delivered by your family physician. It's just human nature.

There's another aspect of the point system that people love: its efficiency. Because aerobics is quantified through the point system, people who don't like to exercise can do the minimum amount to maintain good health.

That's the stance of William F. Buckley, the columnist and novelist. In his characteristically acerbic way, he once wrote that "most of us have no intention of devoting 10 percent of our day to physical exercise. Indeed, I would experience a most awful frustration if, on my deathbed, it were revealed that I had run one foot more, during my lifetime, than was absolutely necessary to keep me fit."

## The Point System's Adaptability

The point system offers another crucial benefit in today's busy world: flexibility.

Women today have exorbitant demands on their time. And change often rules their lives. They may not have the same job or husband or be living in the same apartment or house next year, let alone the same town or city. So, being able to adapt an aerobics program to fluid circumstances has definite advantages.

One case comes to mind. Several years ago, a 38-year-old woman visited the Cooper Clinic. She was a wife and mother with a career as a hospital lab technician. Her family physician had advised her to get into a conditioning program to combat a borderline medical problem. We outlined a combination walking-running-aerobic-dance program for her and then heard nothing for six years.

Just the other day we got a letter from her. She thanked us profusely for introducing her to aerobics, and while she barely mentioned her old medical problem, she did describe in detail how her aerobics regimen had boosted her energy at a time in her life when she needed it most. However, her aerobics regimen today bears no relation to the one we'd originally prescribed. For good reason. Our former patient is now studying to be a doctor and her life has changed radically!

Today, she is a single parent, her children are in college, and she lives in her hometown, both to be near her aging mother and to fulfill the around-the-clock demands of hospital internship. She explained how, through the intervening years, she's been able to alter her exercise program to conform to the rigors of a lifestyle in flux without ever compromising those 30 aerobic points a week she considers her bulwark.

As a busy intern, her new aerobics program revolves around two bicycles—one for getting to and from the hospital and around town on errands, and a stationary cycle that's kept permanently in front of the television set. When she finds time to watch TV, she jumps on the bike and peddles furiously. She says that the two processes have become so linked in her mind that she'd feel strange doing one without the other.

That's what all the point charts in this book are for. They give you the wherewithal to fashion an aerobics program especially for you, one that takes into account your medical needs and personal exercise preferences as well as your time and financial limits.

## Endurance Points

To recapitulate: The aerobic training effect is your goal, and to achieve it you must choose an exercise that is: (1) strenuous enough, and (2) pursued long enough each time. It's analogous to boiling an egg: the water must be *hot enough* to raise the egg's temperature, and the heat must be maintained *long enough* to soft- or hardboil it.

In the case of exercise, how long is long enough?

When we first devised the point system, we overlooked a key issue: the importance of continuous exercise. Our assumption was that running 3 miles in 24 minutes afforded you the same cardio-respiratory benefits as running 3 separate 8-minute miles, with a breather in between. We now know that this is not true.

After further study of the effects of aerobics, we altered our view. Today, all our point charts carry a premium for *endurance points.* These are extra points earned for exercising without letup.

In the case of the 3-mile run, for example, say you earn 5 points for completing 1 mile in just under 8 minutes. You'll earn a total of *17* points—not 15—for completing all 3 miles in just under 24 minutes without stopping. In other words, you'd get 5 points for each mile plus 2 extra points for your endurance, that wonderful ability to keep going.

Endurance points underscore the fact that *the longer the activity is sustained, the greater the aerobic benefit.*

## Weekly Points Indicate Fitness Levels

Research done at the Aerobics Center on several thousand women shows a correlation between fitness levels and the weekly points earned. Note that to place in the "good" category, a woman must earn 30 to 40 aerobic points per week. This is why we urge you to achieve *a minimum of 30 points a week.*

| Fitness Category | Average Points Earned per Week |
|---|---|
| Very Poor | Fewer than 8 |
| Poor | 8–15 |
| Fair | 16–29 |
| Good | 30–40 |
| Excellent | 41–64 |
| Superior | Over 65 |

## Do-It-Yourself Point System

The point system enables you to measure your cardiopulmonary progress as if you were being monitored in a medical research lab. The only "equipment" you'll need is a stopwatch—or a watch with a second hand—and the point chart covering your age group and your preferred exercise. (See charts in Chapter 8 and The Point System Charts in the Appendix.) That's why we like to say that "a point chart is like putting a lab in your pocket."

Unfortunately, there are forms of aerobic exercise you may want to try for which we haven't printed a chart in this book. Or maybe we haven't even compiled a chart for that activity because we haven't found a way to devise one that is universally applicable.

Roller skating, for example, is a free-form type of exercise that's hard to quantify. So are ballet and figure skating.

There's a way around this roadblock, though. As we've said, one objective of aerobics is to elevate your heart to a certain target rate over a sustained period. So, making sure you've achieved that rate is one approach to the problem.

In the absence of a point chart for an activity, here is a four-step formula to make sure your effort is strenuous enough to trigger aerobic benefits.

### Fit Tip: Formula for Monitoring Your Target Heart Rate

- **Step 1. Determine your "resting heart rate."**
  One reason for doing this is simply to learn how to take your pulse. Place the tips of your index and second fingers over your wrist or the carotid artery at the side of your neck, or place your hand over your heart. (Don't press hard at the neck or you may actually slow down your rate.) Count each beat for 10

seconds, then multiply by 6 (or for 15 seconds, multiply by 4). This gives you the number of heartbeats per minute.

- **Step 2. Calculate your "predicted maximum heart rate" (PMHR).**
This will vary according to your age and fitness level. The average woman would subtract her age from 220 to get her PMHR. A 40-year-old woman, for example, has a PMHR of 180—that's 220 minus 40 equals 180.

A well-conditioned woman will have a slightly higher PMHR. She can use the formula for men: 205 minus one-half your age. In the case of a female athlete of age 40, her PMHR is 185—or 205 minus 20 equals 185.

- **Step 3. Calculate your "target heart rate zone" (THRZ).**
Your target heart rate zone is between 60 and 80 percent of your PMHR. In order to trigger the training effect, you want to keep your heart rate in this zone for a minimum of 20 minutes, four times per week.

Using the example of the 40-year-old woman with the PMHR of 180, her THRZ is 108 to 144 heartbeats per minute. To gain any aerobic benefit, she has to make sure her heart rate exceeds 108—and hopefully approaches 144—for a minimum of 20 minutes, five times per week. Or she might aim for a THR of 130 for 30 minutes four times a week. Or a THR of 140 for 20 minutes four times a week. There are a number of possibilities.

## Predicted Maximum Heart Rate (PMHR) by Age

| | | Target Heart Rate Zone (THRZ) | | |
|---|---|---|---|---|
| Age | Predicted Max HR | 60% Max HR | 70% Max HR | 80% Max HR |
| 20 | 200 | 120 | 140 | 160 |
| 21 | 199 | 119 | 139 | 159 |
| 22 | 198 | 119 | 139 | 158 |
| 23 | 197 | 118 | 138 | 158 |
| 24 | 196 | 118 | 137 | 157 |
| 25 | 195 | 117 | 137 | 156 |
| 26 | 194 | 116 | 136 | 155 |
| 27 | 193 | 116 | 135 | 154 |
| 28 | 192 | 115 | 134 | 154 |
| 29 | 191 | 115 | 134 | 153 |
| 30 | 190 | 114 | 133 | 152 |
| 31 | 189 | 113 | 132 | 151 |
| 32 | 188 | 113 | 132 | 150 |
| 33 | 187 | 112 | 131 | 150 |
| 34 | 186 | 112 | 130 | 149 |
| 35 | 185 | 111 | 130 | 148 |
| 36 | 184 | 110 | 129 | 147 |
| 37 | 183 | 110 | 128 | 146 |

| Age | Predicted Max HR | Target Heart Rate Zone (THRZ) 60% Max HR | 70% Max HR | 80% Max HR |
|---|---|---|---|---|
| 38 | 182 | 109 | 127 | 146 |
| 39 | 181 | 109 | 127 | 145 |
| 40 | 180 | 108 | 126 | 144 |
| 41 | 179 | 107 | 125 | 143 |
| 42 | 178 | 107 | 125 | 142 |
| 43 | 177 | 106 | 124 | 142 |
| 44 | 176 | 106 | 123 | 141 |
| 45 | 175 | 105 | 123 | 140 |
| 46 | 174 | 104 | 122 | 139 |
| 47 | 173 | 104 | 121 | 138 |
| 48 | 172 | 103 | 120 | 138 |
| 49 | 171 | 103 | 120 | 137 |
| 50 | 170 | 102 | 119 | 136 |
| 51 | 169 | 101 | 118 | 135 |
| 52 | 168 | 101 | 118 | 134 |
| 53 | 167 | 100 | 117 | 134 |
| 54 | 166 | 100 | 116 | 133 |
| 55 | 165 | 99 | 116 | 132 |
| 56 | 164 | 98 | 115 | 131 |
| 57 | 163 | 98 | 114 | 130 |
| 58 | 162 | 97 | 113 | 130 |
| 59 | 161 | 97 | 113 | 129 |
| 60 | 160 | 96 | 112 | 128 |
| 61 | 159 | 95 | 111 | 127 |
| 62 | 158 | 95 | 111 | 126 |
| 63 | 157 | 94 | 110 | 126 |
| 64 | 156 | 94 | 109 | 125 |
| 65 | 155 | 93 | 109 | 124 |
| 66 | 154 | 92 | 108 | 123 |
| 67 | 153 | 92 | 107 | 122 |
| 68 | 152 | 91 | 106 | 122 |
| 69 | 151 | 91 | 106 | 121 |
| 70 | 150 | 90 | 105 | 120 |

Source: *Group Exercise Leadership Manual,* © 1988 by The Institute for Aerobics Research.

- **Step 4. Monitor your "actual heart rate" (AHR) during exercise.** Unless you can afford to buy one of the new heart rate monitoring devices, you really can't monitor your AHR during exercise, so you have to do the next best thing: take your pulse for 10 seconds immediately after the exercise, multiply by 6, and then adjust for the drop in the heart rate that occurs when you stop exercising. The out-of-shape woman's heart rate drops slowly; the highly conditioned woman's rate drops much more rapidly.

Take the hypothetical case of a woman in peak condition. She should take her pulse within 20 seconds after she stops her aerobic exercise (160), take 10 percent of it (16), then add it (160 + 16 = 176). This yields her AHR during exercise—176. Now she can compare it to her THR to make sure she is exercising aerobically.

The beginning exerciser is another matter. She should take her pulse rate within 20 seconds after she stops exercising, and that is approximately her AHR during exercise.

## Target Zone Exercise Pattern

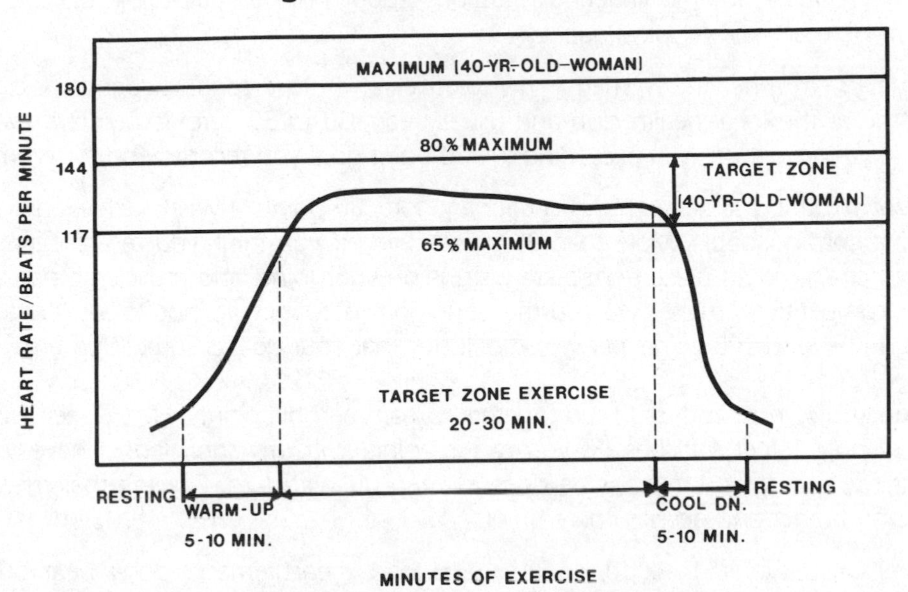


## How to Use The Target Zone

The crucial part of your workout is the length of time you stay in the target zone, the length of time you exercise with sufficient vigor to keep your pulse rate in the 65% to 80% range of maximum heart rate.

The typical exercise pattern should begin with a 5 to 10 minute warm-up of moderate exercise in which the heart rate gradually builds up, followed by more vigorous exercise to bring the heart rate up to the target zone and maintain it there for a period of from 20 to 30 minutes. The 65% level is sufficient to promote fitness; the 80% level is an upper limit which may be sustained if a more intense workout is desired. Exercise in the target zone should be followed by a 5 to 10 minute cool-down in which the exercise intensity is gradually reduced before it is stopped completely. The chart shows the typical target zone exercise pattern for the average 40-year-old woman.

Optimum physical conditioning will result from the performance of this exercise pattern three times weekly with no more than two days elapsing between workouts.

## Putting the Point System to Work for You

You may still have some lingering questions about how to utilize the aerobic point system. Here are some typical queries:

**Fit query:** I'm a healthy woman in my twenties and I love sports. I spend most of my free time at the local health club and usually earn 50 to 55 aerobic points a week. Is there anything wrong with exceeding the 30-point goal you recommend for women?

**Answer:** Nothing at all, with this cautionary note: 30 points a week, achieved without strain, is commendable. More than 85 points, even if you think you've achieved them without strain, could place unnecessary stress on your joints and muscles. Since you're not a competitive athlete, we assume your goal is to get fit, not totally exhausted. Anything beyond 100 points per week indicates that your goal is something else.

•

**Fit query:** My husband and I run together to earn aerobic points. He's 6 feet 3 inches and I'm only 5 feet 4 inches. As you can imagine, with my short legs, I have to take almost twice as many steps as he does to keep up with him. Doesn't that mean I'm exercising harder and deserve more points?

**Answer:** You would think so, but our laboratory measurements don't bear out this supposition. The energy expenditure of tall and short people running on the treadmill has been measured *ad infinitum.* Once you compensate for differences in body weight, the energy cost is the same. Only the very short—those below five feet in height—have to work harder to keep up.

•

**Fit query:** I travel for my job an average of three days a week. Could I double up on the amount of time I exercise and gain all 30 points on the weekends when it's more convenient?

**Answer:** Sorry to disappoint you. You'll be defeating the purpose if you do. To gain the maximum training effect, you must earn your weekly points a little at a time. Trying to cram all 30 points into two workouts per week—referred to as the "weekend warrior syndrome"—may actually be more dangerous than beneficial. And certainly strenuous activity only once a week for a woman past 40 years old is, as we doctors say, "contraindicated."

•

**Fit query:** From the way I feel afterward, it seems to me I should get more aerobic points for running three miles in 30 minutes without stopping than for running three separate miles of 10-minute duration. Am I correct?

**Answer:** Absolutely. Running continuously earns you "endurance points." Studying subjects in our labs we've learned that the training effect increases the longer you can keep going.

•

**Fit query:** A friend and I run together, but we can't agree on one thing about your point system. She believes that speed is what really counts in earning points. I say it's distance. Who's right?

**Answer:** Neither of you. Aerobic points are earned by the interplay of those two factors—that is, the intensity and duration of the activity. As a general rule, we caution against striving for undue speed because it increases strain and fatigue. Besides, what's the rush when you can earn points more safely and comfortably by exercising at a slower rate for a longer time? Keep the charts close at hand and concentrate on earning points, not in setting speed or distance records.

•

**Fit query:** I'm 62 years old and, try as I may, I can't meet the time goals on your charts for women in my age group. What should I do?

**Answer:** First, don't worry about it. Second, just exercise at a slower speed for a longer period of time. Keep in mind that it is more important to earn your points than it is to reach a specific time goal.

Your body is like a car that's been allotted a tank full of gasoline per week. The goal is to empty the tank by the end of each week. You can either do it by tooling around at top speed, burning up fuel quickly. Or you can idle around at a more leisurely pace, conserving gasoline and admiring the view along the way. The choice is yours.

•

**Fit query:** I enjoy aerobics so much I don't feel "right" if I'm not doing it every single day. Is every day too much?

**Answer:** Yes, most definitely. There are limits to every good thing. You shouldn't work out more than five times a week. Even on a five-day schedule, we've got some caveats: Don't exercise to the same vigorous degree each day. Alternate hard days with easier days, also the type of aerobic exercise. Pushing yourself to achieve maximum performance five days straight doing the same exercise could result in cumulative fatigue and will certainly increase the likelihood of muscle, joint, and bone injuries.

## Racing Ahead—Please Don't Do It!

Which brings us to the overall question of pacing—not pacing during one workout but pacing over the multi-week introductory phase of your aerobics program.

When you first begin an aerobics program, we want you to get into the swing of things slowly. We're not saying you have to run or swim or cycle slowly. We're saying you can't start out like gangbusters and earn 30 aerobic points the first week. Not even in the third week, in fact. No, you must earn aerobic points gradually and progressively—so many the first week, a few more the second, and so on.

We've compiled starter program point charts for you to follow based on your age. They appear in the next chapter. You'll note they are graduated.

But before you even get to that stage, you need to know what shape you're in now.

# 5
# The Baseline—What Shape Are You in Now?

Now a respite for a moment from aerobics theory to focus on you and your current physical condition.

This chapter is about testing. It describes the medical exam you may have to undergo before you embark on an aerobics program. It also contains aerobics tests that the conditioned woman can perform to find out how her fitness compares with that of other women in her age bracket. And, for the woman who hasn't been exercising, it outlines a six-week introductory aerobics program to get her started.

## Women Who Can't

You should consult a doctor before embarking on any aerobics program. However, there are women who, for medical reasons, should not undertake aerobics under any circumstances. There are other cases where aerobics could be dangerous—that is, if the activity isn't carefully supervised, perhaps even monitored by a physician who is knowledgeable about exercise physiology.

You're probably thinking, *Where would I ever find a doctor to monitor me during aerobics?*

One place is at our Aerobics Center in Dallas. We have a number of heart-attack victims, for example, whose doctors have sent them to the Aerobics Center for rehabilitative therapy. Every morning you'll see them walking briskly around our indoor track. One of our medical doctors is always there watching them. Their pulse rates and other vital signs are checked both before and after exercise to discern the slightest hint of trouble.

However, it's unlikely that you'll have access to a monitored program like that at the Aerobics Center. So, if you do suffer from one of the following 10 medical conditions, do **not** undertake any form of exercise program—that's **any form of exercise program**, not just aerobics—until the problem has been controlled or corrected.

- Moderate to severe coronary heart disease that causes chest pain from minimal activity (e.g., angina pectoris).
- A recent heart attack. A three-month waiting period is considered standard before a woman starts or returns to a moderately vigorous conditioning program. Even then, as we've said, the program must be medically supervised.
- Severe heart valve defects, usually the result of having rheumatic fever at an early age. Some women with this condition shouldn't exercise at all, even to the extent of walking fast.
- Certain types of congenital heart diseases, particularly those in which exercise makes your skin turn blue.
- A greatly enlarged heart caused by high blood pressure or other types of progressive heart disease.
- Severe heartbeat irregularities requiring medication or frequent medical attention.
- Uncontrolled diabetes where your blood-sugar levels fluctuate constantly.
- High blood pressure not controlled by medication—for example, readings of 180/110 even with medication.
- Obesity, defined as being more than 50 pounds above the weight range for your age, body type, and sex, given on standardized charts. An obese person *must* lose weight on a walking program before she can begin anything more strenuous such as jogging or running.
- Any infectious disease during its acute stage.

## Aerobics by Doctor's Orders Only

The above 10 medical conditions sideline you from exercise. There are ten other conditions, though, that don't place exercise 100 percent off-limits.

If you're a victim of one of the following conditions, you may be able to undertake moderate exercise—but only with your doctor's permission. Actually, the right kind and degree of exercise could even help some of these health problems. Let your physician be your guide:

- Any chronic infectious disease—or one in its convalescent stage.
- Diabetes under control through insulin medication.
- Internal bleeding, recently or in the past. Depending on your specific type of hemorrhage, exercise may not be permitted at all.

- Kidney disease, either chronic or acute.
- Anemia (i.e., fewer than 10 grams of hemoglobin in the body), even if you're under treatment. Wait until the condition is corrected.
- Lung disease, acute or chronic, that causes major breathing problems even with light exercise.
- High blood pressure that, even with medication, can be reduced only to 150/90.
- Vascular disease in your legs that produces pain when you walk.
- Arthritis in your back, legs, feet, or ankles that requires frequent medication to relieve the pain.
- Convulsive episodes that medication has failed to control completely.

## The Pre-Aerobics Medical Exam—Who Must Have It?

Any woman who is 40 years or older *must* get the go-ahead from her doctor before she starts regular aerobics conditioning. We say this unequivocally even if you are—or think you are—in top physical shape.

A pre-aerobics exam is mandatory also for women who smoke; who are 20 pounds or more overweight according to the norms on standardized weight charts; who have a family history of premature heart disease; or who have high blood pressure or a high cholesterol count.

Here are the guidelines for women under age 40:

If you're under age 30, don't start an aerobics program unless you've had a physical exam *within the preceding year* and gotten a clean bill of health. If you're between 30 and 35, the exam should have been *within the preceding six months.* Between ages 35 and 39, *within the preceding three months.*

Actually, a baseline exam at any age is a good idea. It rates your fitness level before aerobics. You can use it later to assess how much your fitness level has improved due to aerobics.

Remember, the fact that you feel fine does *not* necessarily mean you are 100 percent free of medical problems. It just means that any potential diseases are still in the subclinical phase—that the symptoms simply haven't been felt yet.

To be sure you really are as fit as you feel, see if any of these eight key statements apply to you:

### Fit Quiz: Mandate for a Medical Exam

| | True | False |
|---|---|---|
| I become extremely short of breath, sometimes even nauseated, during mild exercise or exertion. | ______ | ______ |
| I have frequent dizzy spells. | ______ | ______ |
| I have chest pain while exercising and sometimes even at other times. | ______ | ______ |
| I feel frequent skipped heartbeats. | ______ | ______ |
| I often feel my heart is racing. | ______ | ______ |
| While exercising or during sudden bursts of activity like running to catch a bus, I've had attacks of blurred vision. | ______ | ______ |
| I have a history of such medical problems as high blood pressure, high cholesterol, heart murmur, or heart attack. | ______ | ______ |
| In the past I've suffered from such musculoskeletal problems as tendinitis and chronic back pain. | ______ | ______ |

If you checked "true" even once, see a doctor before you undertake aerobics. Your symptoms could be transitory and easily treated, or they could indicate something more serious. Either way, check it out to prevent any complications later.

## Preventive Health Care Requires Regular Checkups

Any exam you undergo must be worth the time and money you spend on it. In other words, that exam must be thorough; unfortunately, too many general checkups are not.

A complete physical, at regular intervals, is an important part of preventive health care. A healthy woman in her twenties, with no apparent medical problems, should still have a general examination once every two or three years. In her thirties, when a stress-filled lifestyle could lead to the first signs of high blood pressure, high or unbalanced cholesterol levels, and arteriosclerosis, a woman should have an exam once every eighteen months to two years.

In her forties, when most women become menopausal, the interval narrows even more: once every year to eighteen months. This is when the incidence of serious problems shoots up markedly. A woman should be examined carefully for cancer growths, polyps, coronary disease, osteoporosis, and diabetes.

Between ages 50 and 60, you need annual exams. Now heart and lung diseases, malignancies, arthritis, and osteoporosis are even more likely to be causing problems. A woman over age 60 is probably seeing either a specialist or her family physician anyway for treatment of a specific ailment. Still, she should schedule an annual general checkup.

## Medical Exams by the Cooper Clinic

At the Cooper Clinic, where the thrust is preventive medicine, our exam takes a day to a day and a half and runs the gamut from psychological testing to treadmill stress testing.

However, unless you have reason to suspect a problem, we're not suggesting that any woman under age 40 needs that comprehensive a going-over before starting aerobics. In fact, we recognize the need for shortcut means to test for levels of fitness among the general adult population and have done something about it. Our affiliate organization, the Institute for Aerobics Research, has a computer-generated health/fitness evaluation, called FITCHECK,* which does the job in half an hour.

Here's how FITCHECK works:

Data about your cardiovascular endurance, flexibility, upper-body strength, abdominal strength, and body composition is collected by a health-care or exercise professional and sent in to the Institute for tabulation. This information is compared to standards reflective of the health and fitness levels of average healthy men and women by age

### Fit Facts: Profile of a Thorough Medical Exam

Here's a checklist of the procedures that should be included in any general checkup that purports to be thorough. Compare your doctor's exam against the ideal medical examination, which would include:

- A medical history, a series of detailed questions about other blood relatives' medical problems, the functioning of the major systems of your body, your daily health and habits and any sudden changes, and your diet.
- Opportunities for you to discuss any worrisome symptoms or problems before and during the exam.
- Routine measurements such as height, weight, percentage of body fat, blood pressure, pulse rate, hip and waist measurements, and bone size.

*For more information about FITCHECK, contact the Institute for Aerobics Research, 12330 Preston Road, Dallas, TX 75230.

- Examination of your eyes for signs of disease, high blood pressure, brain tumors, diabetes, and cataracts, as well as to evaluate the way they respond to changes in light and distance. Women over age 40 need a glaucoma test.
- A hearing test.
- Palpation of your thyroid and a probe of your neck, underarms, and crotch area for lymph-node enlargement.
- Listening to your heart, through a stethoscope, while you're in two positions—lying down and sitting up.
- Listening to your lungs for signs of emphysema, asthma, or even such infectious diseases as tuberculosis.
- Listening to the carotid arteries in your neck and femoral arteries in your groin to see if there's any untoward turbulence.
- A breast check for lumps, the same check you should be giving yourself regularly. Women over 40 also need a mammography, which can detect a developing mass in the breast up to two years before it can be felt.
- An abdominal check to detect any enlargement of your liver or spleen or other swelling of internal organs.
- A pelvic exam and Pap smear to test for cervical cancer.
- A rectal exam by finger and stool sample to check for blood. Women over 40 should have their colons examined with a proctosigmoidoscope or a colonoscopy. Both of these instruments are inserted into the rectum for a closeup view. It's believed that nearly all colon cancers can be detected using one of these instruments.
- Examination of your bone structure and musculature through movements that show the range of motion in your limbs. The skeletal check is important because people who are flat-footed or slightly bowlegged are more likely to develop foot and ankle problems if they jog.
- Special strength and flexibility tests to pinpoint muscular or other physical problems. A set of corrective exercises can often lessen or eliminate any problems.
- Skin check for the presence of lesions and minor malignancies that are usually the result of too much sun.
- Reflex tests to screen for neurological problems and brain tumors.
- Examination of the teeth, gums, mouth, and throat cavity. For smokers, the throat and vocal cord check is crucial for discovery of malignancies.
- A spirometry test, in which you take a deep breath and expel as much of it as

possible into a measuring device. It tests your lungs' vital capacity and for emphysema and obstructions in the lungs or throat.

- Blood analysis that can show everything from white blood cell and hemoglobin counts to early signs of anemia, leukemia, diabetes, cirrhosis of the liver, kidney disorders, and a host of other ailments.
- Urinalysis and microscopic scrutiny of the sediment. Like blood analysis, this is a screening mechanism for a whole range of diseases and problems.
- Evaluation of your cholesterol levels and triglycerides as well as your LDL and total cholesterol/HDL ratio.
- For women over 40, a barium enema or colonoscopy to check the entire intestinal system for signs of cancer.
- A chest X ray for better screening of the heart, lungs, and other organs.
- A psychological exam to judge the amount of stress in your life and how well you handle it. Stress is beginning to be regarded as an important risk factor in heart disease, cancer, and other maladies.
- A woman between ages 35 and 39 should have a resting electrocardiogram (ECG). Over 40, she needs both a resting and a stress ECG.
- After the physical, a follow-up educational and motivational discussion with the doctor about the findings.

We also recommend that you leave your doctor's office with results in hand—or with the assurance that a final report will be mailed to you. It's important that you review the facts later in a more leisurely fashion to assess their implications. Besides, you'll want to file these baseline results for future reference and compare them to later results, after aerobics conditioning.

categories. In addition to a performance assessment, you receive an individualized exercise program, some advice about safety, and cumulative data if you've had a FITCHECK previously. Actually, a FITCHECK every six months is an excellent way to measure your improvement.

FITCHECK is a quick assessment. It's by no means intended to take the place of a thorough physical in a doctor's office.

The health-care professionals both at the Institute and at the Cooper Clinic have given a lot of thought to what should comprise an adequate checkup. That's why we view certain procedures as mandatory if you are to gain sufficient knowledge about your body's baseline fitness level before you begin an aerobics regimen.

## The Importance of Treadmill Stress Testing

You'll note that the exam we just described includes, for women over age 40, a treadmill stress test, also known as a "stress" or "exercise" ECG. Even today, not that many doctors have the equipment or the knowledge to administer them. Thus, it may not be practical for most over-40 women to have a treadmill test before they start aerobics. As a precautionary measure, then, we insist that they follow the six-week aerobics starter program outlined later in this chapter.

However, if you're over 40 and you do find a doctor or clinic that will give you a treadmill test, by all means take advantage of it. We think that, correctly done, stress ECGs are an unparalleled way to assess your cardiovascular and pulmonary functioning.

Why is a treadmill test so useful?

The heart is masterful at disguising its problems until they become severe. For some unfortunate people, sudden death is the first and only symptom of underlying, severe coronary artery disease. We all know of people who died of heart attacks when no one—including the victim—knew there was even the slightest problem.

Treadmill stress testing, administered properly, is an excellent way to detect any problem before it manifests in dangerous or perhaps fatal ways.

The benefits of a treadmill test are fourfold: It can expose the presence of obstructed coronary disease; it determines your level of cardiovascular fitness; it helps your doctor design a safe, progressive exercise program just for you; and it's a valuable tool for screening post–heart-attack victims to assess their likelihood to have further problems. In short, treadmill stress testing is both a diagnostic and a prognostic tool.

## How Is a Treadmill Stress Test Performed?

If you visit the Cooper Clinic for a complete physical exam, you can expect the following procedure for your treadmill stress test:

A technician will attach twelve electrodes, or wires, to your body. These send signals to fifteen leads, giving us a complete picture of what's happening to your heart before, during, and after the test. The number of electrodes other doctors use varies, but at least seven are essential.

We know of one case where a doctor—not at the Cooper Clinic—administered the test with only a three-lead system. Not only was this monitoring system inadequate, it was also dangerous. A male patient almost died because the doctor's monitoring system wasn't sensitive enough to assess the man's cardiovascular response to exercise.

In seventeen years of stress testing at the Cooper Clinic, we've never had a fatality and have had to resuscitate only one person. And we have done over 65,000 tests!

Next, prior to starting the active treadmill phase of the test, our technician will take several baseline electrocardiograms. They'll be done while you're in a supine position, a standing position, and after 30 seconds of hyperventilation (rapid, deep breathing).

Before the treadmill is turned on, you'll be given time to acquaint yourself with how it works. Then, the technician will ask you to step on the treadmill belt and grasp the handbar in front of you.

When you give the signal, the machine is turned on, forcing you to take long, languid strides. You'll be encouraged to hold on to the handbar until you've adapted to the rhythm of the machine and feel steady enough to let go. The test doesn't start until you let go, because holding the bar significantly decreases the energy you expend.

At the Cooper Clinic, we use the treadmill test format called the "Balke protocol." This approach requires that we increase the elevation of the treadmill every minute until the twenty-fifth minute, while the speed of the belt remains constant (3.3 mph). After the twenty-fifth minute, the speed is increased 0.2 mph each minute until the patient is too exhausted to continue. The effect is that of walking with increasing speed up an incline that gradually gets steeper.

Our goal is to encourage you to keep going on the machine until you approach your predicted maximum heart rate (PMHR), a concept we introduced in chapter 4. For women, the PMHR is 220 minus your age.

Some doctors have their patients stop when they reach 85 percent of their PMHR. We think this is a mistake. Follow-up statistical analysis on the 65,000 tests we've administered show that we would have overlooked at least a third of the abnormalities that our tests uncovered if we hadn't strongly encouraged our patients to reach their PMHR, or at least close to it.

**Predicted Maximum Heart Rate Adjusted for Age and Fitness**

(If the level of the fitness is unknown prior to treadmill stress testing, use the "Fair" category. Then adjust to another category as is necessary during the test.)

| Age | Very Poor and Poor | Fair | Good and Excellent |
|---|---|---|---|
| 20 | 201 | 201 | 196 |
| 21 | 199 | 200 | 196 |
| 22 | 198 | 199 | 195 |
| 23 | 197 | 198 | 195 |
| 24 | 196 | 198 | 194 |
| 25 | 195 | 197 | 194 |
| 26 | 194 | 196 | 193 |

| Age | Very Poor and Poor | Fair | Good and Excellent |
|---|---|---|---|
| 27 | 193 | 196 | 193 |
| 28 | 192 | 195 | 192 |
| 29 | 191 | 193 | 192 |
| 30 | 190 | 193 | 191 |
| 31 | 189 | 193 | 191 |
| 32 | 188 | 192 | 190 |
| 33 | 187 | 191 | 189 |
| 34 | 186 | 191 | 189 |
| 35 | 184 | 190 | 188 |
| 36 | 183 | 189 | 188 |
| 37 | 182 | 189 | 187 |
| 38 | 181 | 188 | 187 |
| 39 | 180 | 187 | 186 |
| 40 | 179 | 186 | 186 |
| 41 | 178 | 186 | 185 |
| 42 | 177 | 185 | 185 |
| 43 | 176 | 184 | 184 |
| 44 | 175 | 184 | 184 |
| 45 | 174 | 183 | 183 |
| 46 | 173 | 182 | 183 |
| 47 | 172 | 181 | 182 |
| 48 | 171 | 181 | 182 |
| 49 | 170 | 180 | 181 |
| 50 | 168 | 179 | 180 |
| 51 | 167 | 179 | 180 |
| 52 | 166 | 178 | 179 |
| 53 | 165 | 177 | 179 |
| 54 | 164 | 176 | 178 |
| 55 | 163 | 176 | 178 |
| 56 | 162 | 175 | 177 |
| 57 | 161 | 174 | 177 |
| 58 | 160 | 174 | 176 |
| 59 | 159 | 173 | 176 |
| 60 | 158 | 172 | 175 |
| 61 | 157 | 172 | 175 |
| 62 | 156 | 171 | 174 |
| 63 | 155 | 170 | 174 |
| 64 | 154 | 169 | 173 |

| Age | Very Poor and Poor | Fair | Good and Excellent |
|---|---|---|---|
| 65 | 152 | 169 | 173 |
| 66 | 151 | 168 | 172 |
| 67 | 150 | 167 | 171 |
| 68 | 149 | 167 | 171 |
| 69 | 148 | 166 | 170 |
| 70 | 147 | 165 | 170 |

We've established 15 minutes on the treadmill as a minimum realistic goal for the average middle-aged woman. This is roughly equivalent to having the physical capacity to run 2 miles in 20 minutes. If you can make it this far, or longer, you've already reached a high enough level of fitness to be gaining some minimal protection from coronary heart disease.

**Definition of Fitness Categories for Women*, Based on Treadmill Stress Test Results (12,000 Women)**

| | Age Group (years) | | | | |
|---|---|---|---|---|---|
| FITNESS CATEGORY | <30 | 30–39 | 40–49 | 50–59 | 60+ |
| ☐ VERY POOR | <10:09 | <8:59 | <7:29 | <5:59 | <4:59 |
| ☐ POOR | 10:10–12:52 | 9:00–11:29 | 7:30– 9:59 | 6:00– 7:59 | 5:00– 6:29 |
| ☐ FAIR | 12:53–15:59 | 11:30–14:59 | 10:00–12:59 | 8:00–10:38 | 6:30– 9:16 |
| ☐ GOOD | 16:00–19:59 | 15:00–17:39 | 13:00–15:59 | 10:39–13:14 | 9:17–11:59 |
| ☐ EXCELLENT | 20:00–23:01 | 17:40–20:30 | 16:00–18:29 | 13:15–15:55 | 12:00–15:33 |
| ☐ SUPERIOR | 23:02+ | 20:31+ | 18:30+ | 15:56+ | 15:34+ |

*Based on the Cooper Clinic modified Balke treadmill protocol: 3.3 mph (90m/min), 0% for first min, 2% for second min, +1% for each additional min. to 25%, then +.2 mph until exhaustion.

As soon as the test is completed, you'll be told to walk slowly for 3 to 5 minutes before you stop. Then you'll be asked to lie down for at least 10 minutes, during which time several more electrocardiograms will be taken.

## A Controversy in Decline

For years, treadmill stress testing was the subject of heated medical controversy. We're glad to report that the most influential segments of the medical community have now largely come to recognize the test's benefits.

The *New England Journal of Medicine,* which for years criticized treadmill evaluation, is one example. In its July 14, 1983, "Current Concept" column, the editors wrote:

"In patients suspected of having coronary artery disease, the value of the exercise electrocardiogram and the diagnosis of both presence of and severity of the disease is well established."

Any lingering criticism revolves around so-called false-positive and false-negative results. At the Cooper Clinic, we see this as a problem of tests poorly administered, not an inherent problem with the test. And we say this with a history of more than 65,000 tests behind us as of this writing.

First of all, no medical test is 100 percent accurate. To the critics who maintain that 25 percent of all people tested are false positive—in short, the test indicates a problem where there's none—we cite our extensive experience at the Cooper Clinic. Only 11 percent of more than 12,000 women tested have an abnormal test that, theoretically, could be a false positive. And after extensive follow-up research, we determined that the sensitivity level of the test we administer is between 80 and 85 percent accurate. And our sample is probably one of the largest in the country, we might add, because we've been enthusiastic advocates of treadmill stress testing when most doctors were still shunning it.

## The Six-Week Starter Program

This section is for beginners. It doesn't count if you're already a confirmed bodybuilder or weekend tennis player. If you've never undertaken a formal exercise program before, you're a beginner by our definition.

Why this emphasis on progressing slowly?

As we explained in detail in chapter 2, the impact of aerobics on that marvelous biochemical machine, your body, is markedly different—and more life-enhancing—than are the results from other types of exercise. But a powerful exercise tool such as aerobics is a two-sided coin. Utilized improperly, its potential for harm is as great as its potential for good. It's not something to undertake frivolously or without fully understanding what you're doing. Think of it as a potent antibiotic. Used properly, it might cure an infection and save your life. Used improperly, it might cause disastrous side-effects.

Our incremental approach is especially important for women over age 40 who, just prior to starting aerobics, have not had the treadmill stress test we so strongly recommend. In the unlikely event that a woman is suffering from an undiagnosed heart problem, for example, any symptoms that reveal themselves during aerobics should be mild.

For a list of those symptoms, refer back to our "Fit Quiz: Mandate for a Medical Exam" (p. 42). Consider any of the symptoms listed there as warning signs and see your doctor immediately.

The starter program below gives you a choice of four aerobic exercises—walking, running, cycling, and swimming. Choose the one that appeals to you, then follow *to the letter* our guidelines on intensity, duration, and frequency.

One final note: *Never* begin an aerobics workout without an appropriate warm-up or end without a proper cool-down. These before-and-after phases are described in depth in chapter 6. Please read that chapter and follow its advice before you embark on your starter program.

### Six-Week Starter Program for Walking, Age-Adjusted

| Week | Distance in Miles | Time Goals* in Minutes for Women Ages . . . <30 | 30–49 | 50+ | Frequency per Week |
|---|---|---|---|---|---|
| 1 | 1.0 | 16 | 18 | 20 | 4–5 |
| 2 | 1.0 | 14 | 16 | 18 | 4–5 |
| 3 | 1.5 | 22 | 24 | 27 | 4–5 |
| 4 | 1.5 | 21 | 23 | 26 | 4–5 |
| 5 | 2.0 | 30 | 32 | 36 | 4–5 |
| 6 | 2.0 | 28 | 30 | 34 | 4–5 |

*Aim to achieve the time goal by the end of the week. If you cannot meet the goal, then repeat the week.

### Six-Week Starter Program for Running/Jogging, Age-Adjusted

| Week | Distance in Miles | Time Goals* in Minutes for Women Ages . . . <30 | 30–49 | 50–59 | Frequency per Week |
|---|---|---|---|---|---|
| 1 | 2.0 | 31 | 32 | 36 | 4–5 |
| 2 | 2.5 | 38 | 40 | 45 | 4–5 |
| 3 | 3.0 | 45:15 | 48 | 54 | 4–5 |
| 4 | 2.0 | 28 | 30 | 32 | 4–5 |
| 5 | 2.0 | 26 | 28 | 30 | 4–5 |
| 6 | 2.0 | 24 | 26 | 28 | 4–5 |

*Aim to achieve the time goal by the end of the week. If you cannot meet the goal, then repeat the week. To reach the goals for the fourth and sixth weeks, a combination of jogging and walking probably will be required. For women 60 and over, we do not recommend starting with a running/jogging program.

### Six-Week Starter Program for Cycling, Age-Adjusted

| Week | Distance in Miles | Time Goals* in Minutes for Women Ages . . . <30 | 30–49 | 50–59 | Frequency per Week |
|---|---|---|---|---|---|
| 1 | 3.0 | 17 | 18 | 19 | 4–5 |
| 2 | 3.0 | 15 | 17 | 18 | 4–5 |

| | | Time Goals* in Minutes for Women Ages . . . | | | |
|---|---|---|---|---|---|
| Week | Distance in Miles | <30 | 30–49 | 50–59 | Frequency per Week |
| 3 | 4.0 | 20 | 22 | 25 | 4–5 |
| 4 | 4.0 | 18 | 20 | 24 | 4–5 |
| 5 | 5.0 | 25 | 26 | 29 | 4–5 |
| 6 | 5.0 | 22 | 25 | 28 | 4–5 |

*Aim to achieve the time goal by the end of the week. If you cannot meet the goal, then repeat the week. For women 60 and older, use only a three-wheeled bicycle or a stationary one. We do not recommend two-wheeled, outdoor cycling for this age group.

### Six-Week Starter Program for Swimming, Age-Adjusted

| | | Time Goals* in Minutes for Women Ages . . . | | | |
|---|---|---|---|---|---|
| Week | Distance in Yards | <30 | 30–49 | 50+ | Frequency per Week |
| 1 | 200 | 6 | 7 | 8 | 4–5 |
| 2 | 300 | 9 | 9:30 | 10 | 4–5 |
| 3 | 400 | 12 | 12:30 | 13 | 4–5 |
| 4 | 450 | 13 | 13:30 | 14 | 4–5 |
| 5 | 500 | 14 | 14:30 | 15 | 4–5 |
| 6 | 600 | 16 | 17 | 18 | 4–5 |

*Use the stroke that enables you to swim the required distance in the required time. We encourage you to rest, as needed, during the initial weeks and this is accounted for in the time goals. If you cannot meet the goal, then repeat the week.

## Field Testing Your Physical Well-Being

Once you've reached a reasonable level of fitness during the Six-Week Starter Program, you're ready to find out where you fall in the lineup of the thousands of women we've tested in your age group.

We devised three convenient tests to rate your overall fitness. Select one and do it wherever you wish—out on a running track, on a road without much traffic, or on sidewalks around your neighborhood.

Your field test can't be scored unless you know two things: the distance you've covered and the time it took. So, before you leave the starting line, make sure you have with you a pedometer or odometer. (Of course, these aren't necessary if you're fortunate enough to have access to a measured running track or swimming pool.) You'll also need a stopwatch or timepiece with a second hand.

If you are serious about a walking or jogging program, you might want to invest in a special athlete's watch that measures time and distance. There are even super-sophisticated devices that measure heart rate.

If you live 5,000 or more feet above sea level, you will have to compensate for the thin air by making changes in your scores on these tests. Read the section on altitude in chapter 10 and use the charts there to make the necessary adjustments.

The point of this field test is to place you in a fitness category with other women your age. As you saw with our starter program, our age categories are: under 30, 30 to 49, and over 50.

## 3-Mile Walking Test

This is an excellent test for older women whose preferred aerobic exercise is walking. It's simple enough: cover 3 miles in the fastest time possible without running. Take the test when you feel rested, be sure to dress comfortably, and *walk on a flat surface.*

**3-Mile Walking Test (No Running)**
Time (Minutes)

| | Age (years) | | | | | |
|---|---|---|---|---|---|---|
| Fitness Category | 13–19 | 20–29 | 30–39 | 40–49 | 50–59 | 60+ |
| I. Very poor | >47:00* | >48:00 | >51:00 | >54:00 | >57:00 | >63:00 |
| II. Poor | 43:01–47:00 | 44:01–48:00 | 46:31–51:00 | 49:01–54:00 | 52:01–57:00 | 57:01–63:00 |
| III. Fair | 39:31–43:00 | 40:31–44:00 | 42:01–46:30 | 44:01–49:00 | 47:01–52:00 | 51:01–57:00 |
| IV. Good | 35:00–39:30 | 36:00–40:30 | 37:30–42:00 | 39:00–44:00 | 42:00–47:00 | 45:00–51:00 |
| V. Excellent | <35:00 | <36:00 | <37:30 | <39:00 | <42:00 | <45:00 |

* < Means "less than"; > means "more than."

## 1.5-Mile Running Test

Run or jog as fast as you can for 1.5 miles. If you don't have access to a measured running track, measure off a 1.5-mile course beforehand using the odometer of your car. The surface should be level or you will throw off your test results. Don't begin until you've warmed up properly, and cool down appropriately afterward.

**1.5-Mile Run Test**
Time (Minutes)

| | Age (years) | | | | | |
|---|---|---|---|---|---|---|
| Fitness Category | 13–19 | 20–29 | 30–39 | 40–49 | 50–59 | 60+ |
| I. Very poor | >18:31* | >19:01 | >19:31 | >20:01 | >20:31 | >21:31 |
| II. Poor | 16:55–18:30 | 18:31–19:00 | 19:01–19:30 | 19:31–20:00 | 20:01–20:30 | 20:31–21:30 |

| Fitness Category | Age (years) 13–19 | 20–29 | 30–39 | 40–49 | 50–59 | 60+ |
|---|---|---|---|---|---|---|
| III. Fair | 14:31–16:54 | 15:55–18:30 | 16:31–19:00 | 17:31–19:30 | 19:01–20:00 | 19:31–20:30 |
| IV. Good | 12:30–14:30 | 13:31–15:54 | 14:31–16:30 | 15:56–17:30 | 16:31–19:00 | 17:31–19:30 |
| V. Excellent | 11:50–12:29 | 12:30–13:30 | 13:00–14:30 | 13:45–15:55 | 14:30–16:30 | 16:30–17:30 |
| VI. Superior | <11:50 | <12:30 | <13:00 | <13:45 | <14:30 | <16:30 |

* < Means "less than"; > means "more than."

## 12-Minute Walking/Running Test

Again, this test is simply a matter of covering the greatest distance that you can comfortably in 12 minutes. The surface should be level or you'll put yourself at a disadvantage. Warm up and cool down as described in chapter 6. And if any unusual symptoms occur during the test, stop immediately.

**12-Minute Walking/Running Test**
Distance (Miles) Covered in 12 Minutes

| Fitness Category | Age (years) 13–19 | 20–29 | 30–39 | 40–49 | 50–59 | 60+ |
|---|---|---|---|---|---|---|
| I. Very Poor | <1.0* | <.96 | <.94 | <.88 | <.84 | <.78 |
| II. Poor | 1.00–1.18 | .96–1.11 | .94–1.05 | .88–.98 | .84–.93 | .78–.86 |
| III. Fair | 1.19–1.29 | 1.12–1.22 | 1.06–1.18 | .99–1.11 | .94–1.05 | .87–.98 |
| IV. Good | 1.30–1.43 | 1.23–1.34 | 1.19–1.29 | 1.12–1.24 | 1.06–1.18 | .99–1.09 |
| V. Excellent | 1.44–1.51 | 1.35–1.45 | 1.30–1.39 | 1.25–1.34 | 1.19–1.30 | 1.10–1.18 |
| VI. Superior | >1.52 | >1.46 | >1.40 | >1.35 | >1.31 | >1.19 |

* < Means "less than"; > means "more than."

# The Bottom Line—Your Current Fitness Level

After years and years of honing these field-test scores, we can safely say that they're almost as accurate as laboratory measurements made on a treadmill.

With your test results in hand, you know exactly how you rank, fitness-wise, among your peers. Utilizing the information in the next four chapters, it's now time to build on this baseline level of physical well-being.

Some of you may be so out of shape that you can't meet the minimum weekly requirements during the Six-Week Starter Program. If so, just keep repeating the first week's requirements until you succeed.

Another possibility is to progress past the Six-Week Starter Program but limit your exercise to less strenuous activities such as walking. The ultimate minimum goal is the "good" category of fitness, age-adjusted, based on your treadmill time, your field-test results or by earning a minimum of 30 aerobic points each week.

# 6
# Before and After the Main Event

Transitions are important in life, in your career, in your family life, and certainly in your daily aerobics regimen.

The warm-up and cool-down periods before and after your aerobics activity are transitions—transitions for your body. Your body needs these gradual speed-up and slow-down phases or it might rebel. And the form that rebellion could take might be a lot more than you bargained for. In the worst instance, it could even take the form of a heart attack.

Of course, if you've followed our pre-aerobics medical advice in the preceding chapter, you can be confident of having a relatively trouble-free heart before you even begin to exercise. However, ignoring the warm-up and cool-down phases of aerobics, combined with such abrupt changes as sharp temperature increases or decreases, could have catastrophic consequences.

*Warming up and cooling down are as important to your aerobics experience as the main event.* You'd be foolish to think otherwise.

## Warming Up

You wouldn't start your car on a cold winter day and immediately try to drive off, would you? If you've ever done it, you know what happens—your car invariably stalls before you're halfway down the block.

Launching into a vigorous aerobics activity without sufficient warm-up is just as foolhardy. Your body may not "stall" the first time you do it, but it will eventually. Besides, why put your body through such kind of stress when it's so easy to avoid?

The point of a 3-to-5-minute warm-up is twofold:

Warm-ups guard against injuries—those cramps, sprains, shinsplints, and other tendon and musculoskeletal problems that are so aggravating. But they needn't happen at all if you follow the advice outlined below.

A good warm-up routine also works all the muscles of your body—not just those that are directly engaged in your aerobics activity. For example, runners and cyclists get plenty of exercise in their legs and lower bodies but not much in their upper bodies. Swimmers, on the other hand, utilize muscles all over their bodies. The point is to choose a warm-up routine that complements your aerobics activity so that all the muscles of your body have gotten some exercise by the time your finish.

The warm-up routine we insist on at the Aerobics Center focuses on *flexibility* and cardiovascular exercises. These include range-of-motion exercises, brisk walking before jogging, or slow walking before aerobic walking.

We also believe in *strengthening* exercises—but *after* your aerobics activity. Strengthening and weight-lifting exercises build up an oxygen debt. It makes no sense to incur this debt just before an aerobics activity, the whole point of which is to consume additional oxygen. (More about combining aerobics with strengthening exercises in chapter 9.)

## Stretching: What's It All About?

Besides helping you relax mentally and physically, stretching may help prevent injuries and soreness. How? By increasing your flexibility.

Flexibility is the ability to move a part of the body through its full range of motion. For example, drop your head forward and roll it in a half-circle from shoulder to shoulder. Can you do this easily or are there places where you meet resistance or pain? Do this exercise for a while and it will become easier and easier for you. The creakiness of aging may be the only reason your neck has lost some of its agility.

Aside from aerobics, flexibility exercises are good in their own right. You might think of them as preventive measures to reduce the risk of musculoskeletal problems. More than 50 percent of women who have lower back pain can trace the problem to poor abdominal muscle tone and inadequate lower back flexibility. The right stretching and strengthening routine can reduce the pain and eventually eliminate the problem.

Flexibility exercises, judiciously chosen to treat a specific muscular malady, can work wonders. They can reduce muscle tension, decrease soreness, improve coordination, increase range of motion, and help prevent injuries later. Through daily flexibility routines, you can regain the suppleness of youth in any limb where the slow process of decrepitude has set in from lack of adequate use.

Kathleen Munns, a researcher at the Biogerontology Laboratory at the University of Wisconsin, conducted a study that showed just what can be accomplished with twelve weeks of stretching exercises. Twenty people, average age 72, participated. At the end of three months, these senior citizens had increased the range of motion in their necks by 28 percent, in their wrists by 13 percent, their shoulders 8 percent, their hips and backs 27 percent, their knees 12 percent, and their ankles 48 percent.

## Stretching Guidelines

Stretching exercises can be misused, however. Here are some general guidelines to keep in mind before you begin:

All stretching exercises should be performed slowly. Speed is not of the essence here. Indeed, speed is antithetical to stretching, since the whole point is slow, languid movements to elongate your musculature.

There are two ways to elongate your muscles—by ballistic stretching, which involves bouncing and bobbing motions; or static stretching, which is a deliberate, sustained s-t-r-e-t-c-h held for a number of seconds. Although each has its place in a good program, the majority of the flexibility exercises you will find here fall into the static category.

What sensation should you feel if you're executing a static stretching exercise correctly?

Keep in mind that you are stretching a muscle, or set of muscles, beyond its normal length. That's your goal, so feeling your muscles pull is fine. What you must guard against is overstretching. Pain is your signal. When a position starts to hurt, ease off to a more comfortable level and go no further that day trying to deepen that particular movement. However, as you continue to do that same exercise day after day, you will soon be able to stretch farther and farther without pain.

Stretch easily, letting the tension in your muscles ooze out over the course of your exercise routine. If you are new to stretching and your muscles are very tight, don't hold a stretch longer than 10 to 15 seconds. As your flexibility increases, you can increase a stretch in both time and tension.

Think *relaxation* as you do these exercises, relaxing the muscles naturally as you stretch. Breathe slowly and rhythmically to foster this relaxation.

You won't see the benefits from your stretching exercises overnight. Women who have such unrealistic expectations will injure themselves. *Do not ever bounce or attempt violently to stretch a muscle group, thinking that the more pain you can sustain today, the more limber you'll be tomorrow.* To the contrary: what you'll probably be tomorrow is laid up with pulled ligaments, muscles, and tendons.

Stretching before aerobics is mandatory because it helps prepare the muscles for concerted motion when you're stiff from inactivity. An additional stretch afterward is encouraged too and may surprise you. Since your body temperature is raised then, your muscles are warmer and therefore more limber.

## Warm-up Routine

One of the warm-up routines we recommend at the Aerobics Center is outlined below. Study the illustrations and explanatory captions carefully before you attempt the movements.

These are *suggested* warm-up routines, which is not to say you can't do your own exercises or follow your instincts and stretch in a way that feels comfortable for you.

### Fit Tips: Warm-up Routine for Runners

Here's a free-form routine for runners. It encourages you to do some of your favorite limbering-up maneuvers—or to use your imagination and make up some new ones.

- **First two minutes.** Do stretching exercises for the arms, legs, and back.
- **Third minute.** Walk in a circle at a fairly rapid pace.
- **Fourth minute.** Alternate 15 seconds of walking with 15 seconds of jogging in place (a very slow run).
- **Fifth minute.** Jog continuously at a 12- or 13-minute-mile pace.

Now you are ready to break into a full run.

### Fit Tips: Abbreviated Warm-up Routine for Runners

If you are short of time, incorporate the warm-up into your run this way:

- Run the first quarter-mile at a very slow pace.
- During this warm-up jog, do some modified calisthenics. Swing your arms; raise and lower your shoulders; bend your body up, down, and around; find various other imaginative ways to limber up and stretch your upper torso while you move along. Do what comes naturally!

### Fit Tips: 10-Minute General Warm-up Routine

This preparatory routine could precede any form of aerobics. It takes 10 minutes. But, if you're pressed for time, it can be shortened to 2 or 3 minutes. In that case, cut right to the two most important maneuvers—the standing leg stretch and the Achilles tendon stretch. Give yourself adequate room and do:

- **Arms circles.** Extend your arms straight out from your sides, rotate them counterclockwise 10 times, then reverse direction and rotate them 10 more

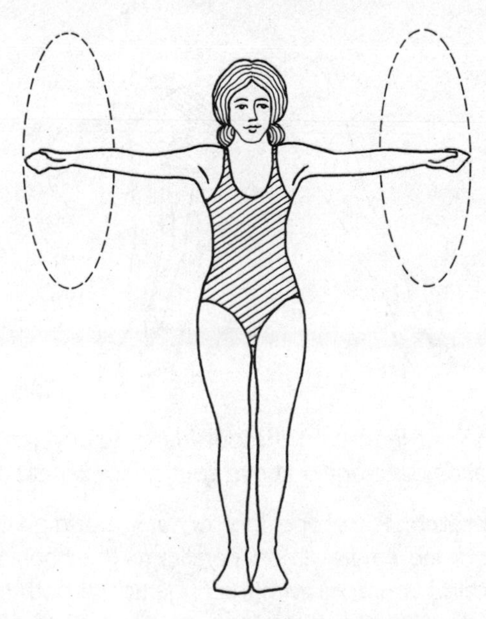

times. Be expansive in your movements, making sure the invisible circle you form in the air has a diameter of at least 2 feet.

- **Twists.** Stand, legs about 30 inches apart, and arms extended as above. Twist your torso all the way to the right, then all the way to the left, letting your arms swing freely as you move. Repeat 10 times.

- **Torso circles.** With your legs still apart as above, clasp your hands above your head. With your hands, bend and touch the outside of your left foot, then the

ground between your legs, then the outside of your right foot. Return to an erect position, hands once again above your head. Repeat 10 times.

- **Standing leg stretch.** Place one foot on a 3-foot-high chair or table and straighten out your leg so it's almost parallel to the floor. Stretch slowly and deliberately, touching your toes with the fingertips of both hands and bowing your head toward your knee. Hold for a count of 10 to 15. Repeat with the other leg. This is an excellent maneuver for limbering up the hamstrings and the big tendons at the hollows of the knees.

- **Sitting toe touches.** (A substitute exercise for the standing leg stretch.) Sit on the floor with your legs spread apart slightly and extended in front of you. Try

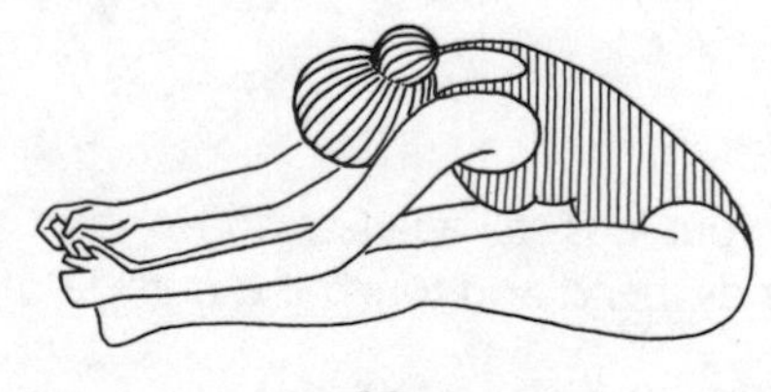

to touch your toes with both hands, bringing your forehead as close to your knees as possible. Don't bounce in an attempt to reach your feet. Just stretch toward your feet as a cat might stretch, v-e-r-y s-l-o-w-l-y. Return to your starting position and repeat 10 times.

- **Sprint.** Assume a squatting position, hands on the floor on either side of your body. Extend one leg straight back as far as possible and gradually transfer some of your weight to that extended leg as you count to 5. Return to your original position. Alternate your legs, then repeat the whole cycle 5 times. This stretches the muscles in your calves.

- **Achilles tendon stretch.** Stand in front of a blank wall, palms resting on it at about eye level. Take one step backward, supporting your weight with your hands. As you lower one heel to the ground, feel your calf and ankle muscles stretching. Hold for 15 seconds. Alternate your legs, then repeat the cycle 5 times. If you have any Achilles tendon problems, do this exercise several times a day.

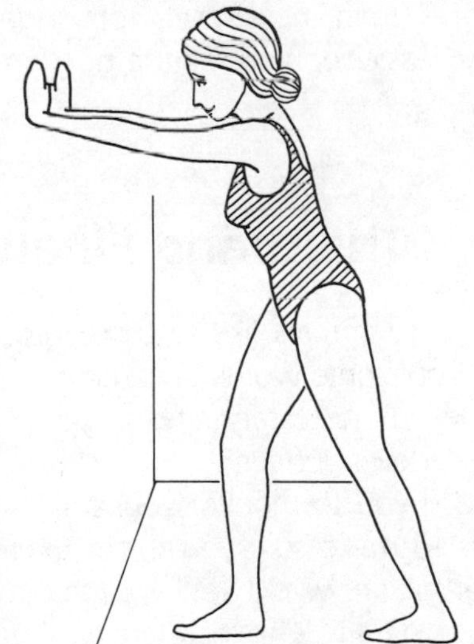

## Cooling Down

It may surprise you to learn that the riskiest phase of aerobics is not the activity itself. It's the seconds after you stop vigorous exercise.

There's a physiological explanation for this:

Recent research shows that during exercise, your adrenal glands produce two natural stimulants called "epinephrine" (known more commonly as "adrenaline") and "norepinephrine." Both rush into the bloodstream during the most strenuous part of your exercise, when your blood pressure is elevated too.

When you stop your exercise, your blood pressure drops, but the levels of these two hormones continue to rise for a time, stimulating your heart and trying to keep your blood pressure up. Their message to the heart: keep pumping fast no matter what other orders you're receiving from other parts of your body.

These adrenal messages explain why people who ignore proper cool-down procedures sometimes faint, experience potentially dangerous irregular heartbeats, or even have heart attacks. Your heart is getting conflicting messages when you stop dead in your tracks after a vigorous workout.

To prevent this cardiac conflict, ease off gradually. Decrease from peak activity to somewhat slower activity until you finally stop 5 or—in the case of a particularly exhausting session—10 minutes later. This gives your body adequate time to stop producing those heart stimulants and allows it to return more naturally to its pre-exercise state.

If you want to let your pulse be your guide, then continue moving until your heart rate drops below 120 beats per minute—or below 100 if you are over 50 years old. If your heart rate stays higher than these levels for longer than the usual 5 minutes it should take to recover, go easier on yourself the next time: don't exercise as vigorously or as long.

## The Grand Finale

Some runners, cyclists, and swimmers like to burst into full speed at the end of their workout. If this describes you, some words of caution:

A 5-minute cool-down is necessary after a typical workout. But after a "kicker" finale, you'll need to recover even longer.

In addition, we advise you to monitor your final sprint carefully. Concentrate on how your body responds to make sure you're not overexerting yourself. If your body meets the challenge, great. Just reward it well with that more leisurely cool-down. You'll find that pampering your body a little at this stage will pay safety dividends in the long run.

### Fit Tips: Cool-down Don'ts

Your goal immediately after aerobics is to make sure that the blood is pumped from your lower extremities back into the central circulatory system. For the first 3 to 5 minutes after aerobics:

- Don't stand still. If you've been running or jogging, start walking. If you're swimming, tread water or walk around the shallow end of the pool. If you're cycling, slow down, then hop off and walk. If you're in an aerobics class, don't skip out before the cool-down phase.
- Don't sit down immediately. If you must take your weight off your legs, then lie down and elevate your feet.
- If you take your pulse, don't stand motionless but walk around while you're doing it.
- Don't become so distracted by conversation with companions that you forget to keep moving.
- If you're running and hit a stoplight or stop sign, don't come to a complete halt. Instead, run in place until you can proceed, or jog a short distance back and forth at the corner until the light changes or the traffic clears.
- Even if you keep moving while you're doing it, don't force your body to adjust to an abrupt change of temperature immediately after aerobics. For example, don't head for a steamroom, sauna, whirlpool, or hot shower right away; nor a warm car on a winter day.

## Beyond Discomfort

There are three indexes of overexertion: (1) how you feel, a purely subjective measurement; (2) your respiration, or breathing rate, after a 5-minute recovery; (3) your heart rate after a 5-minute recovery.

• **Personal overexertion gauge.** The rule of thumb is this: aerobics should make you feel better 5 minutes after you stop than you felt before you started.

If, instead of feeling refreshed, you feel any of a number of negatives—worn out; severely breathless; lightheaded; dizzy; nauseated; doubled over with cramps; tightness, pain, or numbness in your chest or in your left arm or shoulder—realize that these are distress signals from your body. You're overdoing it to the point of danger.

Following are our recommendations for dealing with such exercise emergencies.

• **Your breathing-rate response.** At the end of your 5-minute cool-down, start to monitor your breathing. At this stage you may still be breathing more deeply and faster than normal. But during the next 5 minutes your breathing should return to its normal rate at rest—that's 12 to 16 breaths per minute.

If you're still breathless 10 minutes after you've stopped aerobics, something is wrong. You've clearly been pushing too hard in your workout—or you may have some type of lung or respiratory problem.

• **Your heart-rate response.** Here are the benchmarks for the recovery of your heart rate:

Five minutes after you stop aerobics—that's just as you finish your cool-down—your heart rate should be:

Below 120 beats per minute if you are younger than 50 years of age.

Below 100 for women over age 50.

Ten minutes after you stop aerobics, your pulse should be at or below 100.

This will vary depending on how conditioned you are and your age. The more conditioned you are, the faster your heart will return to its resting rate. The older you are, the slower your heart will beat even during exhausting activity.

## Exercise Emergency: What to Do When You've Overdone It

We hope you never need the advice we're about to give. You shouldn't if you warm up properly, don't push yourself beyond reasonable limits during aerobics, and cool down gradually.

However, should you find yourself feeling lightheaded while exercising or during the cool-down phase, do the following:

- Put your arms above your head and slow down, but, by all means, continue moving for another 3 to 5 minutes. This keeps the blood pressure up and the blood circulating to your heart and head.

If, on the other hand, you feel so spent or nauseated or out of control that you have to stop:

- Don't remain standing. Lie down flat on your back with your feet level with your head. Even better, place your feet higher than your head. You might lie on the floor and perch your feet on the edge of a chair, for example. This position enables the blood that has "pooled" in your legs to return more easily to the upper half of your body—to your all-important heart and head.
- If the negative sensations are severe, consult your physician before resuming any exercise activity.

## More Key Questions about Your Aerobics Routine

Women frequently ask us about the all-important physical problems caused by warm-ups and cool-downs. Here are some typical questions and our answers:

**Fit query:** I recently started an exercise program, a combination of jogging outdoors and stationary running indoors during bad weather. By the second week, my leg muscles were painful and swollen and my joints hurt. I stopped my program immediately and, within a couple of days, the pain went away. Am I babying myself too much?

**Answer:** We'd wager you're a woman starting from zero. You've never run before. Why, then, are you surprised when your stiff muscles and rusty joints let you know about it? They're not used to all this activity. Clearly, they need as much conditioning as your heart and lungs do.

In your case, stopping wasn't necessary. Instead, you should have increased the number of flexibility exercises, especially those aimed at the muscles and joints that caused you the most trouble. You could also have cut down on the intensity but prolonged the duration of your jogging phase for a few days in the very beginning. If that didn't placate your muscles sufficiently, you could have switched to another type of aerobic exercise briefly—swimming, for example. Swimming and jogging put stress on different muscle groups.

Of course, it's also possible that you simply overdid it that first week of your program. Hopefully, you followed our Six-Week Starter Program recommendations (see chapter 5) for the first week's activity for women in your age group. If not, go back and try again, more slowly this time.

•

**Fit query:** There's a circuit training class that I like to take once a week. The only problem is that it's right after work, which means I have to do my usual 20-minute run afterward. Is that all right?

**Answer:** Circuit training involves weight-lifting activities that increase your body's oxygen debt. Circuit training, when done properly, also has an aerobic component. So, on the day you take the class, don't wear yourself out by tacking on an additional endurance activity such as running. It's overdoing it.

•

**Fit query:** I'm a neophyte at aerobics and I confess the idea of getting too out of breath frightens me. Can you allay my fears?

**Answer:** No one has ever died from holding his or her breath. It's impossible. You faint first and then start breathing regularly again. You're just not used to the sensation of deep, rhythmic breathing that aerobics induces. You'll get used to it—and come to crave it as the means to a more invigorated life.

•

**Fit query:** Sometimes I feel quite giddy during or after exercise. Is this normal?

**Answer:** Those symptoms aren't normal. There are two possible explanations:

Yours could be a case of breathing incorrectly. You could be hyperventilating, which means you're breathing faster or even more deeply than you need to for the amount of exercise you're doing. Hyperventilation changes the chemical balance of oxygen and carbon dioxide in your blood. This in turn affects your brain. Besides dizziness, hyperventilation can create buzzing in the ears, tingling sensations in the limbs, and, taken to extremes, a fainting spell.

The second possible cause is more serious. If the sensation was triggered by insufficient blood supply to your brain due to a heart or blood vessel problem, you should not be exercising at all.

Since you don't know which explanation applies to you, visit your doctor to check it out.

•

**Fit query:** I sweat a lot during aerobics. How much and which fluid is best for me to drink to replenish my body's water supply?

**Answer:** Water is your best bet, although fruit juices are fine too. Commercial products with added sugar and salts aren't necessary—unless you are training excessively—because the amount of salt you lose through perspiration is adequately replenished during the average meal. But listen to your body. If you notice unusual fatigue, nausea, and/or muscle cramping, your body may be salt deficient. If so, some of the commercially available electrolyte drinks may be of value. And remember, for good health, your body needs six to eight glasses of water every day, regardless of your level of physical activity.

•

**Fit query:** Can strenuous aerobics induce a heart attack?

**Answer:** Researchers at the Aerobics Center tackled this question in a study entitled, "The Acute Cardiac Risk of Strenuous Exercise," published in the *Journal of the American Medical Association* (October 17, 1980). They studied 2,935 adults who exercised a total of 374,728 hours over a period of five years. Running and walking, this group had covered a total of 1.6 million miles. Only two heart attacks occurred, neither of which was fatal. For women, our researchers concluded that the maximum estimated risk of a heart attack during 10,000 hours of vigorous exercise was 0.2—that's less than one-quarter of 1 percent!

The Aerobics Center data base has grown enormously since then and our researchers have continued to study cardiac risk from exercise. Now, with nearly seventeen years of experience, we have a much larger sample. Collectively, this group has engaged in over 1.25 million hours of exercise, including more than 6 million miles of walking and running. The only additional cardiac event was the death of one man in May 1985. He was in poor shape and didn't follow our guidelines about progressing slowly.

Provided that our basic safety guidelines are followed, our exercise data base—one of the largest in the country—offers incontestable evidence that the risk of sudden cardiac death during exercise is extremely low. Overall, habitual aerobics is associated with just the opposite—a *decreased* risk of heart attack, because aerobics strengthen the cardiovascular system.

•

**Fit query:** What are the guidelines for exercising when I'm fatigued from overwork or lack of sleep?

**Answer:** Exercise is important, but don't be foolish about it. Inordinate fatigue, insufficient sleep, or undue emotional strain combined with strenuous exercise could cause undesirable consequences. You don't want to find out what those undesirable consequences are, so skip exercising for a day or two until you're on a more even keel.

# 7

# Getting Started—The Hardest Part

We're not exaggerating when we say starting an aerobics program is the most daunting part. Here is the odd thing: Interview the average woman in her initial week or two and you'll hear mostly complaints. She'll describe every little ache and pain and how much she really hates what she's doing but through sheer force of will she's doing it anyway. Interview that same woman seven months later, asking her to recall what it was like in the beginning. Chances are she'll stare at you blankly or give you a one-liner and move on to the joys of aerobics.

It's our experience that people who get beyond the six-month point are sold. (Fifty percent of all people who start an aerobics program drop out between the third and sixth months.) They're people committed for the long haul. For them, the benefits they derive from aerobics are so life-enhancing that most have a hard time remembering any negatives.

There are negatives in the beginning. Sore muscles are the least of it. The real barriers are psychological. Actually, they're the same barriers you have to overcome to meet any major challenge in your life. This challenge just happens to be physical.

There are definite plateaus of progress that most people who stick with an aerobics program experience. Here's the typical pattern: first agony, then discouragement, then determination, then minor breakthroughs (at about the six-week point), then success, then smugness.

None of this happens overnight, of course. Most people don't get to the gloating stage until several months into the program.

We're going to assume, for the moment, that you're a beginner. When you put down this book, you'll have sufficient motivation to put on a pair of running, cycling, or aerobic dance shoes and give it a try. That much is almost guaranteed. But your initial burst of enthusiasm will quickly dissipate if you don't have the proper attitude about the commitment you're making.

Let's examine your thoughts during that crucial first six months, when the drawbacks may still loom larger than the rewards.

## Getting the Cobwebs Out of Your Body

Sure, it hurts. What do you expect after months, perhaps years, of sedentary living? Our best advice is to go slowly. Follow the Age-Adjusted Six-Week Progressive Starter Program charts given in chapter 5.

However, if any pain persists longer than three to four days, it may be more than the usual beginner's woes. We suggest you study the section about typical injuries in chapter 11 to make sure you're doing everything possible to prevent injuries—and to find out if your current ailment is serious enough to warrant medical attention.

## That Crucial First Attempt

Maybe the physical tugs are nothing compared to the humiliation you feel about your appearance the first time you put on exercise clothes. "How could I let myself get this out of shape!" is your wail.

If you think your initial attempt out on the track—or on the dance floor or in the swimming pool—was an unmitigated disaster, read on.

In her book *Running Together*, Alison Turnbull, a British journalist and marathoner, interviewed thirty-one of her compatriots, most of whom had started running fairly recently. Here's what they recall about that unforgettable first run—then notice how much they're running today:

**Vicki, 17-year-old student:** "I couldn't run for ¼ mile without stopping to catch my breath." (Now runs 45 miles a week.)

**Lynne, 30-year-old administrator:** "I felt awkward, embarrassed, fat, wheezy, sweaty, positive I wouldn't keep it up." (Now runs 30 miles a week.)

**Lesley, 33-year-old mother:** "I've never smoked in my life, and considered myself to be fairly fit since I walk a lot. But I couldn't stop coughing for about 2 hours!" (Now runs 2½ hours a week.)

**Carol, 34-year-old nurse:** "I felt terrible—as if my lungs would burst and my legs would break. I also remember the pain of my bottom wobbling up and down." (Now runs 35 miles a week.)

**Molly, 39-year-old school secretary:** "I felt foolish! I did not want to be seen, especially by pupils at the school where I work." (Now runs 4 hours a week.)

**Joan, 40-year-old receptionist:** "I felt dreadful, mainly because I tried to run a mile first time out, and I couldn't. I had to stop about six times." (Now runs 2½ hours a week.)

**Maureen, 43-year-old sociologist:** "My throat burned, my legs felt like jelly. I was embarrassed at my pudgy shape. I ran under cover of darkness." (Now running races regularly.)

Embarrassment is common among women when they start an exercise program. Men, in contrast, say they feel "inadequate." This isn't surprising, since male brawn and a macho image are still revered in many segments of our society.

## Dismissing the Excuses from Your Mind

In the beginning, any battle with your body is going to be minor compared to the war in your head. You'll be amazed at the excuses your mind concocts to turn you away from "this madness."

"It's boring"; "It's too time-consuming"; "I'm too tired to exercise"; "I need immediate results to stay motivated"; "I don't have a convenient place to do it"; "I have a bad back, so I really shouldn't exercise"; "Exercise will cut into my social life."

For almost every excuse you can invent, there's a reasonable solution.

Take *"It's boring."* Many runners and cyclists listen to a radio or cassette tapes while they log their daily mileage. Or, if they're like Millie Cooper, they plan their day's activities. Or, if they enjoy communing with nature, they look around at the wonders of the passing scenery.

*"It's too time-consuming"* and *"I don't have a convenient place to do it"* are really weak excuses. The beauty of aerobics is its adaptability. If attending classes takes too much time, choose a solitary form of aerobics you can do anytime, anyplace. Brisk walking is aerobic exercise. Instead of hopping in your car to run an errand, walk—or jog—there. If you demand privacy when you work out, buy a piece of indoor exercise equipment and watch television while you row, walk the treadmill, or cycle.

*"I'm too tired to exercise."* We've already explained how an aerobic session erases fatigue; so being "too tired" isn't an excuse at all. It's a reason to exercise!

*"I need immediate results to stay motivated."* This is the excuse of a person who has a hard time completing any long-term project that involves delayed gratification. Aerobics, like many other worthwhile things in life, takes self-discipline, perseverance, organizational skills, the ability to set and meet goals, and a large measure of commitment. These are success traits, applicable to any endeavor. If you don't possess them, then a lot more than aerobics will go by the boards in your life.

*"I have a bad back, so I really shouldn't exercise."* Depending on your illness or injury, maybe exercise is just what you should be getting—*provided* it's the right form of exercise. Consult your doctor or a sportsmedicine specialist. He or she can recommend activities that will help rehabilitate you if you've had an injury. If you have a chronic condition or disease, they can tell you if and when it's safe to exercise.

*"Exercise will cut into my social life."* In fact, exercise could enhance it. Many

health clubs have snack bars—even elaborate restaurants—where people congregate. People in this setting have something in common, so conversation develops easily. If making new friends is one of your goals, choose a structured aerobics class with a teacher.

There are a few valid excuses beyond the ten medical conditions we listed in chapter 5. They are: temperature-elevating illnesses of a temporary nature (flu, colds, etc.); immunization (lay off exercise for at least twenty-four hours); chronic fatigue (you may be iron deficient); and pregnancy.

Note that we did not include your menstrual period since exercise often helps alleviate cramps. Nor did we include extreme weather conditions. You can always find a way to exercise indoors, regardless of the weather.

Should you have to interrupt your program for more than a few days for one of these valid reasons, make allowance for the time lost. Expect some decrease in your physical abilities. The older you are, the more decrease you can anticipate. Resist the impulse to rush to catch up.

If you're following a program outlined in one of our age-adjusted progressive charts, retreat to the goals several weeks before you stopped. Then monitor your body signals carefully to make sure you aren't overexerting yourself.

Should you drop out of your program for an *in*valid reason, the same advice applies. With this additional word of encouragement:

You're human. So what if you couldn't muster the self-discipline to keep at it and you've made several false starts? That's okay. In fact, with amateur athletes, lapses are the rule rather than the exception. Accept these minor failures. But please don't become so demoralized that you get melodramatic about them and decide to kiss your exercise program goodbye forever.

## Psychological Motivators to Keep You Up and At 'Em

We've got you over the first hurdle—opening the door for the initial week or so of your program. How do we ensure you'll stay with it into the future?

What follows are twenty motivators that have worked for thousands of people all over the world. Some of these hints should strike a resonant chord with you.

Return to this list every time you hit a slump or think you can't go on anymore. Everybody—even the greatest professional athlete in the world—experiences times of confusion and self-doubt. Because this list is fairly comprehensive, we're confident that you'll be able, at any point in your program, to find solace, comfort, and renewed determination here:

- **Know why you're exercising.** There are a myriad reasons why a woman might embark on an exercise program, not the least of which is social. Exercise is a popular leisure activity these days and you may want to join the crowd and meet other men and women who are into it.

However, if this is your only reason, hanging around a health club without ever moving a muscle will serve your purpose just as well. No, we want you to state your exercise goal in terms of your body.

*What do you expect exercise to do for your body?*

You may see exercise mainly as a stress reducer. Or a way to lose weight. To tone your muscles and reconfigure your shape. To improve your cardiovascular fitness. Or simply to make you feel better every day.

Whatever your reason, know what it is and:

• **Write a statement of intent.** A goal put in writing and dated is harder to ignore. But don't make it complicated. Two lines will suffice.

The first sentence should state your goal—for example, "I am exercising to reduce stress and cut down on the alcohol I consume in the early evening for that purpose." The second sentence should state how you intend to reach that goal: "Every weekday, I will swim for thirty minutes right after work when I feel the most wound up; and limit my before-dinner cocktail to one glass of wine."

Leonard Wankel, Ph.D., the graduate program director of the Department of Recreation and Leisure Studies at the University of Alberta, Canada, has studied exercise motivation and thinks "signing up" is crucial. He cites the case of a six-month cardiac rehabilitation program. Of the group who were asked to sign a statement outlining why, when, and how often they would exercise, 65 percent stuck with it. Of those who weren't asked to sign, 42 percent remained faithful. And only 20 percent of the people who refused to sign carried on.

• **Document milestones along the path to your goal.** There's still plenty of room on that sheet of paper headlined "Statement of Intent." Use it to document your progress. Gradually, fill up the page with significant developments.

For example:

> 5/6/87—For the first time, I swam 6 laps without stopping and felt wonderful afterward, not tired at all.
>
> 6/30/87—I seem to be taking the usual crises at work in stride better these days. Thank goodness!
>
> 7/25/87—Won a sprint race against Emma Sue, the Y's number 2 female swimmer. Completed 1 lap in 70 seconds. She couldn't believe it. Neither could I!
>
> 8/10/87—I just realized I haven't had a cocktail before dinner for two weeks now. I haven't even missed it.

• **Adopt your own program, not someone else's.** Exercise, like your choice of occupation and mate, is a highly personal matter. Some women hate swimming; it bothers their sinuses and messes up their hair. Others take to it like a duck to water. Others love aerobic dance but find running boring. Others love cycling, indoors and out.

What's your preference?

There aren't any "shoulds" here. You've got to find your own best exercise—or group of exercises—and ignore your friends' or mate's likes and dislikes. If you adopt their forms of exercise just to be agreeable, you're headed for a fall. When you can't stick with it, you may find yourself unduly demoralized, failing to realize that lack of willpower wasn't the problem at all. The wrong exercise was.

• **Make it fun.** Think of exercise as a wonderful gift you give yourself each day. Change an I-*must*-do-this attitude (the duty-bound approach) to an I-*want*-to-do-this feeling (the hedonistic view).

Find inventive ways to make exercise more enjoyable.

For instance, you might focus on positive thoughts such as the sheer joy of free movement, or how stimulating it is to be alive, or how good it feels finally to be taking better care of your body. Some runners pretend they're a panther skirting across an African plain . . . or an eagle soaring through an azure sky. Or a swimmer might imagine she's a dolphin or a mermaid gliding along.

There are all sorts of visualization techniques and fun mind games you can play with yourself while you're exercising to make the time pass more quickly and enjoyably.

• **Make it convenient.** The bigger production you make out of daily exercise, the faster you'll fail at it. Women who weave their exercise regimen *seamlessly* into their daily schedule are those who easily get some exercise every day.

Many women, like Millie, like to get up earlier than the rest of the family and exercise then. It becomes so routine, it's like part of their daily hygiene. Other people, like myself, see it as a pleasant way to end their day. It's the transition between a harried workday and a leisurely evening. Still others combine commuting with exercise by bicycling to work. More and more office buildings are providing bike racks for those so inclined.

Even if you're really pressed for time, there are always ways to work in aerobics. For example, walk more and faster. Choose the parking spot the farthest away from your office building so you have to cover a half-mile each day to and from your desk. Take the stairs between floors instead of the elevator. Don't hail a taxi; instead walk to appointments.

Where there's a will, there's a way.

• **Choose a pleasant ambience.** Exercising under adverse or stressful conditions is another form of self-sabotage. Make everything about your exercise as appealing as possible.

If you hate your aerobics dance instructor or the music he or she chooses, change classes. If the weather is foul, exercise indoors. If the swimming pool at your health club seems unsanitary, try an exercise machine instead. Or an aerobics dance class. Or running. Or cycling.

In summary, if what you're doing makes you cringe—no matter what the reason—try something else.

• **Develop a pattern but stay flexible.** The standard advice is to work out at the same time each day. The reasoning is sound: if you make a habit of exercise, you'll be less likely to shirk it on days when you feel lazy.

On the other hand, doing the same exercise at the same time in the same place every day can get boring. Then boredom becomes your excuse to give up.

To keep yourself motivated, there are three things you can change: (1) the form of exercise; (2) the time of day; and (3) the place. If your routine is getting too humdrum, try altering one of these things. If you're really fed up, try changing all three at once.

• **Follow the dictates of the seasons.** Choosing seasonal aerobic exercises is one way to inject variety into your program. In winter, for example, go cross-country skiing or play racquetball. In summer, swim and play tennis.

You might also change from individual sports to team sports or vice versa just to keep things interesting.

• **Stay within your comfort zone.** This advice is aimed at compulsive people who approach everything—including leisure and recreation—as if it's a duty.

Easy does it.

Exercise discomfort is a major reason why people drop out. Remember, no one is holding a gun to your head. Exercise at an intensity level that affords some physical rewards without making the experience an ordeal.

• **Seek peer support.** No matter what you're undertaking, it's always helpful to have the backing of family and friends.

Aerobics has a way of bringing family members together. Kids are usually delighted when their parents leave the spectators' bench and become sports participants. Every year, the New York City Marathon seems to attract more running families. In 1986, for example, there was even a mother-son-grandson combination.

Lois Schieffelin, age 75 and a twenty-year veteran of the running track, admits that her 23-year-old grandson John Clifford put her up to entering the grueling 26.2-mile marathon, which no one in her family had ever attempted before. Then the two of them had to coax the 50-year-old John Jay Schieffelin, Jr. Lois Schieffelin told a reporter that she views this cross-generational togetherness as "a family heirloom of sorts."

Dr. Daniel Begel, a Manhattan psychiatrist who specializes in treating athletes and is himself a member of the New York Marathon's psychological support team, says: "Running is a great arena for families to work together. For busy, ambitious people, it's a way to get together that is nonverbal and nonconflictual."

Of course, you may not be so fortunate. Maybe you won't get any support from your family. You can't do much about that. But you can do something about friends who jeer at you: find new friends who share your newfound interest in exercise.

• **Get an exercise partner.** Among your new circle of athletic friends you're sure to find one or two who share your hours and your exercise preference. To cement your commitment, team up with them to exercise. You're less likely to cancel an exercise appointment with a partner, and the company will take your mind off the minor discomfort of exertion. Besides, if you're at all competitive, the fact that your partner can do it will keep you doing it!

• **Have a contingency plan—or plans.** Business trips and vacations are no excuse for temporary reprieves. Maybe your destination makes your usual workout on a rowing machine impossible. But there are plenty of other aerobic substitutes, even if it means packing a jump rope. (See chapter 9 for a rundown of the various aerobic alternatives.)

• **Be serious about it.** It's true that the more you know about a subject, the more interesting it becomes. The same is true of the exercise(s) you select.

These days there are special-interest magazines covering every sport imaginable—and books galore. Read some of them, especially those written by the pros in the field. Find out why they're hooked on a sport and you may get hooked too.

This advice is particularly valuable if you're a very mental person who likes to analyze things before you proceed. You might say it's the getting-to-your-body-by-way-of-your-mind approach.

• **Graft on new goals.** The more you get into a sport, the more you'll discover about it. And the more you discover, the more likely that your initial goal will evolve into several new ones.

If you stick with aerobics, you'll find you're dealing with a dynamic situation much like the tree of life: from an initial seed comes a sprout that gradually becomes a tree trunk from which branches grow. Go where your motivation and inspiration take you.

• **Give yourself tangible rewards.** The intangible rewards of feeling more energetic and alert aren't enough to keep some women exercising. They need something they can see and touch to spur them on. You could call this the "carrot approach" to exercise—as opposed to the "buggy whip."

What would be appropriate incentives?

How about a new exercise outfit the moment you pass the 500-mile point on the running track? Or a jazzy leotard for attending two aerobic dance classes per week for three months? Or a new sweatband if you beat your club's tennis champion in just one set of singles?

• **Teach another person to do it.** This is a guaranteed way to renew your commitment.

Teaching forces you to analyze the process you went through to arrive at your present stage of advancement. In a teacher-pupil relationship, you'll be amazed to discover how much you really know about your exercise. Things you've never verbalized to yourself suddenly become crystal clear in your mind.

You'll also hear yourself coming up with myriad reasons why your student should stay with it despite discouraging workouts and second thoughts. How can you drop out if you're encouraging someone else not to?

• **Compete!** Some people love challenges. They thrive on competition and winning. If you're one of them, inject this element into your exercise. Sign up for clinics, enter contests or races, or take group or private lessons to improve your skills. You may discover a whole new playing field upon which you excel.

• **Recognize when injuries or illness necessitate a change of exercise.** You're in a car accident and you shatter your kneecap; your doctor says it may take months to heal. Indeed, a full recovery is not certain.

This is one of those minor tragedies we all have to endure in life. Clearly, running, which you've grown to love, isn't in the cards for a while, if ever again. But you've got other aerobic choices. Swimming, a nonweight-bearing exercise that builds up your biceps while it's working your lungs, may be just what the doctor orders for rehabilitation. Depending on your knee's progress, cycling may even be possible one day.

There's seldom a reason to give up on aerobics entirely. There are usually viable alternative exercises, no matter what your medical prognosis.

• **Perceive a lapse as a momentary interruption.** Do not see it as a failure forever. That, once again, is compulsive thinking, more harmful than helpful.

Forgive yourself and start again, whether it's for the second time or the twentieth.

# 8

# The Choice Is Yours—The Five Basic Aerobic Exercises

A spokesman for the National Sporting Goods Association recently observed that "the American male may be losing one of his last refuges—the traditional sporting goods store."

Women and the popularity of aerobic sports are the reason. The NSGA reports that twenty years ago a typical sporting goods store was patronized mostly by men and had a product mix of 70 percent equipment and 30 percent clothing and footwear. In the mid-1980s the ratio is reversed because aerobic exercises, greatly favored by women, require minimal paraphernalia—the right shoes and, maybe, some new clothes.

What are the five most popular aerobic exercises among women? Walking, running, swimming, cycling, and aerobic dancing.

## Walking

Walter Matthau, the well-known actor, had a heart attack in 1966 and his doctor prescribed walking for rehabilitation. Matthau is still walking twenty years later at a rate of about 15 minutes per mile. He covers some 5 miles three times a week. One of his favorite perambulatory spots is the beach, with the wide expanse of the Pacific Ocean spread out before him.

"I don't have any strict schedule," he says. "Before breakfast is the best time but I'm never consistent. Having to adhere to a regimen would be stressful for me. Sometimes I take a little radio, especially during the baseball season. I can listen to the ball game and walk seven, eight miles."

Gloria and Jack Amerman in Houston and Ellen and John Dougherty in Edina, Minnesota, also walk to stay fit. But these couples stroll indoors—in their local shopping mall. For years, doctors have been urging their coronary patients to exercise in malls, where the environment is pleasant and controlled and there's no reason to miss a day. Now shopping mall managements, often in conjunction with local hospitals and national organizations such as the American Heart Association, are actively supporting these walking programs.

Although formal shopping mall exercise programs are aimed mostly at postcardiac patients and elderly people, these aren't the only people who can derive benefits from walking. Everybody can—from the obese to those using it as a stepping stone to more intense activity.

Unlike Europeans, Americans have a limited tradition of walking. Older European cities were developed for walkers. Many of the streets are narrow, winding, and picturesque, far more hospitable to people on foot than to machines on wheels. The circumstances are different in the United States, where the distances between towns and cities and the vast size of most cities make cars and public transportation necessary evils.

Vehicles are evil in the sense that they deprive us of the most natural form of exercise there is. There's still some hope for Americans, though. According to the U.S. Census Bureau, more than 5 million Americans, or about 5.6 percent of the working population, now walk to and from work.

Don't dismiss walking as exercise because you think it places too little demand on your body to qualify as an endurance conditioner. Walking and running can yield you the same aerobic benefits as other aerobic exercises *provided* you walk for a longer time each session than you would have to do if you ran.

Dr. Steven Blair, director of epidemiology at our Institute for Aerobics Research, conducted a study on low-intensity exercise programs while he was at the University of South Carolina. It revealed a highly significant improvement in aerobic fitness for young, healthy male subjects who exercised at only 50 percent of their maximum performance for 30 to 40 minutes, five days a week for ten weeks. The conclusion: longer-lasting walking sessions at heart rates even lower than 50 percent of maximum will yield a training effect.

One of the other advantages of walking is that you can converse with a companion while doing it. This makes walking potentially more fun than solitary modes of exercise. You can also vary the routine by walking with a backpack or by carrying hand weights or even walking in a swimming pool.

But walking's greatest virtue is safety. The injury rate is low. Because there is so much less shock involved, walkers avoid the musculoskeletal and orthopedic problems that can plague runners and aerobic dancers. The forces in running are normally 3 times body weight, whereas in walking they are, at most, 1¼ times body weight. That's a big difference.

Walking can be made more challenging, too, without increasing the impact. Hill walking, for example, greatly increases the energy expenditure, depending on the extent of the incline.

To increase their endurance, some people combine jogging with walking. (A jog is a run that's slower than 9 minutes per mile.) They jog as far as they can, then walk until they catch their breath and are ready to start jogging again.

## Fit Check: Good Walking Gait Basics

Because walking is one of the first things we learn to do, we all assume we're experts. But if you're going to walk briskly for health, why not make sure you're doing it right?

Walking is a highly coordinated series of movements. Here is a description of good walking style:

- Begin in an erect standing posture, feet parallel and about 3 inches apart.
- Shift your body weight forward slightly from the ankles.
- Your ankles must be so relaxed that you can roll your weight up through your foot and push off from the toes. Use your toes actively during the push-off of each step.
- Start the leg swing at your hip and move it forward with a minimum of lateral or vertical movement.
- With each footstep, your heel strikes the ground first, then the ball of your foot.
- Keep your stride moderate in length, allowing your knees to remain slightly flexed—never locked—as your legs swing forward and feet strike the ground.
- Point your feet straight ahead—no toeing out or in—and place them just to the left and right of an imaginary center line.
- Swing your arms freely and naturally in opposition to your legs; this keeps your body facing forward without any movement of your head.
- Your head should be lined up on a vertical axis over your body, not jutting forward or hanging down. Imagine a taut string is attached to the top of your head, and keep it aligned properly.
- Keep your shoulders down, as if you are carrying weights in each hand.
- Feel that your weight is always slightly forward over your front foot, ready for the next step, not lagging behind.

## Walking Exercise Program
(Under 30 Years of Age)

| Week Number | Distance in Miles | Time Goals in Minutes | Frequency per Week | Points per Week |
|---|---|---|---|---|
| 1 | 1.0 | 16 | 5 | 5 |
| 2 | 1.0 | 14 | 5 | 10 |
| 3 | 1.5 | 22 | 4 | 14 |
| 4 | 1.5 | 21 | 5 | 17.5 |
| 5 | 2.0 | 30 | 4 | 20 |
| 6 | 2.0 | 28 | 5 | 25 |
| 7 | 2.5 | 36 | 4 | 26 |
| 8 | 2.5 | 35 | 4 | 26 |
| 9 | 3.0 | 43 | 4 | 32 |
| 10 | 3.0 | 42 | 4 | 32 |

By the tenth week, you'll have attained an adequate level of fitness, which you can maintain with a four-times-per-week-schedule. This level equals 32 aerobic points, consistent with the "good" category of fitness for women. For other combinations of distance and time equal to at least 30 points per week, study The Point System charts for Walking/Running in the Appendix.

## Walking Exercise Program
(30–49 Years of Age)

| Week Number | Distance in Miles | Time Goals in Minutes | Frequency per Week | Points per Week |
|---|---|---|---|---|
| 1 | 1.0 | 18 | 5 | 5 |
| 2 | 1.0 | 16 | 5 | 5 |
| 3 | 1.5 | 24 | 5 | 10 |
| 4 | 1.5 | 23 | 5 | 10 |
| 5 | 2.0 | 32 | 5 | 15 |
| 6 | 2.0 | 30 | 5 | 15 |
| 7 | 2.5 | 38 | 5 | 20 |
| 8 | 2.5 | 37 | 4 | 26 |
| 9 | 3.0 | 45 | 4 | 32 |
| 10 | 3.0 | 44 | 4 | 32 |

By the tenth week, you'll have attained an adequate level of fitness, which you can maintain with a four-times-per-week schedule. This level equals 32 aerobic points, consistent with the "good" category of fitness for women. For other combinations of distance and time equal to at least 30 points per week, study The Point System charts for Walking/Running in the Appendix.

## Walking Exercise Program
(50+ Years of Age)

| Week Number | Distance in Miles | Time Goals in Minutes | Frequency per Week | Points per Week |
|---|---|---|---|---|
| 1 | 1.0 | 20 | 5 | 5 |
| 2 | 1.0 | 18 | 5 | 5 |
| 3 | 1.5 | 27 | 5 | 10 |
| 4 | 1.5 | 26 | 5 | 10 |
| 5 | 2.0 | 36 | 5 | 15 |
| 6 | 2.0 | 34 | 5 | 15 |
| 7 | 2.5 | 42 | 5 | 20 |
| 8 | 2.5 | 40 | 5 | 20 |
| 9 | 2.5 | 37:30 | 4 | 26 |
| 10 | 3.0 | 48 | 5 | 25 |
| 11 | 3.0 | 46 | 5 | 25 |
| 12 | 3.0 | 45 | 4 | 32 |

Here we recommend 12 weeks, rather than 10, to allow more time to reach the time goals. By the twelfth week, you'll have attained an adequate level of fitness which you can maintain with a four-time-per-week schedule. This level equals 32 aerobic points, consistent with the "good" category of fitness for women. For other combinations of distance and time equal to at least 30 points per week, study The Point System charts for Walking/Running in the Appendix.

## Walking Maintenance Program Possibilities

| Distance (miles) | Time Requirement (min) | Freq/Wk | Points/Wk |
|---|---|---|---|
| 2.0 | 24:01–30:00 | 6 | 30 |
| or | | | |
| 3.0 | 36:01–45:00 | 4 | 32 |
| or | | | |
| 4.0 | 48:01–60:00 | 3 | 33 |
| or | | | |
| 4.0 | 60:01–80:00 | 5 | 35 |

## Progressive Walking Program Following an Uncomplicated Heart Attack and for Cardiac Patients with Minimal Disease*

| Week | Distance (miles) | Time Goal (min) | Freq/Wk | Points/Wk |
|---|---|---|---|---|
| 1 | 1.0 | 22:00 | 3 | 0 |
| 2 | 1.0 | 21:00 | 3 | 0 |
| 3 | 1.0 | 20:00 | 3 | 3 |
| 4 | 1.0 | 18:00 | 4 | 4 |
| 5 | 1.0 | 17:00 | 4 | 4 |
| 6 | 1.0 | 16:00 | 4 | 4 |
| 7 | 1.5 | 24:00 | 4 | 8 |
| 8 | 1.5 | 23:00 | 4 | 8 |
| 9 | 2.0 | 32:00 | 4 | 12 |
| 10 | 2.0 | 31:30 | 5 | 15 |
| 11 | 2.0 | 31:00 | 5 | 15 |
| 12 | 2.5 | 39:00 | 5 | 20 |
| 13 | 2.5 | 38:00 | 5 | 20 |
| 14 | 2.5 | 37:45 | 5 | 20 |
| 15 | 3.0 | 48:00 | 5 | 25 |
| 16 | 3.0 | 47:00 | 5 | 25 |
| 17 | 3.0 | 46:00 | 5 | 25 |
| 18 | 3.0 | <45:00 | 4 | 32 |
| | or | | | |
| | 4.0 | <60:00 | 3 | 33 |

*This program is to be started 2 months following the heart attack, *only with physician's approval,* and only if the patient is asymptomatic and not requiring medication for relief of pain or prevention of heart irregularities. If these prerequisites cannot be met, the program for patients with moderate to severe heart disease should be used. After this 18-week program, some patients can progress to a standard running program, *but only with their physician's approval.* If approval is given, start the progressive running program at the 2.0-miles-in-25:00-minutes level in your age-adjusted category (e.g., week 4 of the 30–49 age group).

**Progressive Walking Program Following Uncomplicated Coronary Artery Bypass Surgery***

| Week | Distance (miles) | Time Goal (min) | Freq/Wk | Points/Wk |
|---|---|---|---|---|
| 1 | 0.5 | 12:00 | 3 | 0 |
| 2 | 0.5 | 10:00 | 3 | 0 |
| 3 | 1.0 | 22:00 | 3 | 0 |
| 4 | 1.0 | 20:00 | 3 | 3 |
| 5 | 1.0 | 19:00 | 4 | 4 |
| 6 | 1.0 | 18:00 | 4 | 4 |
| 7 | 1.5 | 29:30 | 4 | 8 |
| 8 | 1.5 | 28:00 | 4 | 8 |
| 9 | 1.5 | 26:00 | 5 | 10 |
| 10 | 1.5 | 24:00 | 5 | 10 |
| 11 | 2.0 | 32:00 | 5 | 15 |
| 12 | 2.0 | 31:00 | 5 | 15 |
| 13 | 2.5 | 38:00 | 5 | 20 |
| 14 | 2.5 | 37:00 | 5 | 20 |
| 15 | 3.0 | 48:00 | 5 | 25 |
| 16 | 3.0 | 47:00 | 5 | 25 |
| 17 | 3.0 | 46:00 | 5 | 25 |
| 18 | 3.0 | <45:00 | 4 | 32 |
| | or | | | |
| | 4.0 | <60:00 | 3 | 33 |

*This program should not be started until at least 3 weeks following surgery. After this 18-week program, some patients can progress to a standard running program, *but only with their physician's approval.* If approval is given, start the progressive program at the 2.0-miles-in-25:00 minutes level in your age-adjusted category (e.g., week 4 of the 30–49 age group).

## Racewalking Versus Running

Studies show that the average pace among people walking for exercise is 4 miles per hour. That's a 15-minute mile.

Although jogging and running do burn up more calories than walking at this average pace, the situation changes at 5 miles per hour, a 12-minute-mile pace. At that point, the walker starts to burn as many, if not more, calories than the jogger. A 120-pound woman walker, for instance, will use from 300 to 450 calories in 60 minutes covering 4 to 5 miles an hour.

If you've ever tried to walk at this extremely fast pace, however, you know how uncomfortable it is. That's why a special racewalking gait was developed for speeds above 5 or 6 miles per hour.

The racewalking gait has two basic requirements. Unlike a runner, a racewalker must have her lead foot on the ground when her trailing leg pushes off. And, unlike the regular walker, she must keep her knee straight as her body passes over that leg.

The result is far more arm pumping and pelvic rotation than in either walking or running. That's why racewalkers are often referred to as "hip wigglers." But it's that hip-wiggling movement that is so good for you, especially for your belly and back. A good racewalking session is guaranteed to leave you feeling loose and agile.

Racewalking, or speed walking, is a competitive sport; it's even included in the Olympics. Even if you don't want to race, it's still excellent exercise for advanced walkers ready to graduate to something more strenuous. And strenuous it is. Racewalkers are exercising at a high intensity because they must take more steps than runners to cover the same distance.

Racewalking is right up there with running as a way to boost fitness. A study compared nine national-class competitive racewalkers with distance and marathon runners. It showed that the racewalkers were almost as physically fit as their runner counterparts. The racewalkers had about 85 to 95 percent of the typical aerobic capacity of the runners, but in all other physiological respects the two groups were about equal.

## Running

Walking is the only exercise that beats running for convenience and lack of expense. Buy a good pair of running shoes and you can do it anytime, anywhere, as runners who travel a lot will testify.

One such runner is James M. Markham, a foreign correspondent for *The New York Times*. He believes "the great virtue of running is that it requires so little equipment: shoes, socks, shorts, a T-shirt, Sony Walkman and tapes (latter two optional). All of this can be easily stuffed into a suitcase by a reporter rushing for some airport at midnight; it is probably the ideal sport for the foreign correspondent or the jet-bound executive, since one can do it alone and just about anywhere."

Natalie Tunney, owner of a travel agency in California and the wife of motivational speaker and National Football League referee Jim Tunney, runs for a different reason. "Because of the pressures and long hours I put in at work, the only exercise I have time for is running. I don't have time for structured exercise like tennis."

That's not all. "Looking good is important to me. I don't want to become the typical flabby 40- or 50-year-old. My husband is gone every weekend for seven months of the year, and he's exposed to a lot of people. I know I can stay mentally attractive to him, but I want to stay physically attractive as well."

Women also like running because it's effective. Unfortunately, it's an irony that the potential danger of pounding your feet and legs on the ground is also one of running's major strengths, particularly for women. Because the bones and joints get more pressure exerted on them, they tend to get thicker and stronger. This offers protection from the onset of osteoporosis, the deterioration of the bones that occurs with aging.

If you're overweight, though, running may not be for you. A nonweight-bearing form of exercise, such as swimming or cycling, may be more appropriate, at least in the early stages until you've shed some pounds.

## Jogging Versus Running

Jogging leisurely at a 9-to-11-minute-per-mile pace is like cruising down a country road in second gear. You're going slowly enough to enjoy the sights yet fast enough to feel as though you've accomplished something. In contrast, running is nature's overdrive. It's more like cruising down a superhighway at top speed with your destination as the primary objective.

Women, fortunately, have a much more sensible attitude about running than the average man who comes from the no-pain-no-gain school of thinking, thanks to high school athletics coaches. The macho view is grim: "If you enjoy running, you're not doing it hard enough."

Men also tend to think that more is better. If you can run 5 miles a workout, why not increase it to 6 or 7?

Why not, indeed. Our studies at the Aerobics Center indicate that people who run more than 15 to 20 miles a week increase the risk of injury by a great degree, with only minimal further increases in their cardiovascular fitness.

This fact is best demonstrated by an example. In 1979, we had a male patient in his early forties who came to the Cooper Clinic for a physical. He was running 15 miles a week and tested in the "superior" fitness category with a treadmill time of 24 minutes, 22 seconds. When all the other essential factors—such as cholesterol/HDL ratio, blood pressure, smoking, body-fat ratio, stress, etc.—were taken into account, his overall coronary risk was low.

Nonetheless, being a typical competitive man determined to do better on our treadmill the next time, he increased his training to a minimum of 45 miles per week and eventually ran a 26.2-mile marathon in 3 hours, 8 minutes.

When he returned to our clinic two years later, his treadmill performance had gone up to 28 minutes, 35 seconds, so he was clearly in better physical condition. But here's the rub: even though he tripled the miles he was running each week, his coronary risk profile hadn't changed.

Our conclusion based on this man and the thousands of other men and women we've examined over the years: if you run more than 3 miles, five times a week, you are running for something other than cardiovascular fitness.

It's not that we discourage running more than 15 miles a week, particularly if you are not having any musculoskeletal problems. We just think people should understand why they're doing it. Accept the fact that you're running a greater distance for enjoyment, or competition, or weight loss, or whatever. You're not doing it just for better health. In addition, you must realize that you're increasing your chances of getting injured—and that one of those injuries ultimately may restrict or even terminate your running program.

How about running only 15 miles a week but at a high-intensity level near your anaerobic threshold? That's equally dubious. It gets you nowhere fast, except so out of breath that you can't keep at it very long.

It's much smarter to run the way Dr. Joan Ullyot does, at a pace comfortable enough that she and her female companions can turn the experience into "a roving *kaffeeklatsch.*" Dr. Ullyot, who has been running since 1971, calls it "running in the 'women's way'—this is, with plenty of breath left for talking."

## Running/Jogging Exercise Program
(Under 30 Years of Age)

| Week Number | Distance in Miles | Time Goals in Minutes | Frequency per Week | Points per Week |
|---|---|---|---|---|
| 1 | 2.0 | 31 | 4 | 12 |
| 2 | 2.5 | 38 | 4 | 16 |
| 3 | 3.0 | 45:15 | 4 | 20 |
| 4 | 2.0 | 28 | 4 | 20 |
| 5 | 2.0 | 26 | 4 | 20 |
| 6 | 2.0 | 24 | 4 | 28 |
| 7 | 2.0 | 22 | 4 | 28 |
| 8 | 2.5 | 28 | 4 | 36 |
| 9 | 2.5 | 26 | 4 | 36 |
| 10 | 2.5 | 24 | 3 | 34.5 |

By the tenth week, you'll have attained an adequate level of fitness, which you can maintain with a three-times-per-week schedule. This level equals 34.5 aerobic points, consistent with the "good" category of fitness for women. For other combinations of distance and time equal to at least 30 points per week, study The Point System charts for Running/Jogging in the Appendix.

## Running/Jogging Exercise Program
### (30–49 Years of Age)

| Week Number | Distance in Miles | Time Goals in Minutes | Frequency per Week | Points per Week |
|---|---|---|---|---|
| 1 | 2.0 | 32 | 4 | 12 |
| 2 | 2.5 | 40 | 4 | 16 |
| 3 | 3.0 | 48 | 4 | 20 |
| 4 | 2.0 | 30 | 4 | 20 |
| 5 | 2.0 | 28 | 4 | 20 |
| 6 | 2.0 | 26 | 4 | 20 |
| 7 | 2.0 | 24 | 4 | 28 |
| 8 | 2.5 | 30:30 | 4 | 26 |
| 9 | 2.5 | 28 | 4 | 36 |
| 10 | 2.5 | 26 | 4 | 36 |
| 11 | 2.5 | 25:30 | 4 | 36 |
| 12 | 2.5 | 25 | 3 | 34.5 |

We recommend 12 weeks to allow more time to attain the time goals. By the twelfth week, you'll have attained an adequate level of fitness, which you can maintain with a three-times-per-week schedule. This level equals 34.5 aerobic points, consistent with the "good" category of fitness for women. For other combinations of distance and time equal to at least 30 points per week, study The Point System charts for Running/Jogging in the Appendix.

## Running/Jogging Exercise Program
### (50–59 Years of Age)

| Week Number | Distance in Miles | Time Goals in Minutes | Frequency per Week | Points per Week |
|---|---|---|---|---|
| 1 | 2.0 | 36 | 4 | 12 |
| 2 | 2.5 | 45 | 4 | 16 |
| 3 | 3.0 | 54 | 4 | 20 |
| 4 | 2.0 | 32 | 5 | 15 |
| 5 | 2.0 | 30 | 4 | 20 |
| 6 | 2.0 | 28 | 4 | 20 |
| 7 | 2.0 | 27 | 4 | 20 |
| 8 | 2.0 | 26 | 5 | 25 |
| 9 | 2.0 | 25 | 5 | 25 |
| 10 | 2.0 | 24 | 4 | 28 |
| 11 | 2.5 | 30:30 | 4 | 26 |
| 12 | 2.5 | 30 | 4 | 36 |

By the twelfth week, you'll have attained an adequate level of fitness, which you can maintain with a four-times-per-week schedule. This level equals 36 aerobic points, consistent with the "good" category of fitness for women. For other combinations of distance and time equal to at least 30 points per week, study The Point System charts for Running/Jogging in the Appendix.

## Running/Jogging Exercise Program
(60+ Years of Age)

We don't recommend this type of activity for the totally inactive woman. But jogging is not necessarily contraindicated in the individual who has been jogging/running prior to age 60 and wants to continue. Consult with your physician if you want to start a jogging program—or wish to continue.

### Running/Jogging Maintenance Program

| Distance (miles) | Time Requirement (min) | Freq/Wk | Points/Wk |
|---|---|---|---|
| 1.0 | 6:41–8:00 | 6 | 30 |
| or | | | |
| 1.5 | 10:01–12:00 | 4 | 32 |
| or | | | |
| 1.5 | 12:01–15:00 | 5 | 32.5 |
| or | | | |
| 2.0 | 16:01–20:00 | 4 | 36 |
| or | | | |
| 2.0 | 13:21–16:00 | 3 | 33 |

### Fit Tips: Good Running Motion

Running takes no skill; nobody has to teach you to run. On the other hand, it's important to know what the experts consider a good running motion, because doing it right prevents injuries and streamlines your movements.

- From a standing posture, incline your body forward from the ankles, increasing the degree with speed. If you're jogging, for example, your body should remain almost upright as you run.
- Swing your legs from the hips, following a straight forward and backward line.
- Emphasize forward knee lift.
- Push off forcefully with your toes.

- In a fast run, land on the balls of your feet and your toes. In a jog (or slow run), land on the heel first, then ball and toes.
- Land *lightly* on your feet, with springy ankle and foot action.
- Keep your elbows bent at right angles, your arms close to your sides and swing them in opposition to your legs in a straight forward and backward motion.
- Keep your chin and chest high.
- Keep your shoulders down, relaxed, and their movement held to a minimum and your hands relaxed.
- Avoid making a fist, gripping tightly. In other words, keep your hands relaxed.

## Stationary Running

In bad weather, stationary running can be a godsend. You control the intensity of your workout by varying the height of your knee lift. The higher the lift, the greater the intensity. And don't forget your running shoes just because you're indoors.

### Stationary Running Exercise Program
(Under 30 Years of Age)

| Week | Time Goal (min) | Steps/Min* | Freq/Wk | Points/Wk |
|---|---|---|---|---|
| 1 | 10:00 | 70–80 | 3 | 0 |
| 2 | 10:00 | 70–80 | 3 | 0 |
| 3 | 10:00 | 70–80 | 3 | 0 |
| 4 | 15:00 | 70–80 | 3 | 0 |
| 5 | 15:00 | 70–80 | 3 | 0 |
| 6 | 15:00 | 70–80 | 3 | 0 |
| 7 | 10:00 | 70–80 | 4 | 14.0 |
| 8 | 10:00 | 70–80 | 5 | 17.5 |
| 9 | 12:30 | 80–90 | 4 | 24.5 |
| 10 | 12:30 | 80–90 | 5 | 30.6 |
| 11 | 15:00 | 80–90 | 4 | 31.0 |
| 12 | 15:00 | 90–100 | 4 | 37.0 |

## Stationary Running Exercise Program
(30–49 Years of Age)

| Week | Time Goal (min) | Steps/Min* | Freq/Wk | Points/Wk |
|---|---|---|---|---|
| 1 | 7:30 | 70–80 | 3 | 0 |
| 2 | 10:00 | 70–80 | 3 | 0 |
| 3 | 10:00 | 70–80 | 3 | 0 |
| 4 | 12:30 | 70–80 | 3 | 0 |
| 5 | 12:30 | 70–80 | 3 | 0 |
| 6 | 15:00 | 70–80 | 3 | 0 |
| 7 | 7:30 | 70–80 | 4 | 10.5 |
| 8 | 7:30 | 70–80 | 5 | 13.13 |
| 9 | 10:00 | 70–80 | 4 | 14.0 |
| 10 | 10:00 | 80–90 | 4 | 18.0 |
| 11 | 12:30 | 70–80 | 5 | 24.38 |
| 12 | 12:30 | 80–90 | 4 | 24.5 |
| 13 | 15:00 | 80–90 | 4 | 31.0 |
| 14 | 15:00 | 90–100 | 4 | 37.0 |

## Stationary Running Exercise Program
(50–59 Years of Age)

| Week | Time Goal (min) | Steps/Min* | Freq/Wk | Points/Wk |
|---|---|---|---|---|
| 1 | 5:00 | 70–80 | 3 | 0 |
| 2 | 7:30 | 70–80 | 3 | 0 |
| 3 | 10:00 | 70–80 | 3 | 0 |
| 4 | 10:00 | 70–80 | 3 | 0 |
| 5 | 12:30 | 70–80 | 3 | 0 |
| 6 | 12:30 | 70–80 | 3 | 0 |
| 7 | 5:00 | 70–80 | 4 | 7.0 |
| 8 | 7:30 | 70–80 | 4 | 10.5 |
| 9 | 10:00 | 70–80 | 4 | 14.0 |
| 10 | 10:00 | 70–80 | 5 | 17.5 |
| 11 | 10:00 | 70–80 | 5 | 17.5 |
| 12 | 12:30 | 70–80 | 5 | 24.38 |
| 13 | 12:30 | 70–80 | 5 | 24.38 |
| 14 | 15:00 | 70–80 | 5 | 31.25 |
| 15 | 15:00 | 70–80 | 5 | 31.25 |
| 16 | 17:30 | 80–90 | 4 | 37.5 |

During the first 6 weeks, the requirement is to exercise the required number of minutes, *but not continuously*. Rest frequently and as long as necessary, *but continue to walk slowly while resting*. The time goals represent the combined stationary running and rest periods. Beginning with the seventh week, the time goals represent continuous exercise. Warm up for 3:00 minutes by walking briskly. Cool down for 3:00 minutes after exercise by walking slowly. Exercise on a cushioned surface (e.g., a thick carpet) in athletic shoes that have either a resilient or deep-cushioned sole.

*Count only when left foot hits the floor. Feet must be raised at least eight inches off the floor.

## Stationary Running Exercise Program
## (Age 60 and Over) Not Recommended

## Stationary Running Maintenance Program

| Time Requirement (min) | Steps/Min* | Freq/Wk | Points/Wk |
|---|---|---|---|
| 12:30 | 80–90 | 6 | 33 |
| or | | | |
| 15:00 | 80–90 | 5 | 35 |
| or | | | |
| 15:00 | 90–100 | 4 | 34 |
| or | | | |
| 20:00 | 70–80 | 4 | 32 |
| or | | | |
| 20:00 | 80–90 | 3 | 30 |

*Count only when left foot hits the floor. Feet must be raised at least eight inches off the floor.

To minimize the impact with the floor, which is particularly advisable if you have chronic knee and ankle problems, consider stationary running on a minitrampoline. If you choose this form of exercise, each time period in the charts must be increased by 30 percent to account for the reduced effort required to exercise on a rebounding surface.

# Swimming

The President's Council on Physical Fitness and Sports cites swimming as the nation's number one active sport. According to National Family Opinion, Inc., 95.9 million Americans identify themselves as swimmers. Since many of them may simply lie on the beach, a more telling statistic comes from U.S. Masters Swimming, Inc. In the last decade, the number of registered masters (25 years and older) has jumped from 6,000 to 20,000.

Swimming deserves its popularity, for it's one of the best aerobic exercises. It requires you to use the major muscles of your body yet places minimal strain on your joints and bones. Thus, it's ideal for anyone with orthopedic problems or arthritis.

Swimmers can be compulsive about their sport, covering up to 10 miles *per day* (equivalent to 1,300 points per week) without much danger of pulling a muscle or damaging a joint. For a runner to gain 1,300 points *per week*, she would have to run over 200 miles. Any runner who tried that could expect a serious injury in very short order.

On the other hand, swimming is not 100 percent trouble-free. Swimmers must be on guard to avoid ear and eye infections, sinus problems, and tendinitis.

There are several factors responsible for the growing popularity of lap swimming as well as other aquatic sports.

Water's natural buoyancy makes your body weigh less than 10 percent of your weight on land. For overweight exercisers, this weight-reduced environment is ideal. In addition, the idea of water covering their bodies makes many women feel more comfortable about exercising in public. Chest-deep in water, they have the sense that their body is hidden from view.

A New York City–based freelance writer, who has discarded other exercise choices in favor of swimming, says:

"There's a boredom about repetitive exercise. I can't tolerate running laps or any form of calisthenics. But swimming is something else for me: an adventure of the skin and the muscles, a plunge into a different mentality and medium.

"I try never to make swimming a demand or compulsion, but to keep it as a pure pleasure. Usually, I swim half a mile or half an hour, but I am quite content to swim less if the pool is crowded or I'm in a hurry. Any amount seems to be enough."

## Swimming Exercise Program
(Under 30 Years of Age)

| Week Number | Distance in Yards | Time Goals in Minutes | Frequency per Week | Points per Week |
|---|---|---|---|---|
| 1 | 200 | 6 | 5 | 6.25 |
| 2 | 300 | 9 | 5 | 9.4 |
| 3 | 400 | 12 | 5 | 12.5 |
| 4 | 450 | 13 | 5 | 14 |
| 5 | 500 | 14 | 5 | 15.6 |
| 6 | 600 | 16 | 5 | 18.75 |
| 7 | 700 | 18 | 5 | 24.4 |
| 8 | 800 | 20 | 4 | 30.68 |
| 9 | 900 | 22:30 | 4 | 36 |
| 10 | 1000 | 25 | 4 | 41.3 |

Use the stroke that enables you to swim the required distance in the required time. We encourage you to rest during the initial weeks and this is included in the time goals. By the tenth week, you'll have attained an adequate level of fitness (41.3 aerobic points), but we encourage you to strive for higher levels by swimming longer, faster, or more frequently. Turn to the Appendix to ascertain the point value of various speed-distance combinations.

### Swimming Exercise Program
(30–49 Years of Age)

| Week Number | Distance in Yards | Time Goals in Minutes | Frequency per Week | Points per Week |
|---|---|---|---|---|
| 1 | 200 | 7 | 5 | 0 |
| 2 | 300 | 9:30 | 5 | 9.4 |
| 3 | 400 | 12:30 | 5 | 12.5 |
| 4 | 450 | 13:30 | 5 | 14 |
| 5 | 500 | 14:30 | 5 | 15.6 |
| 6 | 600 | 17 | 5 | 18.75 |
| 7 | 700 | 19:30 | 5 | 24.4 |
| 8 | 800 | 21:30 | 4 | 24 |
| 9 | 900 | 24 | 4 | 28.5 |
| 10 | 1000 | 26:30 | 4 | 33 |

Use the stroke that enables you to swim the required distance in the required time. We encourage you to rest during the initial weeks and this is included in the time goals. By the tenth week, you'll have attained an adequate level of fitness (33 aerobic points), but we encourage you to strive for higher levels by swimming longer, faster, or more frequently. Turn to the Appendix to ascertain the point value of various speed-distance combinations.

### Swimming Exercise Program
(50+ Years of Age)

| Week Number | Distance in Yards | Time Goals in Minutes | Frequency per Week | Points per Week |
|---|---|---|---|---|
| 1 | 200 | 8 | 5 | 0 |
| 2 | 300 | 10 | 5 | 9.4 |
| 3 | 400 | 13 | 5 | 12.5 |
| 4 | 450 | 14 | 5 | 14 |
| 5 | 500 | 15 | 5 | 15.6 |
| 6 | 600 | 18 | 5 | 18.75 |
| 7 | 600 | 17 | 5 | 18.75 |
| 8 | 700 | 20 | 5 | 24.4 |
| 9 | 700 | 19:30 | 5 | 24.4 |

| Week Number | Distance in Yards | Time Goals in Minutes | Frequency per Week | Points per Week |
|---|---|---|---|---|
| 10 | 800 | 22 | 4 | 24 |
| 11 | 900 | 25 | 4 | 28.5 |
| 12 | 1000 | 28 | 4 | 33 |

Use the stroke that enables you to swim the required distance in the required time. We encourage you to rest during the initial weeks and this is included in the time goals. By the twelfth week, you'll have attained an adequate level of fitness (33 aerobic points), but we encourage you to strive for higher levels by swimming longer, faster, or more frequently. Turn to the Appendix to ascertain the point value of various speed-distance combinations.

## Swimming Maintenance Program

| Distance (yards) | Time Requirement (min) | Freq/Wk | Points/Wk |
|---|---|---|---|
| 600 | 10:01–15:00 | 6 | 30 |
| or | | | |
| 800 | 13:21–20:00 | 4 | 30.5 |
| or | | | |
| 900 | 15:01–22:30 | 4 | 36 |
| or | | | |
| 1000 | 16:41–25:00 | 3 | 31 |

## Aqua-Aerobics: Free-Form Water Fun

You might think of aqua-aerobics as aerobic dancing in water. An instructor leads a class through a series of choreographed movements performed to music. Participants copy the movements of the instructor, who is either in the water with them or on the pool deck. However, they're encouraged to work at their own intensity by varying the speed. Classes typically last 45 minutes to 1 hour and are held only at the shallow end of the pool, putting nonswimmers at ease.

Aqua-aerobics are perfect for women who are overweight, sedentary, pregnant, elderly, or recovering from muscular or skeletal injuries. Those of you who don't have access to a class but do have access to a swimming pool might try this aqua-aerobics routine:

## 1 STRETCHING

A. Place right foot flat on pool wall.

B. Stretch forward, moving chest toward knee. Keep the back straight and the chin up.

C. Hold for 10 to 20 seconds and repeat for left leg.

This stretches the hamstrings and the lower back.

## 2 STRETCHING

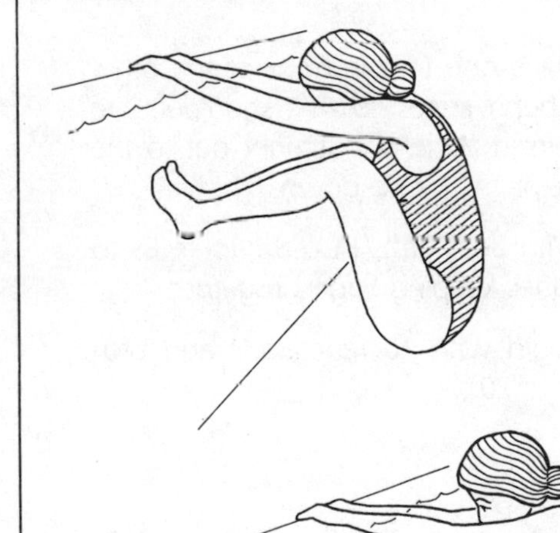

A. Place both feet up on the pool wall and hold on to the edge with hands. Knees and elbows are both bent. Hold for 10 to 20 seconds.

B. Slowly stretch legs out straightening the elbows and knees. Feet are flat on the wall. Hold for 10 to 20 seconds.

C. Repeat 4 more times.

This stretches the hamstrings and the lower back.

## 3 STRETCHING

A. Place left foot behind right foot. Both hands are on the pool wall and toes are pointing straight ahead.

B. Lean hips into pool wall, keeping the back knee straight.

C. Hold for 10 to 20 seconds and repeat for right leg.

This stretches the calf muscle and the Achilles tendon.

## 4 ARMS

A. Place one foot in front of the other and bend knees so that shoulders are immersed. Arms are straight out to the sides, palms facing down.

B. With both arms inscribe figure 8s to the sides keeping fingers together.

C. Begin with 10 repetitions and progress to 20.

## 5 ARMS

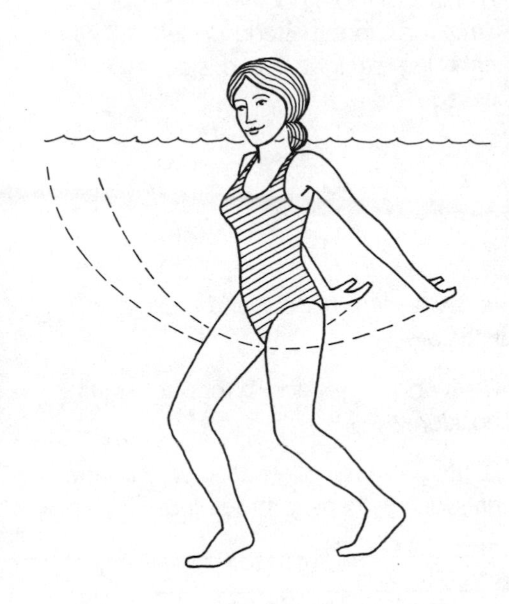

A. Place one foot in front of the other and bend knees so that shoulders are immersed. Arms are straight out front, palms facing down.

B. Swing arms down by sides and behind keeping fingers together.

C. Rotate arms so palms face forward and swing back up.

D. Begin with 10 repetitions and progress to 20.

## 6 THIGHS

A. Place back to the pool wall and use both arms for support. Legs are straight out in front and parallel to the bottom of the pool. Ankles are flexed.

B. Pull legs apart and pull together trying to cross at the thighs.

C. Begin with 5 repetitions and progress to 15.

*Note*: Keep tummy tucked in and lower back pressed against the wall.

## 7 THIGHS

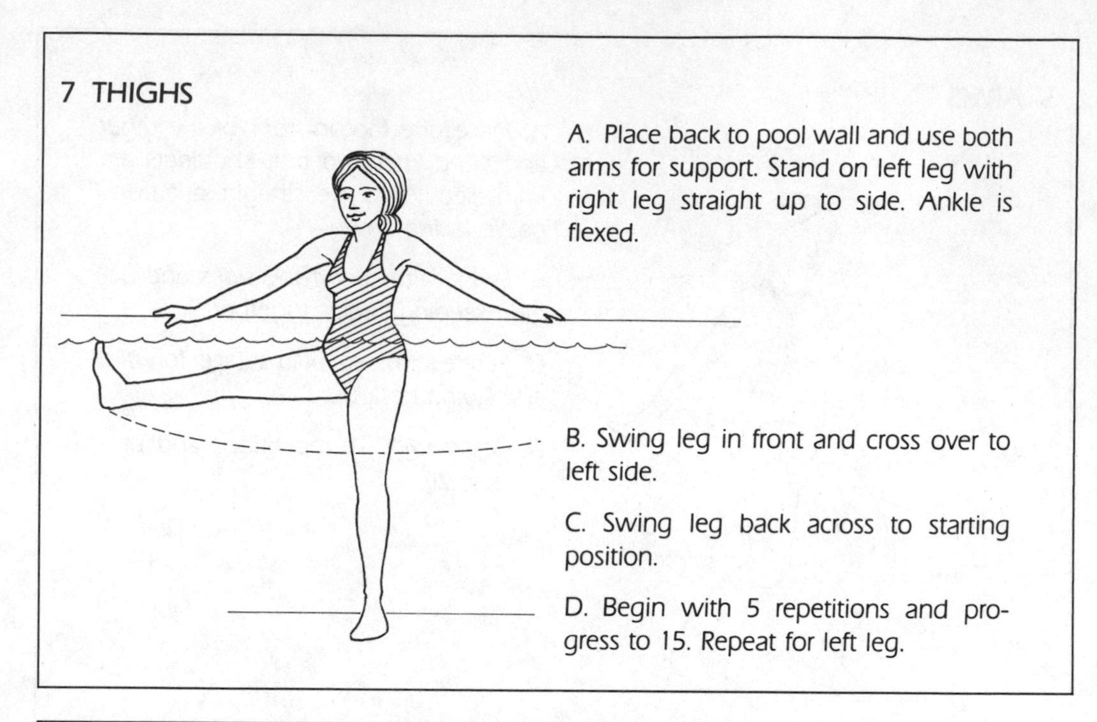

A. Place back to pool wall and use both arms for support. Stand on left leg with right leg straight up to side. Ankle is flexed.

B. Swing leg in front and cross over to left side.

C. Swing leg back across to starting position.

D. Begin with 5 repetitions and progress to 15. Repeat for left leg.

## 8 THIGHS

A. Place both feet on pool wall and hold on to edge with hands. Knees and elbows are straight.

B. Push off with feet and pull legs apart into a straddle position. Elbows will bend as the body moves into the wall.

C. Push off with feet and pull straight legs together returning to original position.

D. Begin with 5 repetitions and progress to 10.

*Note:* Remember to use tummy on this one.

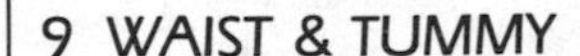

## 9 WAIST & TUMMY

A. Place back to the pool wall and use both arms for support. Legs are straight out in front and parallel to the bottom of the pool.

B. Keep back to the wall and swing both legs to the left side of the wall.

C. Contract abdominals and swing both legs across and to the right side of the pool.

D. Begin with 8 repetitions (4 to the right and 4 to the left) and progress to 16.

## 10 WAIST & TUMMY

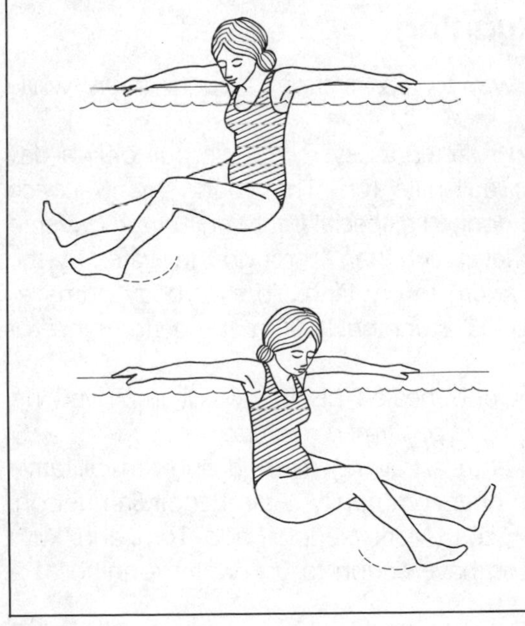

A. Place back toward the pool wall. Suspend from the edge using both arms. Let back come away from the wall.

B. Simultaneously, pedal legs as if riding a bike and twist at hips. Alternate from right and left side. (As right knee comes up toward chest, rotate hips to the left. Then as left leg comes up, rotate hips to the right.) *Note:* The bent knee is always on top and legs are always under the water.

C. Begin with 20 pedals (10 to the right and 10 to the left) and progress to 75.

11 WAIST & TUMMY

A. Crouch so that shoulders are under the water, knees are bent, and weight is on balls of feet.

B. Quickly rotate hips back and forth from right to left—arms will go in the opposite direction from hips. During the twisting movement, your feet will leave the bottom of the pool.

C. Begin with 20 rotations and progress to 50.

*Note:* Hold tummy in tight throughout the exercise!

Source: *Aerobics* newsletter, © 1981, Institute for Aerobics Research

## Water Running

To date, water running is the only known way to recover from a sports injury while improving your performance.

Take the case of a college runner who suffered a severe muscle pull only a day after setting a personal record of 4:18 for a 1-mile run. The young man's coach prescribed water running. For four weeks, he donned a special lightweight vest, lowered himself into the deep end of a pool to neck level, and "ran" through the water. By the fifth week, the young runner was ready to return to dry land. To everybody's amazement, he outdid himself, immediately turning in a stunning 1,500-meter performance of 3:45, equal to a 4:03 mile.

Four weeks of water training had not only healed his injury but improved his performance. Other studies of water running have confirmed this finding.

The effectiveness of water running as both a training method and rehabilitative therapy has not been lost on the marathon runner community. Joan Benoit Samuelson, Mary Decker Slaney, Alberto Salazar, Steve Scott, Mark Nenow, and Tom and Ruth Wisocki are just a few of the top runners who have begun to use water running as a vital part of their training.

Water resistance is the key to this exercise's effectiveness and usefulness for different segments of the population. The faster you move your extremities, the more water resistance you encounter. Because the resistance is within your control, water running (or walking in deep water) is also being used to treat arthritis victims, the elderly, the physically impaired, and cardiac rehab patients.

## Cycling

A National Family Opinion poll identified 88.8 million Americans who consider themselves cyclists of ranging degrees of commitment. If bicycle sales are any indication, it's true that we're slowly becoming a nation of pedalers. Between 1982 and 1985, sales rose from $6.8 billion to $11.4 billion.

Perhaps the biggest boost to American cycling came in 1984 when the American team won nine medals at the Olympics in Los Angeles. Two years later, Greg LeMond became the first American to win the world's oldest, richest, and most important bicycle road race, the Tour de France.

Jogging seems to be among the sports that are losing adherents to cycling. That may be all to the good, since cycling is long on aerobic conditioning and short on injuries. Essentially, it's a nonweight-bearing activity and thus is ideal for the obese or for those with arthritic or orthopedic problems.

Of course, by our definition, an aerobic cyclist is more than just your occasional weekend rider. It's a woman who is out on the road four or five days a week cycling for at least 20 minutes a session at speeds slightly greater than 15 miles per hour. (Note: It should take a beginner at least ten weeks to arrive at this speed.) Generally speaking, speeds of less than 10 miles per hour are worth very little from an aerobic standpoint, whereas speeds in excess of 20 miles per hour are racing speeds.

Moreover, a serious cyclist is someone whose bike is a multi-speed model, since a one-speed bike is too difficult to pedal on hills. A sensible cyclist also takes the dangers of traffic seriously, donning a crash helmet to protect herself in the event of an accident.

Unfortunately, accidents do happen on bicycles. That's why you should always check your tires, brakes, and gears before you go out for a spin. Not all accidents happen *to* cyclists, either. Overly confident riders, who haven't touched a bike since childhood, are often their own worst enemies. Rusty after a long layoff, they no longer have the "feel" of the machine and find themselves tossed over the handlebars from braking too abruptly or negotiating steep declines too fast.

## Cycling Exercise Program
(Under 30 Years of Age)

| Week Number | Distance in Miles | Time Goals in Minutes | Frequency per Week | Points per Week |
|---|---|---|---|---|
| 1 | 3.0 | 17 | 5 | 7.5 |
| 2 | 3.0 | 15 | 5 | 7.5 |
| 3 | 4.0 | 20 | 5 | 12.5 |
| 4 | 4.0 | 18 | 5 | 12.5 |
| 5 | 5.0 | 25 | 5 | 17.5 |
| 6 | 5.0 | 22 | 5 | 17.5 |
| 7 | 6.0 | 26 | 5 | 22.5 |
| 8 | 6.0 | 24:15 | 5 | 22.5 |
| 9 | 7.0 | 30 | 5 | 27.5 |
| 10 | 7.0 | 27:45 | 4 | 36.0 |

By the tenth week, you'll have attained an adequate level of fitness which you can maintain with a four-day-a-week schedule. If higher levels of fitness are desired, cycling farther, faster, or more frequently each week will increase the fitness level. For more specific details, consult the Cycling charts in the Appendix to determine the aerobic point value of various distance-speed combinations.

## Cycling Exercise Program
(30–49 Years of Age)

| Week Number | Distance in Miles | Time Goals in Minutes | Frequency per Week | Points per Week |
|---|---|---|---|---|
| 1 | 3.0 | 18 | 5 | 7.5 |
| 2 | 3.0 | 17 | 5 | 7.5 |
| 3 | 4.0 | 22 | 5 | 12.5 |
| 4 | 4.0 | 20 | 5 | 12.5 |
| 5 | 5.0 | 26 | 5 | 17.5 |
| 6 | 5.0 | 25 | 5 | 17.5 |
| 7 | 6.0 | 30 | 5 | 22.5 |
| 8 | 6.0 | 28 | 5 | 22.5 |
| 9 | 7.0 | 33 | 5 | 27.5 |
| 10 | 7.0 | 30 | 5 | 27.5 |

By the tenth week, you'll have attained an adequate level of fitness which you can maintain with a five-day-a-week schedule. If higher levels of fitness are desired, cycling farther, faster, or more frequently each week will increase the fitness level. For more specific details, consult the Cycling charts in the Appendix to determine the aerobic point value of various distance-speed combinations.

## Cycling Exercise Program
### (50–59 Years of Age)

| Week Number | Distance in Miles | Time Goals in Minutes | Frequency per Week | Points per Week |
|---|---|---|---|---|
| 1 | 3.0 | 19 | 5 | 0 |
| 2 | 3.0 | 18 | 5 | 7.5 |
| 3 | 4.0 | 25 | 5 | 12.5 |
| 4 | 4.0 | 24 | 5 | 12.5 |
| 5 | 5.0 | 29 | 5 | 17.5 |
| 6 | 5.0 | 28 | 5 | 17.5 |
| 7 | 6.0 | 33 | 5 | 22.5 |
| 8 | 6.0 | 31 | 5 | 22.5 |
| 9 | 7.0 | 35:30 | 5 | 27.5 |
| 10 | 7.0 | 32 | 5 | 27.5 |
| 11 | 7.0 | 31 | 5 | 27.5 |
| 12 | 7.0 | 30 | 5 | 27.5 |

By the twelfth week, you'll have attained an adequate level of fitness which you can maintain with a five-day-a-week schedule. If higher levels of fitness are desired, cycling farther, faster, or more frequently each week will increase the fitness level. For more specific details, consult the Cycling charts in the Appendix to determine the aerobic point value of various distance-speed combinations.

## Cycling Exercise Program
### (60+ Years of Age)

We don't recommend this type of activity for women 60 or older. But when a regular cyclist reaches 60, she can continue without restrictions. To avoid problems—including falls and fractures—three-wheeled cycling is encouraged at slower speeds and longer distances.

## Cycling Maintenance Program

| Distance (miles) | Time Requirement (min) | Freq/Wk | Points/Wk |
|---|---|---|---|
| 5.0 | 15:01–20:00 | 5 | 30 |
| or | | | |
| 6.0 | 18:01–24:00 | 4 | 30 |
| or | | | |
| 7.0 | 21:01–28:00 | 4 | 36 |
| or | | | |
| 8.0 | 24:01–32:00 | 3 | 31.5 |

## Stationary Cycling

Accidents are all too common in winter weather, which is why a dedicated cyclist has a stationary machine for indoor workouts.

Compared to a regular bicycle, a stationary cycle has one major drawback: you have to put out considerably more effort to get the same training effect. In an outdoor cycling session on the road, you are not only overcoming the resistance of the bicycle but you're propelling your body weight and dealing with the resistance of the wind and terrain as well. With a stationary cycle, all the resistance is in the pedals. Consequently, your legs tire faster, so you can't keep at it as long.

Twenty minutes of intense pedaling—with a 5-minute warm-up and cool-down—is what most experienced cyclists aim for, usually with their eyes fixed on a television set to ease the boredom.

### Stationary Cycling Exercise Program
(Under 30 Years of Age)

| Week | Speed (mph/rpm) | Time Goal (min) | PR After Exercise* | Freq/Wk | Points/Wk |
|---|---|---|---|---|---|
| 1 | 15/55 | 8:00 | <140* | 3 | 3.0 |
| 2 | 15/55 | 10:00 | <140 | 3 | 3.75 |
| 3 | 15/55 | 12:00 | <140 | 3 | 4.13 |
| 4 | 17.5/65 | 12:00 | <150 | 4 | 6.5 |
| 5 | 17.5/65 | 14:00 | <150 | 4 | 8.0 |
| 6 | 17.5/65 | 16:00 | <150 | 4 | 9.0 |
| 7 | 17.5/65 | 16:00 | >150 | 5 | 11.25 |
| 8 | 17.5/65 | 16:00 | >150 | 5 | 11.25 |
| 9 | 20/75 | 18:00 | >160 | 5 | 18.13 |
| 10 | 20/75 | 18:00 | >160 | 5 | 18.13 |
| 11 | 25/90 | 20:00 | >160 | 5 | 28.33 |
| 12 | 25/90 | 25:00 | >160 | 4 | 30.0 |

### Stationary Cycling Exercise Program
(30–49 Years of Age)

| Week | Speed (mph/rpm) | Time Goal (min) | PR After Exercise* | Freq/Wk | Points/Wk |
|---|---|---|---|---|---|
| 1 | 15/55 | 6:00 | <140 | 3 | 2.25 |
| 2 | 15/55 | 8:00 | <140 | 3 | 3.0 |
| 3 | 15/55 | 10:00 | <140 | 3 | 3.75 |
| 4 | 15/55 | 12:00 | <150 | 4 | 5.5 |
| 5 | 15/55 | 14:00 | <150 | 4 | 7.0 |

| Week | Speed (mph/rpm) | Time Goal (min) | PR After Exercise* | Freq/Wk | Points/Wk |
|---|---|---|---|---|---|
| 6 | 15/55 | 16:00 | <150 | 4 | 8.0 |
| 7 | 15/55 | 18:00 | <150 | 5 | 11.25 |
| 8 | 15/55 | 20:00 | <150 | 5 | 12.5 |
| 9 | 17.5/65 | 18:00 | >150 | 5 | 13.0 |
| 10 | 17.5/65 | 20:00 | >150 | 5 | 14.5 |
| 11 | 20/75 | 18:00 | >150 | 5 | 18.13 |
| 12 | 20/75 | 20:00 | >150 | 5 | 19.38 |
| 13 | 20/75 | 22:30 | >150 | 5 | 22.5 |
| 14 | 25/90 | 25:00 | >150 | 5 | 30.0 |

## Stationary Cycling Exercise Program
(50–59 Years of Age)

| Week | Speed (mph/rpm) | Time Goal (min) | PR After Exercise* | Freq/Wk | Points/Wk |
|---|---|---|---|---|---|
| 1 | 15/55 | 4:00 | <135 | 3 | 1.5 |
| 2 | 15/55 | 6:00 | <135 | 3 | 2.25 |
| 3 | 15/55 | 8:00 | <135 | 3 | 3.0 |
| 4 | 15/55 | 10:00 | <140 | 4 | 5.0 |
| 5 | 15/55 | 10:00 | <140 | 4 | 5.0 |
| 6 | 15/55 | 12:00 | <140 | 4 | 5.5 |
| 7 | 15/55 | 14:00 | <140 | 5 | 8.75 |
| 8 | 15/55 | 16:00 | <140 | 5 | 10.0 |
| 9 | 15/55 | 18:00 | <140 | 5 | 11.25 |
| 10 | 15/55 | 20:00 | <140 | 5 | 12.5 |
| 11 | 17.5/65 | 18:00 | <150 | 5 | 13.13 |
| 12 | 17.5/65 | 20:00 | <150 | 5 | 14.38 |
| 13 | 20/75 | 20:00 | <150 | 5 | 19.38 |
| 14 | 20/75 | 20:00 | >150 | 5 | 19.38 |
| 15 | 20/75 | 25:00 | >150 | 5 | 25.0 |
| 16 | 20/75 | 30:00 | >150 | 4 | 26.0 |

## Stationary Cycling Exercise Program
(Age 60 and Over)

| Week | Speed (mph/rpm) | Time Goal (min) | PR After Exercise* | Freq/Wk | Points/Wk |
|---|---|---|---|---|---|
| 1 | 15/55 | 4:00 | <100 | 3 | 1.5 |
| 2 | 15/55 | 4:00 | <100 | 3 | 1.5 |

| Week | Speed (mph/rpm) | Time Goal (min) | PR After Exercise* | Freq/Wk | Points/Wk |
|---|---|---|---|---|---|
| 3 | 15/55 | 6:00 | <100 | 3 | 2.25 |
| 4 | 15/55 | 6:00 | <110 | 4 | 3.0 |
| 5 | 15/55 | 8:00 | <110 | 4 | 4.0 |
| 6 | 15/55 | 10:00 | <110 | 4 | 5.0 |
| 7 | 15/55 | 12:00 | <110 | 4 | 5.5 |
| 8 | 15/55 | 14:00 | <110 | 4 | 7.0 |
| 9 | 15/55 | 16:00 | <110 | 4 | 8.0 |
| 10 | 15/55 | 16:00 | <120 | 5 | 10.0 |
| 11 | 15/55 | 18:00 | <120 | 5 | 11.25 |
| 12 | 15/55 | 20:00 | <120 | 5 | 12.5 |
| 13 | 17.5/65 | 18:00 | <120 | 5 | 13.13 |
| 14 | 17.5/65 | 20:00 | <120 | 5 | 14.38 |
| 15 | 20/75 | 20:00 | <130 | 5 | 19.38 |
| 16 | 20/75 | 22:30 | <130 | 5 | 22.5 |
| 17 | 20/75 | 25:00 | <130 | 5 | 25.0 |
| 18 | 20/75 | 30:00 | <130 | 4 | 26.0 |

During the first six weeks, warm up by cycling for 3:00 minutes, 17.5 to 20 mph, with no resistance, before beginning the actual workout. At the conclusion of the exercise, cool down by cycling for 3:00 minutes with no resistance.

From the tenth week on, the exercise periods can be divided into two equal periods, performed twice daily.

*Add enough resistance so that the pulse rate (PR) counted for 10 seconds immediately after exercise and multiplied by 6 equals the rate specified. If it is higher, lower the resistance before cycling again; if it is lower, increase the resistance.

## Stationary Cycling Maintenance Program

| Speed (mph/rpm) | Time Requirement (min) | Freq/Wk | Points/Wk |
|---|---|---|---|
| 17.5/65 | 30:00 | 6 | 30 |
| or | | | |
| 17.5/65 | 35:00 | 5 | 30 |
| or | | | |
| 20/75 | 30:00 | 5 | 32.5 |
| or | | | |
| 25/90 | 20:00 | 5 | 28.5 |
| or | | | |

| Speed (mph/rpm) | Time Requirement (min) | Freq/Wk | Points/Wk |
|---|---|---|---|
| 25/90 | 25:00 | 4 | 30 |
| or | | | |
| 30/105 | 25:00 | 3 | 30 |

Add enough resistance so that the pulse rate counted for 10 seconds immediately after exercise and multiplied by 6 equals or exceeds 140 beats per minute.

## Schwinn Air-Dyne Ergometer

These indoor cycles are mushrooming in popularity. They differ from ordinary stationary bikes in that a forward-backward pumping action of the arms accompanies the up-and-down leg movement. The result is a more thorough conditioning session aimed at both your upper and lower body.

### Physiologic and Performance Responses to Arm, Leg, and Combined Arm and Leg Work on the Schwinn Air-Dyne Ergometer

Oxygen uptake, heart rate, energy expenditure, and performance to arm, leg, and combined arm and leg work on the Schwinn Air-Dyne Ergometer was evaluated in 15 men and 15 women by the Institute for Aerobics Research. In both the men and women, maximal exercise values for heart rate, oxygen uptake, and energy expenditure were progressively greater for combined arm and leg work compared to leg work and for leg work compared to arm work. The maximal physiologic values for combined arm and leg work are similar to values on a treadmill test. During submaximal work loads, exercise heart rates and oxygen uptake were higher; and work efficiency was lower for arm work compared to leg work and combined arm and leg work. Our findings indicate that arm and leg work from low to high intensities can be accomplished on the Schwinn Air-Dyne Ergometer. Thus, numerous cardiovascular training and conditioning programs can be conducted on this durable and versatile exercise ergometer. (Information provided by Don Hagan, Ph.D., formerly the Director of Exercise Physiology, Institute for Aerobics Research.)

## Oxygen Uptake and Energy Cost for Work on the Schwinn Air-Dyne Ergometer

| | For Arm Work | | For Leg Work and Arm and Leg Work Combined | |
|---|---|---|---|---|
| Work Load | Gross $VO_2$ ml/kg/min | Gross Kcal/min | Gross $VO_2$ ml/kg/min | Gross Kcal/min |
| 0.5 | 12.5 | 4.7 | 10.5 | 4.0 |
| 1.0 | 17.0 | 6.4 | 14.5 | 5.5 |
| 1.5 | 21.5 | 8.1 | 18.5 | 7.0 |
| 2.0 | 26.0 | 9.8 | 22.5 | 8.5 |
| 2.5 | 30.5 | 11.5 | 26.5 | 10.0 |
| 3.0 | 35.0 | 13.2 | 30.5 | 11.5 |
| 3.5 | 39.5 | 14.9 | 34.5 | 13.0 |
| 4.0 | 44.0 | 16.6 | 38.5 | 14.5 |
| 4.5 | 48.5 | 18.3 | 42.5 | 16.0 |
| 5.0 | 53.0 | 20.0 | 46.5 | 17.5 |
| 5.5 | 57.5 | 21.7 | 50.5 | 19.0 |
| 6.0 | 62.0 | 23.4 | 54.5 | 20.5 |
| 6.5 | 66.5 | 25.1 | 58.5 | 22.0 |
| 7.0 | 71.0 | 26.8 | 62.5 | 23.5 |

## Aerobics Points for Work with the Legs or Arms and Legs Combined on the Schwinn Air-Dyne Ergometer

| Work | Total Time (Minutes) | | | | | | | | |
|---|---|---|---|---|---|---|---|---|---|
| Load | 1 | 5 | 10 | 15 | 20 | 25 | 30 | 35 | 40 |
| 0.5 | 0.06 | 0.3 | 0.6 | 0.9 | 1.2 | 1.5 | 1.8 | 2.1 | 2.4 |
| 1.0 | 0.10 | 0.5 | 1.0 | 1.5 | 2.0 | 2.5 | 3.0 | 3.5 | 4.0 |
| 1.5 | 0.14 | 0.7 | 1.4 | 2.1 | 2.8 | 3.5 | 4.2 | 4.9 | 5.6 |
| 2.0 | 0.21 | 1.0 | 2.1 | 3.2 | 4.2 | 5.2 | 6.3 | 7.4 | 8.4 |
| 2.5 | 0.29 | 1.4 | 2.9 | 4.4 | 5.8 | 7.2 | 8.7 | 10.2 | 11.6 |
| 3.0 | 0.39 | 1.9 | 3.9 | 5.8 | 7.8 | 9.8 | 11.7 | 13.6 | 15.6 |
| 3.5 | 0.50 | 2.5 | 5.0 | 7.5 | 10.0 | 12.5 | 15.0 | 17.5 | 20.0 |
| 4.0 | 0.63 | 3.2 | 6.3 | 9.4 | 12.6 | 15.8 | 18.9 | 22.0 | 25.2 |
| 4.5 | 0.77 | 3.8 | 7.7 | 11.6 | 15.4 | 19.2 | 23.1 | 27.0 | 30.8 |
| 5.0 | 0.93 | 4.6 | 9.3 | 14.0 | 18.6 | 23.2 | 27.9 | 32.6 | 37.2 |
| 5.5 | 1.10 | 5.5 | 11.0 | 16.5 | 22.0 | 27.5 | 33.0 | 38.5 | 44.0 |
| 6.0 | 1.29 | 6.4 | 12.9 | 19.4 | 25.8 | 32.2 | 38.7 | 45.2 | 51.6 |
| 6.5 | 1.50 | 7.5 | 15.0 | 22.5 | 30.0 | 37.5 | 45.0 | 52.5 | 60.0 |
| 7.0 | 1.72 | 8.6 | 17.2 | 25.8 | 34.4 | 43.0 | 51.6 | 60.2 | 68.8 |

## Aerobics Points for Work with the Arms on the Schwinn Air-Dyne Ergometer

| Work Load | Total Time (Minutes) 1 | 5 | 10 | 15 | 20 | 25 | 30 | 35 | 40 |
|---|---|---|---|---|---|---|---|---|---|
| 0.5 | 0.08 | 0.4 | 0.8 | 1.2 | 1.6 | 2.0 | 2.4 | 2.8 | 3.2 |
| 1.0 | 0.12 | 0.6 | 1.2 | 1.8 | 2.4 | 3.0 | 3.6 | 4.2 | 4.8 |
| 1.5 | 0.19 | 1.0 | 2.0 | 3.0 | 4.0 | 5.0 | 6.0 | 7.0 | 8.0 |
| 2.0 | 0.28 | 1.4 | 2.8 | 4.2 | 5.6 | 7.0 | 8.4 | 9.8 | 11.2 |
| 2.5 | 0.39 | 1.9 | 3.9 | 5.8 | 7.8 | 9.8 | 11.7 | 13.6 | 15.0 |
| 3.0 | 0.52 | 2.6 | 5.2 | 7.8 | 10.4 | 13.0 | 15.6 | 18.2 | 20.8 |
| 3.5 | 0.66 | 3.3 | 6.6 | 9.9 | 13.2 | 16.5 | 19.8 | 23.1 | 26.4 |
| 4.0 | 0.83 | 4.2 | 8.4 | 12.6 | 16.8 | 21.0 | 25.2 | 29.4 | 33.6 |
| 4.5 | 1.01 | 5.1 | 10.2 | 15.3 | 20.4 | 25.5 | 30.6 | 35.7 | 40.8 |
| 5.0 | 1.22 | 6.1 | 12.2 | 18.3 | 24.4 | 30.5 | 36.6 | 42.7 | 48.8 |
| 5.5 | 1.44 | 7.2 | 14.4 | 21.6 | 28.8 | 36.0 | 43.2 | 50.4 | 57.6 |
| 6.0 | 1.65 | 8.2 | 16.4 | 24.6 | 32.8 | 41.0 | 49.2 | 57.4 | 65.6 |
| 6.5 | 1.95 | 9.8 | 19.6 | 29.4 | 39.2 | 49.0 | 58.8 | 68.6 | 78.4 |
| 7.0 | 2.23 | 11.2 | 22.4 | 33.6 | 44.8 | 56.0 | 67.2 | 78.4 | 89.6 |

### Fit Checklist: How to Evaluate an Indoor Cycle

Indoor cycles range from junk to exceptionally high-quality equipment with price variants equally wide. Here are some questions to ask to make sure any bike you purchase has the features you need:

| | True | False |
|---|---|---|
| Does the bike have an odometer to show how many miles you've "traveled"? | ______ | ______ |
| Does it have a timer to tell you how long you've labored? | ______ | ______ |
| Does it have a speedometer to let you know your miles per hour? | ______ | ______ |
| Does it have an adjustment for varying the resistance of the pedals? | ______ | ______ |
| Do the pedals have a smooth action—no jerky movements? | ______ | ______ |
| Does the bike have adequate chain guards to protect your pant legs? | ______ | ______ |
| Is the seat comfortable and easy to adjust? | ______ | ______ |

| | True | False |
|---|---|---|
| Is the frame firm and stable? | _______ | _______ |
| Is the handlebar position and grip a good one for you? | _______ | _______ |
| Does it have a heart-rate monitor? (optional) | _______ | _______ |

Do not buy an indoor cycle that is motorized. *You're* supposed to supply the muscle power, not the machine!

Some of the new electronic stationary cycles have variable levels of predetermined time and resistance programs that are excellent. To determine which level is appropriate for you, refer back to chapter 4 to make sure that you are exercising long enough in your target heart rate zone.

## Aerobic Dancing

Aerobic dancing is nothing more than steady, rhythmic movements to the beat of relatively fast music.

Its roots go back to the early 1960s, when Debbie Drake introduced Dancercize. It didn't catch on then because the idea was ahead of its time.

After my book *Aerobics* was published in 1968, Jackie Sorensen tried again with her version which she dubbed "aerobic dancing." By 1970, the public was primed for her version of vigorous exercise choreographed to popular music, and the bandwagon hasn't stopped rolling yet.

By 1986 there was an estimated 23 million Americans, mostly women, dancing aerobically. It's the fastest-growing exercise for women.

A well-orchestrated aerobic dance session works about 75 percent of the body's muscles. A class typically begins with a series of slow-motion stretches and warm-up movements before getting into high-velocity dancing and walking or running in place. After some slower calisthenics done on a floor mat, the session then cools down and ends.

The music reflects the mood and desired pace of exercise, ranging from semiclassical for older women to hard rock for younger.

Unfortunately, the original form of aerobic dance—called "high-impact" or "hard" aerobics—was literally too hard for many who tried it and the injury rate skyrocketed. In response to a ground swell of complaints from injured women who didn't want to desert the exercise floor, a modified form of aerobic dance emerged in California in 1984.

It's called "low-impact" or "soft" aerobics, because one foot remains on the ground at all times, eliminating the foot-pounding aspects of the original aerobic dance.

"Nonimpact" aerobics is a third form of dance exercise. Neither foot ever leaves the ground. Although it's too mild to be an aerobic conditioner, it can still be beneficial to the very obese or the elderly.

Low-impact aerobics is the perfect answer to many a tibia, fibula, and patella's prayer. This relatively misery-free exercise is making it possible for aerobic dance to retain its popularity among an ever-growing cross-section of people, including men.

## High- Versus Low-Impact Aerobic Exercise

No matter what form of aerobic dance you choose, the goal is the same: to elevate (for up to 20 minutes) your heart rate to 60 to 80 or 85 percent of the maximum heart rate for women in your age group.

Which type of aerobic dance does this best?

Comparative studies seem to agree that women who are already quite fit may need a high-impact dance class—or an advanced low-impact class that emphasizes intensity—in order to achieve their heart rate objectives. But for women who are beginners, over age 50, overweight, or have impairments (pregnancy, or problems with joints, bones, or muscles), low-impact is more desirable. It enables participants to get their hearts pumping fast enough to gain some training effect while removing most of the threat of injury.

The theory behind the two forms of aerobic dance is this:

Like walking and running, aerobic dance is an "impact activity." The legs and feet must support the weight of your body, which is doubled or tripled when your feet leave the ground and return with impact. In contrast, swimming and cycling are "supported activities"—supported by water in the first case and by handlebars and the bicycle seat in the second.

Using a laboratory instrument called a force platform, researchers have been able to measure the vertical force on the feet as people undertake impact activities.

A typical high-impact dance exerciser, for example, experiences a vertical force on the ball of the foot that is twice her body weight during the moment the foot comes in contact with the floor. Add more vigorous hops and jumps to a choreographed dance routine and the vertical force on the ball of the foot occasionally exceeds three times body weight. That's a lot of punishment for a woman's feet and legs to endure.

When an exerciser substitutes a low-impact dance routine, the effect is gentler. The feet stay closer to the floor at all times, so the maximum vertical force on the ball of the foot is reduced to about 1½ times body weight.

There's another difference: high-impact aerobics involves more vertical movement (up and down). Low-impact movements tend to be more lateral (side to side), with the knees bent a good deal of the time.

To compensate for the lessened intensity of the average low-impact dance class, instructors have added emphasis to the upper body work. The arms tend to stay at or above heart level and are worked continuously.

## Low-Impact Aerobics

We introduce this form of aerobic dance first because it is more appropriate for beginners.

Even though it goes by such tamer-sounding names as "controlled-impact," "low-percussive," "protective," "no-bounce," "soft," and "fluid," it's a mistake to regard it as an exercise for softies, the infirm, and pregnant women. Nothing could be further from the truth.

Just like high-impact aerobics, low-impact classes are graduated. Beginners should find a low-impact class aimed at their skill level. It will be lower in *intensity* than classes aimed at intermediate or advanced dancers.

What does this mean?

It means that the pace of a beginners' class and the cadence of the music is slower. The workout is less intense even though the dance routine may be similar to the one offered in intermediate classes. On the other hand, a beginner might compensate for this low-intensity by attending longer classes or more classes per week.

One caveat: There are people who may not be able to tolerate even the reduced-weight-bearing nature of low-impact aerobics. Anyone with lower back or neck problems or an existing symptomatic knee problem should stay off the exercise floor.

Since low-impact aerobics is so new, no one is willing to say for certain that it is trouble-free. Researchers are just beginning to study the biomechanics of these new movement patterns to find out if and why injuries may occur.

However, they are already finding more arm and shoulder injuries, especially among dancers used to regular aerobics. In a misguided attempt to intensify their workouts, they tend to exaggerate their arm movements and injure themselves in the process. There is also the problem of poorly educated dance instructors who design low-impact exercises that are not natural to the way people normally move. Strains and pulled muscles often result.

However, professionals in the fitness field do agree that low-impact aerobics is certainly a safer form of dance exercise in all respects than its high-impact counterpart.

### Exercise Programs Conducted to Music— Traditional Aerobics, Low-Impact Aerobics, Aerobic Dancing, Etc.

(Under 30 Years of Age)

| Week Number | Time* in Minutes | Target Heart Rate** Beats per Minute | Frequency per Week | Points per Week |
|---|---|---|---|---|
| 1 | 10 | 124–134 | 3 | 6 |
| 2 | 15 | 124–143 | 3 | 9 |
| 3 | 15 | 134–143 | 3 | 9 |
| 4 | 20 | 134–153 | 3 | 12 |

| Week Number | Time* in Minutes | Target Heart Rate** Beats per Minute | Frequency per Week | Points per Week |
|---|---|---|---|---|
| 5 | 20 | 134–162 | 3–4 | 12–16 |
| 6 | 25 | 134–162 | 3–4 | 12–16 |
| 7 | 30 | 134–162 | 3–4 | 18–24 |
| 8 | 30 | 134–162 | 4–5 | 24–30 |

*Time is in addition to the normal 5- to 10-minute warm-up and the 5- to 10-minute cool-down. Total exercise time would be at least 10 minutes longer than the listed times.

**Heart rates determined at three or more equal intervals during the exercise based on a 10-second × 6 count. *Note:* Low-impact aerobics may produce a slightly lower exercise heart rate than traditional aerobics.

By the eighth to twelfth week, you'll have attained an adequate level of aerobic fitness (24 to 30 aerobics points), which is consistent with the "good" category of fitness for women. Exercising five times per week for 45 minutes would earn 45 points, consistent with the "excellent" category of fitness.

## Exercise Programs Conducted to Music—Traditional Aerobics, Low-Impact Aerobics, Aerobic Dancing, Etc.
(30–39 Years of Age)

| Week Number | Time* in Minutes | Target Heart Rate** Beats per Minute | Frequency per Week | Points per Week |
|---|---|---|---|---|
| 1 | 10 | 111–120 | 3 | 6 |
| 2 | 15 | 111–128 | 3 | 9 |
| 3 | 15 | 120–128 | 3 | 9 |
| 4 | 20 | 120–137 | 3 | 12 |
| 5 | 20 | 120–145 | 3–4 | 12–16 |
| 6 | 25 | 120–145 | 3–4 | 15–20 |
| 7 | 30 | 120–145 | 3–4 | 18–24 |
| 8 | 30 | 120–145 | 4–5 | 24–30 |

*Time is in addition to the normal 5- to 10-minute warm-up and the 5- to 10-minute cool-down. Total exercise time would be at least 10 minutes longer than the listed times.

**Heart rates determined at three or more equal intervals during the exercise based on a 10-second × 6 count. *Note:* Low-impact aerobics may produce a slightly lower exercise heart rate than traditional aerobics.

By the eighth to twelfth week, you'll have attained an adequate level of aerobic fitness (24 to 30 aerobics points), which is consistent with the "good" category of fitness for women. Exercising five times per week for 45 minutes would earn 45 points, consistent with the "excellent" category of fitness.

## Exercise Programs Conducted to Music—Traditional Aerobics, Low-Impact Aerobics, Aerobic Dancing, Etc.
(50–59 Years of Age)

| Week Number | Time* in Minutes | Target Heart Rate** Beats per Minute | Frequency per Week | Points per Week |
|---|---|---|---|---|
| 1 | 10 | 105–113 | 3 | 6 |
| 2 | 10 | 105–113 | 3 | 6 |
| 3 | 12 | 105–121 | 3 | 7.5 |
| 4 | 12 | 105–121 | 3 | 7.5 |
| 5 | 15 | 105–121 | 3 | 9 |
| 6 | 15 | 105–129 | 3 | 9 |
| 7 | 18 | 113–129 | 3 | 10.5 |
| 8 | 20 | 113–129 | 3 | 12 |
| 9 | 25 | 113–129 | 3 | 15 |
| 10 | 25 | 113–137 | 3–4 | 15–20 |
| 11 | 27 | 113–137 | 4–5 | 22–27.5 |
| 12 | 30 | 113–137 | 4–5 | 24–30 |

*Time is in addition to the normal 5- to 10-minute warm-up and the 5- to 10-minute cool-down. Total exercise time would be at least 10 minutes longer than the listed times.

**Heart rates determined at three or more equal intervals during the exercise based on a 10-second × 6 count. *Note:* Low-impact aerobics may produce a slightly lower exercise heart rate than traditional aerobics.

By the eighth to twelfth week, you'll have attained an adequate level of aerobic fitness (24 to 30 aerobics points), which is consistent with the "good" category of fitness for women. Exercising five times per week for 45 minutes would earn 45 points, consistent with the "excellent" category of fitness.

## Exercise Programs Conducted to Music—Traditional Aerobics, Low-Impact Aerobics, Aerobic Dancing, Etc.
(60+ Years of Age)

We do not recommend this type of physical activity for totally inactive women. But it's all right for women who have been involved in aerobic dancing prior to age 60 to continue if they wish. Even the progressive programs are permitted past 60 years of age, provided the exercise can be conducted in a medically supervised environment preceded by an adequate examination.

### Aerobic Dancing and Other Exercise Programs Conducted to Music
(Traditional Aerobics, Low-Impact Aerobics, Aerobic Dancing, Etc.)

| Time (min.) | Heart Rate (beats/min.) | Frequency per Week | Points per Week |
|---|---|---|---|
| 30 | 135–162 | 5 | 30 |
| 40 | 120–145 | 4 | 32 |
| 45 | 120–145 | 4 | 36 |
| 50 | 120–145 | 3 | 30 |
| 55 | 115–140 | 3 | 33 |
| 60 | 115–140 | 3 | 36 |

## High-Impact Aerobics

Some critics have dubbed this exercise "killer aerobics." True, this traditional form of aerobic dance is characterized by pounding and pounding, and shinsplints, stress fractures, and tendinitis are common among the faithful. Still, there are plenty of women who are fit enough to attempt this high-intensity workout and indeed would feel lost without it. They love it enough to risk its dubious safety record.

In fact, many medical authorities don't oppose high-impact workouts for those in shape for it. Rather, they recommend that students alternate high- and low-impact classes. Two low-impact classes interspersed with two high-impact classes per week, for example.

### Fit Tips: Choosing an Aerobics Dance Class

The following statements describe an ideal aerobics dance class (high- or low-impact). Assess any class you plan to join—or are already attending—against these criteria:

- The instructor received formal training (a shocking number haven't). Ideally, she's certified by the American College of Sports Medicine (PO Box 1440, Indianapolis, IN 46206) or the International Dance Exercise Association (I.D.E.A., 4501 Mission Bay Drive, Suite 2F, San Diego, CA 92109) or The Institute for Aerobics Research (12330 Preston Rd., Dallas, TX 75230).
- Participants are screened—asked about their physical condition and goals—in order to determine how advanced a class they should be placed in.
- The composition of classes is relatively uniform as to fitness, age, and skill level. If not, studies show injuries increase.

- A doctor's clearance is required for women over 35 or at least over 40.
- The instructor is aware of any physiological or anatomical shortcomings that could predispose a student to injuries.
- The instructor insists that students wear proper aerobic shoes.
- The instructor chats with women entering her class for the first time, advising them to take it easy in the beginning, even if it means doing fewer repetitions of different movements.
- The instructor cues students adequately both verbally and through her body movements.
- The dance routine does not require students to hold their hands and arms above shoulder level for any extended period of time, because to do so raises blood pressure.
- The choreography is appropriate for the space and number of dancers. The movements are fluid and controlled—never uncoordinated and jerky.
- The class is small enough for the instructor to give individual attention when appropriate.
- The class is structured to include all components of fitness: flexibility (gained through warm-up stretching exercises); cardiovascular conditioning (vigorous aerobic phase); and muscle strength and body composition (calisthenics or the addition of hand weights).
- The pace of the music changes to reflect the transitions from a slow warm-up (5 to 8 minutes) to a vigorous aerobic phase (15 minutes), to a slower calisthenics phase (5 to 10 minutes), winding down even further to the cool-down (5 minutes).
- The music never gets so fast that it's difficult for students to perform side-to-side and backward-and-forward movements with control and safety.
- The type of music fits the class participants and isn't unduly loud. (Senior citizens might enjoy the 1940s big band sound, while young women might prefer rock and pop.)
- The aerobics portion of the class is 30 minutes maximum, unless it's very low in intensity.
- Hand weights are used only in more advanced classes to help elevate the heart rate. (Ankle weights are controversial. Adding weight at the ankles increases the impact each time the feet hit the floor. In a high-impact aerobics class, ankle weights increase the force exerted on the feet over the usual three times a person's body weight.)

- The exercise floor is shock absorbent. According to a 1985 study of aerobic dance injuries, the best floor is a suspended surface such as hardwood over a compressible substance that includes air. The worst surfaces are concrete; carpet directly over concrete; or tile covering a concrete or a brick floor.
- The ventilation and room temperature are satisfactory.
- The lighting is good, neither too dim nor excessively glaring.
- The health club has adequate systems and procedures to deal with emergencies.

## Charting Your Progress

The best way to keep track of your progress is to write it down. We suggest you Xerox the following Personal Progress Chart and use it for that purpose.

### Personal Progress Chart

| DATE | EXERCISE | DISTANCE | DURATION | POINTS | CUMULAT. POINTS |
|---|---|---|---|---|---|
| | | | | | |
| | | | | | |
| | | | | | |
| | | | | | |
| | | | | | |
| | | | | | |
| | | | | | |
| | | | | | |
| | | | | | |
| | | | | | |
| | | | | | |
| | | | | | |
| | | | | | |
| | | | | | |
| | | | | | |
| | | | | | |
| | | | | | |
| | | | | | |
| | | | | | |
| | | | | | |
| | | | | | |
| | | | | | |
| | | | | | |

# 9

# Other Types of Aerobic Exercise

The book *The Aerobics Program for Total Well-Being* singled out thirty-one sports as aerobic. However, it would be more accurate to say that we developed aerobic point charts for some thirty-one sports, many of which don't qualify as aerobic *unless* you do them without stopping for a sufficient period of time.

For example, there are charts for golf and football, not sports that ordinarily occur to you when someone says "aerobic." However, it is possible to earn 3 aerobic points for shooting 18 holes of golf *if* you walk briskly around the course. With football, you earn points only when you are actively participating; 10 minutes of active participation would gain you 1 point.

In this chapter we'll focus on a select group of aerobic activities that hold special appeal for women. Consult the Appendix for The Point System charts that correspond to these exercises.

## Cross-country Skiing

This is *the* best aerobic conditioner—ahead of running, swimming, cycling, and aerobic dance. This sport ranks number one for several reasons:

In downhill skiing, gravity does a lot of the work for you. But in cross-country skiing, which is done on relatively level ground, the muscles of your arms and legs provide the propulsion. Indeed, you're using as many muscles as you do in swimming—and dealing with a greater number of opposing forces than mere water resistance. Surprisingly, the energy required for competitive, international-class cross-country skiing comes mainly from arm activity (70 percent). The legs are responsible for only 30 percent of the energy expenditure.

To get a good aerobic workout, resistance is beneficial, of course. The more resistance, the more strain, the more rigorous your workout.

The heavy clothing that skiers wear provides one form of resistance. The equipment—

skis and ski poles—are heavy too. Moreover, cross-country skiers are often battling the wind at relatively high altitudes.

The high-altitude factor of this sport is actually the major reason why Scandinavian cross-country skiers are the most highly conditioned aerobic athletes in the world. The air is thinner at high altitudes. This forces a person's lungs to work harder to extract the necessary oxygen to meet the body's demands during vigorous activity. The end result: when compared to other athletes, Nordic cross-country skiers have the greatest maximum oxygen consumption of all.

Even if you're lucky enough to live in the right geographic location to cross-country ski on a regular basis, winter ends sooner or later. Off-season, you'll need a substitute activity.

One "summer supplement" for cross-country skiing is a stationary indoor device called the Nordic Track. It simulates skiing movements, requiring you to move your feet and arms in the same way as you would on ski trails outdoors.

The machine has one advantage over skiing outdoors. Outside, you get to rest between poling strokes and on the occasional downhill slide. Inside, you have to keep on striding and using your arms. Indeed, the alternating arm tugs you make on Nordic Track's rope pulley take more effort than real poling. And if your principal concern is to strengthen your upper body, you can even lock the Nordic Track's ski slats in place and use the arm pulls by themselves.

What this machine can't simulate, unfortunately, are the other conditions—the brisk winter air and burden of heavy clothing. In that respect, your indoor workout may be less strenuous.

Still, this type of a machine has merit. However, if you find it too expensive, you might gain access to one in a gym or health club.

## Power Aerobics

At the Aerobics Center, we encourage all our members to pursue a well-rounded exercise program. It has three components: (1) stretching/flexibility exercises (usually done during the warm-up to aerobic exercise); (2) the aerobic activity itself; and (3) muscle-building exercises (usually done either after aerobics or at another time).

There are group exercises designed to hit all three bases. Examples are aerobic dance, aqua-aerobics, and circuit training (discussed at the end of this chapter). Solitary aerobic exercises, such as running and cycling, are another story. Their thrust is to condition your cardiovascular system. While some muscle development does occur, which muscles and how great the toning depend on the exercise.

Walking, running, and cycling, for example, build the leg muscles but do little for the upper body. Swimming, in contrast, is a great builder of muscles, particularly the shoulders. Tennis does wonders for the muscles in the arm you use to swing your racquet, but it won't do much for your other arm; and it has a limited impact on the muscles elsewhere on your body.

What it all adds up to is this:

Your primary aerobic activity probably won't work enough of your body's muscles to get you in top shape. You'll have to supplement this activity with some calisthenics or weight-training aimed at reaching muscle groups that get a free ride during aerobics. You should do these muscle-toning exercises two or three times a week with at least one day between each session.

Your goal is twofold: to increase muscular *strength* and *endurance*. Strength is built up through the overload principle—by increasing, gradually, the amount of weight that you lift. Endurance, on the other hand, comes through adding more repetitions to your workout.

Here are some weight-training guidelines:

Give some thought to the type of strength training you choose, making sure it complements your primary aerobic activity. There's no point in working the muscles already built up during aerobics.

Next, vary your routine from one session to the next to avoid stress on the joints. For example, work your muscles at different angles and through different ranges of motion.

Muscle balancing—or working opposing muscle groups—is equally important. You must work the triceps after you work the biceps, or vice versa, for instance.

## Boning Up Through Strength Training

There are a couple of other reasons, beyond simply firming up your muscles, that you should add strengthening exercises to your workouts.

First, the added toughness you'll gain will make you less prone to injuries during the aerobic aspect of your program.

Second, weight training also increases bone density over time and decreases the chance that you'll develop osteoporosis or "dowager's hump" in old age. Many women mistakenly think that popping calcium pills, or eating lots of dairy products, will eliminate the risk of osteoporosis. It will reduce it to some degree, but exercise is important, too, for reducing risk.

After age 35—when peak bone mass is reached in both men and women—it's alarming how fast sedentary women start losing bone density. They lose it at a rate three times faster than men!

Dr. Everett L. Smith, assistant clinical professor in the Department of Preventive Medicine and director of the Biogerontology Laboratory at the University of Wisconsin, has studied the rate of bone deterioration in women. Beginning at age 35—sometimes even at 30—sedentary women lose .75 to 1 percent of their bone mass per year. It increases to 2 to 3 percent per year after menopause, when the body's estrogen levels drop precipitously. (Another study cites postmenopausal figures as high as a 4 to 6 percent loss per year.) If nothing is done to arrest the process, these percentages can get even higher as a woman moves into old age.

There are young women athletes, involved in sports such as running or gymnastics, who train to excess, however. They also place themselves at risk for osteoporosis. Eventually, their estrogen levels drop and they develop an amenorrhea, which means they stop menstruating. Just as for postmenopausal women, reduced estrogen levels translate, biochemically, into bone mass loss.

There is a solution, however. Reduce the level of physical activity to the point that menstruation returns. At times this may not be possible in the midst of a high-intensity, competitive training program. In such cases, nonweight-bearing activities such as cycling or swimming may be used to minimize the risk of a stress fracture in the presence of low estrogen levels.

## Myths about Muscle Building

Unfortunately, for all its benefits, many women still view weight training with a certain amount of apprehension. It strikes them as a masculine pursuit; even worse, one that will make them look masculine because of bulging muscles.

There's little cause for concern. A myriad of research studies have shown that women who try to build muscles so they'll look like a female Arnold Schwarzenegger fall far short of their goal. Women just don't gain the muscle mass or bulk of a man working out at the same intensity.

One study, by C. H. Brown and J. H. Wilmore, followed seven nationally ranked female track-and-field athletes as they undertook a six-month weight-training program designed to build as much muscle as fast as possible. At the end of the six months, the visual results were hardly startling. The maximum increase in muscle measurement was one-half inch; most measurements were much less. Two of the women actually experienced a decrease in thigh mass because of muscle toning.

There's a biochemical reason for this disparity between men and women. Testosterone, primarily a male hormone, is responsible for muscle bulk. Since women have very little of this hormone, it's improbable that they'll ever match men in muscle size.

Muscle building can be done in more than one way. Here are some choices:

## Calisthenics for Weight Training

A lot of apparatus isn't necessary to build muscles. Strength training can be done using your body weight. Bent-knee sit-ups, leg raises, partial squats, and modified push-ups are calisthenics that build muscular strength.

Lifting weights through the use of elaborate gym equipment, such as Nautilus, is another means to the same end. A third alternative is to carry hand weights or wear a weighted vest while you're engaged in certain aerobic exercises, as described below.

## Walking with Weights

Studies have shown that people who walk briskly carrying 1- to 3-pound hand weights can elevate their heart rates and attain metabolic loads comparable to those of slow jogging—with one proviso: they must move their arms vigorously too. Without these movements, the additional energy expenditure from the hand weights is so small that it can probably be equaled simply by increasing the walking speed very slightly.

What about walking with ankle weights or a heavy vest?

Research indicates that lighter weights on the extremities can produce the same increased work load as a heavier weighted vest. A vest—because the added weight is higher and more centrally located—tends to produce greater forces at the ankles, knees, and hips than do hand or ankle weights. This increases the chance of injury. Conclusion: hand and ankle weights are far more desirable.

Walkers who have back problems are in a special category, however. They probably should eschew hand weights. During the exaggerated walking motion one develops carrying hand weights, the upper body rotates in the direction opposite that of the lower body. At the end of a stride, the muscles of the back and trunk have to stop the rotation in one direction and shift it to the other. Hand weights make it necessary to bring more muscle power into play to change the rotation, thus their danger.

## Jogging with Weights

Jogging with hand weights is another possibility. They increase the intensity of a workout while helping to strengthen the upper body and arms.

Of course, there's a more direct way for a jogger to achieve that goal: speed up to a run (a pace faster than 9 miles per hour).

However, running with hand weights is **not** advised. People's motions are too uncontrolled when they run. Weights tend to throw the body out of alignment at faster speeds. Besides, weights aren't necessary. Runners' hearts are usually pounding fast enough already.

## Aerobic Dancing with Weights

Dancing with weights is the province of advanced exercisers. Beginners who need a more intense workout can simply join a more advanced class. The same goes for intermediate aerobic dancers. In contrast, adding weights makes sense for advanced dancers who want to raise their heart rates. The only other alternative for them is to increase the pace of their workouts.

Even advanced aerobic dancers should resort to hand weights or wrist weights (½ to 3 pounds) only during the *calisthenics* phase of their dance routine. The aerobics phase, involving kicking and lifting and fast movements, is too uncontrolled. Shoulder injuries—rotator cuff and bursitis—and elbow joint strains inevitably result.

Ankle weights are verboten. They increase the effect of gravity on the feet and ankles. Too many aerobic dancers who have tried them end up with hairline fractures of the feet and shin bones, Achilles tendinitis, knee problems, and lower back pain.

## Racquet Sports

We lump racquetball, squash, and basketball together in terms of aerobic points.

If you like team sports, one of these activities should appeal to you. Unfortunately, because of all the stopping and starting they entail, you'll only earn 9 points an hour for them. Your heart rate doesn't stay elevated for continuous stretches of time as it does during one of our five basic aerobic exercises—walking, running, cycling, swimming, and dancing. Thus, it's better to use such sports to augment your primary aerobic activity, not to replace it.

## Indoor Exercise Machines

Bad weather and time constraints are the main reasons why people use indoor exercise equipment for their daily workouts. As corporate wellness programs proliferate, more and more employees are getting exposed to such equipment. Either they have access to it in their company's in-house gym or in a local health club where their company holds a corporate membership.

• **Treadmill.** President and Nancy Reagan are treadmill enthusiasts. In fact, they had a treadmill, designed by a former Cooper Clinic staff member, Bob Parker, installed in the White House. They exercise on it faithfully, as do thousands of other Americans.

There are two basic kinds of treadmills: manual and electric.

The least expensive models are manual. You provide the power, via your leg muscles, to move the belt. It speeds up or slows down when you do. If you can learn to use these models *without* holding on to the side rails—which isn't easy to do—you'll get an effective workout. Otherwise, a session on a motorized treadmill will do you more good.

With a motorized treadmill, you tell the machine what speed you want and the belt accelerates accordingly. The challenge is to keep going at the speed you've chosen, regardless of your desire to slow down.

Almost all treadmills can be adjusted to simulate an uphill run. The treadmill point charts in the Appendix take advantage of this feature. The greater the incline, the more aerobic points you'll earn for your effort.

• **Minitrampoline.** People who don't like stationary running sometimes find a minitrampoline workout more appealing.

This trampoline is just large enough to enable someone to run in place on its surface. Naturally, the risk of muscle and joint injuries on such a device is greatly reduced, since the trampoline runner isn't hitting a hard surface with each step.

Unfortunately, there's a negative side to this coin. On a trampoline, gravity is working for you instead of against you. The trampoline reduces the physical effort required, because trampoliners' legs are "sprung up," while regular runners have to pull up their legs with muscle power.

This translates into fewer aerobic points for the same time put in. Continuous running in place on a minitrampoline is worth 1.6 points for 10 minutes. It's equivalent to a running pace of 1 mile in 12 to 13 minutes.

• **Rowing machines.** Indoor rowing, via machine, and outdoor running are wonderful complementary sports. The crossover effect comes from the fact that rowing strengthens your upper and lower body, while running strengthens mostly your legs.

Rowing machines are extremely challenging even for long-distance runners. A day or two after your first rowing session you'll probably be sore in muscles you never knew you had. A rowing machine workout, unlike many other aerobic activities, demands performance from all the body's major muscle groups—back and arms as well as legs. It's a good total-body exercise.

Rowing does fall short of perfection on two counts, however: you're sitting rather than supporting your body's weight; and your arms and legs work together toward the same purpose, effectively lessening the work load on each.

• **Stair climbing.** Housewives excel at a great indoor exercise and most don't even realize it. It's stair climbing. Navigating flights of stairs for stretches of time every day can actually earn aerobic points. Done consciously in the way I'll describe, it can take the place of a workout.

How one earns maximum aerobic points on stairs may come as a surprise. The woman who walks up and down a flight of stairs continuously for 5 minutes is gaining some benefit. But the woman who keeps going up and down the first three steps of the staircase for the same 5-minute period is doing herself even more good.

Why? The three-step course provides more continuity of effort, an essential factor in earning aerobic points, as we've discussed. The woman negotiating more steps gets more time to rest while she's descending.

Many of us live in apartments, or "flats" as the English call them, for good reason: all the rooms are on one level. In addition, many of us ascend to our apartments in elevators, consequently bypassing stairs. It's too bad. However, innovative manufacturers have come to the rescue. Their answer is stair-climbing machines, which are gaining wider and wider acceptance.

Here's how they work:

While holding on to supporting side bars, you can adjust the speed from slow to fast. A display screen constantly displays the number of floors you've theoretically climbed and the calories you've expended, and some even tell you your heart rate. Yes, it is possible to get an outstanding aerobic workout in a relatively short period of time using one of these ingenious stair-climbing machines.

• **Jumping rope.** Most of us did plenty of this as children on the school playground. You may be delighted to learn that it's equally healthy for adults.

If the weather is bad or you're in a hotel room on a business trip, both stationary running and rope skipping are possibilities. The latter may be the better choice, though. It not only affords you the same training effect as stationary running, but it provides additional exercise for the muscles of your arms, shoulders, and upper torso—and these, remember, support your bust. Rope skipping is also less likely to cause ankle and leg pain and swelling because it lessens the direct impact of your feet against the floor.

You can jump rope in four different ways: (1) with both feet together; (2) alternating feet; (3) on one leg only; (4) stepping over the rope, in something akin to a walking motion, one foot at a time. Modes 1 and 2 are our recommendation.

The speed at which you jump is another variable.

We've all seen movies about professional boxers. In the training scenes at the gym, the boxer is always shown jumping rope at rapidfire pace. We're not suggesting you emulate that speed, although it does afford a terrific workout.

Actually, a rate about the same as in stationary running—70 to 80 steps per minute—is fine. At this pace, it will earn you about the same number of aerobic points as stationary running. Advanced jump ropers may want to progress beyond this, eventually working up to those boxers' speeds of around 110 steps per minute.

Another variation on rope skipping is offered by a "HeavyRope." This is a weighted rope, weighing anywhere from 2 to 6 pounds. It adds a strengthening aspect to this essentially aerobic activity. Exercising with a HeavyRope falls into the same category as walking or jogging with hand weights. It enables you to gain muscle power at the same time as you're increasing your lung power.

## Mixing It Up

In this and the preceding chapter we've introduced you to a host of aerobic exercise choices. Each activity has its own appeal. Our only recommendation is that you try several before you settle into a regimen. And that your regimen include at least two activities—your primary aerobic sport and one to balance it out.

Balance is important. As we've mentioned, aerobic exercises fall into two categories: weight-bearing (e.g., walking, running, aerobic dance, and racquet sports); and nonweight-bearing (e.g., swimming, cycling, and cross-country skiing). You should pick one from each category.

If your primary activity is running, for example, why not give your legs a rest a couple of days a week and do some cross-country skiing? If you did, you'd be following the lead of world-class marathoner Ingrid Kristiansen.

Ingrid Kristiansen's winter training schedule exemplifies cross-training at its best. With a long list of first-place running medals and time records to her credit, Ms. Kristiansen isn't about to let the forbidding Norwegian winters slow her down. Although she considers one outdoor run a week—no matter what the weather—an absolute necessity, she builds her winter training regimen around a treadmill in her basement.

"Treadmill running has made me much more pace-conscious and efficient," she told a reporter for *Runner's World*. "On it, you can spot any inefficiencies in your stride by viewing your form in a mirror for one hour. It's helped me develop a rhythm that translates easily into track and road-racing competitions."

She supplements her twice-daily treadmill sessions with cross-country skiing over snowy hills and dales two to four times per week.

Kristiansen's coach, Johan Kaggestad, says these cross-training choices, including her one outdoor run, all add up to a superior weekly workout.

"Running in the snow, which is often very deep, is a great strength builder. And the combination of running in snow, running on a treadmill, and cross-country skiing is ideal. You develop all areas of the body *and* mind. I have no doubts that our winters make our athletes much tougher competitors."

## Prepackaged Cross-training

Maybe figuring out which sports to combine in your program seems too complicated; you'd rather have some expert make the decisions for you.

One option is *circuit training*, a combination of aerobics and strength training all rolled into a 20-minute exercise program four times per week. A well-designed circuit workout is about as efficient as you can get. Performed correctly, it will help improve your cardiovascular system, build and tone your muscles, and burn calories all at the same time.

During a circuit-training session, ten exercise stations are used and you go through the circuit twice. At each station you are required to perform a different exercise. Some merely involve calisthenics. Others might require you to use Nautilus or other weight-lifting equipment.

Each class is segmented into 30-second stretches. You exercise at each station for 30 seconds, rest for 30 seconds, then go on to the next station, where you do a different set of exercises, again for 30 seconds. At each station, 12 to 14 repetitions of the exercise should be performed, at 65 percent of your maximum capacity.

Each station works on different muscle groups. For the best results, participants must follow the sequence given by the teacher.

One muscle-building sequence is leg muscles first (top of the thighs, back of the thighs, front of the lower legs, and calves); followed by the larger muscle groups of the upper body (abdominals, chest, back, and shoulders); and finishing with the body's smaller muscle groups (fronts and backs of the arms).

A 20-minute, ten-station circuit gives you 4 aerobic points. While research in standard circuit weight training has demonstrated that only minimal aerobic work is accomplished, some studies have documented an average 5 percent increase in aerobic capacity. However, women who start at a very low level of fitness may benefit considerably more.

Here are the keys to obtaining as much aerobic benefit as possible during a circuit weight-training routine:

(1) Perform exercises that incorporate as many major muscle groups at one time as possible. (2) Complete the circuit with little rest in between the exercises. In fact, a modification of circuit training that significantly increases the aerobic benefit is called the "super circuit" training program. Exercising in this manner eliminates the 30-second rest period.

The exercise stations can be set up around a gym floor, and when the 30-second exercise phase is finished you must run for 30 seconds before going on to the next station. In other cases, stationary running, rope skipping, stationary cycling, or running on a minitrampoline can be used between stations. Such continuous activity increases the point valve to 6 points every 20 minutes.

Circuit weight training is very intense and strenuous, and while it is not worth very many aerobic points, it is an excellent way to develop muscular endurance and strength. It is also the recommended weight-training procedure to increase a person's "anaerobic threshold." We recommend circuit weight training as an ideal supplement to a running program, and as the program of choice when space is at a premium.

Training for a *triathlon* is another preordained way to combine activities.

As the name implies, a triathlon competition involves three sports—typically swimming, cycling, and running. The original triathlon was held in Hawaii in 1978 and it wasn't dubbed the Iron Man Triathlon for nothing. Entrants must swim for 2.4 miles, cycle 112 miles, and *then* run a 26.2-mile marathon.

As impossible as this sounds, the Iron Man Triathlon caught on, spawning hundreds of imitators. Most are short triathlons, though. You swim between 800 meters and 1 mile, cycle between 25 and 40 miles, and run between 5 and 13 miles. These distances are much more do-able for most people!

Allison Roe is the former women's world record holder in the marathon. She finished the New York City Marathon in 1981 in 2 hours, 25 minutes, 28 seconds. In 1984, she used triathlon training as a method of rehabilitation following hamstring surgery.

"I want to run marathons again," she told us when she visited the Cooper Clinic in 1985, "but I don't think my leg is yet up to the strain of marathon training, which is very specific. I like triathlon cross-training because it gives me a chance to strengthen different muscles and still compete without having to train specifically for one event."

Within nine months after her surgery, this determined New Zealander had entered six triathlons and won four. On our treadmill, her performance was equally remarkable. Weighing in with a scant 5 percent body fat, she stepped on our machine and proceeded to log 32 minutes, 25 seconds before complaining of a leg pain.

The stress test record for a woman is 33 minutes, 6 seconds, held by the well-known Masters marathoner Joan Ullyot. Allison Roe, competitive athlete that she is, has vowed to top not only the women's record but the overall Cooper Clinic record, held by Brad Erikstadt. On our treadmill, he lasted for a grueling 40 minutes, 2 seconds.

# 10

# When You Exercise Outdoors—Special Considerations

There are certain things you can't predict. One, as we discussed in chapter 7, is whether you're going to feel like exercising when the time rolls around to do it. Another is the weather. You can't predict or control either one, but you can adapt yourself to such eventualities.

Now we will focus on those environmental factors you have to contend with if you do most of your exercising outdoors. We'll also advise you how to avoid hot- and cold-weather mistakes, which, carried to extremes, could have serious, long-term health consequences.

## Sports Apparel

Your closet and drawers are probably filled with appropriate clothing for aerobics. There's no need to "dress the part." For walking, running, or cycling, any garment that is loose, comfortable, and absorbent will be just fine. For aerobic dancing, a leotard and tights are all you need.

The guidelines for active sportswear are straightforward: Choose clothing that is loose enough—in texture as well as fit—to permit your body's heat to escape and is also absorbent enough to foster heat loss through the rapid absorption of perspiration. (We'll discuss the importance of sweat absorption in a moment.)

Cotton knitwear and terrycloth outfits are excellent because cotton has the virtue of "breathing," which synthetics do not. Plus, it acts like a sponge for sweat.

When you're exercising outdoors in the sun, light-colored clothing is best because it reflects the heat. Light colors and reflective clothing are better at night, too, but for visual reasons: passing motorists can see you more easily.

- **Under- and outer garments.** Even if the purpose of your workout is to look better, keep in mind that looking glamorous is your goal *after* aerobics, not *during*. In fact, looking glamorous during aerobics could be a hindrance.

For example, avoid garments that are form-fitting if they in any way restrict your movements or interfere with deep breathing. In that category are numerous undergarments such as tight bras and girdles. Also cast aside shorts, pants, or jumpsuits with tight elastic waists. For that matter, avoid any clothes that are constricting anywhere.

- **Bra.** By all means wear a bra. Choose one that's comfortable and gives you lots of support. This is particularly important for women who have large breasts. A well-made, sturdy bra helps protect the ligaments attaching your breasts to your body. Coincidentally, they're known as the ligaments of Cooper (no relation).

- **Shoes.** Appropriate shoes for aerobics are one thing you probably don't have in your closet. This is likely the one purchase you'll have to make before you begin exercising.

The right footwear is a key factor in avoiding ankle, foot, knee, and leg-muscle problems. Look at it this way: when you walk a mile, you subject the twenty-six little bones in each foot to the full impact of your body weight *at least 2,000 times!* And if you run or take part in an aerobics dance class, jumping up and down hundreds of times, the punishment to your feet grows exponentially. You can ease that burden with top-quality athletic shoes.

Not all sports shoes are alike. Nor are they interchangeable. While basic tennis shoes may suffice for other racquet sports, they won't do for running. Nor can a running shoe pass for an aerobic dance shoe or for bicycling.

Today, if a sport exists, some manufacturer somewhere has designed a shoe for it. Running, aerobic dancing, and cycling all require special footgear, designed with each sport's unique movements in mind.

Running's movements, for example, are all forward oriented, while aerobic dance has more lateral motion. Thus, running shoes have wider soles to foster stability and thicker padding in the heel for shock absorbency. Aerobic dance shoes, in contrast, have more cushioning under the ball of the foot, since that part tends to hit the ground first during routines.

What should you look for when you're buying an athletic shoe—any athletic shoe? Here are some guidelines:

First, a sole that's thick enough to cushion the impact on your body when you exercise on a hard surface. Also, select a sole that gives you the most traction.

Size is crucial. Make sure the shoes you buy are long enough as well as wide enough. Shoes that don't fit properly will create all sorts of problems later.

On your shopping trip, bring along the type of socks you plan to wear during exercise. For example, if you're a woman who wears two pairs of socks (for absorbency and added cushioning), put both on before you try on athletic shoes. Otherwise, you'll end up buying shoes that are too small.

Make sure the shoes have good arch support. This is essential if you're flat-footed. Many runners develop painful knee problems and never realize that poor arch supports are the culprits. Sports orthotics have become popular and, properly fitted, can reduce foot problems.

Finally, check for adequate support at the heel. Shoes should fit snugly around your heel without chafing, and they should have a little elevation.

• **Rubber clothes.** For active sportswear, there is one absolute prohibition. *No rubber suits,* despite the advertisements' claims that these contraptions will aid weight reduction during aerobics. The theory is that if you wear these impervious suits, you'll sweat off water weight. True, you may perspire profusely, but you'll gain any lost pounds right back the moment you quench your thirst.

Not only are these suits a fraud, because they don't do what they're supposed to do, but they're downright dangerous. Why? Clothing that doesn't "breathe" increases the likelihood that you will suffer heat exhaustion, which can lead to heat stroke, which can be fatal. We'll discuss heat-stress reactions later in this chapter.

## Weather or Not

Diehard outdoor runners and cyclists are hard to shackle even when the weather is forbidding. They're out there exercising whether their noses freeze over or their legs fry.

Aerobics outdoors in a range of weather conditions is all right *provided* you diehards take sensible precautions. Since the weather won't always be in the ideal range—from 40 to 80 degrees F., with humidity below 60 percent and wind velocity under 15 miles per hour—you must learn the ways to make it less daunting and uncomfortable, and less dangerous in the case of more extreme heat or cold.

We know: you're wishing for those days in the 40-to-80-degree range. The reality of your environment is probably balmy days for about a quarter of the year, with the balance either raining or freezing cold or sizzling hot with brutal humidity.

Exercising in such unpleasant weather is possible. It just requires common sense and adherence to the tips outlined below.

Before we tackle the triple threats of cold, heat, and humidity, however, one preliminary caveat: if you've just moved from a region with one set of weather and altitude conditions to a place with another—or your region has just been hit with a heat or cold wave—adjust your exercise regimen accordingly. Allow your body to acclimatize itself gradually in this manner:

For the first week, exercise at approximately half your maximum output. If that feels all right, keep the intensity low for a little longer but increase the duration. After two or three weeks, you should start to feel as though you've exercised in these new conditions all your life. At this point, you're ready to resume your normal aerobics schedule.

# Cold-Weather Precautions

Exercising in freezing weather isn't as risky as exercising in high temperature/humidity conditions, believe it or not.

## Fit Tips: Wind Chill Index

Let the Wind Chill Index below be your guide the next time wintry weather makes outdoor exercise dubious. In moderately cold, windy weather (Zones I and II), a lightweight nylon jacket worn over your exercise clothes can help minimize the wind chill without adding weight. Weather that falls in Zones III, IV, and V is too forbidding for exercise.

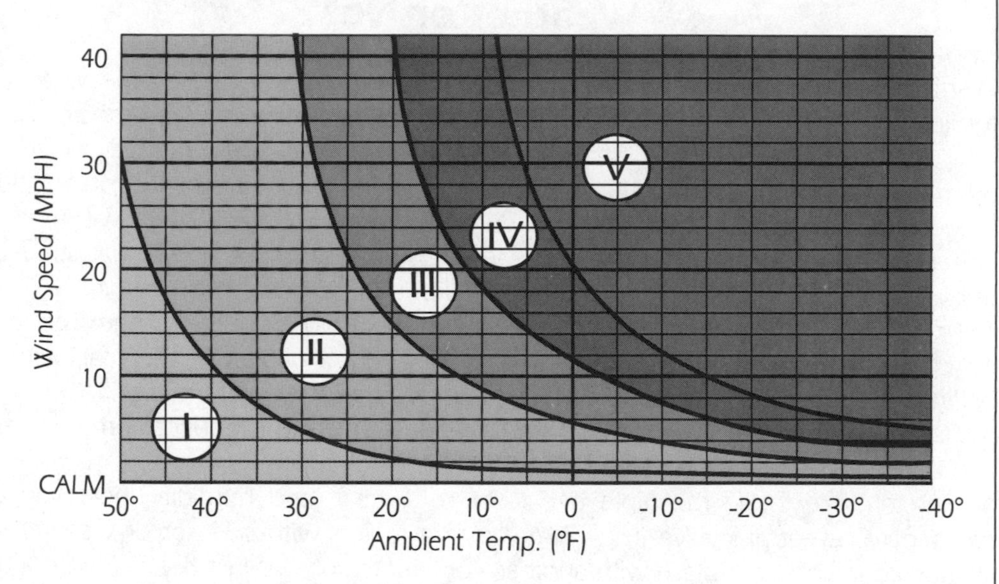


Zone I —Comfortable provided you take normal precautions.
Zone II —Very cold. Exercise is uncomfortable on overcast days.
Zone III—Bitterly cold. Exercise is uncomfortable even on clear, sunny days.
Zone IV—Human flesh could freeze depending upon the intensity of the activity, the amount of solar radiation, and the health of a person's skin and circulatory system.
Zone V —Survival efforts are required. Exposed flesh will freeze in less than one minute.

Adapted from *Group Exercise Leadership Manual* © 1988 by the Institute for Aerobics Research.

For the healthy walker, runner, or cyclist, exercising even in subzero weather is possible. No, your lungs can't get frostbite, although your fingertips, nose, toes, and other extremities can if you don't dress properly and keep moving briskly while you're out there.

On the other hand, there are people for whom cold-weather aerobics isn't a good idea.

For example, you may suffer from spasms in your windpipe due to exposure to very cold air. You start wheezing at a certain point and have to stop aerobics. Even though the symptom disappears as soon as you reenter a warm environment, the experience is an unpleasant one. Better to find an indoor aerobics substitute.

Women with heart trouble who try walking in the cold may get chest pains (angina), particularly if it's windy. They're also candidates for an indoor track when the ground freezes over.

## Fit Tips: Combating Cold Weather

Sure, you can exercise in cold temperatures provided you:

- **Monitor the weather.** A temperature below 10 degrees, combined with a wind velocity of 10 miles per hour or more, is too inclement. Stay indoors and find a substitute form of aerobics.
- **Try to exercise at noon,** or at least during the warmest part of the day.
- **Do your warm-up routine indoors.**
- **Run with the wind behind you.** Return with it against you.
- **Dress appropriately.** Avoid either over- or underdressing, because you'll get chilled. Too many clothes not only hamper your movements, they make you perspire excessively since exercise raises your body temperature almost immediately.
- **Layer your upper-body clothing.** This is a better approach than bulky, heavy garments that impede movement and can't be shed easily if they prove too warm.
- **Assess your outfit by three criteria:** Does it absorb perspiration, insulate, and break the wind? Next to the skin, a cotton or polypropylene fabric will soak up sweat to prevent chilling. For the second layer, a wool garment or sweatshirt provides good insulation. The outer layer should be a windproof fabric such as nylon or Gore-Tex.
- **Cover your head.** A hooded sweatshirt or a cap that covers your ears is ideal.
- **Cover your face if the wind is gusty or the temperature is below zero.**

A ski mask is one possibility. Other women prefer a dental or surgical mask worn over the mouth and nose, although this does make breathing more difficult. Substitutes are a terrycloth or cheesecloth "veil" or a loose-knit scarf or muffler.

- **For extra comfort, drape a scarf or towel around your neck.**
- **Wear mittens or gloves.** Most experts recommend mittens because they trap the heat from your fingers into one small, enclosed space.
- **Go light on socks.** If your shoes fit perfectly with one pair of socks, don't wear two pairs thinking that will make your feet warmer. The opposite will happen. Tight shoes impair circulation, making your feet colder.
- **Put on a jacket or windbreaker during your cool-down**—if you're not wearing one already. Your body's temperature is dropping during this 5-minute winding-down phase and you could develop a chill.
- **Cool down for 5 minutes outdoors**—or in the same weather conditions in which you exercised.
- **After your cool-down, get warm and dry.** Change into dry clothing if yours are damp, or take a bath or hot shower.
- **Be sensible. If it's icy or slippery, stay indoors.**

## Outdoor Swimming When It's Cool

This can be tricky. If the water is much warmer than the air temperature, you're asking your body to endure a shock when you get out of the water. This can be mitigated somewhat if you stay in the warm water for an extralong cool-down period. However, it's still not the ideal exercise environment.

Water that's colder than 75 degrees is also problematic, especially if you have a heart condition. For a cardiac patient, the mere shock of entering cold water can induce cardiac arrhythmia; and if that's not treated immediately, it could be fatal. Also, just the sensation of cold (from air or water) on the face can suppress the heart rate, thereby increasing the heart's work load.

In general, people lose body heat much more rapidly in water than in cold air. On land, you can exercise to raise your body temperature. When you're immersed in cool water, you can't.

## Hot-Weather Precautions

As much as possible, try to avoid heat-stress conditions. They can be lethal—far more lethal for exercisers than most cold-weather conditions.

The risk of heat stress starts when the temperature is above 80 degrees combined with humidity higher than 60 percent. When the thermometer tops 90 degrees and the humidity 40 percent, minimize outdoor exercise. It's potentially quite dangerous.

If it's summer or you live in a tropical/semitropical climate, plan to exercise in the relative cool of the morning or the evening. On the other hand, if your schedule permits

### Fit Tips: The WBGT Index for Hot, Humid Weather

The Wet Bulb Globe Temperature (WBGT) Index was devised to alert people to dangers of heat stress from exercising in hot, humid weather. To calculate the four zones, readings from three different types of thermometers (measuring dryness, humidity, and radiant heat) are combined in a formula. The result is a highly accurate reading of heat stress intensity.

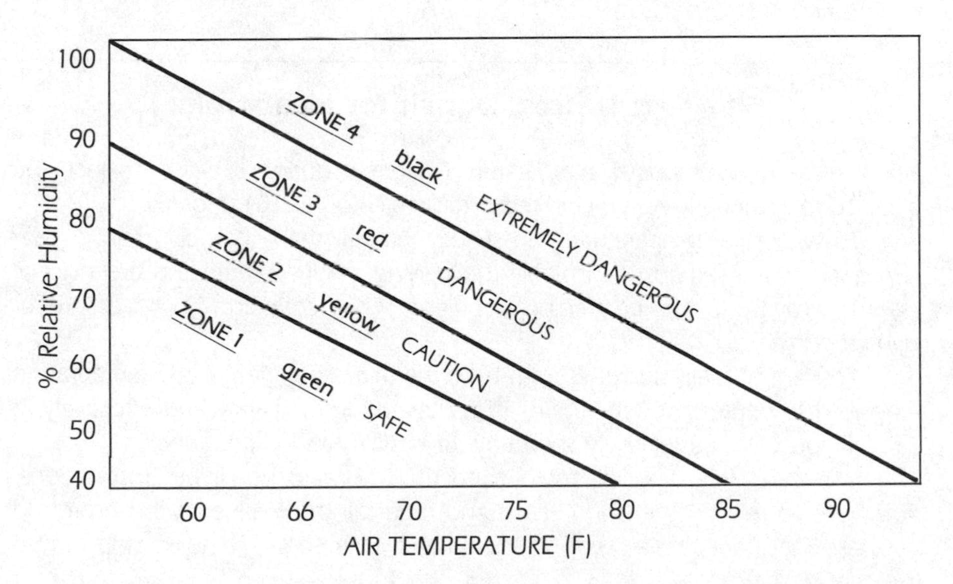


At the Aerobics Center in Dallas, colored flags are flown near the start of the track to alert members of hazardous heat conditions:

Zone 1 (Green Flag)—Weather conditions are no deterrent to unrestricted physical activities . . . WBGT is less than 85.

Zone 2 (Yellow Flag)—Only people who have been working out in similar heat for a minimum of 10 days should engage in much exercise outdoors . . . WBGT between 85 and 87.

Zone 3 (Red Flag) —Only people who have been exercising in similar heat for a period of 30 days or more should work out in such weather . . . WBGT between 88 and 90.

Zone 4 (Black Flag) —Don't exercise vigorously outdoors regardless of your conditioning or heat acclimatization . . . WBGT more than 90.

Adapted from *Group Exercise Leadership Manual* © 1988 by the Institute for Aerobics Research.

exercise only in the heat of the day, give your body a break: Cut down on speed and intensity and compensate with increased duration. In short, exercise at a lower rate for a slightly longer time. You'll still gain your points, but you'll earn them more safely.

Remember to replace what you lose in perspiration by drinking lots of liquids. And *un*dress for comfort. This does not mean exposing a lot of skin to the sun's rays. It means wearing thin, loose, cotton tops with short or three-quarter-length sleeves and comfortable shorts. You might add a hat with a brim or visor to shade your face.

## Fit Alert: Distress Signals for Heatstroke

An increase in your body's temperature is normal during exercise. In fact, the average marathoner's core racing temperature is around 104 degrees.

However, a temperature just slightly higher than that can cause *heat exhaustion.* Heat exhaustion isn't life-threatening but it's a definite distress signal on the way to a life-threatening condition. That condition is *heatstroke* or *hyperthermia.*

You are officially suffering from hyperthermia when your body temperature reaches 106 degrees. If hyperthermia isn't treated immediately and effectively, it can kill you within a relatively short time or impair you for life.

You can't treat yourself for hyperthermia because you'll be unconscious. You have to rely on the good sense and medical knowledge of those around you, an important reason why you shouldn't exercise all alone in hot, humid weather.

Here are the physiological changes that occur when your body's core temperature rises during exercise. If precautions aren't taken at the heat-exhaustion level, around 104 or 105 degrees, your body's temperature will keep rising until it finally rages out of control. (Keep in mind that the conditioned or acclimatized woman's body temperature will rise more slowly.)

- **98.6 degrees**—Normal core body temperature.
- **100 degrees**—Your skin flushes and you begin to sweat. If the perspiration doesn't evaporate quickly enough because of high humidity, your temperature continues to rise.
- **102 degrees**—You experience rapid dehydration. This fluid loss impedes the blood flow to your skin. Your blood pressure starts dropping.
- **103 degrees**—Although a rise in core temperature to this level is normal during exercise, the decreased blood flow to the brain can cause disorientation, pallid color, and hyperventilation in some people.
- **104 degrees**—Your brain temperature increases. Your heartbeat could become irregular and your decreasing blood flow may trigger muscle breakdown.
- **105 degrees**—You stop perspiring as your sweat glands shut down. You develop severe blood clot problems, often causing internal hemorrhaging.
- **106 degrees**—This is the clinical threshold of hyperthermia. Most victims go into shock or delirium. An uneven heartbeat and blood leaking into organs can produce fluid in the lungs.
- **107 degrees**—You'll probably suffer from acute kidney failure requiring emergency dialysis. You'll also experience liver damage.
- **108 degrees**—Permanent heart damage is likely. A massive heart attack is possible.
- **108 to 110 degrees**—You're in a coma. Your brain literally "cooks," causing serious brain damage that can't be reversed even if you do live. Massive heart damage occurs in 15 percent of the cases studied.

## Tragic Story of a Heatstroke Victim

Unfortunately, what follows is a real case history of a tragic death that could have been prevented if the victim had just taken a few simple precautions.

Douglas Zefting, a 34-year-old runner and professional man, entered the annual Manufacturers Hanover Trust Lilac 10K Road Race in Rochester, New York, in May 1986. Some 2,600 other runners surrounded him that day in unexpected heat. Instead of the usual mid-May coolness, the thermometer hit 78 degrees, with humidity estimated at 73 percent. (Note that this is Zone 4, extremely dangerous on the Heat Index Chart—p. 141.) There was no wind to moderate the bright, hot rays of the sun beating down unrelentingly on the participants.

These conditions might not seem daunting to runners in other parts of the country who are acclimated to heat and humidity, but, in reality, they are dangerous for any runner. And in Rochester, New York, such people aren't prepared for this kind of weather until the middle of summer. By that time, runners have had a chance to get used to the heat gradually as the seasons change.

Rochester race officials knew that the unanticipated heat could create problems, so they advised entrants not to try for personal records; to consume large quantities of water prior to the race and at the two "pit stops" set up along the route; and to listen to their bodies for signs of heat exhaustion.

Despite the warnings, the finish line "looked like a war zone" in the words of one observer. More than 300 runners were treated for heat stress, 17 were hospitalized, and Doug Zefting died.

## Fit Tips: How to Beat the Heat and Humidity

Should you choose to ignore our warning and exercise anyway when the temperature is over 90 degrees and the humidity over 60 percent, at least do the following to reduce the risk of heat-caused injuries:

- Even if you don't feel thirsty, drink water frequently to avoid dehydration. Marathon runners should drink a minimum of 1 to 2 cups of water 10 to 15 minutes before a race and should continue to do so every 3 to 4 kilometers—or more often.
- Avoid salt tablets or commercial electrolyte solutions. The average American diet contains a lot of salt—and that's in addition to the salt you get every time you reach for the shaker. If you must take salt tablets, you'll have to drink even greater amounts of water, because both salt and sugar slow down your body's ability to absorb water from the small intestine. Commercial electrolyte solutions contain high concentrations of sugar, so they must be diluted to half strength if you insist upon drinking them. In general, body fluid losses during exercise are much greater than electrolyte losses.
- Stop exercising and immediately seek medical attention should you experience any severe symptoms of heat-related injury: headache, "goose flesh" on the chest and arms, chills, overbreathing, fainting, nausea, vomiting, muscle cramps, a staggering gait, or mental disturbances ranging from incoherence to unconsciousness.
- If your symptoms are relatively mild, signaling heat exhaustion rather than heat-stroke, you may still be aware enough of what's happening to direct your own treatment. The goal is to lower your body temperature by applying ice packs to your neck, abdomen, armpits, and groin.

Zefting was no neophyte. He'd entered the event in previous years and finished with no problems. Just the week before the race, Zefting and a friend had run the course in about 50 minutes, once again with no untoward effects. His companion recalled that the distance had been so easy for Zefting; in fact, that he'd "talked the entire way." The friend also pointed out that they'd run in the evening, a fairly warm and humid one, but *there was no sun.*

Of all the people in the race, Zefting did not appear to be the most likely candidate for a fatality. So what went wrong?

Zefting did not stop for water at the 5K point, presumably because of the crowd of other runners assembled there. Zefting was worried about his time. Nor is there any evidence that he stopped further on at the 8K point.

Fewer than 100 yards from the finish line, Zefting collapsed, unconscious. By this time, so many of his fellow runners needed assistance, too, that Zefting was ignored briefly. When he did arrive at a nearby hospital, all the hazard signs of hyperthermia were apparent. They included kidney failure and, because of his blood's inability to clot, bleeding from multiple sites. He died without regaining consciousness. The fate that befell this heatstroke victim need not befall you. The simple precautions on page 144 will ensure your safety.

## How's Your Altitude?

The air is thinner the higher the altitude. Thinner means the oxygen pressure is lower, forcing your body to work harder to compensate for the seeming lack of oxygen in the air. Count on this fact to have a decided impact on your breathing during aerobics performed in high altitudes.

Attention was focused on this altitude difference in 1968 when the Olympics were held in Mexico City (elevation: 7,300 feet above sea level). The athletes who had trained at comparable altitudes were at a decided advantage in those games. Kenyan distance runners, for example, tend to train at altitudes above 6,000 feet, forcing their lungs and hearts and the rest of their cardiovascular systems to adjust to the thin air. The end result is runners with a lot more oxygen-carrying hemoglobin in their red blood cells and more blood volume in general.

One way to train the superathletes of tomorrow, in fact, would be to make them work out at altitudes of 10,000 feet in 95-degree, dry heat. That's fine for men and women who devote their lives to sports, mind you. It's not fine for you who are exercising simply to look and feel better and live longer.

Indeed, we've devised special altitude compensation charts especially for you. If you exercise in the rarefied atmosphere 5,000 feet or more above sea level, consult the charts that follow to ensure you aren't slighting yourself when you take our three fitness tests described in chapter 5. Also, make sure you adjust for altitude on a daily basis when you figure your aerobics points.

## Walking or Running 1 Mile at Various Altitudes

| Time (min: sec) Standard | 5,000 Feet | Point Value | 8,000 Feet | 12,000 Feet | Point Value |
|---|---|---|---|---|---|
| 19:59–14:30 | 20:29–15:00 | 1 | 20:59–15:30 | 21:29–16:30 | 1 |
| 14:29–12:00 | 14:59–12:30 | 2 | 15:29–13:00 | 16:29–14:00 | 2 |
| 11:59–10:00 | 12:29–10:30 | 3 | 12:59–11:00 | 13:59–12:00 | 3 |
| 9:59– 8:00 | 10:29– 8:30 | 4 | 10:59– 9:00 | 11:59–10:00 | 4 |
| 7:59– 6:30 | 8:29– 7:00 | 5 | 8:59– 7:30 | 9:59– 8:30 | 5 |
| under 6:30 | under 7:00 | 6 | under 7:30 | under 8:30 | 6 |

## 3-Mile Walking Test, Adjusted for High Altitudes

| Altitude in Feet at Which Acclimatized | Times to Be Added to the Age Requirements for Walking 3 Miles* |
|---|---|
| 5,000** | 2 minutes |
| 6,000 | 3 minutes, 15 seconds |
| 7,000 | 4 minutes |
| 8,000 | 4 minutes, 30 seconds |
| 9,000 | 5 minutes, 30 seconds |
| 10,000 | 7 minutes |
| 11,000 | 8 minutes |
| 12,000 | 9 minutes |

*Refer to 3-Mile Walking Test in chapter 5, p. 53.

**Up to 5,000 feet, use the 3-Mile Walking Test without altitude correction.

## 1.5-Mile Run Test, Adjusted for High Altitudes

| Altitude in Feet at Which Acclimatized | Times to Be Added to the Age Requirements for Running 1.5 Miles* |
|---|---|
| 5,000** | 30 seconds |
| 6,000 | 40 seconds |
| 7,000 | 50 seconds |
| 8,000 | 1 minute |
| 9,000 | 1 minute, 15 seconds |
| 10,000 | 1 minute, 30 seconds |

| Altitude in Feet at Which Acclimatized | Times to Be Added to the Age Requirements for Running 1.5 Miles* |
|---|---|
| 11,000 | 1 minute, 45 seconds |
| 12,000 | 2 minutes |

*Refer to 1.5-Mile Run Test in chapter 5, p. 53.

**Up to 5,000 feet, use the 1.5-Mile Run Test without altitude correction.

## 12-Minute Walking/Running Test, Adjusted for High Altitudes

| Altitude in Feet at Which Acclimatized | Distances to Subtract from Age Requirements for Walking/Running 12 Minutes* |
|---|---|
| 5,000** | .05 miles |
| 6,000 | .06 miles |
| 7,000 | .08 miles |
| 8,000 | .10 miles |
| 9,000 | .125 miles |
| 10,000 | .150 miles |
| 11,000 | .175 miles |
| 12,000 | .20 miles |

*Refer to 12-Minute Walking/Running Test in chapter 5, p. 54.

**Up to 5,000 feet, use the 12-Minute Walking/Running Test without altitude correction.

# Smog Alert

We get letters frequently from women in cities such as Los Angeles and Phoenix, cities which commonly exist under a cloud of "smog"—a devastating combination of soot and dirt and car exhaust fumes.

These women are concerned that they may be harming themselves by breathing in this smog during aerobics.

To answer their concerns, we've searched the scientific literature and found no studies showing that smog has long-term deleterious effects on joggers or runners. In the short run, though, it could cause some temporary lung irritation or make you cough.

Crisp, clean air undoubtedly is preferable. On the other hand, if your choice is between aerobics with smog or no aerobics, we recommend the former. To exercise and breathe in the smog is certainly better for your health than to sit around in the smog and let your body atrophy because you're afraid to exercise in it.

Having said this, there are a few precautions you can take. If possible, place yourself upwind from the smog. Even better, drive to a place where the smog isn't as thick. The smog is at its highest concentrations within 30 feet of a busy road or expressway. It is like an umbrella hanging over the highway and reaches a peak level while the sun is shining.

To avoid these problems, exercise in a place farther than 30 feet from a busy highway. And exercise before sunup and after sundown, particularly during the hot months. On those days when your city's air quality index reaches the "unsatisfactory" or "warning" level, don't venture outside at all for aerobics. Try in-place running or some other form of indoor workout until the air quality improves.

## Surfaces Do Matter

To reduce the risk of injury, it's important for joggers and runners to find a comfortable surface. Grass or other springy turf is best. Next best, in order of desirability, are: composition track, cinder track, dirt road, asphalt, and concrete.

Naturally, the fewer pedestrians you have to dodge, the better—another reason why concrete sidewalks can be hazardous. Curbs and potholes are other perils to watch out for.

Also avoid running for any distance on steeply graded shoulders of road. A curved or slanted surface is hard on your knees and your hips. Try to run on the part of the road where it's level. In lieu of that, keep alternating between the right and left shoulders of the road.

If you run or cycle on urban streets or country roads at night or when it's foggy, remember this important detail: *put several strips of reflective tape on your shoes or exercise outfit so that passing motorists can see you easily.*

### Footprints in the Sands of Time

People often ask if they deserve extra points for running on the soft sand of the beach. They report it's a glorious outdoor ambience, uplifting for the spirit, but more of a struggle for the body because the sand shifts constantly under your feet.

Yes, running on soft sand is more difficult than running on a solid surface. Although we haven't worked out the precise aerobic points, it probably merits a 20 percent upward adjustment in time because, for the same energy output, it will take you longer to cover the same distance. For example, a hard-surface mile in 12 minutes would likely be equal to a sand mile in 14.5 minutes.

# 11

# Injuries Don't Have to Happen

In chapter 10, we outlined the environmental risks of outdoor exercise. They're multiple, ranging from frostbite to heatstroke, not to mention the greater burden placed on the body when a person works out at high altitudes.

In this chapter, we'll discuss musculoskeletal injuries, in which environment is not a determining factor. These types of injuries could occur anywhere, indoors or out. They might be mere transitory annoyances or they could be serious enough to warrant a physician's care. They could damage joints, fracture bones, or tear soft tissue, causing pain or inflammation.

However, these types of injuries do have one thing in common: cautious exercisers who have no physical abnormalities needn't get them. Apply an ounce of prevention and it's unlikely you'll sustain an injury during aerobics, at least anything more than a minor one.

## The Injury Controversy

How often exercise does result in injuries is a raging debate right now, one we want to address head-on.

There's a welter of misinformation about the frequency of injuries due to exercise. In actuality, there aren't that many epidemiological studies on the subject of exercise-induced injuries, and those that do exist tend to be poorly designed. As a consequence, the statistical results are often distorted.

No matter to the popular press, unfortunately. In the mid-1980s, many widely circulated newspapers and magazines have trumpeted high injury-rate statistics, scaring off many potential exercisers. The scare tactics are working. The number of people exercising in America is now leveling off, even declining.

This is a shame, and in this chapter we want both to allay your fears and to give you guidelines about how to prevent injuries. We're realistic about injuries, though. We realize that no matter how careful a person is about exercise, accidents do happen occasionally. At the end of the chapter, we'll catalog typical sports-related injuries and treatments.

## Studies of Questionable Merit

Any competent academic researcher, looking at the average exercise-injury study, can cite serious flaws in its design.

First of all, hardly any of the papers compare exercise injuries with injuries sustained by a sedentary control group. There are 70 million unintentional injuries in the United States each year that have nothing to do with exercise. A comparison group is necessary in order to judge the net exercise-injury rate, taking into account injuries that would happen regardless of exercise.

The definitions of "injury" are another problem. They vary considerably. Some studies even categorize the slightest ache or pain—including sore muscles—as an injury. This is silly, since most exercisers have sore muscles occasionally, especially if they're beginners or even high-conditioned but changing from one form of aerobics to another.

Some studies lack a time frame. To say a sample of X number of women sustained X number of injuries without computing those figures in terms of a time period tells you very little. A good study comes up with an incidence rate stated in these terms: ______ new injuries per ______ participants per ______ (time period, such as year or month). Prevalence rates are stated: ______ total injuries (new and old) per ______ participants per ______.

We'll now describe several of the most publicized studies and tell you what's wrong and right with them.

## Aerobic Dance: Bouncing Your Way to a Battled Body

That's certainly the impression you have if you believe the popular press.

One of the most widely quoted studies was published in 1985. The authors are Drs. Peter and Lorna Francis, physical educators at San Diego State University; and a graduate student, Kim Welshons-Smith. Their study focuses on injuries sustained over an unspecified period of time by 135 aerobic dance instructors, most of whom were women aged 20 to 35.

The authors found that 103 of the instructors had one or more injuries from aerobic dancing. That's 76 percent, an astonishing figure! Sixty-four percent of the injuries were new ones, while 36 percent were old injuries that had been aggravated. The most common injury was to the shin, followed by the foot, back, ankle, and knee.

The figures aren't so astonishing, however, when you realize that the instructors could define "injury" in any way they liked. The authors offered no definition whatsoever.

Another factor helps explain the high injury rate: the aerobic dance instructors in this particular sample were, in the authors' own words, "minimally qualified to teach any form of aerobic exercise." They were surprisingly naïve about several key issues.

For example, the instructors wore various types of shoes. Many wore running or court shoes, while a large portion couldn't even identify the specific model of their shoes. Nor did they show any understanding of the role of shoes in reducing impact injuries. The majority felt that the most important feature of an aerobic dance shoe was lightness; second, that it offer arch support. As any sportsmedicine specialist knows, the primary feature of an aerobic dance shoe should be shock absorption, but this group ranked cushioning as the third most desirable feature.

Despite the fact that Reebok, the sports shoe manufacturer, sponsored the study, the authors did *not* conclude that inappropriate shoes or the interaction between bad footwear and rigid floor surfaces was the main cause of injuries. Rather, it was overuse—too much weekly weight-bearing exercise that's too intense for too long. The instructors were exceeding their body's tolerance to mechanical stress by teaching an average of 1.7 classes per day for 4.2 days per week—an overall average of 7.14 classes per week per instructor.

A study with far sounder methodology was conducted at about the same time by Dr. James G. Garrick, director of the Center for Sports Medicine in San Francisco and Jane Fonda's consultant. His sample consisted of 411 aerobics participants (351 students and 60 instructors) in six private dance programs in California.

Garrick made an effort to distinguish true injuries from transient complaints. A level I complaint, by his definition, is an annoyance, uncomfortable but not reason enough to interfere with daily activities or drop out of dance class. A level II problem interferes with dance classes but not everyday activities. A level III injury is more serious and interferes with both daily and aerobic-dance activities. And a level IV injury necessitates some form of medical assistance.

During the 16-week study period, the participants collectively logged almost 30,000 hours of dance. Of the 327 complaints reported during the course of the study, only 84 fell into the level III category; in short, it took 345 hours of dancing to produce a single level III injury among students and 385 hours for instructors. Only 7 injuries, or 2.1 percent, required medical treatment.

The shin/leg, foot, and ankle accounted for nearly two-thirds of the injuries. Aerobic dancers most likely to be injured were those who had prior orthopedic problems and those who didn't participate in any other fitness activities.

Dr. Garrick's conclusion: "Injury rates were influenced by the design and conduct of the aerobic program but not by brand of shoe or type of flooring. Aerobic dance appears to offer students the potential for fitness enhancement with a minimal risk of injury."

## What Is Known about Exercise Injuries

Unfortunately, most information about exercise injuries comes from case reports. Although useful, case reports do not take into account the population-at-large from which the injuries occur. This makes it difficult to draw valid conclusions.

Kenneth E. Powell, M.D., from the National Centers for Disease Control, Atlanta, looked at the *causes* of running injuries from an epidemiological perspective (*The Physician and Sports Medicine*, vol. 14, no. 6, June 1986). In general, his conclusions were that more research into the causes of injuries is needed and should be directed to those factors over which the exerciser has some control. We think this is a valid suggestion, regardless of the type of exercise being done.

Yet, the myriad anecdotal case histories in the medical literature give some insight into the types of injuries associated with different sports.

Swimmers are prone to swimmer's ear, conjunctivitis, dental enamel erosion, and shoulder and arm injuries, for example. Runners and aerobic dancers are at risk for foot, ankle, and leg injuries. The head, eyes, legs, and elbows are typical racquet-sport injury sites. And cyclists are at risk for head injuries, broken limbs, abrasions and lacerations, knee problems, and tendinitis in the feet, legs, and hands.

Based on the available data, the risk of injury increases with exposure. The greater number of miles run per week or the number of hours of aerobic dancing seem to relate directly to the number of injuries. Age, gender, body build, experience, and even speed appear not to influence the risk of injury, according to Dr. Powell. To the contrary, past injuries, physiological abnormalities, individual susceptibility, a sudden increase in training intensity or mileage, and the type of shoe are almost certainly related to the risk of injury. However, data is not yet available to establish firmly the relationship.

Dr. Powell's conclusions are that form, stretching, weight training, "appropriate" warming up and cooling down, terrain, surface, climate, and time of day may or may not be related to the risk of injury.

Injuries related to other types of aerobic activities are also poorly defined, but, surprisingly, the injury rate in nonexercisers is not that much different from that observed in exercisers. Dr. Steven Blair, Director of Epidemiology at the Institute for Aerobics Research, studied 2,102 men and women runners and compared them with 724 nonrunners seen at the Cooper Clinic. Rates of injuries for the foot, knee, hip, back, shoulder, and elbow were examined. Only knee injury rates were significantly higher in runners. The overall injury rate was relatively low, approximately 12 percent per year, and comparable in both groups.

The National Centers for Disease Control in Atlanta also did a study to ascertain the *probability* of injury among runners. The sample was 693 men and 730 women who run regularly.

The researchers found that those who log an average of 19 miles a week will get hit by a thrown object once in 12 years, bitten by a dog once in 26 years, and hit by a car once in 135 years. Clearly, not problems to worry about.

Unfortunately, runners are far more likely to suffer musculoskeletal injuries. Fortunately, this risk factor is under runners' control to a great extent because it's directly related to: (1) the number of miles covered every week; (2) frequency of running; and (3) increases in weekly mileage. People who run fewer than 10 miles a week are injured on average once every three years, whereas those logging 30 or more miles are likely to suffer two injuries over the same period.

## Fit Test: Your Exercise Injury Risk Profile*

Let's find out how likely you are to injure yourself during exercise. Here are a series of statements regarding the frequency and severity of your injuries. These statements may or may not describe you. Check each "true" or "false." If a statement applies only to runners, say, and you're a swimmer, skip it and go on to the next.

| | True | False |
|---|---|---|
| I'm not overweight, nor is my body/fat ratio above 22 percent. (See chapters 12 and 13 for discussions of ideal weight and body/fat ratios.) | ______ | ______ |
| The arches in my feet are relatively normal—not too flat or too high. | ______ | ______ |
| My feet, when they hit the ground, do not over- or underpronate. (*Overpronation* means you tilt your feet inward excessively. Shoe heels broken down along the inside are a tip-off. Heels broken down on the outside indicate *underpronation*.) | ______ | ______ |
| I'm not bowlegged to any great degree. | ______ | ______ |
| I'm not knock-kneed. | ______ | ______ |
| Both my legs are the same length. Or, if there is any discrepancy, it's not more than ¼ inch. | ______ | ______ |
| I have sufficient flexibility in my calf muscles. (Lock your knees and bend your foot up as far toward your knee as you can. Your foot should be able to flex up at least 15 degrees from its perpendicular position.) | ______ | ______ |
| I have sufficient flexibility in my hamstrings. (Lie on your back and lift your leg as far as you can while keeping | | |

| | True | False |
|---|---|---|
| your knee locked. You should be able to form at least a 90-degree angle with your other leg.) | _______ | _______ |
| I have been involved in a primary aerobic activity for more than four months. | _______ | _______ |
| I always warm up and cool down sufficiently. | _______ | _______ |
| I'm careful not to overexert myself during the aerobics phase and I monitor my heart rate regularly to make sure. | _______ | _______ |
| I do a minimum of 10 minutes of strengthening exercises twice each week. | _______ | _______ |
| I do a well-rounded strengthening exercise routine, making sure all the major muscle groups of my body get a workout. | _______ | _______ |
| If I participate in two or more aerobic activities, I choose them because they complement each other, using different muscles and placing different stresses on my body. | _______ | _______ |
| I wear shoes specifically made for my sport. | _______ | _______ |
| I never exercise barefoot. | _______ | _______ |
| If I'm involved in a weight-bearing sport, I'm careful to avoid surfaces that have virtually no resilience, such as concrete. | _______ | _______ |
| I alternate any weight-bearing sport with a nonweight-bearing one such as swimming or cycling. | _______ | _______ |
| I seldom jog/run more than 15 miles a week. | _______ | _______ |
| I seldom swim more than 6 miles a week. | _______ | _______ |
| I seldom cycle more than 100 miles a week. | _______ | _______ |
| As an aerobic dancer, I never attend more than four classes a week (total of 4 hours) and never two days in a row. | _______ | _______ |
| As an aerobic dancer, I alternate high- and low-impact aerobics classes. | _______ | _______ |
| I don't do my outdoor exercise on busy streets wearing headphones that limit my awareness of my surroundings. | _______ | _______ |
| I'm careful not to increase the intensity or distance I cover more than 10 percent per week. | _______ | _______ |

| | True | False |
|---|---|---|
| After any injury that requires an interruption of my exercise regimen, I return to my activity gradually, working back to my former mileage and/or intensity slowly. | ______ | ______ |
| I seldom enter races or other exercise competitions. | ______ | ______ |
| If there is equipment involved in my sport, I make sure I know all about its proper use and maintenance. | ______ | ______ |

*All these factors are felt to be closely related to the presence or absence of running injuries, but more valid research is needed to ascertain their absolute effect.

The more check marks you have in the "true" column, the more likely you are to avoid injury during exercise. The more check marks you have in the "false" column indicates just the opposite—you're more at risk of being injured.

## Women: The Likelier Sex

When it comes to exercise injuries, women seem to have a worse track record than men. They may be at greater risk due to hereditary and anatomical reasons, although at this time such problems are more anecdotal than substantiated by valid research.

However, some problems may be due to anatomical differences. Women's hips, for instance, tend to be wider than men's, which means that their feet strike the ground at a wider angle. The immediate result: *overpronation*, an excessive inward rolling of the foot. A possible long-term result: such painful leg ailments as shinsplints and "runner's knee."

Women's bones are also smaller and more delicate than men's, so they don't absorb the shock of impact as well. Women's susceptibility to osteoporosis (brittle bones) is another disadvantage that translates into more stress fractures, particularly following menopause.

What's more, women's tissues are more elastic than men's. For example, look at the number of women who can easily touch their toes, and then compare them with men.

Another example: Because of women's wider pelvises, inward-angling thighbones, and weaker muscles in the fronts of their thighs, women's kneecaps may be more vulnerable to the pain and stiffness known as "runner's knee." This occurs when the kneecap shifts sideways and rubs against nearby cartilage.

To counteract these gender-based tendencies, it's important for women to do some muscle-strengthening exercises. It's also especially important for them to wear the proper athletic shoes—perhaps with special internal supports that help counteract any of their body's biomechanical abnormalities.

## Dr. Cooper's Injury Prevention Formula

Women as well as men can guard against injury by taking certain commonsense precautions. We've incorporated five key safety precautions into an easy-to-remember formula.

The formula won't surprise you because it combines everything we've discussed in the last few chapters. It's:

**4 S's minus 0**

or

**S**tretching + **S**hoes + **S**tyle + **S**urface – **Overuse**

Let's take each item one by one:

• **Stretching.** Your warm-up involves the slow, languid stretching of muscles. Although debatable in some circles, we believe it's very important. Cold, stiff muscles may tear or be injured during rigorous exercise. In addition, a gentle, progressive warm-up may minimize some heart problems such as irregularities or angina pectoris. These problems can occur in susceptible people if vigorous exercise is begun too rapidly.

Our advice: *Never skip your warm-up, no matter how rushed you are.*

• **A good pair of shoes.** Wearing the correct shoes cannot be emphasized enough. You may exercise in clothes straight out of a rag bag. Fine. But your shoes should befit royalty.

What you want from a good athletic shoe are cushioning and stability, particularly if you're involved in an impact sport.

Take running, for example. During a 10-mile run, each shoe lands on the ground almost 10,000 times. For a woman weighing 120 pounds, this means that a cumulative force of several tons is delivered through the shoe. Imagine the stresses that places on her feet, ankles, knees, hips, and spine. Women who undertake a weight-bearing exercise wearing inadequate shoes will surely develop orthopedic problems.

• **Proper exercise style.** Impact exercisers can tell a lot about their style by examining the soles of a well-worn pair of their athletic shoes. If you're doing everything right, your soles should be worn down evenly.

• **Resilient surface.** Concrete and blacktop—or any surface that has no "give"—constitute a danger to exercisers involved in impact aerobics. For runners, the ideal terrain is soft and spongy, such as a tarmac or cinder track, grassy field, or smooth dirt road. An ideal floor for aerobic dancers is hardwood over airspace or hardwood with a spring base over airspace.

• **Avoid overdoing it.** Too much exercise can cause musculoskeletal problems.

Many studies, including the National Centers for Disease Control running study, have shown this to be true.

More recently, it was borne out by a landmark study published in 1986 in the *New England Journal of Medicine.* It concluded that although physical activity does increase longevity, those who regularly burn more than 3,500 calories a week in exercise are likely to have problems that negate, to some extent, the health benefits. They may even die earlier than do moderate exercisers. In comparable terms, 3,500 calories is roughly equivalent to 7½ hours of lap swimming, 9 hours of cycling, or 10 hours of aerobic dancing.

At the Aerobics Center, we'd rather err on the cautious side. We think even these ceilings for swimming, cycling, and aerobic dancing represent too much weekly activity for the average amateur athlete. We think the threshold point at which the risk of injury starts to cancel out cardiovascular benefits is lower.

With running, we cite 15 miles a week as the critical juncture. Run more than that and you're inviting injury. With swimming, cycling, and cross-country skiing—because they're all nonweight-bearing activities—you can do more with less threat of incurring problems. Cautious swimmers should keep their mileage below 6 per week; cyclists, below 100 miles. For cross-country skiers, the maximum is 6 hours per week; and for aerobic dancers, the limit is four 60-minute classes per week, with a rest day in between each; preferably, you should also alternate low- with high-impact workouts.

If these restrictions strike you as too limiting, there are two ways you can modify your weekly exercise regimen without increasing, to any great degree, your chances of injury.

First, you might follow the hard-easy principle. A hard, strenuous workout—whether longer distances or higher speeds—should be followed by an "easy" day. The easy day may mean complete rest or half your normal daily effort.

Second, there's the option of cross-training. Augment your basic aerobic activity with another one that uses different muscles and, perhaps, is less likely to cause injury. Do one impact sport and one nonweight-bearing sport each week.

## Beginners' Woes Do Not an Injury Make

Beginners tend to have three complaints, none of which are injuries. Rather, you might label them "physical annoyances."

• **Sore muscles.** It's the exceptional beginner who doesn't moan and groan about sore muscles. Sore muscles are painful, to be sure, but they're not debilitating. If you suddenly start using muscles that haven't done much work for you recently, of course they're going to rebel. Pain is their rebellion.

Perseverance is the treatment for sore muscles. What you should *not* do is give in and stop exercising until the soreness goes away. It will go away, all right, but it will also return as soon as you resume exercise. All you'll have done is postpone the inevitable. Accept the fact that you're going to hurt in strange places for the first week or two of a new exercise program until your muscles gain some strength.

• **Abdominal "stitches."** "Stitches" are the pains in the sides of the abdomen induced by exercise. Again, only beginning exercisers tend to get them.

Nobody really knows what causes stitches. Medical authorities have put forth various theories: they're a spasm of the diaphragm; liver congestion; gas in the large intestine; an area of the diaphragm that may not be getting enough blood; or weak abdominal muscles.

Although we cannot pinpoint the cause, we can assure you that stitches are nothing to be alarmed about. There are several things you might do about them:

You may want to reduce your exercise intensity or duration to see if that helps. If the pain isn't that great, keep on exercising and concentrate on your breathing—especially deep exhalations. You may have heard the expression "breathe through the pain." Breathing techniques are a common Oriental pain-control practice.

On the hunch that gas is the culprit, before you run, have a bowel movement.

Finally, try strengthening your abdominal muscles by doing sit-ups. Work up to 40 or 50 a day.

• **Cracking knees.** If you just hear the sound—some people liken it to that of crumpling cellophane—but have no pain, there's no cause for concern.

Sometimes small pieces of cartilage break off from the back of the kneecap and are loose within the joint. When you move your knee, they make a snapping, popping, or cracking noise. Unless there is pain or discomfort, try to ignore the sound, because there's not much you can do about it.

People who suffer from chondromalacia, or "runner's knee," sometimes report hearing a sound too. But this is a different matter. You'll definitely feel pain. (See p. 160 for more on this malady.)

## Common Exercise Injuries

• **Foot trouble.** A sudden turn can shear the gristly band of connective tissue that runs along the bottom of the foot. The band is called the "plantar fascia," hence the medical term for the injury—"plantar fascitis." Its symptom is pain in the arch of the foot or the heel.

People at risk for this problem tend to have one or more of the following: high arches (underpronation when the feet roll outward), tight plantar fascia, and tight Achilles tendons. As a consequence, the balls of their feet must absorb the brunt of the shock during impact sports.

Treating this malady can be tricky. We heard from a runner once who had tried everything—orthotics, heel padding, injections, ice, as well as taking some long layoffs from her running routine. What worked best for her, though, was an unorthodox approach she hit upon through trial-and-error.

She started to run barefoot on the beach and her pain disappeared. This woman obviously had far more rigid feet than average, and the shifting sand under her moving feet helped her to run more flat-footedly. Like all high-arched people, her goal was to remove her weight from the balls of her feet. Barefoot sand running and, later, a return to plain, no-frills running shoes on harder surfaces was her answer. However, for most runners, an arch support or medically prescribed orthotic device is of value in controlling the problem.

• **Ankle problems.** If you've got Achilles tendinitis, you'll have these symptoms: swelling around your ankle, which lessens movement; a grating sensation when you touch the tendon behind your ankle bone; and pain when you rise on your toes or run in place.

The Achilles tendon runs from the heel to the calf. Any impact exerciser who overdoes it or tends to exercise continually with her weight on the balls of her feet and toes risks injury to this tendon.

Inflammation of the Achilles tendon should be treated with the R.I.C.E. method (see p. 161). Unfortunately, this tendon doesn't have a good blood supply, so small tears and other injuries don't heal quickly.

To prevent this problem, stretch the muscles of your calves sufficiently during your warm-up. Heel raises are excellent for this purpose.

• **Shinsplints.** Impact exercises breed shinsplints, or pain in the shins. Shinsplints happen mainly when your legs are out of shape or you're doing weight-bearing exercises to excess. There are four recognized causes:

The most common—responsible for about 75 percent of exercise-induced shin pain—is muscular. It's a fatigue tear of the fibers of the posterior tibialis muscle at its insertion into the tibia. This muscle originates in the back of your lower leg bone and holds up your arch. If you've got flat feet which makes you overpronate (turn your feet inward), you're at greater risk of developing shin pain. Another frequent cause is running or exercising on a different or particularly hard surface.

An inflammation of the lining covering the lower leg bone (called the "tibial periostitis") is occasionally the culprit. A third, more serious cause is an interruption or lessening of the blood supply to the three muscles in the front of the lower leg—sometimes referred to as "anterior compartment syndrome." It can require surgery. Finally, a stress fracture, even a hairline one, in the lower leg bone (tibia) could be responsible.

Shinsplints usually go away with rest. Treat shin pain with R.I.C.E. (p. 161) and stop exercising for a week or more.

If your doctor indicates that flat-footedness is partially or totally to blame, you'll have to use an orthotic device inserted in your shoes. This foot support—whether it's custom-made or purchased over-the-counter—will lift your arch, thus eliminating the constant tugging on your posterior tibial muscle-tendon. Even with this shoe correction, though, it will take two or three weeks more for your muscle injury to heal completely. You may resume less intense exercise activity about a week before it's healed completely.

• **Runner's knee.** Knee injuries account for 30 to 50 percent of all running-related injuries. Technically known as chondromalacia, runner's knee is caused by constant pounding and overpronation (feet rolling inward). As a result, the back of the kneecap rubs against the thighbone (femur) and you feel pain on either or both sides of the kneecap.

A sufficient rest followed by a program that strengthens the front thigh muscles and stretches the back thigh muscles is the best way to treat the problem and prevent a relapse. Knee extensions on a weight-training machine help to build the right muscles. In the future, you will also need to be more aware of the resilience of your exercise surfaces, seeking out those that have "give." You may also need orthotics to correct your inwardly angled foot-support pattern. In turn, this will create better alignment between your kneecap and femur.

• **Other leg ailments.** Rapid acceleration has been known to snap or pull the muscle in the back of the thigh known as the "hamstring." This is more liable to happen if your hamstrings are shortened and inflexible from lack of adequate, gradual stretching—one more reason not to overlook your warm-up.

## Fit Facts: Defining Your Injury

The following are some common exercise-related injuries and their descriptions:

**Bursitis** —An inflammation of the bursa (fluid-filled sac) located near certain joints of the body. The affected joint swells up and its movement is painful.

**Contusion**—A blow to the body causes pooling of blood under the skin. Otherwise known as a "bruise."

**Fracture** —A break or crack in a bone.

**Sprain** —A ligament stretched too far or torn. (Ligaments connect one bone to another.) A twisted ankle is an example of a sprain.

**Strain** —A muscle or muscle-tendon stretched too far or torn. Painful calf, thigh, or back muscles represent a strain.

**Tendinitis**—Tenderness and inflammation of a tendon, usually caused by prolonged irritation in the same area. (A tendon is a sinew of dense, tough, inelastic, fibrous tissue that connects a muscle with a bone or some other structure.)

## Fit First Aid: The R.I.C.E. Approach

The acronym R.I.C.E. stands for: *R*est . . . *I*ce . . . *C*ompression . . . and *E*levation. It's a well-known method for treating athletic injuries.

**Rest:** As soon as you feel significant pain or notice the injury, stop exercising. Too many women aggravate a small injury by trying to ignore it. Eventually, it becomes too painful to overlook. In the process of being stoic, they sometimes turn a minor irritation into a major medical problem.

**Ice:** You can't go wrong by applying an ice pack or cold water to an injury, but you can increase the severity of an injury by applying heat. Ice decreases swelling and reduces bleeding from torn blood vessels. It also helps relieve pain. For 48 hours (maximum 72 hours), apply ice intermittently, but never for more than 20 minutes at a time. Always wrap the ice in a towel or encase it in some protective covering before placing it against your skin.

**Compression:** Compression—the tight wrapping of the injured part—also helps reduce swelling and blood pooling. But don't make the wrap too tight, as this will completely cut off the blood supply. Leave the bandage on for 30 minutes, loosen, then reapply.

**Elevation:** Elevate the injured part so it's higher than your heart. This enables gravity to help reduce the pressure of fluids (blood, etc.) on the injured area. Keep it elevated even while sleeping.

• **Backaches.** Doing a low-impact aerobics routine with hand or wrist weights that are beyond your strength capabilities can result in backaches. How?

Say you're trying to lift these too-heavy weights over your head but your shoulder muscles aren't strong enough to allow you to do it while keeping your body in proper alignment. So, you compensate by thrusting your pelvis forward, arching your back, and using your entire body to try to lift the weights over your head. Do this very often and you're liable to throw your back out. In fact, it's almost guaranteed that, repeated often, any unbalanced movement such as this that throws your body out of proper alignment will spell trouble for you eventually.

To prevent backaches, strengthen your abdominals, be a stickler about good posture, make sure your form is correct during exercise, and keep your back stretched out and flexible.

• **Arm/Shoulder injuries.** Swimming and low-impact aerobics, because both place so much emphasis on arm movements, can lead to injuries in the neck and shoulder areas. With low-impact aerobics, the risk increases if you work out with heavy hand-held weights.

There are two kinds of hand-held weights: those with a Velcro strip that secures the weight to your hand, and those that require you to grip continuously. The latter can cause tendinitis in the elbow and wrist. The former can also be a hazard if they're too loosely wrapped, for sliding weights put stress on the shoulder and elbow.

# 12

# Good Nutrition and Exercise—To Increase Your Chances of Living Longer

With a name like the Aerobics Center, you might think that our focus is strictly exercise to foster physical fitness but that's not entirely true.

Yes, we have aerobics instructors, exercise physiologists, and sportsmedicine practitioners on our payroll. But we also have nutritionists, psychologists, health-care researchers, weight-loss experts, and medical doctors.

Contrary to the name, our real thrust is preventive medicine and our vision is long-range. Our attention is focused not just on health here and now but on the prevention of illness in the future, when middle and old age could start to wreak havoc on the body.

Note the use of the word *could*. Aging, as we discussed in chapter 2, doesn't have to be synonomous with poor health. That's why the message that permeates all our programs at the Aerobics Center, the Cooper Clinic, and the Institute for Aerobics Research is not simply "exercise for good health." It's "do whatever is necessary to promote good health over the long term."

What's necessary?

Exercise, indeed. A heightened understanding of stress and how to manage it, certainly. And there's a third factor, at least as critical: proper nutrition.

Just like exercise, the right diet, in and of itself, cannot guarantee good health. But it can definitely help. Good eating habits, based on moderation and variety, are the foundation upon which health and fitness rest.

## The Principles of Healthful Eating

We've codified six key nutrition principles, which we describe in this chapter. These principles are aimed at women who are trying to maintain their ideal weight. If extra pounds are your problem and weight loss your goal, you'll find special diet advice in the next chapter.

But now let's concentrate on the role good nutrition should play in all women's lives.

## Nutrition Principle

### Know Your Ideal Body Weight and Strive to Stay Within It

At the Aerobics Center, we use two formulas for estimating ideal weight.

The first is the Mahoney formula. If you are small- or medium-boned, take your height (in inches), multiply by 3.5, and subtract 108. For instance, a woman who is 5 feet 6 inches should weigh around 123 pounds—that's 66 inches times 3.5 equals 231, minus 108 equals 123.

You are large-boned if your wrist size is greater than 6½ inches. In that case, add 10 percent to the ideal weight you've calculated via the above formula. Our hypothetical 5-foot-6-inch woman's ideal weight then becomes 135.3 pounds.

Our In-Residence Weight Reduction Program uses another calculation called the Hamwi formula. Assign yourself 100 pounds for being 5 feet tall. Then add 5 pounds for each inch above 5 feet—or subtract 5 pounds for each inch below.

**Determination of Desirable Weights**

| Build | Women | Men |
|---|---|---|
| Medium | Allow 100 lb for first 5 ft of height, plus 5 lb for each additional inch | Allow 106 lb for first 5 ft of height, plus 6 lb for each additional inch |
| Small | Subtract 10% | Subtract 10% |
| Large | Add 10% | Add 10% |



Using this system, our 5-foot-6-inch woman *of medium build* should tip the scales at 130. However, if she's small-boned, she should subtract 10 percent from this weight, which would place her target weight at 117. If she has a large frame, she'd do the opposite—add 10 percent, giving her an ideal weight of 143.

## Nutrition Principle

### Determine Your Daily Caloric Intake to Maintain Your Ideal Weight and Peak Energy Level

Women often think of all calories as being bad: too many of them make you fat.

While that may be true, too few calories can turn you into the human equivalent of a limp dishrag. And that's what we're concerned about here—gauging the maximum number of calories you need to keep your body running at optimum strength but without adding any extra fat.

Everything you eat and drink contains calories. These calories are your body's energy sources. Adequate quantities of calories are necessary to sustain life processes and give you sufficient get-up-and-go. Excess calories, on the other hand, are stored as fat for reserves, for the odd day when you eat very little or don't eat at all and have to burn body fat to keep going.

Figuring out the correct daily caloric intake for your body is a multistep process.

• **Step 1. Determine your baseline daily caloric intake.** Again, we fall back on a formula. This one takes your age into account:

If you're relatively sedentary and you're under 50 years of age, you would multiply your ideal weight by 12.

For example, let's pretend our 5-foot-6-inch woman is a 25-year-old secretary in a company located in the suburbs. Aside from occasional Saturday nights at the local disco, she doesn't exercise at all. Her inactive lifestyle requires a daily caloric intake of 1,476. In short, she multiplied her ideal weight of 123 pounds by 12 and got 1,476 calories a day.

If she were 50 years or older, however, this same relatively inactive woman would multiply by a factor of 11 instead, since older women require fewer daily calories to maintain their weight. Thus, her baseline daily caloric intake would be 1,353.

If she were 60 or older, she'd multiply by a factor of 10. She'd only need 1,230 calories.

• **Step 2. According to your activity level, adjust your baseline calories upward to reach your target daily caloric intake.**

Now we start adding calories to that baseline figure for those of you who have an active lifestyle. These extra calories represent the allowance you have to make depending on how much energy you expend in a typical day.

For example, a woman who stays on her feet most of the day, doing housework or some other active pursuit, needs more calories to keep going than a woman who drives to and from work and sits at a desk for eight hours.

Suppose you're a highly active woman, age 49 or younger. You should multiply your ideal weight by a factor of 15, instead of 12. If you're 50 or older, multiply by a factor of 13.

Since you're reading this book, we assume you either exercise aerobically already or are about to. This will have an effect on your daily caloric needs, increasing them even more. Because we don't know how much strenuous aerobic exercise you're getting, it's better to describe the theory to you and let you do your own calculations.

Just sitting there reading—or undertaking any other passive pursuit—you burn off approximately ½ calorie per pound of body weight per hour. However, doing an aerobic exercise, you could, in less than an hour, burn off 200 calories or more.

If you've already reached your ideal weight—so your exercise goal is not to shed excess pounds—you should raise your caloric intake by the number of calories you expend in the course of exercising.

## Fit Facts: Calorie Expenditure in 1 Hour for Various Activities

| Activity | Body Weight (lbs) 100 | 125 | 150 | 175 | 200 |
|---|---|---|---|---|---|
| PERSONAL NECESSITIES | | | | | |
| Sleeping | 48 | 60 | 72 | 84 | 96 |
| Sitting (reading or TV) | 48 | 60 | 72 | 84 | 96 |
| Sitting (talking) | 72 | 90 | 108 | 126 | 144 |
| Dressing or washing | 130 | 162 | 192 | 222 | 252 |
| Standing | 58 | 72 | 84 | 102 | 114 |
| Eating (sitting) | 62 | 78 | 96 | 108 | 120 |
| Writing | 77 | 96 | 120 | 138 | 156 |
| LOCOMOTION | | | | | |
| Walking downstairs | 274 | 342 | 402 | 468 | 528 |
| Walking upstairs | 720 | 900 | 1,050 | 1,212 | 1,374 |
| Walking 2.5 mph | 115 | 144 | 174 | 198 | 228 |
| Walking 4 mph | 211 | 264 | 312 | 366 | 420 |
| Running 9 min/mile | 523 | 654 | 786 | 918 | 1,044 |
| HOUSEWORK | | | | | |
| Making beds | 158 | 198 | 234 | 270 | 312 |
| Washing floors | 182 | 228 | 276 | 318 | 360 |
| Cleaning windows | 163 | 204 | 240 | 282 | 324 |
| Cooking | 130 | 162 | 198 | 228 | 264 |
| Mowing grass | 307 | 384 | 456 | 534 | 612 |
| Ironing | 173 | 216 | 264 | 306 | 348 |
| Knitting | 62 | 78 | 96 | 108 | 126 |
| Weeding | 197 | 246 | 294 | 342 | 390 |
| Food shopping | 168 | 210 | 252 | 294 | 336 |
| SEDENTARY OCCUPATION | | | | | |
| Typing (electric) | 72 | 90 | 108 | 132 | 150 |
| Standing (light activity) | 96 | 120 | 144 | 168 | 192 |
| Light office work | 115 | 144 | 174 | 204 | 234 |
| RECREATION | | | | | |
| Dancing (moderate) | 139 | 174 | 210 | 246 | 276 |
| Dancing (vigorous) | 456 | 570 | 690 | 804 | 918 |
| Volleyball | 134 | 168 | 204 | 240 | 270 |
| Basketball | 374 | 468 | 564 | 660 | 750 |
| Racquetball | 360 | 450 | 540 | 630 | 720 |
| Tennis | 298 | 372 | 444 | 522 | 594 |

• **Step 3. Determine the average number of calories you consume daily.** You probably have no idea how many calories are in the foods you eat. Take a typical day and write down everything you eat and the estimated calorie amounts. Next, consult the calorie-per-serving charts on pp. 205–211.

• **Step 4. Compare your actual to your ideal caloric consumption.** Completing this step will either leave you pleasantly surprised at your prudence or slightly horrified at your indulgence.

## Nutrition Principle

### Maintain a 50/20/30 Ratio among the Three Main Food Types Each Day

This should make clear to you that, to a great extent, *your energy level is within your control.* Those superachievers you respect so much weren't just born that way. Their living habits have a lot to do with that dynamism and stick-to-itiveness you admire—and undoubtedly wish to emulate.

Good news. You *can* be like them!

There is a workable—and quite simple—formula identifying the categories of food, and combinations, that will most efficiently boost your daily stores of energy. It was developed by government researchers after much painstaking, scientific study of the impact of foods on the human body.

The formula requires that you distribute your daily intake of calories so that at least 50 percent come from complex carbohydrates, 10 to 20 percent from protein, and 20 to 30 percent from fats. You might remember it this way:

**50% CCs + 20% PRs + 30% FTs = 100% ENERGY**

The issue here is the *quality* of the calories you consume, not just the quantity.

You've probably heard the phrase *empty calories.* This refers to foods that contain a lot of calories but very little nutrient value. Foods and beverages that fall into this category are alcohol, caffeine drinks, and many sweet desserts. No matter how pumped-up they make you feel immediately after consuming them, they contain virtually nothing that is nutritious.

In contrast are the kinds of calories contained in complex carbohydrates, proteins, and fats. Foods in these categories are high in nutrient value, which is why they should be the staples of your daily diet. Except for that occasional splurge you're entitled to if you exercise regularly—*eating foods that have high nutrient value should always be your goal.*

To implement the 50% + 20% + 30% energy formula, you need to know four things: (1) which foods are the best sources of complex carbohydrates; (2) which foods are the best sources of protein; (3) which foods contain the healthiest kinds of fats; and (4) the number of calories contained in a single serving of these foods.

In the latter case, consult the calories-per-serving charts on pp. 205–211. For more information on sources of complex carbohydrates, protein, and fats, however, read on:

• **Complex carbohydrates.** These should be given the highest priority—comprising at least 50 percent of your diet—because they are the chief and most efficient source of energy. Sugar, a *simple carbohydrate*, is a quick-energy source, but it's loaded with calories and lacking in vitamins and minerals.

A lot of different types of food are complex carbohydrates, so you've got maximum latitude here in designing a varied menu.

Complex carbohydrates range from vegetables and fruits to starches and high-fiber breads and cereals. In all their different forms, complex carbohydrates pack large amounts of vitamins and minerals. And they deliver other benefits as well.

For example, fibrous complex carbohydrates promote digestion, reduce constipation, and decrease the risk of colon cancer and other intestinal ailments. For these reasons, you should eat some high-fiber foods every day.

Dietary fiber, or "roughage," consists of any plant material that doesn't break down fully in your digestive tract. Under this classification falls everything from breads and cereals made from whole-grain bran, oats, wheat, corn, rye, barley, and oatmeal to fresh fruits and vegetables, beans, nuts, and seeds.

Many complex carbohydrates are also high in water content, which is crucial to normal body functioning. Water aids temperature control, waste excretion, digestion, and absorption of nutrients.

• **Fats and Protein.** Are you surprised that our 50/20/30 ratio downgrades fats and protein? True, this departs from the typical American diet, but remember that Americans are famous for overindulging in protein and fats.

The world over, people will tell you that the average American meal consists of a hamburger, french fries, and a Coke. Let's analyze this:

Beef is red meat, high in protein but also high in animal fat. Frying that hamburger ensures that the grease is sealed in. French fries, too, are basically desirable—potatoes are a complex carbohydrate—but once again the frying process adds saturated fat.

Odds are that the hamburger roll is made with white flour; this means that the most nutritious part of the wheat has been removed to produce bread with a smooth, spongy texture. Far better if the roll were mottled-looking and its texture crunchy, indicating it had been baked with a whole-grain flour.

And what about the cola drink? These days, it's liable to be a diet drink, which helps reduce caloric intake. Still, a natural fruit juice or water would be preferable, because they have some nutritive value, whereas diet beverages contain virtually no nutrition.

We reduce protein as well as fat in our 50/20/30 ratio diet because the two are related.

There are two major categories of fats: unsaturated, which come from vegetable sources; and saturated, which usually come from animals, but can be vegetable (coconut oil, palm oil, and cocoa butter). Fats from vegetable sources (such as corn and most other vegetable oils, margarine, mayonnaise, salad dressings, nuts, and seeds) are always preferable to animal fats (such as butter, cream, whole-milk dairy products, lard, meat fat, and bacon).

One reason we suggest cutting down on the protein in your diet—particularly red meats—is that by doing so, you're reducing your consumption of animal fats, those saturated fats you want to avoid. On the other hand, meats, fish, and fowl contain other essential nutrients that may be hard to obtain if you eliminate these foods entirely.

Whole-milk dairy products are another big source of protein as well as saturated fat. However, the calcium and other nutrients in dairy products make them too essential to eliminate. Instead, we suggest you replace them with skim-milk or low-fat milk products.

Diets high in saturated fats are dangerous because they cause your body to produce too much low-density lipoprotein (LDL) to your system. (More about LDL and cholesterol in a moment.) Moreover, research indicates an association between such high-fat diets and increased incidence of cancers of the colon, breast, ovaries, pancreas, prostate, and rectum.

Another important reason to limit the fats in your diet:

Fats may be high in calories but, paradoxically, those calories are relatively inefficient sources of energy. Unlike calories that come from complex carbohydrates and protein, fat calories are for *reserve* energy: they are activated later, after the quick-action calories from complex carbohydrates, first, and protein, second, are depleted.

*Moral:* Make it a rule to cut down on all fats in your diet. Begin by being judicious in your use of margarine, mayonnaise, and salad dressings, for instance. And make sure those fats that you're still eating are polyunsaturated ones.

Replacing saturates in your daily fare with polyunsaturates shouldn't be too difficult. For example, don't fry food; bake it or broil it instead. You will have to avoid sauces, gravies, rich desserts, cold cuts, hot dogs, and excessively large portions of meats, however. Finally, use only vegetable oils in cooking and food preparation, including baked goods that call for butter.

The accompanying chart and sample daily menu will make the 50% + 20% + 30% formula easier to remember. You might want to make copies of them and affix them to your refrigerator door or a kitchen cabinet.

## Fit Facts: The 50% + 20% + 30% Formula at a Glance

Daily Menu Goal: Consume 50% COMPLEX CARBOHYDRATES + 20% PROTEIN + 30% FAT to achieve 100% ENERGY

| Food Type | Benefits | Quality Food Sources |
|---|---|---|
| **Complex carbohydrates** | Most efficient energy source. | Fresh fruits and vegetables |

| Food Type | Benefits | Quality Food Sources |
|---|---|---|
| | Rich in vitamins/ minerals.<br>Supplies essential fiber.<br>Reduces need for protein as an energy source. | Legumes (beans, lentils)<br>Whole-grain breads and cereals<br>Starches (potatoes, rice, pasta; unsalted popcorn and pretzels) |
| **Protein** | Body's building-block material in tissues, organs, bones, muscle, hormones, and enzymes.<br>Regulates body's acid-base balance.<br>Helps body resist disease. | Dried beans and peas (also considered complex carbohydrates); fish, poultry, and veal (10 meals per week)<br>Lean red meats (4 meals per week)<br>Low-fat dairy products<br>Eggs (3 per week) |
| **Fat** | Long-term reserve energy source.<br>Contains fatty acids essential for skin and health.<br>Vehicle for fat-soluble vitamins. | Polyunsaturated fat found in vegetable sources (safflower, corn, sunflower oil; margarine, mayonnaise, Italian and French salad dressings, most nuts)<br>Monounsaturated fat found in olive oil, peanut oil, avocados, and some nuts |

## Sample 50/20/30 Daily Menu

At each meal, eat a mix of complex carbohydrates, protein, and fats. You don't have to adhere strictly to the 50/20/30 ratio at each meal *provided* all three meals balance out to that ratio.

| Food Type | % of Calories | Food & Portion |
|---|---|---|
| **Complex carbohydrates** | 50 | 4–8 fruits and vegetables (at least 2 raw and as many fresh as possible) |

| Food Type | % of Calories | Food & Portion |
|---|---|---|
| | | 4–8 starches, including 1+ whole grains (bread/cereal/ crackers) |
| **Protein** | 20 | 4–6 oz. fish, poultry, lean meat, or legumes (dried peas/beans) 2 cups skim or low-fat milk/ yogurt (or 2 oz. low-fat cheese) |
| **Fat** | 30 | 3–6 teaspoons added fats (margarine, vegetable oil, salad dressing) Eat only baked or broiled foods —no fried |
| **Water** | | 4 glasses (1 quart) minimum |
| **Other beverages** | | 4 glasses (1 quart) of other fluids (containing limited amounts or no sugar, sodium, caffeine, or alcohol) |

# Nutrition Principle

## Understand Cholesterol and Its Impact on Your Body

Every woman's body metabolizes fats a little differently. Nothing proves this more than blood cholesterol comparisons made among women with the same bad diets high in saturated fats. A small proportion of such women will maintain reasonable blood cholesterol levels despite their poor eating habits. However, the majority of such women won't. Assume you fall in the latter category. It's safer that way.

This statement generally holds true: *People who eat a lot of saturated fats, foods high in cholesterol, and other excess calories will increase the level of cholesterol in their blood.* And that's not good!

People with high blood cholesterol levels have a greater chance of developing the circulatory problem known as "hardening of the arteries" (arteriosclerosis) and of having a heart attack or a stroke someday. Their chances go up even more if they also have high blood pressure and are smokers.

Arteriosclerosis is caused by fatty cholesterol deposits that build up on the inside walls of blood vessels. These are visible proof that your body is awash with more cholesterol than it needs.

Cholesterol is a waxy substance found only in animals. Despite its bad press, it is essential to many of the body's functions, including that of the brain. It is a vital component of cell linings and is involved in the creation of certain hormones. In fact, the body produces cholesterol in the liver. The excess cholesterol found in so many people's bloodstreams tends to come not from internal production but from excess amounts of cholesterol in the foods they eat.

Cholesterol is carried in the bloodstream by three types of proteins. Two of them—low-density and very low-density lipoproteins (LDLs and VLDLs)—encourage a harmful buildup of cholesterol-laden plaque on arterial walls. That's why they're termed *bad cholesterol.* High-density lipoproteins (HDLs), on the other hand, do just the opposite. They coat arterial walls with a protective layer that impedes this buildup. In addition, if dangerous fatty deposits are already narrowing your blood vessels, HDLs may help dissolve them, scouring out passageways so that your blood can once again flow more freely.

Clearly, the greater the HDLs and the lower the LDLs in your bloodstream, the better off you'll be, now and in the long term.

Fortunately, you can to a great extent control your overall cholesterol level and the HDLs and LDLs in your blood. You can do this by changing your diet and exercising regularly. Proper nutrition helps lower levels of the bad LDLs, while exercise helps increase the beneficial HDLs. Now let's concentrate on diet.

There are three kinds of dietary fats that have a direct bearing on cholesterol and lipoprotein levels in the blood: saturated fats, mostly from animal sources; monounsaturated fats, found largely in olive oil and avocados; and polyunsaturated fats, from plant sources. The latter two kinds of fats, in moderation, are the best for you because they tend to lower the damaging LDLs and VLDLs in your blood, thus raising the percentage of HDLs. Saturated fats, in contrast, raise your total cholesterol level and create more LDLs.

Certain animal products, such as eggs and organ meats, contain great amounts of cholesterol. They, too, raise the level of that substance in your blood.

Not very long ago, it was thought that maintaining a low-cholesterol level, in and of itself, would protect a person from heart disease. However, the prevailing thinking now is more sophisticated. Today, most medical experts feel that the ratio between your total cholesterol and your HDLs is the real key to maintaining a relatively clean cardiovascular system.

In other words: a low total cholesterol count offers no guarantee against heart disease. Nor is a high HDL level any guarantee if it's accompanied by a high cholesterol level. Rather, it's the two together, in the right proportions, that help you avoid heart disease.

What is an advantageous proportion, or ratio?

It differs for men and women. Actually, women are fortunate because they have a genetic predisposition for more HDL in their bodies. For women, the ratio of total cholesterol (HDLs and LDLs) to HDLs alone should always be under 4.5, and preferably under 4. Put another way, a woman's HDL amount should comprise at least 25 percent of her total cholesterol count (HDLs plus LDLs). Even better if it's 30 percent or higher.

If you have the right percentage of HDLs in your blood—and the only way to find out is to have a lab test—you can be pretty sure that your arteries aren't hardening. Indeed, with enough HDLs at work some dissolving of plaque may be taking place, thereby reversing the artery-hardening process. But if you have less than the minimum percentage of HDLs, watch out: the chances are good that you're steadily developing arteriosclerosis.

Triglycerides are another form of fat found in the blood and in some of the body's stored fat. Your triglyceride level is also important to monitor because triglycerides seem to be inversely proportional to the good HDLs. High triglycerides often indicate low levels of HDL. The normal adult triglyceride range is 30 to 120 mg. per deciliter.

## Fit Query: How Do Your Blood Lipids Rate?

| Component | Age | Optimal Range Female | "High Risk" Level Female |
|---|---|---|---|
| Total cholesterol | 20–29 | below 152 | above 220 |
| | 30–39 | below 166 | above 240 |
| | over 40 | below 190 | above 260 |
| HDL cholesterol | 20–29 | above 60 | below 45 |
| | 30–39 | above 64 | below 45 |
| | over 40 | above 70 | below 45 |
| LDL cholesterol | 20–29 | below 88 | above 130 |
| | 30–39 | below 100 | above 140 |
| | over 40 | below 118 | above 165 |
| Total/HDL ratio | 20–29 | below 2.5 | above 6.0 |
| | 30–39 | below 2.6 | above 6.5 |
| | over 40 | below 2.7 | above 7.0 |
| Triglycerides | 20–29 | below 78 | above 146 |
| | 30–39 | below 90 | above 175 |
| | over 40 | below 100 | above 190 |

If you've had a cholesterol count done recently and know you've got a problem, there are four ways to get your cholesterol/HDL ratio back in the right balance: (1) change your diet; (2) shed pounds if you're overweight; (3) exercise; and (4) use prescription medications for that purpose.

We're going to tell you how to change your diet and leave the drug therapy to your doctor. Our weight-loss program is described in chapter 13.

- **Fish oil.** Many animals—such as dogs, rabbits, and dolphins—don't have problems with cholesterol buildup because they have high levels of HDLs in their bodies—sometimes as high as 75 percent of total cholesterol.

Just as animal species differ when it comes to cholesterol levels, so do nations of people. For example, Americans have higher blood cholesterol levels than do Eskimos and Scandinavians. Americans also have a much higher incidence of heart disease.

Why?

One crucial variable is dietary. While Americans are wolfing down their high-fat cheeseburgers, Eskimos and Scandinavians are probably munching on fish. And recent scientific research has focused on sea creatures as one of nature's most healthful foods.

This new evidence emphasizes what earlier generations of mothers knew all along. They weren't being cruel when they fed their children cod-liver oil; the latest studies show that fish oils—specifically Omega-3 fatty acids—help guard against coronary disease, can lower blood pressure, and may even help alleviate migraines, arthritis, and some allergies. In short, Omega-3 oils seem to do an even better job than Omega-6 oils—those found in polyunsaturated vegetable fats—at keeping arteries clear of potentially lethal fatty deposits.

In one study, Dutch researchers followed the dietary habits of 852 middle-aged men for twenty years. Those men in the sample who had eaten more than 1 ounce of fish daily were half as likely to have a heart attack than those who rarely ate fish.

Where once the leaner cuisine of the sea (monkfish, sole, flounder, haddock, ocean perch, shark, swordfish, clams, and scallops) took precedence over their oilier counterparts, these new studies turn that thinking on its ear. Now, the oilier the fish, the better. Hence, the newfound popularity of such cold-water fish as salmon, cod, mackerel, sardines, herring, and bluefish.

Interestingly, the Omega-3 acids in cold-water fish have a greater amount of eicosapentaenoic acid (EPA) than their warmer-water counterparts. And EPA has a beneficial blood-thinning effect that may work to keep human blood flowing in much the same way as it acts as an antifreeze for fish swimming around in the deep, dark waters of the North Atlantic and Pacific.

## Fit Tips: Do Your Heart a Favor— Lower Cholesterol and Those Dangerous LDLs

You claim you're determined to lower your intake of high-cholesterol foods and saturated fats, hence lower the amount of LDLs in your bloodstream. This checklist will ascertain the strength of that commitment.

| | True | False |
|---|---|---|
| **I can truthfully say that I:** | | |
| **Eat no more than three egg yolks a week.** (Egg white contains no cholesterol.) | ______ | ______ |

| | True | False |
|---|---|---|
| **Rarely eat sausages, hot dogs, or bacon.** | ____ | ____ |
| **Substitute chicken and turkey cold cuts for other types of processed and cured luncheon meats.** | ____ | ____ |
| **Buy only the very leanest cuts of red meats (filet, flank, chuck, rump and arm roasts, tenderloin)**—that is, veal, beef, lamb, pork, and venison. | ____ | ____ |
| **Trim any visible fat from red meat before cooking.** | ____ | ____ |
| **Sharply limit my consumption of organ meats**—that is, kidneys, liver, etc. (Along with eggs, they pack the most cholesterol.) | ____ | ____ |
| **Eat small portions (3 to 4 ounces) of red meat on the infrequent occasions when I still do eat it.** | ____ | ____ |
| **Substitute poultry and fish for red meats most of the time** (ten times a week). | ____ | ____ |
| **Make sure I eat enough (8 to 16 ounces) of the cold-water, oilier fish that are high in beneficial Omega-3 fatty acids** (e.g., salmon, mackerel, sardines, herring, bluefish). | ____ | ____ |
| **Remove the skin from poultry before cooking.** | ____ | ____ |
| **Reduce by half the amount of red meat called for in recipes for casseroles and soups, and in its place add cubes of tofu, cooked legumes, cooked grains, or vegetables.** | ____ | ____ |
| **Prepare meat, poultry, and fish by baking, broiling, grilling, boiling, poaching, or steaming**—never by frying or stewing. | ____ | ____ |
| **Pour or drain off any excess fat after cooking no matter what method I've used.** | ____ | ____ |
| **Drink low-fat or skim milk instead of whole milk.** | ____ | ____ |
| **Substitute low-fat (2%) or skim milk (½%) products for whole-milk products** (e.g., the low-fat or skim-milk versions of cottage cheese, plain yogurt, mozzarella, ricotta, etc.). | ____ | ____ |
| **Limit my intake of high-fat cheeses, which are also high in salt, to 3 to 4 ounces a week.** | ____ | ____ |

| | True | False |
|---|---|---|
| **Substitute nonfat evaporated milk for heavy or whipping cream.** | ______ | ______ |
| **Substitute sherbet, ice milk, or frozen yogurt for ice cream.** | ______ | ______ |
| **Substitute corn-oil and safflower-oil margarine for butter.** | ______ | ______ |
| **Substitute the softer, tub margarine for the stick variety because the latter is more saturated.** (Rule of thumb: all "hydrogenated" or "hardened" vegetable oil is more saturated than in its liquid form.) | ______ | ______ |
| **Avoid the few vegetable fats that contain saturated fats:** cocoa butter (the fat in chocolate); coconut oil; and the palm (kernel) oils used in nondairy creamers and some frozen desserts, cake mixes, crackers, and breakfast cereals. | ______ | ______ |
| **For cooking or baking, replace solid shortening—butter or lard—with liquid vegetable oil** (1 cup solid shortening equals ⅞ cup liquid oil)**.** | ______ | ______ |
| **In baked goods, substitute two egg whites for one whole egg.** | ______ | ______ |
| **Avoid sour cream and cream cheese altogether.** | ______ | ______ |
| **Rarely eat saturated-fat toppings and condiments,** such as butter, margarine, cream, sour cream, creamy salad dressings, gravies, and sauces. | ______ | ______ |
| **Substitute low-fat plain yogurt for sour cream in recipes for dips.** | ______ | ______ |
| **Replace the sour cream in hot-food recipes with a low-fat cottage cheese substitute consisting of 1 cup cottage cheese, 2 tablespoons skim milk, and 1 tablespoon lemon juice.** (Add to hot foods after they're removed from the heat.) | ______ | ______ |
| **Seldom eat in fast food restaurants; and when I do, stick to the salad bar and other low- or nonfat offerings.** | ______ | ______ |
| **Exercise regularly to lower my body-fat ratio, at the same time improving the cholesterol/HDL ratio in my bloodstream.** | ______ | ______ |

## Nutrition Principle

### Be Knowledgeable about Your Body's Special Nutritional Needs

There is no ideal diet for every woman because every woman's nutritional needs vary depending on her size, physical activity, genetic makeup, and special conditions such as pregnancy or illness. In addition, women's nutritional needs change as they age.

So, all we can do is point out what some of your body's unique requirements may be and let you and your doctor make the decisions.

We've compiled the following "Nutrient Guide" to give you a quick overview of other foods we didn't discuss earlier. Read through the list carefully. In some cases, you'll want to raise your intake of a nutrient; in other cases, you'll want to restrict it.

### Fit Facts: Nutrient Guide

| Nutrient | Why Needed | Food Sources |
|---|---|---|
| **Sodium** | Normal water balance inside and outside cells. Blood pressure regulation. Electrolyte and chemical balance. | Salt, processed foods (ham, bacon, crackers, pickles, sauces, soups, fast foods, pizza); protein foods (meat, cheese); bread and bakery products |
| **Potassium** | Balance and volume of body fluids. Prevent muscle cramping, weakness. Normal heart rhythm. Electrolyte balance in blood. | Citrus fruits, leafy green vegetables, potato, tomato, whole grains and bran. |
| **Zinc** | Appetite; taste acuity; growth; healthy skin; wound healing. Structural part of cells in body. | Lean meat, liver, milk, fish, poultry, shellfish, whole grain cereals. |
| **Iron** | Formation of red blood cells. Oxygen transport to cells. Prevents nutritional anemia. | Liver, lean meats, dried beans, peas, eggs, dark green leafy vegetables, whole grain cereals, dried fruit. |
| **Vitamin A** | Normal vision, healthy eyes. Prevents night "blindness." Healthy skin, mucous membranes. Resistance to infection. Tissue growth & repair. | Liver, dark green or yellow-orange fruit and vegetables (spinach, carrots, broccoli, cantaloupe, apricots, plums, tomato). |

| Nutrient | Why Needed | Food Sources |
|---|---|---|
| **Vitamin D** | Promote calcium and phosphorus absorption; normal growth; healthy bones, teeth, nails. | (Vitamin D is formed by action of sunlight on skin.) |
| **Vitamin E** | Prevents spoilage of fats. Preserves foods. Protects cell membranes. | Vegetable oils, margarine. (You need 3 teaspoons daily!) |
| **Thiamin ($B_1$)** | Energy production; appetite; digestion; functioning of nerves, heart, muscle; growth; fertility. | Pork, liver, meat, enriched and fortified whole grains, legumes, nuts. |
| **Riboflavin ($B_2$)** | Energy production; good vision; healthy skin and mouth tissue. | Low-fat dairy products, lean meat, liver, eggs, enriched and fortified whole grains, green leafy vegetables. |
| **Niacin ($B_3$)** | Energy production; healthy skin, tongue; digestive and nervous system; appetite, digestion. | Liver, lean meats, pork, poultry, fish, nuts, legumes, enriched and fortified whole grains. |
| **Pyrodoxine ($B_6$)** | Energy production; red blood cell formation; growth. | Liver, pork, lean meats, fish, legumes, enriched and fortified whole grains, green leafy vegetables. |
| **Pantothenic acid** | Energy production; growth and maintenance of body tissues. | Liver, eggs, lean meats, low-fat milk, whole grains, legumes, potato. |
| **Folic acid** | Red blood cell formation; energy production. | Liver, lean meat, fish, legumes, nuts; green leafy vegetables, whole grains. |
| **Vitamin $B_{12}$** | Healthy nerve tissue; normal red blood cell formation; utilization of folic acid; energy production. | Liver, lean meat, poultry, fish, eggs, low-fat dairy products. |
| **Vitamin C** | Promotes growth, wound healing; resists infection, bone, teeth formation/repair; increases iron absorption. | Citrus fruits, cantaloupe, strawberries, potato, tomato, green vegetables (greens, broccoli, cabbage, kale, collards), liver. |

| Nutrient | Why Needed | Food Sources |
|---|---|---|
| **Calcium** | Strong bones, teeth, nails. Muscle tone; prevents cramping. Blood clotting; nerve function. Heart beat; prevents osteoporosis. | Low-fat dairy products (milk, yogurt, cheese, etc.). Dark green leafy vegetables (broccoli, spinach, etc.). Eat at least 3 dairy products daily. |
| **Phosphorus** | Strong bones and teeth growth; energy production; regulates blood chemistry and internal processes. | Lean meat, fish, poultry, low-fat dairy products. |
| **Magnesium** | Energy production; normal heart rhythm. Muscle/nerve function; prevents muscle cramps. | Whole-grain cereals, nuts, legumes, seafood, dark green leafy vegetables. |

Source: "Optimal Nutrition" pamphlet by Georgia Kostas and Kimberly Rojohn, © 1985 by the Cooper Clinic.

There are two dietary deficiencies that are common to women: iron deficiency anemia and calcium deficiency. You should be aware of them and modify your diet to make sure you're not, unknowingly, contributing to the onset of these problems.

• **Iron deficiencies.** Iron deficiency anemia, which you hear so much about in the advertisements for iron supplements, is a way station on the road to full-blown anemia, which is a very serious matter.

You're iron deficient when your body isn't getting enough iron daily, so it has to draw on reserves in your liver, bone marrow, spleen, muscles, and lymphatic tissue. Anemia results when those reserves are depleted and your body starts utilizing the iron in your red blood cells, where half your body's iron is stored.

The classic symptoms of iron deficiency are malaise and fatigue, but there are others, ranging from anxiety, depression, and sleeplessness to heartburn, cramping, changes in appetite, and headaches.

Iron deficiency affects 20 to 25 percent of American women, but only 5 percent are actually anemic. Women ages 11 to 50, those who are pregnant or lactating, and vegetarians are at greatest risk of iron deficiency. Younger women, too, are candidates for iron deficiency if they have low iron intake, heavy menstrual periods, fall prey to fad dieting, and eat too little vitamin C, which enhances iron absorption in the system.

Iron deficiency is a problem for vegetarians because heme iron—the iron-rich red pigment in blood hemoglobin—is found in abundance only in red meat, not in vegetables. Your body can absorb 10 to 30 percent of the heme iron you consume but only 3 to 10 percent of the nonheme iron found in certain plants such as broccoli, wheat germ, and dried apricots.

Athletes involved in weight-bearing exercise—distance running, racquet sports, aerobic dance—are also prone to iron deficiencies. Marathon runner Alberto Salazar found this out the hard way in 1984 after a string of bad races. During a television interview, he admitted that he'd been plagued with insomnia for a year and felt irritable and unmotivated. A Canadian doctor, an expert on sports-induced iron deficiency, happened to be watching the broadcast and called Salazar's coach with a diagnosis. Sure enough, Salazar tested negative for anemia (his hemoglobin count was normal) but positive for a ferritin deficiency (the iron stores in other parts of his body were depleted). After two months of taking iron supplements, he was running well enough again to make the Olympic team.

A recent study at the University of South Carolina's Human Performance Laboratory checked the iron levels of 126 adult female runners against those of 87 healthy but inactive women. Sure enough, the runners showed more iron depletion and iron deficiency than the control group.

Since many female marathon runners have diminished menstrual periods or none at all due to their heavy training schedules, what accounts for this tendency toward iron deficiency?

Athletes lose a lot of iron through sweating. Heavy training also suppresses their appetites, and many avoid red meat. Even making a special effort to eat more iron-rich foods doesn't solve the problem, because athletes absorb less iron in their system than do inactive people. The reason: food passes through athletes' intestinal tracts so fast—because of exercise as well as their typical high-roughage diets—that there isn't as much time for iron absorption to take place.

Perhaps even more causal is the phenomenon of hemolysis, first noted in soldiers following long marches. Hemolysis is the process by which red blood cells break down prematurely due to repeated pounding.

Distance runners are compressing the red blood cells (RBCs) in their feet every time their soles hit the ground. In addition, a buildup of lactic acid from heavy workouts destabilizes the RBC membranes, making them more susceptible to breakage, which inevitably happens. To compensate for the constant RBC losses in the bloodstream (the lost iron filters out through the urine), athletes' bone marrow must produce more new RBCs than usual, thus draining stores of iron from the marrow and other organs.

Athletes who take aspirin to kill pain aren't helping their iron stores either. This anti–inflammatory drug can cause minor internal bleeding. Even 1 grain of aspirin per day can be responsible for blood loss of 1 milliliter. That amount, small though it may be, contains between ½ and 1 mg. of iron.

There's another sports-related iron phenomenon you should be aware of. It's variously called "transient anemia," "sports anemia," or "pseudoanemia." It sometimes occurs in the early stages of an aerobics program when your body begins reaping the benefits of the "training effect" (see chapter 2).

At a certain point, your blood plasma expands—in short, your blood becomes more diluted with water. This decreases the ratio of red blood cells and hemoglobin to your total blood volume. Your blood, in effect, becomes thinner, which some researchers now think may be an advantage for carrying oxygen more efficiently. However, until your body's blood ratios (plasma to hemoglobin) get back into balance—usually in about six weeks—any blood test you have will indicate that you're anemic. Unless you are experiencing symptoms of fatigue, don't worry about it.

## Fit Tips: How to Up Your Intake of Iron

The best way to increase the iron in your system is to watch what you eat. Both professional athletes and amateur exercisers should increase the iron in their diets because this essential nutrient promotes their bodies' energy production process.

This checklist will help you put *more iron* in your diet. Ask yourself, **"Am I:**

| | True | False |
|---|---|---|
| **Eating meat, fowl, or fish several times a week (6 to 8 ounces daily)?** (In general, red meats contain more high-absorption heme iron than fish or poultry. Pork and calves' liver, oysters, and clams contain the highest amounts of all.) | ______ | ______ |
| **Eating lean red meat cuts four times a week (3 to 4 ounces per serving)?** | ______ | ______ |
| **Eating dried fruits because they're excellent sources of nonheme iron?** (E.g., raisins, prunes, apricots, peaches.) | ______ | ______ |
| **Including fruits and vegetables rich in vitamin C in my daily diet?** (Vitamin C substantially increases absorption of both nonheme iron and the additive iron in mineral supplements.) | ______ | ______ |
| **Reading labels to make sure that the processed grains I buy are "enriched" or "fortified"?** (White bread, rolls, crackers, rice, pasta, and cereals to which iron has been added.) | ______ | ______ |
| **Using at least one iron pot or skillet when I cook?** (When you cook acidic foods, such as tomato sauce, in an iron pan, it will leach some core material into the foods.) | ______ | ______ |
| **Limiting my consumption of tea and coffee with meals?** (When consumed with a meal, tea can inhibit the body's ability to absorb iron by as much as 87 percent; coffee by as much as 39 percent. Drink caffeinated beverages two hours after meals to enhance iron absorption.) | ______ | ______ |

| | True | False |
|---|---|---|
| **Always sure to drink orange juice or some other fruit juice high in vitamin C when I eat breakfast?** (The adverse effect that tea and coffee have on iron absorption can be countered somewhat by vitamin C.) | ______ | ______ |
| **Careful not to overdo a good thing with dietary fiber?** (High amounts of bran and the phytates in high-fiber foods can interfere with iron absorption. Once again, vitamin C can come to the rescue. Dried beans and lentils are fibrous foods that contain some iron.) | ______ | ______ |
| **Mindful to eat good vitamin C sources and nonmeat foods rich in iron if I'm a vegetarian?** (Substitute dark green leafy vegetables [broccoli, spinach, romaine lettuce, greens] high in iron and vitamin C and consider taking a supplement containing no more than 18 mg. of iron.) | ______ | ______ |
| **Aware that some medications—especially alkaline antacids and oral tetracycline—are iron inhibitors?** | ______ | ______ |
| **Aware that milk and egg yolks act as iron inhibitors?** (They bind nonheme iron to them, thus blocking iron absorption from the small intestine.) | ______ | ______ |
| **Aware that nuts, spinach, and other dark green leafy vegetables may be high in iron but also contain their own iron inhibitors (oxalates and phytates)?** | ______ | ______ |

Eat moderately and vary the foods you consume. This way, you're more likely to balance the iron-absorption inhibitors in your system with the iron-absorption boosters.

• **Calcium deficiency.** You may shortchange your body on calcium when you're younger and not notice any negative effects. But the chickens will come home to roost later, as they say. After menopause, you'll start to experience the symptoms brought on by those earlier years of calcium starvation: bones that are brittle and shrinking due to leaching calcium.

This condition is called osteoporosis. Fortunately, it can be prevented through dietary means. And, once it's established, it can be reversed to some extent.

Recently, calcium deficiency has been associated with other problems. The *New England Journal of Medicine* (November 28, 1985) published a study showing a relationship between calcium deficiency and cancer of the colon. In another study, calcium was used to treat a medical condition. A dosage of 1,000 mg. per day over an eight-week period lowered blood pressure in selected hypertensive patients.

Clearly, a diet containing adequate calcium is important no matter how old you are, and regardless of whether you have symptoms of osteoporosis.

The best sources of calcium are dairy products. However, as we've discussed, whole-milk dairy products are high in saturated fat, which you want to avoid. The answer: keep eating dairy products, by all means. Just make sure you're eating the low-fat or skim-milk versions of such foods as cheeses, yogurt, and both the milk you drink and the milk you add to your tea or coffee.

## Fit Facts: Calcium-Rich Foods

The average woman consumes only 500 to 600 milligrams (mg.) of calcium daily, not nearly enough to meet the recommended daily allowance (RDA) of 800 to 1,500 mg. Here is a list of foods high in calcium, ranging from dairy products to nuts. Those of you who cannot tolerate lactose—about 3 million Americans can't—have plenty of other choices:

| Food Group | Amount | Elemental Calcium (mg.) | Calories |
|---|---|---|---|
| **Dairy Group** | | | |
| Low-fat yogurt, plain | 1 cup | 455 | 158 |
| Parmesan cheese | 1 oz. | 390 | 129 |
| Low-fat yogurt, fruited | 1 cup | 345 | 231 |
| Ricotta cheese, part skim | ½ cup | 335 | 170 |
| Skim milk | 1 cup | 302 | 86 |
| Low-fat milk (1%) | 8 fl oz. | 300 | 102 |
| Low-fat milk (2%) | 8 fl oz. | 297 | 121 |
| Whole milk | 8 fl oz. | 291 | 150 |
| Gruyère cheese | 1 oz. | 287 | 117 |
| Buttermilk | 1 cup | 285 | 99 |
| Chocolate milk (whole milk) | 8 fl oz. | 280 | 208 |
| Swiss cheese | 1 oz. | 272 | 107 |
| Ice cream, vanilla, soft | 8 fl oz. | 236 | 376 |
| Provolone cheese | 1 oz. | 214 | 100 |
| Monterey cheese | 1 oz. | 212 | 106 |
| Cheddar cheese | 1 oz. | 204 | 114 |
| Muenster cheese | 1 oz. | 203 | 104 |
| Gouda cheese | 1 oz. | 198 | 101 |
| Colby cheese | 1 oz. | 194 | 112 |
| Brick cheese | 1 oz. | 191 | 105 |

| Food Group | Amount | Elemental Calcium (mg.) | Calories |
|---|---|---|---|
| **Dairy Group** (continued) | | | |
| Mozzarella cheese, part skim | 1 oz. | 183 | 72 |
| Ice milk, vanilla | 1 cup | 176 | 184 |
| American cheese | 1 oz. | 174 | 106 |
| Ice cream, vanilla, reg. | 1 cup | 164 | 310 |
| Mozzarella cheese, whole milk | 1 oz. | 147 | 80 |
| Cottage cheese, low-fat (2%) | ½ cup | 77 | 101 |
| **Fish Group** | | | |
| Sardines (with bones) canned in oil, drained | 3 oz. | 313 | 173 |
| Salmon (with bones), canned | 3 oz. | 219 | 118 |
| Oysters, raw (7–9) | ½ cup | 113 | 79 |
| Shrimp, canned | 3 oz. | 98 | 99 |
| **Vegetable Group** | | | |
| Spinach, boiled | ½ cup | 122 | 18 |
| Broccoli, boiled | ½ cup | 105 | 27 |
| Collards, boiled | ½ cup | 74 | 13 |
| Mustard greens, boiled | ½ cup | 54 | 11 |
| Kale, boiled | ½ cup | 47 | 21 |
| **Combination Foods** | | | |
| Quiche, plain, 8″ pie | ⅙ | 252 | 293 |
| Cheese pizza, homemade, 14″ pie | ⅙ | 192 | 205 |
| Tomato soup prep w/whole milk | 1 cup | 159 | 161 |
| Macaroni and cheese | 1 cup | 126 | 266 |
| Cheese pizza, commercial, 12″ pie | ⅙ | 114 | 197 |
| **"Other" Group** | | | |
| Tofu (processed w/Calcium Sulfate) | ½ cup | 175 | 70 |
| Dried figs (6) | ½ cup | 162 | 286 |
| Pudding, all types | ½ cup | 150 | 160 |
| Baked custard | ½ cup | 150 | 160 |
| Cheesecake | ⅛ pie | 141 | 277 |
| Blackstrap molasses | 1 tbsp. | 137 | 43 |
| Pancakes, buttermilk, 4″ diameter | 2 | 119 | 109 |
| Almonds | ¼ cup | 97 | 203 |
| Filbert nuts | ½ cup | 68 | 232 |
| Brazil nuts | ½ cup | 62 | 230 |
| Garbanzo beans (chick-peas) | ½ cup | 41 | 138 |

Adapted from Supri pamphlet © 1986 by General Foods Corp.

Women up to age 30 should eat two to three dairy products per day, equivalent to drinking two to three glasses of milk. Between ages 30 and menopause, women need a daily intake of three glasses of milk, or their calcium equal. Postmenopausal women should aim for four glasses a day.

Elderly women should be especially mindful of their need for calcium. They have to increase their calcium intake even more because their bodies absorb less of it. In addition to eating calcium-rich foods, some women should take calcium supplements.

Older women seem caught in a dietary dilemma. Compared to men, the average woman of any age has more knowledge about food and nutrition. Still, when women get older and find themselves alone, they tend to fall prey to an "it doesn't matter anymore" attitude about food.

Because such women no longer have to cook for a family, they may grab something that's quick and easy at odd times of the day. Since their appetites are diminished, they may no longer see the need for regular meals with all the trimmings. Many don't bother to buy healthful fresh fruits and vegetables because they're too perishable or because their false teeth make chewing high-fiber foods more difficult.

While older, more sedentary women should eat less, *what* they do eat should be packed with nutritive value per calorie. Sadly, what many of these women do eat are convenience foods high in sodium, sugar, and empty calories. Instead of helping their aging bodies function better, they're fostering their further disintegration.

## Nutrition Principle

### Eat the Right Foods to Stay Healthy and Don't Rely on Vitamin and Mineral Supplements to Do the Job

Popping pills is the lazy woman's route to health and fitness.

Sorry to tell you, but in most instances the supplement "cure" doesn't work very well. It's no shortcut to anything. Far better to change your diet to recapture the essential nutrients you're lacking.

Why is a more healthful diet a better way to go?

For one thing, your body better absorbs natural sources of vitamins and minerals. Second, if you change your diet and also take small supplemental amounts of the needed nutrient, your body will be more accepting of the nutrient in its artificial, pill form.

Still, we're not advocating self-treatment via pills. In fact, unless you know what you're doing, you could actually do more harm to your system than good. Vitamins, minerals, and other nutrients react to one another in a multitude of ways. Dietitians understand these relationships and interactions. The average person and even many doctors don't.

We're not saying that certain conditions and maladies don't respond well to dietary modes of treatment. Many do. Two outstanding examples are women in their childbearing years, who often need to take iron supplements to replace the iron they lose through menstrual bleeding; and pregnant or breast-feeding women, who often need more iron, folic acid, vitamin A, calcium, and additional calories.

What we're saying is this: Let a registered dietitian, nutritionist, or your doctor guide you in this very specialized area, particularly if large doses of a vitamin or mineral may be necessary to reverse or retard your particular symptoms.

# 13

# Exercise and Weight Loss— A Synergistic Duo

Americans are getting fatter, year by year, inch by inch. The National Center for Health Statistics used 1980 census data to compile the most recent definitive picture of the nation's girth. A pretty picture it is not. The findings: since the 1960s, the average adult has become 6 pounds heavier, and is only a ½ inch taller.

The root of the problem certainly isn't inactivity, or at least not predominantly, since we've become a nation of joggers, aerobic dancers, and iron-pumpers over the same period. No, we have to look elsewhere—at the dinner table. The United States Department of Agriculture's index of per capita food consumption tells us that every American now eats 5 percent more than he or she did ten years ago.

America's food consumption patterns indicate that we're all fooling ourselves. Collectively, we've learned more about nutrition, but we don't apply what we know uniformly. Yes, we eat more chicken and fish, but as soon as beef prices plummet, red meat consumption goes in the opposite direction—up.

We've also become hooked on baked potatoes with saucy toppings and various rich and delicious cakes, cookies, and gourmet ice creams. In 1985, each of us put away an average 150.9 pounds of sweeteners, 5 pounds apiece more than the year before and a full 20 pounds more than in 1976. While sales of sugar may have declined, sales of soda pop—diet and otherwise—and high-calorie desserts have soared.

Alarmingly, the Metropolitan Life Insurance Company, publisher of a highly respected ideal height-and-weight table, has adjusted its table accordingly. So-called optimum weights are now up to 13 pounds heavier than those shown on its previous chart, compiled in 1959. The company now claims that "today's adults can weigh more than their 1959 counterparts and still anticipate favorable longevity."

We dispute that claim, along with the American Heart Association, which urges doctors to retain the 1959 tables as their weight guide. You won't find any Metropolitan charts, new or old, in this book, but you will find other height-weight formulas that conform to a leaner view of human fat deposits.

We don't want you to just "think thin," which, as these belt-busting statistics show, many people are already doing, to no avail. Rather, we want you to *get lean*, not just because you'll look and feel better, but because it will increase the chances that you'll live longer.

## The Principles of Weight Loss

The Aerobics Center weight-loss program is built on eight weight-loss precepts. We'll go through them one by one in this chapter.

Our precepts aren't gimmicks. In fact, much of what follows will strike you as old-fashioned, unadulterated common sense. But in the weight-loss field, unfortunately, common sense isn't common. It's extremely rare.

Unlike other programs, ours is relatively easy to follow. After all, we can cover this subject in one chapter, while most so-called diet experts require one whole book.

Most important of all, *our program works!* One reason it works is because it's not solely dependent on dietary change. Our program is holistic. We link calorie reduction to exercise to better nutrition overall. We emphasize that eliminating your weight-loss problem depends as much on altering your attitudes and behavior patterns as it does on putting less food in your mouth. To be sure, your problem may not be the amount of food you eat; it may simply be the poor quality of those foods.

We think it's terrific if some popular diet has helped you get down to your ideal weight and stay there. Some of those diets do work for some people some of the time. We don't denigrate success even if another diet regimen is responsible, as long you do not lose your health, slow down your metabolism, or lose muscle. But in our program we say you've still got a *potential* obesity problem until you commit yourself to the principles of good nutrition we enunciated in chapter 12.

### Weight-Loss Precept #1

#### Accept the Facts: Obesity Can Kill You

If you're overweight, even by a mere 10 or 15 pounds, losing weight is not just a matter of vanity. That extra flab you're carrying could be fatal. Yes, eventually it could kill you!

Excess weight has been isolated as a risk factor in a great many medical problems. It's associated with heart, gallbladder, and renal disease. It can trigger strokes and various cancers as well as such chronic medical conditions as diabetes, high blood pressure, and increased levels of blood fats (cholesterol and triglycerides). That's why a panel of experts at the National Institutes of Health in 1985 issued an alert labeling obesity a "killing disease." They urged the medical community to treat it with the same urgency now reserved for smoking, high blood pressure, and a family history of life-threatening illness.

Obesity is implicated the most strongly in coronary disease. The two go together like a horse and carriage.

The American Heart Association (AHA) lists obesity as one of eleven risk factors for heart disease. This means that fatness, in and of itself, raises your chances of having a heart attack even if none of the other risk factors are present. But if you're overweight, it's probable that some of the other ten risk factors are present too. The reason: excess weight also contributes to the development of diabetes, hypertension, and elevated blood lipid levels—and each of these three conditions is on the AHA's list too. This adds up to a fourfold linkage between coronary artery disease and obesity!

A bibliography of studies supporting the cause-effect relationship between obesity and various life-theatening disease states would go on for pages, so we'll just summarize some of the most startling findings:

• Overweight individuals tend to die younger. Their increased mortality rate is due mainly to cardiovascular disease.

• There is a strong and consistent relationship between obesity and hypertension, with the incidence of high blood pressure estimated at two to four times greater among the obese. Put another way: approximately 60 percent of hypertensive patients are also obese.

• If a person has high blood pressure—either the upper (systolic) or lower (diastolic) figure—his or her condition usually will improve following weight loss. And with that reduction comes a reduction of the chances of suffering a stroke. Indeed, strokes are the most common result of high blood pressure.

• Over the past forty-five years, various animal studies have shown an association between obesity, high dietary fat intake, and cancers of the colon, prostate, pancreas, breast, ovary, kidney (among women), endometrium, and gallbladder. A 1985 cancer prevention booklet, *Taking Control*, published by the American Cancer Society, states: "Obesity is linked to cancers of the uterus, gallbladder, breast, and colon. Exercise and lower calorie intake help you avoid gaining a lot of weight."

• A recent study of rats by Michael Pariza, Ph.D., of the Department of Food Microbiology and Toxicology at the University of Wisconsin, showed that a high-calorie diet, regardless of the food sources of those calories, increased the animals' risk of developing cancer.

Having said all this, we hope you'll develop a *healthy* fear of fat. We emphasize "healthy" because a growing number of women have an *un*healthy fear of fat. They are the victims of bulimia and anorexia nervosa, compulsive eating disorders that experts estimate some 2 to 8 million American women have suffered from at some point in their lives. Today, these disorders have reached epidemic proportions among young women aged 13 to 30.

Bulimic women seem to love food—in public. In private, however, they rid their bodies of what they've eaten by inducing vomiting or by using laxatives or diuretics. Their binge-and-purge merry-go-round is physically dangerous, not to mention mentally unhealthy. It can cause a chemical imbalance that can lead to pancreatitis, kidney malfunction, and irregular heartbeats, even death.

Anorexic women, on the other hand, don't engage in this sort of behavior. Their obsession with thinness is straightforward. Their weight-loss method is starvation, which can trigger nutritional deficiencies, menstrual irregularities, infertility, hair loss, skin changes, cold intolerance, severe constipation, psychiatric disturbances, and other complications. Anorexia nervosa has the highest mortality rate of all psychiatric syndromes, with an estimated 5 to 10 percent of severe cases culminating in death.

To say that bulimia and anorexia are just dieting gone haywire misses the point. Both have deep-seated emotional roots that may take years of psychological counseling to expose.

Both bulimics and anorexics have a distorted view of their own body image. They look in the mirror and instead of seeing a slim body—it may even be emaciated—they see rolls of fat. Such women are frequently obsessed with exercise, simply another manifestation of their underlying problem.

If you have bulimic or anorexic tendencies, don't even read this chapter. Go back to chapter 12, which deals with nutrition, and adhere steadfastly to what we say there, and seek the counsel of an expert psychologist who specializes in bulimia and anorexia.

## Weight-Loss Precept #2

### Your Goal Is Twofold: Ideal Weight as Well as Body-Fat Ratio

We've established why weight control is important—*vitally* important. But there's more to it than merely lowering your weight reading on your bathroom scale. The percentage of your weight that is body fat versus the percentage that is muscle, bone, and other solid components is also important.

A study we conducted at the Cooper Clinic in 1980 sheds more light on this matter, for it shows the correlation between body fat and high cholesterol, a heart disease risk factor.

Our sample consisted of 2,000 healthy men, ranging in age from under 30 to over 60. We began with the assumption that the mere fact of aging contributes to elevated cholesterol levels. Yet, when we studied the data, this hypothesis was too simplistic, since, with advancing age, the men's HDL, or good cholesterol, remained nearly constant. It was their LDLs, or bad cholesterol, that increased.

We looked at several other variables that could account for the deteriorating lipid profile in our older men and finally found one. *Body fat.*

Whereas our younger men were relatively lean, with around 18 percent body fat, the men 40 and older suddenly jumped to around 23 percent body fat. Forty was also the age that showed a large increase in LDL cholesterol.

Our conclusion: As people grow older, their percentage of body fat increases even though their body weight may remain the same. This is even more true for women. That's why at age 40 your weight could be the same as it was at age 21, yet your waist measurement is considerably larger.

This bulge at the midriff and the unfavorable balance in your blood lipid levels don't have to occur, of course. By watching what you eat *and* exercising (which we will discuss fully under Precept #6, p. 203), you can decrease your percentage of body fat and keep those bad LDLs from congregating.

Over the years, we've followed the medical histories of thousands of men and women who come for regular physical exams and treadmill stress tests at the Cooper Clinic. Those data show a direct correlation between age-adjusted levels of physical fitness and body weight and fat. When you exercise, your percentage of body fat—and your HDLs—go down, while your body's lean muscle mass goes up.

In chapter 12 we outlined two formulas for calculating your ideal weight. Yes, you must know your ideal weight and strive to achieve it. But you must also know your ideal percentage of body fat and get that into line too.

Now we are going to make what may appear a paradoxical statement: *Obesity is not necessarily the same as being overweight.*

Commonly accepted obesity categories are:

| Percentage above Ideal Weight | Diagnosis |
|---|---|
| 10–20 | Overweight |
| 20–30 | Mild obesity |
| 30–50 | Moderate obesity |
| 50–100 | Severe obesity |
| 100% + (or more than 100 pounds overweight) | Morbid obesity |

## Cooper Clinic Percent Body Fat Goals, Age and Sex Adjusted*

| FEMALES | | | MALES | | |
|---|---|---|---|---|---|
| Age | Acceptable | Ideal | Age | Acceptable | Ideal |
| <30 | 19.5% | 15.6% | <30 | 12.9% | 8.4% |
| 30–39 | 20.6% | 16.8% | 30–39 | 16.6% | 12.8% |
| 40–49 | 24.1% | 20.0% | 40–49 | 18.9% | 15.2% |
| 50–59 | 27.1% | 22.7% | 50–59 | 20.7% | 16.9% |
| 60 + | 28.2% | 22.9% | 60 + | 21.2% | 17.2% |

*Data obtained from the percent body-fat determination using underwater weighing and/or skinfold measurements of 4,997 women and 18,917 men tested at the Cooper Clinic. *Acceptable* levels indicate the top 35 percentile; *ideal* the top 15 percentile.

This is fine as far as it goes. But to really know where you stand, weightwise, you must differentiate between the muscle, adipose tissue (fat), and bone mass in your body.

For women of average build, the ideal percentage of body fat should be in the 18-to-22 range; for men, the range is 15 to 19.

In other words, to be in a state of physical equilibrium, your ratio of fat to solid mass (muscle and bone) should stay within this range. Unfortunately, the average woman 32 years old has a body-fat ratio just above 30 percent. That says a lot about female health, since a body-fat ratio exceeding 22 percent automatically places any 30-year-old woman at greater risk of heart disease.

Not surprisingly, very athletic women have the lowest body-fat ratios, but that has its drawbacks too. If a woman's body fat drops below 15 percent, for example, she may experience menstrual irregularities. Below 12 percent and her fertility could be impaired. (More about this problem in chapter 15.)

At the Aerobics Center, we have two highly accurate methods for measuring a woman's percentage of body fat. First, we measure, with calipers, the skinfold thickness at seven sites: (1) under the collarbone; (2) the armpit, or axilla; (3) the triceps, or back of the upper arm; (4) below the shoulder blade (subscapular); (5) at the waist; and (6) above the iliac crest. The seventh and final measure is the front of the thigh. Then we weigh the woman while she's totally submerged in water.

You can avail yourself of one of these methods. Ross Laboratories (Dept. 441, 625 Cleveland Ave., Columbus, OH 43216; 614-227-3333) sells a caliper kit for individuals who want to measure body fat.

You can also estimate whether your body fat is within a safe range by figuring your waist-to-hip ratio. For women, it shouldn't be any higher than 0.8.

Here's how to do it:

Measure your waist in a relaxed state and divide this measurement by your hip measurement. If your waist measures 24 and your hips 36, your waist-to-hip ratio is 0.6, well within the acceptable range.

Several studies have shown that a high waist-to-hip ratio is correlated to coronary artery disease, stroke, and other causes of premature death. In other words, *where* the fat tissue is deposited on your body, not just the existence of excess fat, can be important. Since women's fat tissue tends to collect below the waistline and men's at the waistline in the form of potbellies, men have the more serious problem.

Moral: Women have to look beyond their weight and know their bodies' percentage of fat to solid mass (muscle and bone). It's the only way to truly balance the weight scales.

## Weight-Loss Precept #3

### Understand the Theory Behind Weight Loss: Calories Out Must Exceed Calories In

Losing weight is largely a matter of arithmetic, not to play down the need for self-discipline and perseverance. But, stripped of its mystique, weight loss simply means burning more calories each day than you consume.

Your objective is to burn away fat deposits in your body. Body fat is nothing more than calories that have accumulated during periods when you ate more calories than you expended in activity. Now that you've decided to lose weight, you must reverse the process: exercise more and eat less.

It takes about 3,500 calories to make 1 pound of body fat. (Visualize 1 pound of body fat as four sticks of butter.) It only stands to reason, then, that to lose 1 pound, you have to burn 3,500 excess calories.

How to do it?

To lose weight, you must reduce your daily caloric intake below what it takes to maintain your ideal weight. (In chapter 12 we explained how to determine your daily caloric intake to maintain your ideal weight and peak energy level.)

Simple arithmetic says that lopping off 500 calories a day from your ideal-weight caloric intake will cause you to lose 1 pound a week (500 calories × 7 days = 3,500 calories).

Losing 1 to 2 pounds a week is all you should ever aim for. Even that amount is pretty dramatic when you consider that total starvation creates a maximum of only a ¾ pound weight loss each day. Fast weight loss like this, even for short periods, is not only deceptive—most of the initial weight loss is due to glycogen and water loss, not fat—it's self-defeating. And not just because it can lead to malnutrition, which will eventually kill you. But for a reason related to body metabolism that we'll explain in a moment.

While a drop of 500 calories in daily food intake is one route to weight loss, it's not advisable. As we explained in Precept #2, when we discussed body fat and lean body mass, your goal is not just to lose weight but to lower your body-fat ratio. That's done through a combination of diet and exercise. Better to cut only 250 calories a day and burn off the other 250 calories through some form of exercise that tones your muscles while you're shedding fat.

There is another advantage to exercising rather than only dieting to lose weight. Dr. Marcia L. Stefanick of Stanford University's Center for Research in Disease Prevention in Palo Alto, California, compared men who jogged 10 miles a week with those who merely cut 300 calories a day from their diets. In this two-year study, she discovered that both groups lost the same amount of weight, approximately 9 pounds each. Yet, the exercisers increased significantly their good or HDL cholesterol levels compared to the dieters; and the joggers had much lower levels of bad or LDL cholesterol. Both of these changes among the exercisers should substantially reduce their heart disease risk.

Dr. Stefanick has now started a new study that will include women. The prediction is that the results will be comparable to those seen in men.

Following our prescription for weight loss, you'll avoid a situation so common among women who go on crash diets or resort to starvation methods. They may achieve their goal weight but they're still displeased with their appearance when they stand naked in front of a mirror. Their flesh sags and their muscles have no tone. But if they get any thinner they'll look gaunt, which they may look already.

The problem has to do with the ratio of muscle to fat on their bodies and the poor condition of their muscles. Even though their total weight is within the ideal range, they have excess fat on their bodies.

A contradiction? Not at all.

Because their muscles are weak and unconditioned, they weigh less than normal, firm muscles. So, their lighter-weight muscles compensate for the slight excess fat on their frames, making their total weight seem proper.

The same reasoning explains why a bodybuilder may be "overweight" using the formulas we cited, yet still look tip-top. It's because her "excess" weight is in the form of extraordinarily developed muscles and lean body mass, not fat.

If exercising as well as cutting food calories is still too onerous a proposition for you, look at it this way:

Suppose you continue to eat as you always have but add 30 minutes a day of moderate exercise to your schedule. (A good rule of thumb is that running or walking briskly for 1 mile uses about 100 calories.) You would still lose weight—about 15 pounds per year. Think of what you could lose if you exercise and changed your diet in tandem!

## Weight-Loss Precept #4

### For Faster Initial Weight Loss, for 2 Weeks Follow the Formula: 200 + 425 + 225 = 850 Calories a Day

In the beginning of a weight-loss program, people need to see quick results to motivate them to continue. Because we understand this, we suggest that women drop down to 850 calories a day for the initial two weeks. But this is merely to get you started.

Unless you're a very petite woman, an 850-calorie-a-day diet is too restrictive, especially since you'll be exercising more and will need to maintain a higher energy level to support this.

The 1,000-calorie-a-day diet we describe is the one we prefer. Combined with exercise, it guarantees safe weight loss over a reasonable period of time.

Although most obese women are not particularly athletic, it may be instructive here to describe a condition called "nutritional arrhythmia," which can occur in hard-training athletes because of insufficient food.

Dr. Thomas J. Bassler, in a *Journal of the American Medical Association* article, reported on the sudden deaths—mostly in their sleep!—of twelve top-notch marathoners. All were in the process of severely restricting their diets. The exact cause of these deaths is unknown, although the term *nutritional arrhythmia* has come into vogue to explain the semistarvation circumstances surrounding the mortalities.

What happened? Apparently, the marathoners starved themselves by eating too little food to support the enormous amount of exercise they were getting.

There's little chance that obese women will follow in the footsteps of these marathoners. Rather than overdo exercise, they're more likely to *under*do eating. For this reason, here is our caveat:

On a two-month diet/exercise weight-loss program, you can go on this low 850-calorie, two-week diet once. Over a three-month period, you can go on it twice, provided there's an interval of six weeks between when you're on the 1,000-calorie diet that follows.

## Aerobics Center Positive Eating Program for Weight Loss and Maintenance

These Positive Eating Program (PEP) menus are designed to let you mix-and-match them according to your changing weight-loss goals. For example, if your goal is:

- **Quick Weight Loss**–Eat 850 calories a day, distributed as shown, but for two weeks only:

**200 (Breakfast) + 425 (Lunch) + 225 (Dinner) = 850 calories**

- **Slower, Safer Weight Loss**—Eat 1,000 calories a day until you reach your ideal weight:

**250 (Breakfast) + 500 (Lunch) + 250 (Dinner) = 1,000 calories**

To maintain present weight, each woman will have a slightly different daily calorie total depending on her activity level. However, 1,500 calories is probably average. Those calories should be eaten:

**300 (Breakfast) + 500 (Lunch) + 700 (Dinner) = 1,500 calories**

Design your own maintenance menus utilizing the information on the chart on p. 205, "Exercise Equivalents for Food and Beverage Calories."

*Note:* Calories for weight loss at approximately 25 percent breakfast, 50 percent lunch, 25 percent dinner. This distribution promotes faster weight loss. Since it is not always possible to eat this way, lunch can be made smaller and dinner larger, but do not allow more than 50 percent of the day's calories to stack up at night.

Source of PEP menus: "Eating on the Run" pamphlet by Georgia Kostas and Kimberly Rojohn, © 1985 by the Cooper Clinic.

## Quick and Easy Breakfast Ideas
### (200–300 Calories)

| FOOD | | | |
|---|---|---|---|
| Fruit (40) | 2 T. raisins | ½ banana | ½ cup blueberries |
| Starch (70) | ½ cup bran flakes | ¾ cup cornflakes | ½ cup grapenut flakes |
| Protein (80) | 1 cup skim milk | ¾ cup 2% milk | ½ cup whole milk |
| Fat (45) | | | |
| Calories | 200 | 200 | 200 |
| Fruit (40) | ½ cup orange juice | 1 apple | 1 orange |
| Starch (70) | 1 whole wheat toast | 4 crackers* | ½ cup oatmeal |
| Protein (80) | 1 egg, poached or boiled | 1 oz. low-fat cheese | 1 cup skim milk |
| Fat (45) | 1 tsp. margarine or 2 tsp. honey | | 1 tsp. margarine or 2 tsp. honey |
| Calories | 235 | 200 | 235 |
| Fruit (40) | ½ grapefruit | 6 oz. tomato juice* | 1 pear |
| Starch (70) | ½ bagel | ½ English muffin | 1 corn tortilla |
| Protein (80) | 1 oz. turkey | 1 oz. lean ham* or beef | 1 oz. low-fat cheese, grated, melted |
| Fat (45) | 1 T. Neufchâtel cheese | 1 tsp. margarine | |
| Calories | 235 | 235 | 190 |
| Fruit (40) | ½ cup applesauce | ¼ cantaloupe | ¾ cup strawberries |
| Starch (70) | ½ whole wheat pita pocket | ½ whole wheat pita pocket | 3 T. grapenuts |
| Protein (80) | ½ cup skim ricotta cheese | ⅓ cup low-fat cottage cheese | 1 cup skim milk yogurt |
| Fat (45) | Toast pita; top w/ cinnamon; broil | 3 tsp. diet margarine | 1 T. chopped nuts |
| Calories | 200 | 235 | 235 |
| Fruit (40) | 1 small pear | 1 medium peach | 1 small apple |
| 2 Starch (140) | 1 cup dry cereal mix (rice, wheat, corn, bran chex, shredded wheat, pretzels*) | 1 cup vegetable soup* 4 melba toast | 1 English muffin or 1 bagel or 1 bran muffin |

FOOD, continued

| | | | |
|---|---|---|---|
| Protein (80) | 1 oz. farmer's cheese | 1 cup skim milk | ¾ cup 2% milk |
| Fat (45) | | | 3 tsp. diet margarine |
| Calories | 260 | 260 | 300 |
| 2 Fruit (80) | 1 cup fruit salad | ½ banana + ¾ cup strawberries | 1 banana |
| Starch (70) | 1 small baked potato | 4 rye crackers* | 2 thin whole wheat bread |
| Protein (80) | 1 oz. mozzarella cheese, grated | 1 cup skim milk (Blend fruit and milk as shake) | 1 T. peanut butter* |
| Calories | 230 | 230 | 230 |
| Fruit (40) | ⅛ honeydew | 1 orange | ½ cup pineapple |
| Starch (70) | ½ English muffin | 1 whole wheat toast | 1 whole wheat toast |
| 2 Protein (160) | 1 egg, poached + 1 oz. low-fat cheese (Make open-faced sandwich) | 1 egg (or egg substitute) + ¼ cup skim ricotta cheese (Make omelet, cooked without fat) | 1 oz. low-fat cheese ¾ cup 2% milk |
| Calories | 270 | 270 | 270 |
| Fruit (40) | 12 grapes | ½ cup grapefruit juice | ½ cup orange juice |
| Starch (70) | 2 thin whole wheat bread | ½ English muffin | 2 thin whole wheat bread |
| 2 Protein (160) | 1 oz. low-fat cheese 1 oz. lean ham* or chicken | 2 oz. lean pork broiled | 2 oz. hamburger patty (tomato, lettuce, mustard*) |
| ½ Fat (25) | 2 tsp. diet margarine | 2 tsp. diet margarine | 2 tsp. diet mayonnaise |
| Calories | 295 | 295 | 295 |

P = protein
C = complex carbohydrate
F = fat

*High-sodium. For low-sodium intake, select unsalted or low-sodium varieties.
Note: "Low-fat cheese" refers to mozzarella, farmer's, skim ricotta and 1–2% fat cottage cheese.

## Quick and Easy Brown Bag Lunches
### (300–500 Calories)

**SANDWICHES**

| | |
|---|---|
| 2 slices thin whole wheat bread (C) (70)<br>2 oz. chicken/turkey/lean beef (P,F) (120)<br>1 tsp. mayonnaise (F) (45)<br>lettuce, tomato slices (0)<br>1 small orange (C) (40)<br>25 stick pretzels* (C) (70) | 2 slices thin whole wheat bread (C) (70)<br>½ cup tuna* (P,F) (110)<br>3 tsp. diet mayonnaise (F) (45)<br>lettuce, pickle* (0)<br>1 medium apple or 6 oz. apple juice (C) (80) |
| Calories 345 | 305 |
| 2 thin slices whole wheat bread (C) (70)<br>1 T. peanut butter* (P,F) (90)<br>1 banana (C) (80)<br>1 cup skim milk (P,C) (80) | 1 pita pocket (C) (140)<br>1 cup vegetables (C) (50)<br>1 oz. grated mozzarella cheese (P,F) (80)<br>1 medium apple (C) (80) |
| Calories 320 | 350 |
| 2 slices whole wheat bread (C) (140)<br>egg salad: 1 egg (P,F) (80)<br>1 T. diet mayonnaise (F) (50)<br>lettuce (0)<br>carrot sticks (C) (25)<br>1 small pear (C) (40) | Fast food hamburger* (P,C,F) (400)<br>(¼ lb. meat, no mayonnaise)<br>1 small apple (from home) (C) (40)<br>water (0) |
| Calories 335 | 440 |

**OTHERS**

| | |
|---|---|
| 1 cup soup* (C) (70)<br>6 whole wheat crackers* (C) (105)<br>1 oz. low-fat cheese (P,F) (80)<br>12 grapes (C) (40) | Salad (C) (25)<br>1 T. salad dressing* (F) (80)<br>1 large baked potato (C) (140)<br>1 oz. mozzarella cheese (P,F) (80) |
| Calories 295 | 325 |
| 1 cup plain skim milk yogurt (P,C) (90)<br>1 cup fresh strawberries (C) (50)<br>4 graham crackers or 8 whole wheat crackers* (C) (140) | ½ oz. box raisins (4 T.) (C) (80)<br>4 graham crackers or 1 cup dry cereal mix (shredded wheat, bran, rice, corn chex, pretzels*) (C) (140)<br>1 cup 2% milk (P,C,F) (120) |
| Calories 280 | 340 |

OTHERS, continued

| | |
|---|---|
| ½ cup low-fat cottage cheese (P,F) (100)<br>½ cup pineapple chunks (C) (40)<br>½ cup strawberries (C) (30)<br>½ banana, sliced (C) (40)<br>Topping: 3 T. grapenuts (C) (70) | Low-calorie frozen meal (i.e., Lean Cuisine,* Weight Watchers,* etc.) (P,C,F) (300 or less calories per meal)<br>1 fruit (C) (40) |
| Calories 280 | 340 |

## COLD SALADS

| | |
|---|---|
| **combine:**<br>½ cup spaghetti (C) (70)<br>1 cup raw vegetables (C) (25)<br>1 oz. grated mozzarella cheese (P,F) (80)<br>1 T. low-fat Italian dressing* (F) (25)<br>1 fresh fruit (C) (40) | **combine:**<br>½ cup cooked rice (C) (70)<br>1 cup raw vegetables (C) (25)<br>1 oz. cooked chicken (P,F) (60)<br>3 tsp. diet mayonnaise (F) (45)<br>1 fresh fruit (C) (40) |
| Calories 240 | 240 |

## Other Ideas:

1. Pick up sandwich at local deli at lunch or before work (some delis are in grocery stores). Add fresh fruit from home.
2. Pack leftovers.
3. Keep supply of soup, frozen meals, cheese and crackers, peanut butter, fruit, juice, at work.
4. See breakfast and supper ideas.

P = protein
C = complex carbohydrates
F = fat

*High-sodium. For low-sodium intake select unsalted or low-sodium varieties.
Note: "Low-fat cheese" refers to mozzarella, farmer's, skim ricotta, and 1–2% fat cottage cheese.

## Quick and Easy Dinner Ideas
**(250–535 Calories)**

| Soup/Sandwich/Fruit (470) | Chalupa or Taco/Milk or Juice (410) |
|---|---|
| 1 cup chicken noodle soup* (C) (70)<br>Sandwich: 2 slices whole wheat bread (C) (140) | 1 corn tortilla (C) (70)<br>2 oz. lean ground beef (P,F) (160)<br>1 oz. low-fat cheese (P,F) (80) |

Soup/Sandwich/Fruit, continued

3 oz. lean meat (P,F) (180)
mustard,* lettuce, tomato (0)
1 large fruit (C) (80)

## Soup/Salad/Fruit (415)

1 cup vegetable soup* (C) (70)
Tossed salad with raw vegetables (C) (25)
2 T. Italian dressing* (F) (160)
1 oz. grated low-fat cheese (P,F) (80)
1 large fruit (C) (80)

## Taco Salad/Fruit (535)

Lettuce, chili peppers, chili powder, hot sauce (0)
2 oz. lean ground beef or chicken (P,F) (160)
cooked in ½ oz. tomato sauce* (C) (35)
1 oz. grated low-fat cheese (P,F) (80)
½ cup pinto or kidney beans (P,C) (150)
1 corn tortilla (toasted, broken in salad) (C) (70)
¾ cup strawberries (C) (40)

## Cheese Toast/Fruit Salad/Juice (280)

1 slice whole wheat toast (C) (70)
1 oz. low-fat cheese (P,F) (80)
1 cup fruit salad (C) (80)
1 cup V-8 juice* (C) (50)

Chalupa or Taco/Milk or Juice, continued

2 slices tomato (C), 2 T. chopped onion (C) (20)
lettuce, pepper, hot sauce (0)
1 cup skim milk (P,C) or 1 cup orange juice (C) (80)

## Baked Potato/Salad/Fruit (445)

1 large potato (C) (140)
1 oz. low-fat cheese (P,F) (80)
(or 2 pats margarine) (F)
Tossed salad with raw vegetables (C) (25)
2 T. French dressing* (F) (120)
1 large fruit (C) (80)

## Chicken or Fish/Vegetable/Rice/Fruit (420)

3 oz. chicken (no skin) or fish (P,F) (180)
seasoned with 2 T. diet Italian dressing* (F) (40)
½ cup steamed spinach, etc. (C) (25)
½ cup steamed carrots, etc. (C) (25)
½ cup brown or wild rice (C) (70)
1 large fruit (C) (80)

## Mini Pizza/Fruit (360)

1 oz. lean ground beef (P,F) (80)
1 oz. low-fat cheese (P,F) (80)
½ cup raw mushrooms (C) (15)
½ cup tomato sauce* (C) (35)
on pita pocket half or tortilla or English muffin half (C) (70)
1 large fruit (C) (80)

### Stuffed Vegetables/Fruit/Bread (430)

Fill tomato, green pepper, squash or eggplant (C) (50)
with 2 oz. lean ground beef (cooked) (P,F) (160)
(or ½ cup of tuna [in water],* chicken or salmon* salad)
½ cup cooked rice (C) (70)
1 large fruit (C) (80)
1 whole wheat dinner roll (C) (70)

### Omelet/Toast/Vegetable/Fruit (495)

2 eggs (P,F) (160) + ¼ cup low-fat cottage cheese (P,F) (50)
2 slices whole wheat toast (dry) (C) (140)
(or 1 large boiled or broiled potato, sliced) (C)
4 slices tomato (C) (25)
1 cup apple juice (C) (120)

### Stir-Fry Vegetables/Rice/ Fruit Salad/Yogurt (475)

2 cups vegetables (C) (100) cooked in ½ T. corn oil (F) (60)
with ½ cup tuna (in water)* (P,F) (120)
(or chicken or turkey)
½ cup rice (C) (70)
1 cup fruit salad (C) (80)
½ cup plain skim yogurt (P,C) (45)

### Steamed Vegetables/Rice/Cheese/ Fruit (490)

2 cups mixed steamed vegetables (C) (100) over
1 cup rice (C) (140), topped with
1 oz. grated low-fat cheese (P,F) (80)
1 cup plain skim yogurt (P,C) (90)
and 1 cup mixed fruit (C) (80)

### Cold Plate (480)

Raw vegetables (C) (25)
with ½ cup low-fat plain yogurt dip (P,C) (75)
2 oz. low-fat cheese (P,F) (160)
8 whole wheat crackers* (C) (140)
1 large fruit (C) (80)

### Tuna Melt Sandwich (445)

1 whole wheat bun or English muffin (C) (140)
½ cup tuna (in water)* (P,F) (120)
1 oz. mozzarella cheese, melted (P,F) (80)
1 cup raw vegetables (carrots, broccoli, tomato slices, cucumber) (C) (25)
1 large fruit (C) (80)

### Shrimp Creole/Salad/Fruit (515)

Mix and heat:
1 cup rice (C) (140)
1 cup tomato sauce* (C) (70)
Steamed celery, onion, seasonings (0)
10 frozen cooked shrimp (P,F) (120)
Tossed lettuce with raw vegetables (C) (25)
with 1 T. oil and vinegar (F) (80)
1 large apple (C) (80)

### Low-Calorie Frozen Dinner/Salad/ Fruit (350-500)

Low-calorie frozen meal (i.e., Lean Cuisine,* Weight Watchers,* etc.) (P,C,F) (300 or less calories per meal)
Tossed lettuce salad with raw vegetables (C) (25)
with 1 T. oil and vinegar (F) (80)

Steamed Vegetables/Rice/Cheese/Fruit, continued

(optional sugar substitute for sweetness)

## Tuna-Noodle Vegetable Casserole (500)

Mix and heat until cheese melts:
½ cup tuna (in water)* (P,F) (120)
1 cup noodles (C) (140)
1 cup vegetables (C) (50)
1 oz. grated low-fat cheese (P,F) (80)
¼ cup 2% milk (P,C) (30)
1 large fruit (C) (80)

## Steak/Potato/Vegetable/Salad (455)

3 oz. broiled filet (P,F) (210)
1 small potato (C) (70)
Tossed lettuce with raw vegetables (C) (25)
with 1 T. salad dressing* (F) (80)
½ cup steamed green beans with mushrooms (C) (25)
3 tsp. diet margarine (F) (45)

Low-Calorie Frozen Dinner/Salad/Fruit, continued

1 cup fresh fruit salad (C) (80)

## Grilled Patties/Vegetables/Salad/Fruit/Bread (415)

Mix ½ cup tuna (in water),* salmon* or chicken (P,F) (120)
with seasonings (onion, parsley, etc.) (0)
plus 1 raw egg (P,F) (80)
Mold into patties and grill in a nonstick pan.
½ cup broccoli (C) (25)
Lettuce wedge (0) + 1 T. Italian dressing* (F) (80)
½ cup fruit cocktail (in own juice) (C) (40)
1 slice whole wheat bread (or 2 thin slices ) (C) (70)

## French Toast/Fruit/Tomato Slices (425)

French toast: Mix 1 whole egg (P,F) (80) +
1 egg white (P) (0)
¼ cup 2% milk (P,F) (30)
½ tsp. vanilla extract (0)
Soak 2 slices whole wheat bread (C) (140) in the mixture.
Cook on grill with nonstick cooking spray (0)
1 T. honey, jelly, syrup or 2 T. lite syrup (C) (70)
1 cup grapefruit sections (C) (80)
4 tomato slices (C) (25)

P = protein
C = complex carbohydrates
F = fat

*High-sodium. For low-sodium intake, select unsalted or low-sodium varieties.
Note: "Low-fat cheese" refers to mozzarella, farmer's, skim ricotta and 1–2% fat cottage cheese.

## Weight-Loss Precept #5

### For Slower, Safer Weight Loss over an Indefinite Period, Follow the Formula: 250 + 500 + 250 = 1,000 Calories a Day

The ideal weight-reduction program is one that satisfies all your nutritive needs—except for calories—yet leaves you with a minimum of fatigue at the end of the day. That's why we prefer a well-balanced 1,000-calorie-a-day diet to those that are more miserly.

You'll notice that both the 850-calorie diet and the 1,000-calorie diet distribute daily calories so that lunch is your biggest meal. This is by design. We refer to it as the 25-50-25 Rule.

This is the typical eating pattern of an obese woman:

She eats no breakfast, hardly any lunch, but loads up at dinnertime, when she consumes 70 percent of her daily calories. The problem with this pattern is that it goes counter to human beings' natural circadian (24-hour) rhythm.

Most people's internal systems reach their peak activity level in midday. (We're excluding, of course, people who work a night shift or, for some other reason, turn night into day.) This being the case, it's only logical to eat the largest meal of the day at a time when your system is primed to convert food into energy the fastest and most efficiently. Eating a big meal at the end of the day when you're winding down and preparing for sleep is illogical, is it not?

When you add the variable of exercise to your daily schedule, you do alter somewhat the circadian rhythm we just described. However, we still think it advisable to eat more calories at midday and fewer at dinner than is the American norm.

## Weight-Loss Precept #6

### Incorporate Aerobic Exercise into Your Weight-Loss Program

It's well known that women who get hooked on fad diets—many of which are extremely restrictive and unbalanced—often fall victim to the yo-yo syndrome. They lose weight all right, but they put it right back on the moment they try to eat normally again.

There's a logical, physiological explanation for this phenomenon. It concerns your metabolism.

Metabolism is that complex biochemical process by which food is converted to energy in your body. Dieting has a profound effect on metabolism. Unfortunately, dieting has the wrong effect—just the reverse of what you are trying to achieve. The crux of the problem is this:

When you go on an extreme diet without exercising, your metabolism swings into survival mode. Denied food, your body tries to conserve its reserves—those fat deposits you want to rid yourself of. Instead of burning fat faster, it burns it more slowly—and last. That initial weight loss you experience isn't the loss of adipose tissue at all. More likely it is the loss of glycogen, water, and muscle tissue. (Glycogen is the storage fuel in your muscles.)

Perhaps the bitterest irony of all: the longer you stay on your extreme diet, the more difficult it becomes to lose weight. Once your metabolism settles into low gear, it converts body tissue—fat tissue or otherwise—into energy at a much slower pace than before you began your diet. This is why some obese people, perennially on diets, "eat like birds" and still get fatter.

That's not the worst of it. When you go off your diet, your metabolism doesn't go off it with you. It continues on the slow course you set for it during your diet. The result: you'll gain weight more easily than ever before.

One Swedish study of men who had been on a 600-calorie powdered protein diet showed that they still had a lowered metabolic rate more than one year after going off the diet. Studies also show that every time people put weight back on after a severe diet, they tend to lay down arterial plaque at an accelerated rate as well as increase the size of fat cells in their bodies. They end up getting fatter and fatter with each yo-yo episode.

Exercise is the antidote to this metabolic dilemma. Unlike the color of your eyes or hair, your metabolism is not fixed at birth. You can control it to some extent—through exercise.

While severe dieting slows your metabolic rate, exercise raises it, sustaining it at an elevated level long after the period of vigorous activity has ceased. A metabolism in high gear, of course, is burning off fat tissue—precisely what you're trying to accomplish. This is why exercise is the perfect complement to a *moderately restrictive* diet.

We say "moderately restrictive" because exercise requires a minimum energy level. For this reason, we recommend for exercisers a diet of no fewer than 1,000 calories per day for any period of time.

At the Aerobics Center, we counsel many extremely athletic patients about weight loss. A woman who swims many hours every week, for example, may have to adhere to a diet higher than 1,000 calories per day. But because of all the calories she's burning off in the swimming pool, she'll still lose weight.

As we said earlier, it's just a matter of arithmetic—figuring the calories you take in versus the calories you expend every day. The following chart, "Exercise Equivalents for Food and Beverage Calories in Minutes," will help you with your daily calorie addition and subtraction calculations.

## Exercise Equivalents of Food and Beverage Calories in Minutes*

| Cooper Clinic Exercise Constants | | 12.50 | 5.62 | 7.81 | 9.09 | 12.04 |
|---|---|---|---|---|---|---|
| | | Walking 4 mph | Running 6 mph | Swimming 30 yds/min. | Stationary Bicycling | Aerobic Dance** |
| Food | Calories | min. | min. | min. | min. | min. |
| BEVERAGES | | | | | | |
| Beer 12 oz. | 150 | 33 | 15 | 21 | 24 | 32 |
| Carbonated soft drink 12 oz. | 160 | 35 | 16 | 22 | 26 | 34 |
| Coffee, sugar and cream 1 cup 1 tsp. 1 T. | 50 | 11 | 5 | 7 | 8 | 11 |
| Gin, rum, vodka, whiskey 1 oz. | 70 | 15 | 7 | 10 | 11 | 15 |
| Lemonade 8 oz. | 90 | 20 | 9 | 12 | 14 | 19 |
| Manhattan cocktail 3½ oz. | 165 | 36 | 16 | 23 | 26 | 35 |
| Martini cocktail 3½ oz. | 140 | 31 | 14 | 19 | 22 | 30 |
| Milkshake, homemade 12 oz. | 420 | 92 | 42 | 58 | 67 | 89 |
| Old-fashioned cocktail 4 oz. | 180 | 40 | 18 | 25 | 29 | 38 |
| Tom Collins 10 oz. | 180 | 40 | 18 | 25 | 29 | 38 |
| Wine 3½ oz. | 80 | 17 | 8 | 11 | 13 | 17 |
| CANDY | | | | | | |
| Candy, hard (all flavors) 1 oz. | 110 | 24 | 11 | 15 | 18 | 23 |
| Fudge, chocolate 1 oz. | 110 | 24 | 11 | 15 | 18 | 23 |
| Hershey bar 1.02 oz. | 160 | 35 | 16 | 22 | 26 | 34 |
| Mars bar 1.7 oz. | 230 | 51 | 23 | 32 | 37 | 49 |
| Snickers bar 2 oz. | 270 | 60 | 27 | 37 | 43 | 57 |

| Cooper Clinic Exercise Constants | | 12.50 | 5.62 | 7.81 | 9.09 | 12.04 |
|---|---|---|---|---|---|---|
| | | Walking 4 mph | Running 6 mph | Swimming 30 yds/min. | Stationary Bicycling | Aerobic Dance** |
| Food | Calories | min. | min. | min. | min. | min. |
| **CEREALS** | | | | | | |
| Dry cereal, nonsugar 1 oz. | 110 | 24 | 11 | 15 | 18 | 23 |
| Oatmeal, cooked ¾ cup | 110 | 24 | 11 | 15 | 18 | 23 |
| **CHEESE** | | | | | | |
| Cheese, American 1 oz. | 95 | 21 | 9 | 13 | 15 | 20 |
| Cheese, Brie 1 oz. | 95 | 21 | 9 | 13 | 15 | 20 |
| Cheese, cheddar 1 oz. | 115 | 25 | 11 | 16 | 18 | 24 |
| Cheese, cottage, low-fat ½ cup | 100 | 22 | 10 | 14 | 16 | 21 |
| Cheese, cream 1 oz. | 100 | 22 | 10 | 14 | 16 | 21 |
| **COMBINATION FOODS** | | | | | | |
| Beef and vegetable stew 1 cup | 220 | 48 | 22 | 30 | 35 | 47 |
| Bacon, lettuce, and tomato sandwich, with mayo on white bread | 280 | 61 | 28 | 39 | 45 | 59 |
| Cheeseburger | 320 | 70 | 32 | 44 | 51 | 68 |
| Chicken salad sandwich on whole wheat bread | 250 | 55 | 25 | 34 | 40 | 53 |
| Chili, canned 1 cup | 320 | 70 | 32 | 44 | 51 | 68 |
| Frozen "Lite" dinner 1 average | 300 | 66 | 30 | 41 | 48 | 64 |
| Pancake, with 2 T. butter and 1 tsp. syrup | 300 | 66 | 30 | 41 | 48 | 64 |
| 1 T. Peanut butter and 1 tsp. jelly sandwich, on 1 slice white bread | 170 | 37 | 17 | 23 | 27 | 36 |

| | Cooper Clinic Exercise Constants | 12.50 | 5.62 | 7.81 | 9.09 | 12.04 |
|---|---|---|---|---|---|---|
| | | Walking 4 mph | Running 6 mph | Swimming 30 yds/min. | Stationary Bicycling | Aerobic Dance** |
| Food | Calories | min. | min. | min. | min. | min. |
| COMBINATION FOODS, continued | | | | | | |
| Pizza, pepperoni, frozen ¼ of 14″ pie | 360 | 80 | 36 | 50 | 58 | 76 |
| Spaghetti with tomato sauce 8 oz. | 180 | 40 | 18 | 25 | 29 | 38 |
| Taco | 175 | 39 | 17 | 24 | 28 | 37 |
| Turkey sandwich, with lettuce on whole wheat bread | 240 | 53 | 24 | 33 | 38 | 51 |
| **DESSERTS** | | | | | | |
| Banana split | 540 | 119 | 53 | 74 | 86 | 115 |
| Brownie 1 piece | 130 | 29 | 13 | 18 | 21 | 28 |
| Cinnamon roll, with icing 1 small | 120 | 26 | 12 | 17 | 19 | 25 |
| Chocolate cake, with icing, 1 piece (2″ × 3″ × 2″) | 230 | 51 | 23 | 32 | 37 | 49 |
| Cookie, chocolate chip 1 cookie | 50 | 11 | 5 | 7 | 8 | 11 |
| Cookie, oatmeal 1 cookie | 80 | 18 | 8 | 11 | 13 | 17 |
| Doughnut, cake 1 average | 105 | 23 | 10 | 14 | 17 | 22 |
| Doughnut, with jelly center 1 average | 226 | 50 | 22 | 31 | 36 | 48 |
| Ice cream 1 cup | 270 | 59 | 27 | 37 | 43 | 57 |
| Ice cream bar, with chocolate coating 1 bar | 160 | 35 | 16 | 22 | 26 | 34 |
| Ice milk 1 cup | 185 | 41 | 18 | 25 | 30 | 39 |
| Pie, fruit 1 slice | 400 | 88 | 40 | 55 | 64 | 85 |

| Food | Cooper Clinic Exercise Constants | 12.50 | 5.62 | 7.81 | 9.09 | 12.04 |
|---|---|---|---|---|---|---|
| | | Walking 4 mph | Running 6 mph | Swimming 30 yds/min. | Stationary Bicycling | Aerobic Dance** |
| Food | Calories | min. | min. | min. | min. | min. |
| DESSERTS, continued | | | | | | |
| Pie, pecan 1 slice | 500 | 110 | 49 | 69 | 80 | 106 |
| **EGGS** | | | | | | |
| Egg, boiled 1 large | 80 | 18 | 8 | 11 | 13 | 17 |
| Egg, fried or scrambled, with 1 tsp. oil 1 large | 125 | 28 | 12 | 17 | 20 | 27 |
| Egg omelet, plain 1 egg | 100 | 22 | 10 | 14 | 16 | 21 |
| **FATS** | | | | | | |
| Bacon, fried 1 slice | 35 | 8 | 3 | 5 | 6 | 7 |
| Butter or margarine 1 tsp. | 40 | 9 | 4 | 6 | 6 | 8 |
| Salad dressing, blue cheese 1 T. | 80 | 18 | 8 | 11 | 13 | 17 |
| Salad dressing, French 1 T. | 70 | 15 | 7 | 10 | 11 | 15 |
| Salad dressing, low-calorie 1 T. | 25 | 6 | 2 | 3 | 4 | 5 |
| Sour cream, cultured 1 T. | 30 | 7 | 3 | 4 | 5 | 6 |
| **FISH** | | | | | | |
| Catfish, fried 3½ oz. | 220 | 48 | 22 | 30 | 35 | 47 |
| Salmon, broiled 3½ oz. | 180 | 40 | 18 | 25 | 29 | 38 |
| Tuna, canned in water 3 oz. | 110 | 24 | 11 | 15 | 18 | 23 |

| | Cooper Clinic Exercise Constants | 12.50 | 5.62 | 7.81 | 9.09 | 12.04 |
|---|---|---|---|---|---|---|
| | | Walking 4 mph | Running 6 mph | Swimming 30 yds/min. | Stationary Bicycling | Aerobic Dance** |
| **Food** | **Calories** | **min.** | **min.** | **min.** | **min.** | **min.** |
| **FRUITS** | | | | | | |
| Apple, raw 1 medium (2½" diam.) | 80 | 18 | 8 | 11 | 13 | 17 |
| Apricots, dried 10 halves | 80 | 18 | 8 | 11 | 13 | 17 |
| Banana 1 medium | 105 | 23 | 10 | 14 | 17 | 22 |
| Cantaloupe 1 cup | 60 | 13 | 6 | 8 | 10 | 13 |
| Grapes 1 cup | 60 | 13 | 6 | 8 | 10 | 13 |
| Orange juice 8 oz. | 105 | 23 | 10 | 14 | 17 | 22 |
| Raisins ⅔ cup | 300 | 66 | 30 | 41 | 48 | 63 |
| **GRAIN PRODUCTS** | | | | | | |
| Bagel 1 small | 160 | 35 | 16 | 22 | 26 | 34 |
| Bread, whole wheat 1 slice | 60 | 13 | 6 | 8 | 10 | 13 |
| Crackers, graham 2 squares | 60 | 13 | 6 | 8 | 10 | 13 |
| Crackers, Ritz 4 crackers | 70 | 15 | 7 | 10 | 11 | 15 |
| Crackers, soda 4 crackers | 48 | 11 | 5 | 7 | 8 | 10 |
| English muffin, with butter (4" diam.) 1 tsp. | 180 | 40 | 18 | 25 | 29 | 38 |
| French toast, with 2 T. syrup 1 slice | 165 | 36 | 16 | 23 | 26 | 35 |
| Melba toast 4 pieces | 60 | 13 | 6 | 8 | 10 | 13 |
| Noodles ⅗ cup from 1 oz. dry | 110 | 24 | 11 | 15 | 18 | 23 |

| Cooper Clinic Exercise Constants | | 12.50 | 5.62 | 7.81 | 9.09 | 12.04 |
|---|---|---|---|---|---|---|
| | | Walking 4 mph | Running 6 mph | Swimming 30 yds/min. | Stationary Bicycling | Aerobic Dance** |
| **Food** | **Calories** | **min.** | **min.** | **min.** | **min.** | **min.** |
| GRAIN PRODUCTS, continued | | | | | | |
| Pancake, plain 1 large | 160 | 35 | 16 | 22 | 26 | 34 |
| Rice, instant, cooked, ⅔ cup | 125 | 28 | 12 | 17 | 20 | 27 |
| **MEATS** | | | | | | |
| Beef tenderloin 3 oz. | 222 | 49 | 22 | 31 | 36 | 47 |
| Ham, cured 3 oz. | 140 | 31 | 14 | 19 | 22 | 30 |
| Peanut butter 1 T. | 90 | 20 | 9 | 12 | 14 | 19 |
| Pork, loin chop 3 oz. | 310 | 68 | 31 | 43 | 50 | 66 |
| Veal cutlet, cooked 3 oz. | 240 | 53 | 24 | 33 | 38 | 51 |
| **MILK** | | | | | | |
| Milk, skim 8 oz. | 86 | 19 | 9 | 12 | 14 | 18 |
| Milk, whole 8 oz. | 150 | 33 | 15 | 21 | 24 | 32 |
| Yogurt, with fruit 1 cup | 225 | 50 | 22 | 31 | 36 | 48 |
| Yogurt, plain, low-fat 1 cup | 150 | 33 | 15 | 21 | 24 | 32 |
| **POULTRY** | | | | | | |
| Chicken, roasted without skin 3½-oz. breast | 140 | 31 | 14 | 19 | 22 | 30 |
| Chicken, fried with skin 3½-oz. breast | 330 | 73 | 33 | 45 | 53 | 70 |
| Turkey, dark meat, smoked 3½ oz. | 120 | 26 | 33 | 16 | 19 | 25 |

| Cooper Clinic Exercise Constants | | 12.50 | 5.62 | 7.81 | 9.09 | 12.04 |
|---|---|---|---|---|---|---|
| | | Walking 4 mph | Running 6 mph | Swimming 30 yds/min. | Stationary Bicycling | Aerobic Dance** |
| Food | Calories | min. | min. | min. | min. | min. |
| **SNACKS** | | | | | | |
| Peanuts 1 oz. | 170 | 37 | 17 | 23 | 27 | 36 |
| Popcorn 1 cup | 54 | 12 | 5 | 7 | 9 | 11 |
| Potato chips 10 pieces | 115 | 25 | 11 | 16 | 18 | 24 |
| Pretzels 1 oz. | 110 | 24 | 11 | 15 | 18 | 23 |
| **SOUPS** | | | | | | |
| Bouillon, chicken 1 cup | 20 | 4 | 2 | 3 | 3 | 4 |
| Minestrone 1 cup | 90 | 20 | 9 | 12 | 14 | 19 |
| **VEGETABLES** | | | | | | |
| Asparagus, cooked ⅔ cup | 20 | 4 | 2 | 3 | 3 | 4 |
| Avocado, raw ½ medium | 160 | 35 | 16 | 22 | 26 | 34 |
| Broccoli, raw 1 stalk | 30 | 7 | 3 | 4 | 5 | 6 |
| Carrots, cooked ⅔ cup | 30 | 7 | 3 | 4 | 5 | 6 |
| Corn, sweet, with 1 tsp. butter 1 ear | 140 | 30 | 14 | 19 | 22 | 30 |
| Potato, baked 1 large | 140 | 31 | 14 | 19 | 22 | 30 |
| Potato, french-fried 20 pieces | 280 | 62 | 28 | 39 | 45 | 59 |
| Three-bean salad ⅖ cup | 75 | 17 | 7 | 10 | 12 | 16 |

*This chart is calculated for a 125-pound reference person. To estimate the exercise equivalent in minutes for different weights: Minutes = Calories × Cooper Clinic Exercise Constant × $\frac{2.2}{\text{Weight in pounds}}$

**Calories burned will vary depending on intensity of aerobic dance workout.

A cautionary word to women who aren't used to exercising:

*Begin slowly.* A brisk walking program is all a severely obese woman should expect to do for several months until she loses some weight. As we explained in the F.I.T. formula in chapter 4 (p. 29), walking can burn just as many calories as running. A walker just has to stay out on the track for a longer time each day than the runner.

Obese exercisers are also more susceptible to hot weather, so they should take to heart all our environmental advice in chapter 10.

**Progressive Walking Program for the Excessively Overweight Individual***
(To Be Used in Conjunction with Dieting)

| Week | Distance (miles) | Time Goal (min) | Freq/Wk | Points/Wk |
|---|---|---|---|---|
| 1 | 2.0 | 40:30 | 3 | 3 |
| 2 | 2.0 | 39:00 | 3 | 9 |
| 3 | 2.0 | 38:00 | 4 | 12 |
| 4 | 2.0 | 37:00 | 4 | 12 |
| 5 | 2.0 | 36:00 | 5 | 15 |
| 6 | 2.0 | 35:00 | 5 | 15 |
| 7 | 2.5 | 45:00 | 5 | 20 |
| 8 | 2.5 | 43:00 | 5 | 20 |
| 9 | 3.0 | 52:00 | 5 | 25 |
| 10 | 3.0 | 51:00 | 5 | 25 |
| 11 | 3.0 | 50:00 | 5 | 25 |
| 12 | 3.0 | 49:00 | 5 | 25 |
| 13 | 3.0 | 48:00 | 5 | 25 |
| 14 | 3.0 | 47:00 | 5 | 25 |
| 15 | 3.0 | 46:00 | 5 | 25 |
| 16 | 3.0 | <45:00 | 4 | 32 |

*After completing the progressive program, either continue with the final program listed above or select one of the maintenance programs that follow the progressive programs; or develop a program of your own from The Point System charts in the Appendix.

When you're exercising to lose weight, the length of each exercise session is key. Work out at a pace that you can sustain for more than half an hour. Why? During the first few minutes of each workout, your body is burning mainly carbohydrates. Only as your exercise period continues does adipose tissue become the predominant fuel supply. Thus, the intensity of your effort is less critical than time when you're focusing on weight loss.

## Weight-Loss Precept #7

### Exercise before Eating, Preferably before Dinner

The timing of exercise also figures into the weight-loss equation.

Unfortunately, when to exercise to facilitate the greatest loss of body fat is still a controversial subject. Some studies show that morning exercise or exercise right *after meals* is the most effective. Other research, including studies here at the Aerobics Center, pinpoints exercise *before meals*, particularly before dinner, as the optimum time.

People attending our In-Residence Weight Reduction Program exercise for 30 minutes *before* each meal. Contrary to expectations, vigorous exercise does not make them ravenous. Rather, it suppresses their appetites. That's all to the good. Since our women participants are on our most restrictive diet for the two weeks that they're here, suppressing their food cravings stretches those 850 calories, making them seem more adequate than they would under other circumstances.

There's another reason we recommend exercise before meals—preferably before dinner if you exercise only once a day. As we explained, exercise speeds up your metabolism. If your metabolism is going at top speed while you're eating, it will burn more of the food calories passing through your system.

On the other hand, some experts argue that exercise right after a meal has the same effect. This may be true, but it's not always pleasant to exercise on a full stomach, and it may be dangerous if you have undiagnosed heart disease.

We think the appetite-suppression mechanism that before-meal exercise triggers is reason enough to add it to your arsenal of weight-loss weapons. Anything that makes dieting more pleasant—and also works, as before-meal exercise does—is worth deploying.

While the studies focusing on when to exercise haven't given us a definitive answer, they have proved something else:

Regardless of the time of day that you work out, weight-reduction programs that couple exercise with moderately low-calorie diets result in maximum fat-tissue loss and minimum muscle-tissue loss. Some of these studies have even shown muscle gain.

At the opposite end of the spectrum are diets with no exercise component. They invariably burn up muscle tissue.

## Weight-Loss Precept #8

### To Stay Slim, Change Your Thinking as Well as Your Eating Habits

We have yet another formula for you. This one is very easy. It will help you change your thinking as well as your behavior on the way to developing that svelte profile you dream about.

The thought-jogger is:

**4Ws and an H**

It stands for:

**What** you eat
**Where** you eat
**Why** you eat
**When** you eat
and
**How** you eat

If you've never thought about your eating habits in this way before, do so now.

Given your druthers, *what* do you eat? In chapter 12 we discussed what you *should* eat. Compare what you do eat with our recommendations.

*Where* you eat: Sometimes we make strange associations between places and food. For example, you may be a person who can't go to sleep at night without a little snack. That's a bad habit; break it. You might make a rule: *The only time I will eat in my house is at the table.*

*Why* you eat: All sorts of feelings and situations can trigger hunger. For some people, it's boredom; for others, stress. This isn't true hunger. It's sublimation. For a two-week period, ask yourself "Why?" every time you put food in your mouth, and see what you discover.

Monitor *when* you eat every day. Regular eating habits, centered around three balanced meals a day, is the best practice. For weight loss, distributing your calorie intake so it conforms to the 25-50-25 Rule (see p. 203) is advisable. If weight loss is not necessary, follow a 25-30-45 pattern.

*How* involves style. Do you eat on the run? In such a haphazard, grab-a-bite way that it seems as if you're always eating? Hardly at all some days, and like a person just released from a concentration camp the next? Eat three nutritious meals a day and make sure each meal has a beginning, a middle, and an end to it. Remember, sensible people eat to live. Only gourmands—fat ones at that—live to eat.

## Fit Tips: Behavior Change to Keep Fat off My Frame

Let's find out how far you're really willing to go to eliminate your weight problem. The following statements focus on counterproductive attitudes and habits that could be sabotaging your weight-loss efforts or your ability to maintain your ideal weight once you achieve it.

The following are negative behaviors. Checkmarks next to any of them mean you've still got some work to do to keep your weight in line.

**I have to admit that:**

| | True | False |
|---|---|---|
| **I eat only when I'm hungry. I eat a lot some days and next to nothing on other days.** | ____ | ____ |

This shows no self-control. Establish consistent eating patterns based on three meals a day, consumed every five to six hours. This stabilizes your blood sugar, which regulates appetite, energy levels, and your ability to handle stress. Scheduled eating will also help stop you from bingeing when you get a sudden urge.

**I eat fast.** ____ ____

You'll find food more satisfying if you savor it. Devote at least twenty minutes to each meal. No matter how much you've eaten, it takes this long for your stomach to tell your brain that you're full.

**I sometimes keep eating beyond the point when I feel full in order to clean my plate.** ____ ____

Listen to your body's messages—and don't feel guilty if you can't finish everything. Be thankful if your appetite is growing smaller.

**I prefer "soft" foods to "crunchy" foods.** ____ ____

Crunchy foods, such as apples, take longer to chew than soft foods, such as bananas. For this reason alone, jaw-workout food is more satisfying. Besides, we *need* to chew. It relieves stress and tension.

**I eat what's available when mealtime rolls around.** ____ ____

Planning and regularity are the essence of weight loss and maintenance. Think before you grocery shop. Then, when mealtime arrives, you can follow the adage: Same time, same place, same categories of wholesome foods, same calorie totals each day.

**I force myself to eat specific foods, day in and day out, when I'm on a strict reducing diet.** ____ ____

You're punishing yourself needlessly. Eat a variety of foods based on the 50 percent (complex carbohydrates) + 20 percent (protein) + 30 percent (fat) equation. Just don't go beyond your daily calorie ceiling.

**I hate counting calories, so I guess.** ____ ____

In the beginning, you must write down your daily calorie intake and expenditure. Later, you won't need to be so meticulous. You can let experience be your guide.

| | True | False |
|---|---|---|
| **I don't own a food scale and estimate each portion.** | ______ | ______ |

There's only one way to be sure you're consuming only X number of calories. That's by knowing how much each portion of food weighs or measures, or by reading the labels on processed foods. Any other way and you're fooling yourself. But you're not fooling your body!

**I consider a big dinner one of the highlights of my day.** ______ ______

Be rational. You don't have to stuff your stomach to enjoy the conviviality of an evening meal with family or friends—or any celebratory event, for that matter. Psychologically sever the association between fun and food.

**I look forward to second helpings so I serve food in bowls, family-style.** ______ ______

Get used to putting the correct portions on your plate at the stove. Don't have serving dishes on the table—go back to the stove for more.

**I feel deprived when I see those moderate portions on my plate.** ______ ______

Substitute a smaller plate so that the food on it will look more plentiful.

**I like to linger at the table and talk.** ______ ______

Tables and food go together. When you've finished eating, get up and go into another room to chat.

**I drink alcohol almost every day to relieve stress.** ______ ______

Exercise is a much better relaxer. And there are others—hobbies, socializing, reading "escape" fiction, and so on. Limit yourself to 1 beer, a 2-ounce cocktail, or 6 ounces of wine per day. Those are the equivalent of 150 non-nutritive calories.

**I eat mostly processed diet food because it saves time.** ______ ______

Fresh fruits and raw vegetables don't take any time to prepare and they're better for you. Add them to your daily fare.

**I drink a lot of coffee, tea, and/or diet soda.** ______ ______

Your body needs six to eight glasses of fluids every day. The more you stay with water, the better. Other

| | True | False |
|---|---|---|
| healthful substitutes are low-fat milk, unsweetened fruit juices, and low-salt soups. | | |
| **I avoid starchy foods I consider fattening such as bread, potatoes, rice, pasta, and corn.** | ______ | ______ |

These are excellent complex carbohydrates. Don't cut them out of your diet. Just reduce the portions.

**I cheat sometimes and snack.** ______ ______

Snacking isn't all bad—although one snack a day should suffice. It's the food you choose that makes the difference. Eat low-calorie snacks: unbuttered popcorn; puffed cereals; broth; diet candy; unsweetened yogurt; raw fruits and vegetables.

**I can't seem to resist those hunger pangs when I watch television (or read, or go to the movies, or sew).** ______ ______

You'd be surprised at the odd cues that switch on people's appetites. Be aware of yours. Then break the association. Try sipping a tall glass of refreshing ice water during the next episode of your favorite sitcom. Drinking fluids helps you to feel full.

**I hop in the car to run errands when I could just as easily do them on foot.** ______ ______

The more calories you expend through activity and exercise each day, the more calories you can take in without adding pounds. Think about it the next time you get lazy and reach for the car keys . . . or buy an appliance that eliminates the need for elbow grease . . . or turn down a chance to play tennis in favor of doing something sedentary.

*Your weight is within your control. So control it!*

## Summing Up: Your Weight-Loss Goals

- Lose 1 to 2 pounds per week.
- Lower your body-fat ratio.
- Build lean body mass (muscle) through exercise.

- Count calories to make sure you are consuming fewer than you expend through activity and exercise.
- Eat a sufficient number of calories to prevent fatigue.
- Prevent a slowdown of your metabolic rate through exercise.
- Plan nutritionally balanced meals based on the 50 percent (complex carbohydrates) + 20 percent (protein) + 30 percent (fat) formula.
- Maintain your ideal weight once you achieve it by changing negative habits and attitudes.

## A Weight-Loss Success Story

Since 1984, Ann Morgan has been one of the Aerobics Center's most active members. Slimming down was her initial impetus for joining, but other factors have kept her here, as she explains:

> My family isn't especially athletic but they're not obese either. I was the one with the weight problem. As a child and young woman, it made me feel different and unhappy.
>
> My mother never nagged me. But every once in a while she would say, "When are you going to do something about your weight, Ann?"
>
> I guess the message finally sank in. I'll never forget it. I suppose the same kind of thing happens to people who suddenly become motivated to give up smoking or alcohol. I just woke up one morning—I was 22 years old—and I said to myself, "I'm going to do something about these useless pounds *right now.*"
>
> When I joined the Aerobics Center, I weighed 225 pounds; I'm 5 feet 4 inches tall. That put me in the "severe obesity" category, since my ideal weight is around 130.
>
> Today, after thousands of hours of exercise and a different eating pattern, I weigh 150. I'm still losing, slowly now, ounce by ounce, but steadily. In fact, the whole process was more gradual than it was dramatic.
>
> In the very beginning, I followed a meal plan that added up to about 850 calories a day. But I don't feel I ever went on a "diet." An Aerobics Center dietitian just taught me about eating healthful foods in the right amounts. I did cut out sweets, though.
>
> Now, I eat around 1,000 calories a day since I'm still trying to shed pounds. I know approximately how many calories are in things and I'm careful without being obsessive about it.
>
> I started out walking 2 miles a day. Next, I added a workout on the Schwinn Air-Dyne stationary bicycle. I found I enjoyed exercising so much that I've tried just about everything the Center has to offer. To keep my interest up, I

mix and match things. I run 6 miles a day. Then, I may do the Air-Dyne for 30 minutes, swim, lift weights, or take an aerobics dance class.

I feel so much better when I exercise. Not long ago, I had my gallbladder removed. The operation was on a Thursday and I was back at the Aerobics Center the next Tuesday walking around the track. My doctor said walking was all right, so I got back to it as soon as possible.

Ann has become so engrossed in this subject that she has now gone back to college and is working toward a master's degree in exercise physiology.

## Other Success Stories—You Can Be One of Them

The Aerobics Center sponsors formal wellness/weight-loss programs, called the In-Residence Programs. The programs attract people from all walks of life, ranging in age from 19 to 75.

Improving overall health is what the programs are all about. Each thirteen-day program, with its maximum of twenty participants, usually has about half women. While weight loss is often an important goal for our female participants, it's by no means the only one.

Following are some typical results achieved by three women who attended our programs:

**Name:** C. A.
**Age:** 49
**Height:** 62.75 inches
**Ideal weight:** 135
**Diagnosis:** moderate obesity

| | Before Program | After 2 Weeks | After 1 Year |
|---|---|---|---|
| Actual weight: | 189.5 lbs. | 182.5 lbs. | 136 lbs. |
| Body fat: | 37.5% | — | — |
| Cholesterol: | 205 | 158 | — |
| Chol/HDL ratio: | 3.5 | 3.2 | — |
| Triglycerides: | 64 | 62 | — |
| Treadmill time: | 9:44 minutes (poor category) | 11:20 minutes (fair category) | — |

### Exercise Workout Schedule

**0–3 months:** WALKING 7 times a week/80 minutes each session (5 miles)
**3–6 months:** WALKING 7 times a week/35 minutes each session (2.5 miles)
**6–12 months:** WALKING 5 times a week/35 minutes each session (2.5 miles)

### Diet

No sweets or fried foods. Decreased red meats. Increased fruits and vegetables.

**Name:** Beth Perry
**Age:** 31
**Height:** 66.25 inches
**Ideal weight:** 155
**Diagnosis:** mild obesity

| | Before Program | After 2 Weeks | After 10 Months |
|---|---|---|---|
| Actual weight: | 196 lbs. | 186.75 lbs. | 169 lbs. |
| Body fat: | 36.5% | — | 27% |
| Cholesterol: | 194 | 141 | 191 |
| Chol/HDL ratio: | 4.7 | 2.9 | 3.5 |
| Triglycerides: | 124 | 87 | 85 |
| Treadmill time: | 13 minutes (fair category) | 17:16 minutes (good category) | 22 minutes (superior category) |

### Exercise Workout Schedule

| | |
|---|---|
| Running: | 3–4 times a week/30 minutes each session (3+ miles) |
| Outdoor Cycling: (in season) | 1–2 times a week/30–60 minutes each session (10–25 miles); 1 time a week (30–40 miles) |
| Weight training: | 3 times a week/30–45 minutes each session |
| Wind trainer or Air-Dyne: (mostly winter) | 3–4 times a week/30 minutes each session |

"I alternate the above activities. For example, if I run on Monday, I try to ride on Tuesday. Weight training is a Monday-Wednesday-Friday venture. The wind trainer/Air-Dyne workout occurs at home whenever the mood strikes and time allows."

—Beth Perry

**Name:** B. C.
**Age:** 51
**Height:** 63.5 inches
**Ideal weight:** 165
**Diagnosis:** severe obesity

| | Before Program | After 1 Year 6 Months |
|---|---|---|
| Actual weight: | 226 lbs. | 158 lbs. |
| Body fat: | 42.5% | — |

| | Before Program | After 1 Year 6 Months |
|---|---|---|
| Cholesterol: | 169 | 190 |
| Chol/HDL ratio: | 2.4 | — |
| Triglycerides: | 97 | 84 |
| Treadmill time: | 5:54 minutes (very poor category) | — |

**Exercise Workout Schedule**

| | |
|---|---|
| Swimming: | 3 times a week/45 minutes each session (½ mile) |
| Low-impact Aerobics: | 3 times a week/30 minutes each session |

# A Question about Cellulite

I'd like to share a letter we received recently from Sue Ann Smith, a Houston woman worried about cellulite. Since I suspect she's not alone in her concern, her query and our reply ought to prove helpful:

> I feel odd actually writing to ask someone about this, but I have read so many different opinions about it, I'm confused.
>
> I'm a 28½-year-old female, 5 feet 4 inches, 115 pounds (about 10 pounds overweight) and I have an awful case of cellulite. I know that cellulite is fatty tissue but it doesn't seem to go away evenly like the rest of my fat when I'm dieting or exercising.
>
> I've read the cottage-cheese appearance is due to the fibers that bind the fat. If that's true, how do you get rid of the fibers? Some say the only way to get rid of cellulite is through intense, painful massage. Some say you need to get down to your ideal weight—in my case, 105. Is this true? Does all other fat have to be off your thighs and buttocks before you can hope to see the beginning of the disappearance of cellulite?
>
> I started getting cellulite about six years ago. It's gotten worse and is slowly but surely moving down my thighs. This year, I'm afraid to wear shorts, let alone suffer the humiliation of a swimsuit. I have a very athletic boyfriend who loves to swim, as I do; and I'm going to embarrass him in public, as well as myself, if I can't find a way to do something about it.
>
> I read also that walking an hour a day for five days a week helps more than running because your walk stride is different and concentrates more on the thighs, hamstrings, and buttocks, where a woman's cellulite is located.
>
> This year, I've decided to start a new "healthy" life. I exercise four to five hours a week. I quit smoking on New Year's Eve but I gained 7 pounds from that so I started a diet on February 1. I'm taking it nice and slow and losing an average of a pound a week. I'm eating healthy food and feeling better. I know

that with continued exercise and good food, I can get down to my ideal weight but I worry constantly about the ugliness of my legs and rear-end. I refuse to believe that it's there for life, edging further and further down my legs until even my Achilles' heel is dimpled!

SOS! Please help with what cellulite is and *how to get rid of it!* A diet is frustrating when you look in the mirror and see a slimmer you, but still horribly dimpled.

Our reply:

I can assure you that your frustrations are shared by many women.

To assist you I first want to clarify the confusion about cellulite. Cellulite is a popular term—not a *medical* term—used to describe formation of fat below the skin.

The best approach to deal with the problem is to continue your exercise program and keep body fat at a desired level. For a female below 30 years of age, body fat of 16 to 18 percent is acceptable. It is likely that some people are normal weight but overfat.

An ideal way to measure body fat is to have your body composition measured by skinfold calibration and hydrostatic, or underwater, measurement. This test can also assist you in determining desirable weights. In your case, you may find 115 pounds is more acceptable!

Congratulations on your healthy lifestyle—no more smoking and a good eating program. Yes, we recommend a slow weight loss as well as an eating program high in complex carbohydrates, moderate in protein, and low in fat.

Again, Sue, keep in mind that women tend to deposit fat more often below the waist. Individuals vary in their patterns of fat distribution, and offspring are likely to follow the same patterns as their parents. There is always that chance that the "cellulite" cannot be altered.

One final suggestion: along with your aerobic exercises, you may want to consider weight training and calisthenics for toning and strengthening.

# 14

# Stress and Depression—It Can Hit at Any Age

You hear the word *stress* all the time nowadays, and for good reason. In this pressure-cooker age when nothing seems permanent, a large portion of the global population is feeling its debilitating effects.

Stress defies easy definition. Dr. Hans Selye, the author of *Stress Without Distress*, describes it as "the non-specific response of the body to any demand made upon it." He's saying, in effect, that stress is the body's natural and necessary reaction to challenging situations.

"General adaptation syndrome" (GAS) is how Dr. Selye labels the changes that take place inside the body of a person under stress. GAS has three phases:

During phase 1—sometimes called the "fight or flight" reaction—your body releases adrenaline and other hormones. Your blood pressure, heart rate, and respiration increase, all normal physiological responses to threatening stimuli.

This initial acute reaction graduates into phase 2. The body is suspended in a state of readiness, like the lioness crouched in the grass, waiting for the best time to attack her prey. This second phase can be enormously productive *provided* you know how to channel your body's newly released energy to get the maximum amount accomplished.

But if you try to sustain this level of arousal for too long, you're asking for trouble. Eventually, you'll cross over into the danger zone—phase 3—when that suspended state of readiness turns into chronic exhaustion. You've pushed yourself too far.

Many people in this third phase of GAS lose all sense of themselves and the fact that they've become extremely irritable, argumentative, and illogical. They ignore the expressions of concern from their friends and family and keep driving themselves down the same hazardous road.

It takes bouts of insomnia, heart palpitations, gastrointestinal disorders, skin problems, headaches, back pain, and more to make some people realize they're running on nervous energy that is almost depleted. Other people, in order to relax, become addicted to drugs such as Valium, Equanil, or alcohol before the alarm bell rings. But the saddest people are those who don't heed any of the warning signals: a complete mental or physical breakdown is the only thing that makes them see the error of their ways.

# Stress—It's Not All Bad

Stress is *not* all bad. In fact, Dr. Selye calls stress "the spice of life." He points out that it can be a positive force, goading people into peak performance, utilizing skills and capacities they didn't realize they possessed.

Positive stress—or the mastery of challenge—is an absolute prerequisite to having a sense of fulfillment and excitement in life. Think back over your achievements for a moment and you'll realize that some of the most rewarding times of your life were those of great stress. It's all a question of striking the right balance between stress and relaxation. It's a matter of learning how to *manage* stress constructively.

## Fit Facts: Truisms about Stress

People have a lot of misconceptions about stress. To set the record straight, here are some facts about stress that may surprise you. Should you be feeling a lot of tension and not know why, perhaps this list will help clarify your thinking:

- Some stress is good for you, making you more alert and productive.
- Your environment may be a source of stress if it is too hot, cold, damp, noisy, crowded, light, dark, etc., and you are extremely sensitive to such matters.
- Age-related changes—such as puberty or menopause—often create stress.
- Overload—*too many demands* made on you at home, work, or even in your social life—can cause stress.
- Boredom—when *too few demands* are made on you by others—is a source of stress unless you're an unusually inner-directed person.
- For most people, loneliness—too little social contact—creates stress.
- Too much stimulation or social contact (overload) is not necessarily more stressful than too little (deprivation).
- Major life changes (job change, relocation, marriage, separation/divorce, death of a close family member, etc.) are stressors.
- The more major life changes that occur simultaneously, the more stress you experience.
- The small stresses of everyday life—traffic jams, frustrations, family fights, run-ins with the boss—if they're constant and accumulate, can in the long run be more harmful than major life changes.

- The stress produced by a situation or event depends more on your perception of it than on the situation or event itself.
- Symbolic stressors, involving your perceptions, are affected by your prior life experiences, attitudes, and values.
- You will feel great stress in any situation in which you see yourself as useless, powerless, or out of control.
- A particularly stressful job is one that carries a lot of responsibility but minimal autonomy and decision-making power.
- When under stress, you may feel confused and unable to concentrate. This, in turn, lowers your performance and increases your chances of having an accident.
- Stress can impair the functioning of various systems in your body—especially the cardiovascular, respiratory, neurological, endocrine, and gastrointestinal.
- Stress often weakens your body's defenses against disease. During stress periods, you may be sick often.

If you don't know how to control stress, it can cross over that fine line that separates a positive life force from a roadblock to success. Indeed, too much stress, as we've described, is a very bad thing. It's been implicated in all manner of psychological problems ranging from disorientation to depression to such major illnesses as asthma, cancer, high blood pressure, and heart disease.

Once again, the optimum amount of stress depends on the individual. It might be defined as the amount that keeps you on your toes, improving your performance without producing harmful emotional or physical side effects.

## Stressors—You're Surrounded by Them

A lot of people have the mistaken idea that stress means time pressure: it's caused by too much to do and too little time to do it in. As you're beginning to see, stress is a far more complicated matter than that.

Stressors can be almost anything—an event, circumstances, certain places, people, feelings, even your own attitudes.

What makes stress complicated is the fact that people respond differently to the same stressors. The stress produced by any given situation always depends more on a person's perception of it than on the situation itself.

Since this isn't a psychology book, we're going to tread lightly on the causes of stress in your life. We're more interested in two things: (1) the amount of stress you feel, and (2) the specific ways you cope with it.

## Personality Types—A and B

We all know about Type A personalities since cardiologists Drs. Meyer Friedman and Ray Rosenman published their 1974 bestseller *Type A Behavior and Your Heart.*

Type A people are competitive, often hostile, and feel a compulsive need to excel and dominate. Because they feel there aren't enough hours in the day to accomplish their many goals, they do everything with a sense of urgency. Even worse, Type A people tend to mistrust everyone and channel these negative emotions inward. As a consequence, they are more prone to heart disease than people who have lower levels of stress.

At the other end of the spectrum, according to Drs. Friedman and Rosenman, are the so-called Type B people. They seem to take everything in stride even if their world is crumbling around them. They may not get too much accomplished in life, but one thing can certainly be said about them—they're easygoing.

### The Female Type A

The notion of personality types is useful because it helps explain the different ways people deal with stress. For years, the classic Type A personality was a middle-aged, highly successful business executive destined to die young on the golf course from a massive heart attack. That stereotype has given way over the last decade as more women have arrived in the executive suite. Women's career ascendance has been marked by a growing incidence of heart attacks within their ranks, too, proving that job-related stress is certainly no respecter of sex.

It's not only the superachievers who have to pay a physical price for their success; occupational psychologists now tell us that everyone else is at risk too. You don't have to be at the top of the corporate pyramid to suffer from stress. The National Centers for Disease Control in Atlanta recently issued a report that concluded: job-related stress and its accompanying health problems are on the increase at all occupational levels.

Dr. Alex Cohen, chief of applied psychology for the National Institute for Occupational Safety and Health, which prepared the report, lays the blame on the massive shift we are undergoing in the job market. We are moving away from physically demanding jobs to mentally demanding ones that are more repetitive. Moreover, many of the new jobs are service positions that pay less than the old factory jobs. Instead of occupational safety and health problems due to mechanization, Cohen says, in the future we're going to be seeing more health problems of a psychological nature.

The computer is one of the biggest culprits. In the past, many jobs demanded that workers get up and move around—to retrieve a file, talk to a colleague, consult a chart.

Now, the ubiquitous computer terminal has made most of these movements unnecessary. The "workstation," where workers sit immobile for hours, is a breeding ground for muscle tension and stress.

The disorders of the "information age" are wide-ranging, from neuroses and depression to more physical complaints—headaches, allergies, backaches, drug abuse, insomnia, irritable colon, hypertension, and heart disease.

Already, workers' compensation claims for job stress, rarely seen a decade ago, account for 11 to 14 percent of all lawsuits and are rising the most rapidly in younger age groups and among women. Experts estimate that job stress costs American industry $150 billion annually in absenteeism, diminished productivity, employee turnover, and direct medical insurance and compensation costs.

## What Personality Type Are You?

Automation and the white-collar society it fosters are here to stay. No doubt about that. Human beings will just have to adapt to the stresses and constraints. The question is—can a Type B function in today's demanding world?

### Fit Quiz: My Stress Profile

| | True | False |
|---|---|---|
| I have no family history of chronic depression. | ______ | ______ |
| No one in my family, including me, is a victim of alcoholism or other obsessive or addictive behavior. | ______ | ______ |
| I rarely experience tension headaches, lower back pain not caused by injury, or neck and shoulder tightness. | ______ | ______ |
| I rarely suffer from sleep disorders—insomnia or sleeping excessively. | ______ | ______ |
| I tend to wake up feeling fresh and rested. | ______ | ______ |
| Tension rarely causes me to lose my appetite or to overeat. | ______ | ______ |
| I'm seldom unhappy, irritable, or depressed without sufficient cause. | ______ | ______ |
| I can usually concentrate for periods of time without a problem. | ______ | ______ |
| I don't feel I'm constantly racing against the clock. | ______ | ______ |

| | True | False |
|---|---|---|
| After a normal day's work, I can usually relax without trouble—and without relying on alcohol or drugs. | ______ | ______ |
| My life usually affords me an adequate amount of time for recreation, relaxation, and rest. | ______ | ______ |
| I generally keep my temper under control. | ______ | ______ |
| I know the cause of most negative emotions I'm feeling. | ______ | ______ |
| My responses to small daily frustrations seldom get so out of hand that people say I'm overreacting. | ______ | ______ |
| I rarely experience stomach problems—heartburn, indigestion, tightness, and the like. | ______ | ______ |
| To my knowledge, I've never had psychosomatic symptoms that could be stress-related. | ______ | ______ |
| I'm not unduly sensitive to such environmental factors as temperature, noise levels, lighting, decor, etc. | ______ | ______ |
| I feel prepared to handle most things that come up in my life. | ______ | ______ |
| I feel I have a reasonable amount of control over my life. | ______ | ______ |
| I have a good amount of energy and vitality and seldom feel totally worn out and exhausted. | ______ | ______ |
| In my opinion, people don't expect too much from me. | ______ | ______ |
| I rarely feel bored or lonely—but when I do, I try to do something positive about it. | ______ | ______ |
| People generally think of me as cheerful. | ______ | ______ |
| Overall, I like myself. | ______ | ______ |
| I seldom feel worthless or that my life is hopeless. | ______ | ______ |
| I feel that I treat myself well, both inside and out. | ______ | ______ |

If all your checkmarks are in the True column, we tip our hat to you. You're the picture of mental and emotional well-being. You're also unusual. The average woman will have several checkmarks in the False column. The more marks *you* have in that column, the more you should take to heart the advice we're about to offer about managing stress.

In truth, neither the Type B nor the Type A is the person you should emulate. They're both extremes. Neither approach to life is balanced.

The Type A person may receive enormous praise, but she'll probably die young or suffer from a series of debilitating stress-induced illnesses. The Type B may live longer but wonder why. Boredom and a lack of challenge in one's life can lead to feelings of worthlessness and hopelessness. People feeling this way may *wish* they were dead.

No matter where you fall on the Type A-B continuum, there's hope for change. Anyone can learn to deal with stress in a healthier fashion. It takes some lifestyle and personality changes, it's true. But it can be done.

Let's probe your stress profile and find out if any change is warranted—and if so, how much.

## The C Zone Personality—The Type to Emulate

In 1984, a full ten years after the world first read about Type A personalities, two psychologists came up with a concept equally compelling. Drs. Marilyn and Robert Kriegel, in their book *The C Zone—Peak Performance under Pressure*, discuss Type C behavior, which they define as "being able to perform under pressure *without* suffering the debilitating effects of stress."

In the Kriegels' lexicon, "C" stands for commitment, confidence, and control. People operating in the Kriegels' C Zone have a constant cycle of challenge and mastery in their lives. C Zone people have enough challenge to feel some stress yet enough mastery to spark a sense of achievement. In this zone, stress is necessary and important but it remains positive because it's always well controlled. This optimum level of stress actually *promotes* physical and mental health.

The Kriegels' version of the Type A personality is someone existing in what they call the "Panic Zone." These are people with too much challenge and stress in their lives and not enough mastery. They are overcommitted, overconfident, and completely out of control most of the time.

In contrast, the Type B personality, according to the Kriegels, slouches along in the "Drone Zone." Drones are highly stressed, too, but for the opposite reason. They're short on risks and challenges and long on mastery. They're uncommitted, underconfident, and overcontrolled—and terribly bored, not to mention totally enervated.

## Managing Stress—A Key to Success

The Kriegels emphasize that C Zone behavior is predicated, to a great extent, on top physical conditioning. It requires the ability to avoid or delay the onset of fatigue; a good mental attitude; and, of course, skill and knowledge in your chosen field.

Think about your life for a moment. Stress is probably something you feel almost every day, like it or not. You might as well get used to the fact that you can't totally stress-proof your life, because stress is an integral part of being alive. Fortunately, you can stress-guard your body—by learning coping techniques.

Let's face it. Getting to the top—whether your goal is the top of a mountain or the top of your profession—demands strength, endurance, and energy. On the road to success, stress control will gain you a lot of extra mileage.

To be sure, there's more than one appropriate way to cope with stress. There are also many inappropriate, unhealthy ways.

Which category do your stress responses fall into?

## Fit Checklist: My Response to Stress—Is It Healthy?

Check the statements that describe the way you typically respond to stress.

**To alleviate feelings of tension and stress I often:**

(1) ____ read.
(2) ____ watch television.
(3) ____ immerse myself in a hobby, such as painting, cooking, gardening, crafts, etc.
(4) ____ listen to music.
(5) ____ go for a drive.
(6) ____ make love.
(7) ____ go to sleep.
(8) ____ cry.
(9) ____ pray or involve myself in some other religious activity.
(10) ____ meditate or rely on some other relaxation technique.
(11) ____ do some kind of exercise.
(12) ____ talk to a relative, friend, or co-worker.
(13) ____ deny that I'm feeling it.
(14) ____ eat.
(15) ____ get angry or "blow my top."
(16) ____ smoke a cigarette.
(17) ____ take a drug.
(18) ____ have an alcoholic drink.

Statements 1 through 12 describe appropriate responses to stress. They take your mind off the stressor for a while and give your body a chance to recuperate from the tension. Statements 13 through 18 are unhealthy responses. These activities may help you forget your immediate problems, but your body will suffer in the long run.

## Exercise Tops the List of Stress-Control Techniques

Granted, there's more than one good stress-control method, but physiologically, at least, exercise is the best. Exercise at the end of the workday, prior to the evening meal, is an excellent way to alleviate tension, increase your energy supply, and ward off any impending depression.

There are any number of studies, designed by respected scientists at well-known research institutions, showing that aerobic activity helps people control anxiety reactions. Many of these studies focus on the change in heart rates of individuals as they shift from a resting, unpressured state to a high-anxiety situation.

The average, unconditioned woman has a resting heart rate of 75 to 80 beats per minute. But even after minimal aerobic conditioning, her resting pulse rate drops significantly. This will make a big difference the next time she's thrown into a high-pressure situation. In contrast to her pre-aerobic reaction, she'll notice that she now stays calmer and more in control of her emotions throughout the ordeal.

Why?

Her conditioned heart will not be as greatly affected by various "fight or flight" adrenal secretions because it's become more efficient. Her conditioned heart can pump more blood with each beat. Hence, even when pushed, it beats slower.

## Endorphins—Nature's Tranquilizer

We discussed endorphins briefly in chapter 2. We return to the subject now because it's endorphins, the body's own natural tranquilizer, that can calm that raging beast within you, stress.

It's been a little over ten years since scientists discovered that the body produces its own analgesic. Dubbed "endorphins," these strong, hormonal painkillers enter the bloodstream during times of duress and circulate there for several hours. Actually, it's still unclear what events trigger endorphins' release, although there's no doubt that vigorous exercise is one of them. Scientists believe that endorphins account, at least in part, for the relaxed, self-confident feeling that so many regular exercisers report.

We're still learning about endorphins, but this much is known:

Beta endogenous morphine (or endorphins) is produced primarily by the pituitary gland and possibly other organs of the body. Once released into the bloodstream, its beneficial effects last two to three hours.

Endorphins seem to be the catalysts for two important, and very positive, organic responses. They kill pain to a degree that's astounding, and they give people a sense of euphoria and well-being—a feeling that all's right with the world.

Researchers have tested the endorphin levels in people with various medical conditions and made some interesting observations.

For example, it's been shown that severely depressed people have low endorphin levels. That's one reason why many psychiatrists and psychologists incorporate exercise into their depressed patients' treatment regimens.

Thomas Stephens, Ph.D., a visiting scientist in the Office of Analysis and Epidemiology at the National Center for Health Statistics in Hyattsville, Maryland, conducted an exhaustive study that probed the relationship between exercise and mental health. Utilizing data on 75,000 American and Canadian adults, all mildly to moderately depressed, he came to this preliminary conclusion:

"No matter what your definition of exercise, there is a positive connection—that up to a point, the more people exercise, the better their mental health."

Endorphins' painkilling ability has also come under clinical scrutiny. Researchers have discovered that during acupuncture, for instance, people's endorphin levels are high. Likewise during pregnancy. And during natural childbirth, when a woman's pain threshold needs to be high, endorphin levels are, researchers report, extremely high.

## Endorphins—The Bane of Pain

There's no doubt that endorphins are very powerful painkillers. It's been demonstrated that, dose per dose, they're two hundred times more powerful than their synthetic counterpart, the drug morphine. That's powerful!

A study conducted at the University of California School of Dentistry in San Francisco showcases how the body mediates pain by marshaling its endorphin forces:

Postoperative dental patients were given a placebo (a sugar tablet) and told that this tablet would completely control their pain. In many of the patients, it did so. When tested, researchers discovered why. These patients' endorphin levels were high, suggesting that the mind has a role to play in the release of endorphins. However, when these same patients were given naloxone, a substance that neutralizes the effects of morphine (and endorphins), their pain immediately returned.

Perhaps the most incredible example of endorphins' painkilling power occurred during the 1982 Boston Marathon. One of the entrants was a 39-year-old male who previously had qualified for the race by running a marathon in less than 2 hours, 50 minutes.

Describing the race in retrospect, this runner remembers that everything was fine until the 7-mile point, when he heard something snap. He thought he'd stepped on a twig or stick. Then a severe pain shot through his right thigh. He stumbled along for several paces but soon regained his balance and continued on, with the pain gradually subsiding. For the next 19 miles, his average speed was about 6:30 per mile.

He crossed the finish line in less than his qualifying time, establishing a new personal record. But as soon as he slowed down and relaxed the muscles of his leg, he collapsed and fell to the pavement. It was then discovered that the snap he had heard two hours earlier was a fracturing femur (the large bone above the knee). It took almost five hours for the orthopedic surgeons to correct this problem by placing an intramedullary pin through his fractured femur.

How could this occur?

The physicians who handled his case said, "His thigh muscles were so strong, they splinted the broken bone. And his endorphin levels were so high, he didn't feel the pain."

If you're a first-time exerciser, you'll thank your lucky stars for endorphins. The only reason you'll be able to get through your early exercise attempts is because of those amazing painkilling endorphins. Without them, your muscle pain would be so severe during exercise that you'd have to stop almost immediately. As it is, you won't escape pain altogether. About twenty-four hours after your sessions, when you no longer have any residual effect from endorphins, you'll probably have some pain or discomfort.

In deconditioned people, it appears that peak endorphin levels are reached sometime *after* they stop exercising. In such people, endorphins help to spread out the pain so it isn't so intense all at once. In conditioned people, however, peak levels of endorphins seem to occur *during* exercise, which may account for the "runner's high" —that feeling of invincibility and euphoria experienced by some runners.

## The Personality-Change Principle

Now we're moving into an area where science has yet to formulate answers. To support our statements, all we can offer is anecdotal testimony from people who have written to us or visited the Aerobics Center over the years. But we can tell you this much with certainty: thousands of people have similar things to say about the psychological benefits of aerobics.

It is our conclusion that people who continue to exercise, year after year, don't do it because their triglyceride or cholesterol level goes down, or because their blood pressure drops, or because their heart rate slows. They do it because *regular exercise makes them feel better.* They tell us that they're more productive at work, they have more energy, and their self-image improves.

We realize these seem like odd, intangible benefits to attribute to something as physical and tangible as exercise. But we must do so all the same. Too many people report these results even if we don't have fully worked-out, scientific answers to explain them yet.

## Reports from the Field

Dr. Elizabeth Doyne, a clinical assistant professor at the University of Rochester (New York) Medical Center and a psychologist in private practice, uses exercise to treat her depressed patients whenever she can. Her belief in exercise as an antidepressant stems from personal experience. A number of years ago, she went through her own "blue period," a long and deep depression that she couldn't seem to shake—until she took up aerobics. Biking and tennis were her palliatives.

Beyond quantitative biochemical hypotheses, there are various qualitative theories about why exercise helps relieve stress and depression. Some researchers think it works because it distracts sufferers from their suffering. Or because people benefit from the social reinforcement that accompanies some sports. Or because exercise over time enables them to see measurable improvement.

Dr. Doyne, among others, suggests that "there's something besides an aerobic 'training effect' going on. My theory is that people feel a sense of mastery with achievement, a sense of control. Nobody is giving them a pill."

That could be part of it. Many exercisers have told us that they've been able to carry over the strengths they developed in aerobics to other areas of their lives. One executive said that after working up to 2 miles per run, he was able to apply that seemingly unachievable distance to his professional life. Just as running for miles didn't seem impossible anymore, overwhelming amounts of work didn't seem impossible either. He said, "I seem to have more tolerance for emotional stress."

He went on to describe the effects of his exercise in almost mystical terms:

"Now, many days when I run several miles, I have a much greater awareness of my body than I ever had before. Sometimes, at the end of a good run, my body seems to be working like a well-oiled machine. I may start the run in a fragmented emotional state, with many concerns and worries plaguing me. But by the end of the session, I feel whole. My mind and body become one."

Here are some other testimonials we've heard over the years:

"There's more respect in business for a fit person," a Texas CEO states.

"Without exercise, I lose the ability to handle stress," according to a New Jersey executive.

"Most of all, I feel a great sense of calmness," says a woman executive from New York.

Whatever the underlying physiological mechanisms, it seems evident that aerobics can and does help control stress and depression. As thousands of such testimonials attest, it seems also to enhance one's sense of well-being. That's certainly a bonus nobody is going to reject.

# 15
# Aerobics and Pregnancy

This letter from a woman in upstate New York is typical of many we receive from pregnant women:

> I have been jogging off and on for about seven years. For the last eight months I have been running seriously, doing 3 miles per day (in under 24 minutes), five times a week.
>
> I have just become pregnant for the first time, am now in my seventh week, and have continued jogging. My doctor, however, has discouraged jogging since he has not seen enough pregnant joggers to be able to justify it. He suggests brisk walking instead. I feel good running and know I would *not* do enough walking to keep in the fit state I am now.
>
> Can this jogging motion really hurt my baby? I have unconsciously slowed down so I know I am not pushing myself. I am 32 years old, in very good health, do not smoke or drink (coffee and black tea included), and have been following a natural food diet for many years.

The best counsel we can offer this woman is to cite cases—not the famous cases of marathoners such as Ingrid Kristiansen, who ran right up until the time they delivered, but cases of dedicated amateurs every woman can identify with. At the Aerobics Center, we have many female members who continue to run or jog throughout their pregnancies.

There's Margie Archer. She ran 6 miles a week until the seventh month of her first two pregnancies. In the fifth month of her third pregnancy, her exercise regimen was running 1 mile and walking ¾ of a mile each day and going to exercise class three times a week. Later, she switched to swimming.

Margie has this to say about what exercise did for her:

"I always hear complaints about muscle cramps, backaches, and water retention from women who don't exercise during their pregnancies. I've never had any of these problems. Exercise has helped me keep my muscle tone and get back into shape faster after each baby was born."

## Other Examples

Mary Speight has run many marathons and averages about a 7-minute mile for the 26.2-mile length of the course. She's so dedicated, in fact, that she ran a 13-mile marathon just three weeks before delivering a healthy, 8-pound daughter. She had no problems throughout her pregnancy or with labor. Perhaps the most wonderful part of it was the rapidity with which she recovered from the postpartum phase. Her highly conditioned state during pregnancy was responsible.

A freelance writer made a particularly eloquent case for running while pregnant in an essay she wrote for *Women's Sports* magazine:

> Since I had been running for exercise for several years, it seemed only natural to keep on going while I was pregnant. By the time [my daughter] was born, she had been a passenger on 4- or 5-mile runs for almost nine months.
>
> Running through those nine months yielded up such incredible experiences—physically, emotionally, spiritually. Doctors often make a woman a passive agent in her own pregnancy, issuing decrees on weight gain and allowed activities. But I felt so good being actively involved in my own physical and mental well-being, to feel responsible for it.
>
> Running allowed me to tune in on all the different levels of this thing I call my "self." Focusing on the physical changes made me feel at home with my body. It must be such a frightening thing to feel your body is foreign to you—and that could easily happen to a woman during pregnancy.
>
> On a psychological level, the biggest help that running offered was the assurance that I could still do what I had always done despite the huge change in my life. I could incorporate this new life into my old one.
>
> About ten days before [my daughter] was born, I set off on a run only to find that my legs were working sideways instead of forward. I had always thought that waddling pregnant women were out of shape, but there was nothing I could do to stop looking like a running duck. It turns out there is a hormone called relaxin, released sometime in the last few weeks of pregnancy, that relaxes ligaments around the pelvis.
>
> Running had helped to prepare me, having taught me endurance, pacing,

acceptance of a little fatigue, and the discipline to push on to that marvelous second wind.

## Benefits of Moderate Exercise for the Would-be Mother

The women we've just quoted are exceptional. And we don't recommend jogging your way to the delivery room as they did.

Our advice, even to women who are committed runners and have no problems that might complicate their deliveries, is to substitute a less impactful form of exercise during the last three months of pregnancy. Many women do so much earlier than that because jogging becomes too uncomfortable.

There are many myths concerning the effects of exercise on the mother and fetus. Research results, however, have been limited and somewhat inconclusive.

In general, studies show that moderate exercise has few negative effects on the expectant mother who has no complications, such as high blood pressure, vaginal bleeding, previous abortions, and so forth. This is in line with the American College of Obstetricians and Gynecologists' official position statement that says: "Any exercise prescription should be based on the individual's medical and exercise history and any complications during pregnancy."

Based on our experience at the Aerobics Center and from the letters we receive, we can make these assertions about women who exercise throughout their pregnancies: (1) they have fewer cesarean-section deliveries; (2) they have shorter second-phase labor; (3) their recovery time is reduced.

We've also found that exercise helps expectant mothers (a) gain weight within the optimum range as well as control body fat; (b) reduce constipation, which can be a real problem for pregnant women; (c) sleep better despite the discomfort of an enlarging stomach; (d) reduce tensions and better cope with the physical and emotional stresses of pregnancy; (e) increase energy; (f) protect against back pain from postural shifts; and (g) improve postpartum muscle tone.

## Physiological Changes During Pregnancy

When you're carrying a child, a number of major physiological changes take place in your body. It's these changes that affect your ability to exercise with the same *f*requency, *i*ntensity, and *t*ime—the F.I.T. formula, once again—as you did before.

For one thing, your blood plasma will increase in volume some 30 percent to meet the demands of the placenta. Both heart rate and cardiac output (the amount of blood pumped by the heart) rise accordingly. These changes reduce cardiac reserve, which will limit your capacity for exercise during the first trimester.

Naturally, you'll gain weight, but it should be controlled. About 20 to 30 pounds is usual. The increased blood volume, coupled with this additional weight, will make you reach your target heart rate with less vigorous activity than during your prepregnancy workouts.

A lot of your newfound weight, of course, is in your abdomen, so your posture changes. You'll find yourself leaning back to compensate for your belly. The result: the familiar swayback or lordosis (curvature of the spine) and waddling gait.

There are several consequences of this postural shift. You'll find you have a tenuous sense of balance. Pregnant women often complain that they feel like a boat about to capsize. Your new center of gravity will also put more pressure on the muscles and ligaments of the back, which may well cause lower back pain.

Later on in the third trimester, the hormone relaxin comes into play. It softens the connective tissue and ligaments so that you'll be wondrously flexible in all your joints—from your pelvis to your ankles, feet, hips, knees, and shoulders. While this may be a pleasant surprise, we advise you to be careful. Don't overdo it and stretch your ligaments beyond their normal range of motion. This warning stays in effect for the first six to sixteen weeks after the birth of your child too. It takes that long for relaxin to return to normal levels.

As a result of these pregnancy-induced physiological changes, sports that require agility, balance, and strength—sports such as skiing, horseback riding, gymnastics, and tennis—pose a risk, particularly after the first trimester and on into the postpartum phase. Your new instability can easily lead to accidents.

Another change: Near the end of your pregnancy, your enlarging uterus will push your diaphragm upward and cause you to breathe in a more pronounced manner. During mild exercise, this hyperventilation will become more noticeable. During moderate or strenuous exercise, you'll surely feel its effects.

## The Exercise Prescription

We've just told you about the physiological changes that will make exercising a little more difficult during pregnancy. On the other side of the issue, there are also a couple of pregnancy-related problems that can be relieved better through exercise than any other means.

For example, pregnant women are prone to circulation problems. When the weight of the fetus presses on the main leg artery in the groin, it cuts off some blood flow. Fainting, swelling, and muscle cramps are the possible symptoms, and aerobic activity—such as walking, biking, or swimming—is the best antidote.

Slack pelvic-floor muscles can be another problem. These are the muscles that support the abdominal organs. They are connected like a hammock between the tailbone and the front of the pelvis. These muscles need to be contracted during pregnancy in order to retain their tone and strength. After delivery, they must be strengthened so that the mother can regain proper bladder control.

Exercise, once again, can help, but a type other than aerobics is required. Frequent contraction of the urethral sphincter—as you do when you finish urinating—is the exercise of choice. Practiced regularly, this should help immensely in correcting urinary incontinence and regaining complete bladder control.

## General Guidelines

As a general rule, if you have not been exercising vigorously prior to pregnancy, you shouldn't begin a strenuous program now. Walking should be about it for you.

This is the advice dispensed by the average obstetrician. It's a conservative approach, perhaps far more conservative than wise, however.

Giving the lie to this approach is a five-year study at Madison General Hospital in Wisconsin. The Madison study enrolled a large number of previously sedentary, pregnant women and placed them in a supervised workout program. Neither they nor their babies showed any ill effects. To the contrary, they were as healthy at birth as the babies of women who didn't exercise.

Active women who follow challenging exercise programs before pregnancy pose more of a dilemma to the typical ob-gyn. There's no unanimity among doctors about how to counsel them. The advice runs the gamut: "Cut back to walking and swimming" is the cautious doctor's litany. "Continue what you've been doing at a slower pace" is the liberal doctor's theme.

We fall somewhere in between, leaning toward liberal. Our advice is to continue your program, but reduce its intensity, especially during the first and second trimesters—provided, of course, your doctor has assured you that you have no medical or obstetrical complications.

In the third trimester, though, we encourage our patients to switch to "safe" exercises such as swimming and walking. But despite our counsel, many of our diehard exercisers, particularly the runners, continue doing whatever they've been doing. We've no ill effects to report.

All this advice is well and good, but we should point out that Mother Nature has a tendency to disrupt the best-laid plans of the most well-intentioned exerciser or her physician.

For one thing, during the first 13 weeks of pregnancy at least 50 percent of women experience bouts of nausea. During the final 23 weeks, hormonal changes, particularly a rise in progesterone, may cause fatigue and lack of motivation. In addition, during the last 12 weeks of that period, women often lose some mobility in their ankles and wrists and experience some weakness in their hands.

Even if you don't suffer these changes, you should decrease your level of training commensurate with your weight gain, particularly from the fifth month on. The extra weight alone will make your normal workout more difficult.

## Special Considerations

There are some special exercise considerations for pregnant women who remain aerobically active.

For example, as an expectant mother, you need to practice good posture at all times—even during exercise—to avoid strain on the back and abdomen. As we've mentioned, the added weight of the fetus tends to draw the pelvis forward, which increases the hollow of the back, a posture known as "lordosis." The proper posture is to stand tall, head erect, back straight, abdomen and chest held high.

Because pregnancy renders your ligaments more lax and joints more unstable, your risk of sustaining a musculoskeletal injury increases. This is the prime reason we want our patients in the third trimester to switch from jerky, high-impact exercise to something more gentle. Avoid especially exercises involving deep-knee flexion.

## Women Who Walked

Brenda Lawrence, an Aerobics Center regular, continued her low-impact exercise program until two days before her son was born. It consisted of walking 8 to 12 miles a week and going to exercise class three times a week. On this regimen, she had no problems. "It helped me keep my weight down and lose it quickly once the baby was born."

Mona Fontenot, on the staff for the Institute for Aerobics Research, walked 2 miles a day and attended exercise class twice a week until a week before delivery.

### Fit Tips: Exercise Dos and Don'ts During Pregnancy

The point of exercise during pregnancy is to *maintain your current fitness level,* not to improve it. The F.I.T. formula should be modified during pregnancy in this way:

***Frequency:*** Exercise every other day.

***Intensity:*** Do not exceed 70 percent of your maximum age-predicted heart rate.

***Time:*** Exercise 20 to 40 minutes each session.

Monitor your heart rate immediately upon stopping your 5-minute cool-down. It should be below 120 beats per minute.

The temperature and humidity during exercise is a key consideration. Do not let your body temperature rise above 101 degrees F. when you exercise or you could retard fetal development. A fetus is unable to dissipate excess heat, so hyperthermia becomes a real danger. Hot, humid weather can increase core body temperature quickly, so cut back on intensity and duration during this weather. Also avoid hot tubs, whirlpools, and saunas, because they have the same effect.

You need to drink extra fluids during pregnancy, especially during exercise. Force yourself if you have to. You'll probably find, maybe to your displeasure, that you retain more fluid during pregnancy: you feel bloated. This is normal and should not be interfered with. Studies show that taking diuretics or restricting sodium can reduce infant size at birth.

In addition to this general advice, there are a number of exercise precautions to keep firmly in mind.

**AVOID:**

- Contact sports such as football, basketball, hockey, and volleyball, because of the potential of injury.
- Water skiing, because you may fall, risking an unintentional vaginal douche with contaminated water.
- Scuba diving, because of the pressure it puts on the body.
- Snow skiing, ice skating, and equestrian sports, since the potential for injury due to a fall is significant.
- Any exercise that requires quick movements such as jumping, twisting, and sudden changes in direction. Reason: the change in a pregnant woman's center of gravity affects her balance and coordination, so falls become more likely.
- Weight training. Pregnancy, in and of itself, is a form of weight training.

**AFTER FIVE MONTHS:**

- Sit-ups may create too much pressure on the uterus and cervix. If so, substitute abdominal curls.
- Back hyperextensions, such as donkey kicks, should be avoided, because the lower back has enough pressure on it and has already been weakened enough during this time to take any additional stress.
- Because the belly is heavy, a supine position (lying on your back) could block the return of blood from the lower part of the body to the heart. If you attempt this position, monitor how you feel very carefully.

"I've never had more energy or felt better in my life," she says about that time. "I didn't experience any of the physical or emotional problems of pregnancy, and I firmly believe it's because of my personal fitness program."

Cindy Pardue was going to exercise class and walking 6 to 8 miles a week well into her pregnancy:

"My doctor is big on exercise as long as you don't overdo it," she says. "My exercise program hasn't changed much since I got pregnant. I believe in lots of exercise in moderation. It's important to your peace of mind to stay in shape. You feel better and look good."

## Labor and Delivery

There's no scientific study proving that exercise during pregnancy has a positive effect on labor and delivery. Indeed, marathon runner Mary Decker Slaney had a difficult, extremely painful nine hours of labor, presaged by the fact that, in the later stage of her pregnancy, she couldn't run any farther than 400 yards at a time due to cramping.

Of course, I can cite just as many cases of avid exercisers who had easier deliveries seemingly because they remained active. It seems logical that endurance exercise will increase your endurance during natural childbirth. Whether it will cut down on pain or shorten overall delivery time is something else.

What I think you can realistically expect exercise to do for you during the blessed event is to increase your sense of joy and well-being. And there's a lot to be said for that!

## Postpartum

Barring any complications during birth, your doctor will probably allow you to start an easy walking program quite soon after you leave the hospital.

An episiotomy, by the way, is a complication. If you've had one, you can exercise, but avoid movements that stretch your perineum (the area between your vagina and your anus, where the episiotomy was done). Examples are inner and outer thigh lifts, leg lunges, and straddle stretches.

Unless you're an elite athlete, we wouldn't recommend renewing serious training until five or six weeks after delivery. Our experience is that physically fit women lose their weight gain within the first three months after giving birth without straining to do so.

Are you comfortable exercising? That's the question you must keep asking yourself both before and after delivery. Staying in touch with your body is very important. It offers the best guidelines of all about how to proceed.

## Breast-Feeding

Women who intend to breast-feed sometimes ask whether exercise will decrease their milk production. It won't, *provided* your exercise remains moderate and you keep your caloric intake up. When you're nursing, a weight-reducing diet should be the farthest thing from your mind.

If you insist on running great distances or exercising to excess, yes, your breast-feeding ability could be adversely affected. But we'd be surprised if you could exercise too vigorously with large nursing breasts anyway—it's too uncomfortable.

# 16

# For Competitive Athletes: Strenuous Exercise and Menstrual Irregularities

Strenuous exercise over a period of time can have a negative impact on the reproductive functions of women.

You may have heard this before. It deserves some clarification.

First of all, it probably doesn't apply to you, for this reason: Before a woman's menstrual cycle is affected in the slightest way, that exercise must be *extremely* intense and continue for months—maybe years. We're talking about the kind of all-out training effort that highly competitive female athletes engage in.

If you're the average woman who joins an aerobic dance class or gets out on the track for health and fun, you're not a candidate for menstrual irregularities due to exercise. You may want to skip this chapter, in fact. A professional athlete or serious amateur athlete should read on, however. If you fall into either of these categories, you may have noticed changes in your cycle and wondered why.

At least three distinct disorders are seen increasingly in females engaged in endurance training. For young girls, it's delayed menarche (the start of menstruation). In adult women, it's amenorrhea (absence of menstruation) and oligomenorrhea (light or infrequent menstruation).

## The Young Girl as Athlete

Athletic young women were liberated in 1972 by federal legislation—Title IX—that put girls, for the first time in the nation's history, on an equal footing with boys on the athletic field. Since then, many young women have taken full advantage of their newfound equality. In fact, some young girls are so fired up by sports that they could be risking harm to their maturing bodies.

A number of studies focus on the effects of endurance exercise training on prepubescent girls. Some of the conclusions may give pause to parents of extremely athletic girls.

Jo E. Cowden, a researcher at the University of New Orleans, reviewed the existing literature and identified four major areas of concern regarding the effect of distance running—one form of endurance training—on boys and girls. Viewed collectively, Cowden says these studies show that young runners, compared to adults, are: (1) more vulnerable to musculoskeletal injuries caused by overuse; (2) less able to endure stress on the cardiovascular system; (3) less able to adapt to temperature stresses on their bodies; and (4) less able to endure the psychological pressures of competition.

To date, there haven't been enough longitudinal studies of young girls engaged in competitive aerobic sports to draw any strong conclusions. However, it is clear that endurance training often delays menarche; some studies indicate a delay of five months or more for every year of training.

Whether the delay of menarche has any deleterious long-term effects, we don't know. Researchers are still posing serious questions.

For example, since it's been shown that the loss of menstruation in adult women is accompanied by bone loss, how does the similar condition of delayed menarche affect the athletic adolescent? Does delayed menarche in the young woman, who may not have adequate bone mass to begin with, mean she'll never hit the peak bone mass that she should? And if she starts with low bone mass and loses mass at the same rate as everybody else, will the point at which she is at a high risk of fracture be earlier?

## The Cooper Clinic Prescription for Youthful Exercisers

Naturally, we're pro exercise for girls. But, given all these open questions, we're for exercise *within reason.* Clearly, consideration should be given to the type, intensity, and stress of the exercise as well as to the age at which it begins.

We advise parents of girls up to about 10 years of age to concentrate more on teaching them athletic skills than to push endurance sports such as distance running. At the fifth- or sixth-grade level, we suggest introducing them to some competitive lifetime sports. Running is all right, but we discourage long-distance running of more than 3 miles (or 5 kilometers) until age 12 or later.

However, once a girl reaches puberty—say, 14 years of age—we think an aerobics program is in order and is safe. In fact, we encourage it as a preventive measure against heart disease later in life, an affliction that increasingly befalls women as well as men (see chapter 18).

## Adult Women Who Compete

While studies on young female athletes are sparse, researchers have done much more extensive studies on adult female athletes and have arrived at some preliminary conclusions.

First, there is significant incidence of menstrual irregularities among women who reach a high level of competition in endurance sports. Some researchers claim as many as 50 percent of female athletes have the menstrual problems amenorrhea and oligomenorrhea. Of the two, amenorrhea is more troublesome.

The causes of amenorrhea—when a woman stops having menstrual periods—fall into two categories: serious disorders unrelated to exercise, such as diabetes mellitus and diseases of the thyroid, ovaries, adrenal, or pituitary glands; and disorders associated with intense endurance exercise.

Any woman athlete who starts missing her period—or notices a marked change in her menstrual pattern—should have a complete medical exam to rule out serious disease conditions. If none are present, then exercise moves to front and center stage as a causal factor.

Endurance training, the low-calorie diets, and the low body fat and weight of competitive athletes are all implicated in amenorrhea. They can bring about a fundamental change in the body chemistry known as hypoestrogenism, or a lower-than-normal estrogen level.

The mechanism that links endurance exercise with hypoestrogenism and anovulation, which we'll discuss below, is unclear. One hypothesis suggests that the endorphins in abundance in the body during strenuous exercise may inhibit the pituitary gland's release of LH and FSH, the female hormones that regulate the menstrual cycle.

Amenorrhea isn't the only symptom of hypoestrogenism by any means. Some women report hot flashes, reduced muscle tension, a delay in clitoral response time, a decrease or absence of vaginal lubrication, or painful uterine contractions during orgasm. Notice that these are the same symptoms that menopausal women experience, again because of drops in estrogen levels.

By far the most serious effect of hypoestrogenism, however, is the loss of bone mineral content. It's ironic that a moderate amount of weight-bearing exercise can help build up and strengthen bone tissue. But excessive exercise triggering hypoestrogenism can have just the opposite effect, robbing the body of bone mass. The condition is known as osteoporosis (see chapter 17); and, as you've just learned, postmenopausal women are not the only females at risk for it.

An endurance female athlete suffering from borderline osteoporosis can expect to sustain a higher-than-average number of stress fractures. Studies bear this out. One wide-ranging, three-phase study, published in *Medicine and Science in Sports and Exercise,* vol. 18, no. 4, involved some 500 recreational female distance runners. It concluded that "premenopausal women who have absent or irregular menses, while engaged in vigorous exercise programs, are at increased risk for musculoskeletal injury."

## Treatment for Amenorrhea

In treating amenorrhea in premenopausal female athletes, doctors often prescribe birth control pills, a calcium-rich diet, and calcium supplements. However, some runners eschew contraceptive pills because they tend to lower oxygen capacity and increase breathlessness. Researchers have validated this reaction in clinical studies.

The most reliable—and safest—approach to the problem is, unfortunately, something most serious athletes won't consider. That's to markedly reduce or stop exercise altogether for a while, which increases body fat and weight. Doctors who have treated such women report that menstrual function usually reverts to normal within one or two months. Whether the bone mass they've lost can ever be recovered is something else. Treatment can arrest osteoporosis, but whether it can reverse its effects to any great extent is still in doubt.

### Myth: Amenorrhea as a Contraceptive Method

Some amenorrheic athletes make the mistake of assuming that the absence of periods means they aren't ovulating. Thus, they don't bother with birth control.

However, amenorrhea cannot be viewed as an absolute form of birth control, because some amenorrheic women still ovulate. Ingrid Kristiansen, the marathon runner, is a prime example. She hadn't been bothered by menses for months, so she didn't realize she was pregnant until she was several months along and her racing times began to suffer.

Amenorrheic women, on the other hand, who are actively trying to get pregnant may need hormone treatments both to regulate their cycle and to induce ovulation.

## Oligomenorrhea

Another exercise-induced symptom is oligomenorrhea, when the menstrual period is scanty, with only a very small amount of blood.

Just as amenorrhea can indicate that a woman is suffering from hypoestrogenism, oligomenorrhea may be associated with anovulation and reduced progesterone levels. As a consequence, the luteal (postovulatory) phase of a woman's menstrual cycle is shortened, meaning that ovulation occurs fewer than ten days before the onset of her next cycle. In most cases, ovulation simply occurs later in the cycle than before, so the total cycle length may not be affected.

## Fit Facts: Exercise and Your Menstrual Cycle

Studies of elite female athletes indicate that intense training is likely to affect their menstrual cycles, either with obvious symptoms or in subtle biochemical ways that may go unnoticed. Here is a glossary of these menstrual conditions as well as some related gynecological terms:

**Amenorrhea**—Missed menstrual periods. Causes can range from low body fat or hypoestrogenism induced by intense exercise to serious disorders totally unrelated to exercise (e.g., diabetes mellitus and diseases of the ovaries, thyroid, adrenal, or pituitary glands).

**Anovulation**—Suspension or cessation of ovulation.

**Dysmenorrhea**—Painful menstrual periods.

**Endometriosis**—Often painful condition marked by the presence of functioning uterine tissue outside the uterus or womb but usually confined to the pelvis. It may be found on the outside surface of the uterus, on the ovaries, bladder, intestine, or various other places.

**Female sex hormones**—Estrogen and progesterone, hormones from the ovaries secreted during the pre- and postovulation phases, respectively, of a woman's menstrual cycle. Gonadotropins—LH (luteinizing hormone) and FSH (follicle-stimulating hormone)—are the pituitary hormones that stimulate the ovaries and regulate the menstrual cycle.

**Hypoestrogenism**—A lower-than-normal estrogen level that increases the risk of bone-density loss (osteoporosis). It tends to manifest itself in menstrual irregularities, such as amenorrhea, or in such symptoms as hot flashes, reduced muscle tension, a delay in clitoral response time, a slowing or absence of vaginal lubrication, or painful uterine contractions at orgasm.

**Menarche**—The onset of menstruation, which signals the beginning of puberty. The national average age at menarche is 12.8 years. Menarche is often delayed in lean young girls (body fat content of lower than 17 percent) who exercise intensely before age 10 or 11.

**Menstrual irregularity**—Bleeding more often than every 25 days or less often than every 35 days, counting from the first day of one period to the first day of the next.

**Oligomenorrhea**—The menstrual period is scanty, with only a very small amount of blood loss. Oligomenorrhea can indicate the presence of a condition known as "anovulation" (see definition above).

**Premenstrual stress syndrome (PMS)**—A set of symptoms—irritability, mood changes, depression, nervousness, water retention, bloating, constipation, headache, fatigue, cravings for sweet or fatty foods, or breast tenderness—occurring several days prior to the beginning of menstruation. Exercise is one method recommended for controlling these symptoms.

## Do the Rewards Justify the Risks?

You have to have some goal, other than fitness, to justify exercising to the point of inducing menstrual irregularities. If you're a professional athlete, we know why you're doing it. If you're an avocational athlete, though, you should be doing some serious soul-searching and put your exercise regimen in perspective.

Are the trade-offs worth it to you? Even if you do eventually cut back on training and regain a normal menstrual cycle, there are still many unanswered questions about the ultimate effects on bone mass in women who have long histories of amenorrhea, for example. We're still not sure that calcium and estrogen therapy can completely reverse bone loss. The question is: Do you want to risk it?

## Intensity Guidelines for the Amateur Athlete

With so much media attention focused on exercise safety, the American College of Obstetricians and Gynecologists (ACOG) finally issued guidelines in 1986. They're intended to help physicians answer active women's questions about exercise—how much is too much, and what organic changes to expect when they do exercise to excess.

The ACOG guidelines draw on earlier guidelines formulated by the American College of Sports Medicine (ACSM). ACSM's formula, though, is the one now widely accepted:

ACSM recommends 15 to 60 minutes of aerobic activity, three to five days a week, at 60 to 90 percent of aerobic capacity.

These figures represent *minimum levels of exertion the average woman might engage in to maintain a minimum level of fitness.* The ACOG guidelines do not say a woman should necessarily limit herself to that amount.

Dr. Harrison Visscher, ACOG's director of education, explains that the purpose of the guidelines was simply to offer counsel to entry-level exercisers while minimizing the risks associated with starting an exercise program. With the guidelines, ACOG wanted "to get more people started in aerobics of a moderate nature so we'll have some chance of holding them to a lifestyle that involves exercise."

Dr. Patricia Potter, former chief medical officer of the U.S. Olympic Committee and a member of the Women's Sports Foundation medical advisory board, clarifies further: "There's no reason for women to limit their exercise to this small quantity. Women should not be discouraged from exercising more intensely, more frequently, and for longer durations [than the minimum described in the ACOG guidelines]. Recreational athletes may choose to exercise in greater amounts, and competitive athletes will need to."

## Your Cycle's Influence on Athletic Performance

We've been discussing the effect of exceptional athletic performance on your body. Now let's reverse gears and discuss the effect of your monthly period on your performance.

Most of the information on this subject is purely anecdotal. Reports from female athletes reveal no clear-cut pattern. Some women claim their performances are so adversely affected by menstruation that they use oral contraceptives to modify their cycles. Other women have set world records during their periods.

Linda S. Lamont, Ph.D., an exercise physiologist in the cardiac division of Cleveland Metropolitan General Hospital, decided to infuse these anecdotal reports with scientific evidence in a study focusing on blood lactate levels of menstruating female athletes during one hour of moderate exercise.

Without sufficient oxygen, the muscles produce lactic acid, which accumulates in the blood. A low level of blood lactic acid during exercise, then, signifies great endurance capacity.

Dr. Lamont studied nine exercising women twice—at the beginning and near the end of their menstrual cycles. She found that blood lactate levels did increase during exercise in both phases, but it did not differ significantly between phases. She concluded: "The menstrual cycle exerts no effect on blood lactate concentrations during moderate–intense, steady-state exercise."

What's missing from Dr. Lamont's study is blood lactate information about the same nine women on typical exercise days when they're not menstruating. The few other studies that exist are, like the anecdotal reports, divided about fifty-fifty between those that say menstruation impedes performance and those that say it enhances it. Clearly, the jury is still out on this matter.

# 17

# Aerobics as Prevention and Treatment for Osteoporosis

One out of every four American women is now, or will be, a victim of osteoporosis. That's a startling statistic. A woman is even more at risk if she's fair-skinned and of northern European, Japanese, or Chinese descent. Such ancestry gives a woman a genetic predisposition to this bone-wasting disease.

## Osteoporosis—Elderly Women's Waterloo

For women, osteoporosis is a common condition of middle and old age. It's characterized by too little bone mass. In addition, the bone that remains is brittle, weak, and extremely susceptible to fracture. Because the skeletal structure is so weak, even the slightest amount of stress can cause an osteoporotic woman to break her hip, wrist, or spine.

Each year, almost 200,000 American women break their hip bones dues to osteoporosis; 15 to 20 percent of them die within three months from ensuing complications. Those who do survive are often incapacitated and need continuing care.

Osteoporosis is also the reason why so many older women have dental problems: the jawbone, too, is affected by the disease. As a consequence, women may lose their teeth, and if too much of the jawbone ridge is lost, their dentures won't seat properly. Difficulties in chewing may cause these women to avoid the much-needed high-fiber foods, which can lead to nutritional problems.

Clearly, osteoporosis is more than just a physical ailment. It has nutritional ramifications and often leads to psychological problems as well. As stricken women develop such deformities as "dowager's hump"—an extremely stooped posture—they lose all confidence in their appearance and withdraw from contact with the outside world.

Hiding indoors not only increases feelings of isolation and depression but may cause a vitamin D deficiency from lack of sunlight. This further aggravates the basic problem, because vitamin D aids in calcium absorption and calcium is an important component of bone tissue.

## Are You at Risk for Osteoporosis?

In truth, all women are at risk. But if you haven't yet reached those postmenopausal years when the incidence of osteoporosis shoots up dramatically, you can do a lot to reduce your chances of developing the problem later in life.

Bone loss is tied to advancing age; it's normal and inevitable. Bone mass reaches its peak in women at approximately age 35, then decreases at a rate of about 10 percent per decade, until menopause, when it accelerates for five to ten years. About age 60, it slows down somewhat, which is not to say it stops entirely even then. (The loss in men begins some ten to fifteen years later and proceeds at about one-half the rate of women.)

The bottom line is that by age 65, half of all women have a bone mineral density below the normal fracture threshold of a 20-year-old woman. By age 85, *all* women are below this fracture threshold.

## Its Causes Are Many

Many factors contribute to the development of osteoporosis. There's the inheritance factor we already mentioned. There's the nutritional factor. Too little calcium in the diet increases your chances of falling prey to the disease. There's also the role of exercise, specifically weight-bearing exercise. Research not only shows that such exercise builds up bone mass and helps *prevent* osteoporosis, but one pioneering study among elderly women even showed a small reversal of the problem through exercise therapy.

There are other, less well-established causes that have also received mention in the medical literature. These "hidden causes" range from thyroid disorders, major stomach surgery, paralysis, and surgical removal of the ovaries, to chronic use of steroids or anticonvulsives. Cigarette smoking, heavy drinking, frequent consumption of large amounts of protein, and a chronic lack of vitamin D (which aids in calcium absorption) have also been implicated.

But the factor that most experts pinpoint as the disease's cause is hormonal. They believe that a *lack of adequate estrogen* is the main culprit, a theory that explains why postmenopausal women develop the disease in droves and why amenorrheic female athletes are particularly susceptible (see chapter 16).

## If Prevention Is Your Goal . . .

It is a mistake for young women to write off osteoporosis as an old woman's disease, since, once stricken, there's very little a woman can do to reverse the debilitating effects of the disease. At best, a victim can just stop the problem from getting worse.

To help you gauge whether you'll be one of the stricken ones in later life, we've devised the following risk factor test:

### Fit Quiz: My Osteoporosis Risk Factor Profile

| | True | False |
|---|---|---|
| 1. I have a family history of osteoporosis. | ______ | ______ |
| 2. My ancestors are from the British Isles, northern Europe, China, or Japan. | ______ | ______ |
| 3. I'm very fair-skinned. | ______ | ______ |
| 4. I'm small-boned. | ______ | ______ |
| 5. I'm over 35 years old. | ______ | ______ |
| 6. I've had my ovaries removed. | ______ | ______ |
| 7. I breast-fed my baby. | ______ | ______ |
| 8. I'm allergic to milk and milk products. | ______ | ______ |
| 9. I avoid milk and cheese in my diet. | ______ | ______ |
| 10. My daily routine is stressful. | ______ | ______ |
| 11. I smoke. | ______ | ______ |
| 12. I classify myself as a moderate to heavy drinker. | ______ | ______ |
| 13. I get very little exercise. | ______ | ______ |
| 14. I get so much high-intensity exercise that I'm amenorrheic (stopped menstruating). | ______ | ______ |
| 15. I consume a lot of soft drinks. | ______ | ______ |
| 16. My diet is very high in protein. | ______ | ______ |
| 17. My exposure to bright sunlight and dietary intake of vitamin D is low. | ______ | ______ |

When it comes to osteoporosis, these statements are all negative. If you answered True to just two of them, you are at risk for developing osteoporosis. The more checkmarks in the True column, the greater your risk. We should point out that it's the rare woman who can honestly say none of these statements applies to her.

But the good news is that risk does not necessarily become future reality—that is, if you're determined to prevent it. Evidence from many clinical studies strongly suggests that osteoporosis is preventable. While you cannot control the risk factors in statements 1 through 8 in the above quiz, you can do plenty to change the behaviors and habits described in statements 9 through 17. The choice is yours.

## A Prevention Regimen

If you're premenopausal, your prevention program should be built around a diet containing 1,500 mg. of calcium per day (see chapter 12), and a regular program of weight-bearing exercise.

The medical community first became aware of the causal relationship between certain kinds of exercise and bone density in the early years of the space program. It was found that astronauts, even in the short time they're in a weightless state during flights, experience measurable bone loss. As a result of that discovery, today's astronauts are required to exercise regularly while in space.

A battery of studies has established the fact that *exercising against gravity*—walking and running, for example—builds bone mass. Studies comparing the bone mass of athletes to that of sedentary individuals are especially revealing. All show that bone mineral content as well as bone width are significantly higher in the athletes. In addition, the athletes show the greatest bone development in the limbs they rely on most—the arm tennis players use to wield their racquet, for instance.

In short, the more bone mass you have to begin with, the better off you are when the normal aging process begins to rob you of vital bone minerals. That's why men, with their larger bones, have a distinct advantage.

The form of exercise you choose is critical, as the case of Anne Buckner underscores. Anne is one of our patients at the Cooper Clinic. In her sixties, she's a very fit woman, as evidenced by her diet and treadmill stress test results. Nonetheless, Anne has a moderate degree of osteoporosis. We can explain this only by the fact that Anne is a swimmer. Although she's been swimming regularly for years, this nonweight-bearing form of aerobics offered her little protection against osteoporosis.

## ERT—Controversial but, Perhaps, What You Need

Once you are menopausal, consider carefully, through discussions with your doctor, beginning estrogen replacement therapy (ERT). Estrogen is a key element in staving off osteoporosis because it helps the body better utilize calcium.

Higher calcium intake alone won't do much to arrest postmenopausal bone loss, as a new study, published in the *New England Journal of Medicine*, points out. For two years, researchers monitored bone loss in 43 Danish women who were taking calcium supplements of 2,000 mg. a day. They lost bone rapidly, just about as fast as a second group of female controls who took no extra calcium.

Granted, ERT is controversial, since studies have linked it to an increased risk of developing cancer of the uterus lining (endometrial cancer). But as researchers have learned more about this form of cancer and about ways to administer estrogen more effectively and safely, it appears that ERT no longer has to increase cancer risk.

In considering ERT, keep in mind the following: First, endometrial cancer is rare even among women on ERT. Moreover, women who, for other reasons, are at high risk for this cancer can, through careful medical scrutiny, be identified *before* ERT is prescribed. Finally, endometrial cancer is slow-growing and is nearly always diagnosed while still curable.

Granted, the latter statement may provide little incentive to proceed with ERT. However, consider some of the even more recent evidence.

Studies now show that the risk of developing endometrial cancer can be greatly reduced, perhaps eliminated, when estrogens are given in cycles of 3 weeks on and 1 week off, and are combined with the hormone progesterone in the last 7 to 13 days of each cycle. The latest and best studies also show that ERT does *not* promote cancer of the breast. Indeed, it may offer some protection against it. And breast cancer is a far more common death threat to women than endometrial cancer.

On the other hand, not all women are candidates for ERT for other reasons: either they're too sensitive to its side effects, or they have other medical problems that make it too risky.

In some women, ERT induces nausea, vomiting, tissue swelling or abdominal bloating, and cyclical vaginal bleeding resembling a brief menstrual period on days when the hormone therapy is stopped. ERT is also not recommended for women who already have endometrial or breast cancer, blood clots, strokes, coronary artery disease, a history of migraines, liver disease, or undiagnosed vaginal bleeding.

## Treatment Once You Have It

Barring a medical history that includes any of the above conditions, it is recommended you seriously consider ERT if you're already showing signs of rapid bone loss. But how do you ascertain the rate at which your bones are shrinking?

There are two new high-tech bone-scanning methods that make detection possible. They are dual-photon absorptiometry (DPA) and quantitative computed tomography (QCT). Both are noninvasive, definitive ways to spot ominously rapid declines in bone mass in either the spine or the hip. They also offer doctors the opportunity to monitor the effects of bone-building treatments and to keep on top of bone loss due to chemotherapy or other iatrogenic (physician-induced) causes.

One important federal watchdog has lined up recently in favor of ERT. In April 1986, the federal Food and Drug Administration (FDA) approved the use of oral estrogen to retard bone loss in postmenopausal women. The agency also emphasized that ERT was not enough, however. It had to be combined with adequate calcium intake of 1,500 mg. a day and a regular program of weight-bearing exercise.

However, if you already suffer from osteoporosis, you must be particularly careful about any exercise you undertake. Don't ever forget that your bones fracture easily. A walking program is safest. Safer still are walks taken in the company of a companion with whom you can link arms for support when needed. Also, walk outdoors in the sunlight as much as possible. The vitamin D in sunlight helps metabolize calcium.

Most osteoporosis experts claim that current treatment methods only *retard* further bone loss. They cannot *reverse* it. However, we know of two instances where reversal was achieved.

In the first, elderly women, ranging in age from 69 to 95, were involved in a three-year treatment program. All had advanced cases of this bone-wasting disease. The women, all nursing-home residents, took calcium and vitamin D supplements and did chair exercises for 30 minutes three times a week. Dr. Everett L. Smith, the program designer and head of the Biogerontology Laboratory at the University of Wisconsin, reported a 2.3 percent increase in the mineral content of his patients' leg bones, whereas a comparable group of nonexercisers showed a 3.3 percent loss.

The other great success story occurred right here in the Cooper Clinic in Dallas. Mrs. Frances Elverda Allsup came to us some four years ago with an advanced case of osteoporosis. She was in such bad shape that we couldn't risk putting her on any program of weight-bearing exercise. The odds that she would break a bone were too great. Instead, we sent her to a bone specialist in Dallas. He biopsied her bone tissue, analyzed its composition, and then developed a treatment regimen that included various types of injections including fluorides. Her condition improved dramatically.

The last time we saw Frances was at a wedding here in Dallas. We watched this 82-year-old woman and her 86-year-old husband dance together, almost nonstop, for several hours.

# 18
# The Battle Against Heart Disease

When it comes to heart disease, be thankful you're a woman. It leads to premature death in men far more frequently than in women. In fact, up to the age of 60, the incidence of heart disease in women remains five to six times lower than in men. Thereafter, the rates in women catch up quickly. By the age of 80, the incidence is about the same.

Thus, you could say that sex—being born male rather than female—is a major risk factor in cardiovascular disease. Why this is so is still a matter of medical debate.

It's certainly to women's benefit that they tend to have higher levels of the good high-density lipoproteins (HDLs) in their bloodstreams. Authorities also cite female reproductive hormones, such as estrogen, as protective mechanisms. This would explain why heart disease is so rare among women in their childbearing years but increases dramatically *after* menopause, when estrogen levels decline.

Indeed, estrogen was once viewed as such a significant immunizing factor in coronary disease in women that some physicians, on an experimental basis, actually used estrogen treatments on men, particularly after they'd had heart attacks. Unfortunately, so much estrogen was required to achieve protection that it also produced feminizing effects: the men started to develop breasts and lose their beards and deep voices. The therapy was halted, for obvious reasons.

Let us caution you against smugness, though. Just because you're a woman, do not assume you'll escape the ravages of heart disease. For the truth of the matter is this:

*Overall, heart disease kills more women in our society than does any other medical problem.*

Thousands of woman die of heart attacks every year. And many more suffer from the pain and disability of cardiovascular disease even if it isn't fatal.

In this chapter, we'll tell you what you can do to increase your chances of avoiding this fate.

## Heart Disease—The Modern-Day Plague

Until this century, the major causes of disability and death were infectious diseases—smallpox, diphtheria, typhoid, dysentery, tuberculosis, and the like. But modern-day epidemics are a different story. In Westernized countries, deaths from infections are relatively rare, whereas coronary heart disease and cancer are major killers.

Interestingly, our contemporary killers are almost unheard of in Third World and developing countries. The work of Dr. Dennis Burkitt, a surgeon in an East African teaching hospital, bears this out. Over a twenty-year period, he accumulated an enormous amount of data from postmortem examinations performed on Africans who had died in his hospital. He found that less than one case of coronary heart disease occurred each year among the 98 percent of Africans in his sample.

Clearly, the causes of mortality in "civilized" society are far different from those in primitive cultures, even today. Dr. Burkitt's findings suggest that the disparity is due to lifestyle factors. We smoke, overeat, drink too much, and otherwise behave in ways that are detrimental to our health. In contrast, primitive people's lives and habits are inherently more protective against coronary heart disease.

Cancer, heart disease, and similar noninfectious killers are often referred to as the "diseases of civilization." The irony is that such diseases are, to a great extent, self-inflicted. Many of us freely choose to ruin our health despite the fact that we have at our disposal far more scientific knowledge about the human body and its functions than any previous generation.

But enough of the bad news. The good news is that a great many people in Westernized societies have seen the light over the last twenty years. Our headlong flight into personal self-destruction has been arrested somewhat, although much remains to be done.

## A Short History, A Long Shadow

Before 1940, heart disease was a rarity, even in America. It accounted for only some 200,000 deaths a year. But soon thereafter it started its rapid ascent. By 1968, the figure was about 500,000, and the disease had become the single greatest cause of death in every Westernized country.

In 1968, heart disease peaked. Since then, I'm happy to report, the picture has improved markedly. By 1987, the incidence of coronary deaths had dropped some 37 percent. And if this downward trend continues at the current rate, by the year 2015 the average lifespan of an American child born that year will be in excess of 80 years. Compare that to the life expectancy facing children born in America in 1986: a male child could expect to live to be 72 years old; a female child, to 78 years.

## One-Man Survey

Why this improvement?

Since 1968, when my first book, *Aerobics,* was published, I've traveled all over the world, promoting the concept of preventive medicine. I now have a broad sense of how people feel about personal health care.

I see five predominant reasons for the reduction in the incidence of heart disease over the last two decades:

People are smoking less. Modern technology can detect and treat hypertension better. We have greater knowledge about the harmful effects of stress. More people are exercising. And more people are concerned about their diets—their eating habits have improved.

Statistics bolster my case:

In 1964, more than 50 percent of the American male population smoked cigarettes. Currently, the figure is less than 30 percent. Women haven't exercised as much self-restraint, unfortunately. Those women who do smoke seem to find it much harder to quit.

In the late 1960s, only 10 to 15 percent of the hypertension in this country was detected, treated, and effectively controlled. By 1984, more than 50 percent of people with high blood pressure were receiving adequate treatment.

While modern life seems to contain more and more sources of stress, at least we now recognize stress as the enemy and are devising methods to better cope with it.

According to a Gallup poll, in the early 1960s, only about 24 percent of adults exercised regularly. By 1984, the number had increased to 59 percent.

By 1979, almost two-thirds of all Americans had changed their eating habits for reasons of health. The result: among middle-aged men in the 1960s, average cholesterol levels were in the 230s. By the early 1980s, the figure had dropped to the 215-to-220s range.

## A Class Difference

The reasons for these improvements, I believe, all involve changes in lifestyle. Unfortunately, certain segments of the population have been more amenable to such changes than others, a statement borne out by an exhaustive scientific inquiry, often referred to as The Du Pont Study. Dr. Sidney Pell, an epidemiologist, authored the study, which was published in the April 18, 1985, issue of the *New England Journal of Medicine.* Dr. Pell probed the incidence of heart attacks among Du Pont employees from 1957 to 1983. His sample population was basically male, and total numbers varied from 88,000 in 1957 to 109,000 in 1983.

Over the 26-year period of the study, Dr. Pell discovered that the incidence rate fell 28.2 percent among all employees. But when the rate was broken down by salaried employees versus hourly wage workers, the situation was different. The white-collar workers experienced a 38 percent drop, the blue-collar workers only an 18 percent drop.

This discrepancy is large and warrants comments.

It would appear there's a socioeconomic factor at play here. That is, the better educated have changed their lifestyles more than have the less educated. The blue-collar worker is still stubbornly clinging to his or her beer can and high-cholesterol fried foods, while his or her boss is starting to heed the message of wellness advocates.

Just as being born male places a person at greater risk for heart disease, being in a lower socioeconomic bracket may too. My personal experience and knowledge of the wellness movement supports this assertion.

I'm sorry to have to admit it, but I'll wager that 90 percent of the women who read this book are reasonably well educated and affluent. And I suspect that wager will hold true in any country where this book is eventually sold. I haven't yet figured out how to reach a broader class spectrum with my wellness message, but it's certainly one of my major goals.

## Lifestyle Change

The lifestyle changes required to slash your chances of developing heart disease will be harder for some of you than others. It depends on your current physical condition.

If you haven't engaged in any physical exercise beyond housework for years, a major summoning of resolve may be necessary. On the other hand, if you've already given up smoking, reached your target weight, and found ways to minimize the stress in your life, you're halfway home.

Instituting any major change in your life is a two-part process. The first part involves education—gaining a thorough understanding of why change is in order. The second half of the change process involves action. Good intentions are fine, but they come to naught unless you act on them. You can't just talk about giving up cigarettes, for instance. You have to *do* it. You can't just join a health club. You have to go there regularly and work out.

## The 11 Coronary Risk Factors—Some You Can Change, Some You Can't

If you read health articles, you see the phrase *risk factors* all the time. Risk factors are hereditary traits, personal habits or behaviors, or environmental factors that increase your chances of getting certain diseases.

Risk factors fall into two categories: those you can control and those you can't. The risk factors of age, sex, race, and heredity are acts of God; you can't do anything about them. Other risk factors—such as smoking, overeating, and sedentary living—involve decisions you've made, consciously or unconsciously. These factors are within your control. Concentrate your energies on them.

Cardiovascular disease has 11 risk factors associated with it. The list grew out of pioneering research conducted by the National Institutes of Health (NIH) in 1949. The NIH's Framingham Study analyzed the health of some 5,000 men and women in that Massachusetts town, nearly the entire community, to determine the role that various factors played in causing heart disease.

The American Heart Association, the nation's premier force for cardiovascular health, has updated the original list as new research comes to light. Today, the list encompasses:

Family history
Abnormal resting (ECG)
Stress, personality behavior patterns
Hypertension
Cholesterol, triglycerides
Diet rich in fats and cholesterol
Obesity
Inactivity—sedentary living habits
Cigarette smoking
Oral contraceptives
Glucose—diabetes

You can control most of the factors on this list. Let's go through them, one by one:

• **Family history.** This is one of those things you can't do anything about. If you have blood relatives who died or suffer from heart disease during early adulthood or middle age, you are more susceptible to heart disease yourself. That's a fact.

We all know of seemingly fit people who died suddenly, at a relatively young age, of heart attacks. It's a surprise to everyone. But it's not so surprising if you review their family medical history. The key to the puzzle often lies in their genes. Many such victims had relatives who also suffered from heart attacks—maybe or maybe not fatal—before age 50.

There's no certainty as to why coronary disease runs in families. In some cases, it's just that bad habits, such as overeating, inactivity, and smoking, run in families.

In other cases, where family members are health-conscious, a genetic link is the more obvious answer. Some hereditary weakness predisposes family members to cardiovascular deformities. Or the weakness manifests itself in a tendency to develop the precursors to heart disease—high blood pressure, hyperlipidemia, or diabetes, for example. Indeed, all three of these medical conditions are coronary risk factors in their own right.

This is not to scare those of you who have a strong family history of cardiovascular disease. Even if your family is riddled with it, this does not mean you will *inevitably* suffer premature disability or death. Again, there are other risk factors over which you can exert control, thereby lessening your chances of falling victim to your relatives' fate:

• **Abnormal resting electrocardiogram (ECG).** An abnormal resting ECG and family history of heart disease are risk factors in the sense that they help you *predict* heart function problems. They aren't causal agents in the sense that obesity or other factors are.

An abnormal resting ECG is a serious matter, possibly signaling the presence of moderate to severe coronary disease. A woman with such a condition cannot undertake an exercise program until it has been adequately diagnosed and treated.

You are definitely ahead of the game if you know you have an abnormal resting ECG. However, you would be much further ahead of the game if you had discovered your cardiovascular problem earlier, before it reached this obvious and more serious stage. This is why we believe so fervently in treadmill stress tests. They are an excellent diagnostic tool for detecting problems *before* they reach the acute stage. It's the reason why we insist that any woman over 40 have one before she begins a vigorous exercise program. And, at the very least, we insist that women between ages 35 and 39 have a resting ECG (see chapter 5).

• **Stress, personality behavior patterns.** We devoted chapter 14 to the causes and remedies for stress. We pointed out that your personality type, to a great extent, determines how you deal with stress and, in turn, how likely you are to suffer tension-induced organic symptoms—headaches, hypertension, back pain, and the like.

We also pointed out that work-ethic–driven puritans, the so-called Type A personalities who disregard stress in the name of superhuman achievement are courting self-destruction. Why? Because unrelieved stress over a long period of time will eventually disable you and possibly kill you. The knockout punch will probably come in the form of either a stroke or some other cardiovascular-related ailment.

If there's chronic stress in your life, our advice to you is urgent and straightforward: Do something immediately to minimize it.

How? By applying the Triple-A Strategy, the best way we know to analyze and reduce the threat of stress in your life.

When confronted with a recurring stressful situation, stop and think for a moment. Ask yourself, "In the future, how can I *a*void it? *A*lter it? Or, if those aren't possible, *a*dapt to it, changing my way of handling the situation to make it, at the very least, more tolerable?"

• **Hypertension.** Hypertension, or high blood pressure, is called "the silent killer." It's "silent" because its symptoms aren't apparent—until something devastating occurs, such as a stroke, heart attack, or kidney failure. Hypertension accelerates hardening of the arteries. It contributes to 30 percent of all deaths due to kidney failure annually and is implicated in an even greater percentage of deaths annually due to heart attack, cardiovascular disease, and stroke.

This quiet murderer is also pervasive. A large segment of the adult population in Westernized countries suffers from it—some 15 to 20 percent.

A little background: We all have a certain level of blood pressure within our circulatory systems. If we didn't, blood wouldn't course through our bodies in a normal manner. It's the *level* of our blood pressure that's important and enables our doctors to decide whether it falls in the normal or high range. (There's no real medical problem with "low blood pressure," by the way. Lower-than-normal blood pressure is a good thing unless there are symptoms associated with it. Fainting frequently or constantly feeling light-headed are the most common hypotensive symptoms.)

Another thing about blood pressure: it changes throughout the day. Stress, eating, exercise, dealing with a surly bus driver—all affect your blood pressure level. During exercise, blood pressure is particularly high, but it drops swiftly, or should, as soon as you stop.

Every time you have a medical exam, a doctor or nurse takes your blood pressure. In an attempt to standardize readings by minimizing influences that raise blood pressure, they'll probably ask you to lie down and relax. Then they'll put a cuff around your upper arm, inflate it, and listen to your artery through a stethoscope as the cuff deflates. They end up with a "blood pressure reading."

A blood pressure reading is composed of two numbers, separated by a slash. The top number, which is always higher, is the systolic reading. That indicates the maximum pressure in your arteries exerted by each heartbeat. The bottom number, which is always lower, is the diastolic reading, or the pressure in your arteries between heartbeats. A blood pressure less than 140-over-90, or 140/90, is considered normal.

At exactly what point normal blood pressure enters into the abnormal realm remains arbitrary since everyone's body tolerances are different. However, for the purpose of definition, we'll use the World Health Organization's guidelines. It defines borderline hypertension as a systolic reading between 140 and 160 and diastolic between 90 and 95. When the diastolic pressure moves up to between 96 and 104, mild hypertension is diagnosed. Moderate hypertension is when diastolic is between 105 and 114; and severe, when the diastolic pressure is 115 or greater.

There's a controversy in the medical profession about whether mild hypertension needs to be treated. But no one disputes that moderate to severe hypertension needs serious medical treatment.

In 95 percent of the cases, the cause of the hypertension is essential, idiopathic, or, in other words, unknown. In the other 5 percent, the cause is related to something obvious such as kidney problems, rare disturbances of the hormone-secreting system, or tumors.

This is not to say that medical science hasn't studied hypertension extensively and that a lot of well-documented statements can't be made about it. For example, we know that blacks are more prone to high blood pressure than whites and that a tendency toward hypertension can be inherited.

In terms of sex, hypertension is more common among young adult men than women of the same age. After age 50, though, the incidence in both sexes is about the same. Indeed, in the 55 to 65 age range, some 35 to 40 percent of both men *and* women have higher than normal blood pressure, for this is one medical condition closely correlated with advancing age. In the normal course of events, blood pressure increases slightly with age. This is why a blood pressure reading that physicians might regard as acceptable in a 70-year-old woman might be considered elevated in a 30-year-old.

Dietary factors also come into play. It's known that a diet high in salt and saturated fat increases blood pressure in many people. A number of studies underscore the connection, with salt being the worst culprit. Perhaps the most telling evidence involves the people of northern Japan. They have both the highest salt consumption (26 grams per day) and incidence of hypertension (40 percent) in the world today. Nations with low salt consumption have the lowest incidence.

When it comes to salt, Americans err on the high side. The average American consumes between 10 and 15 grams (2 to 3 teaspoons) daily, or 12 pounds per year. This is still far too much, since man's physiological requirements call for 200 mg. (one-tenth of a teaspoon) daily.

How does sodium chloride increase blood pressure? The following scenario has been proposed to explain it:

High intake of salt stimulates the nervous system and causes the body to retain water, making the blood vessels "waterlogged." This heightened nerve stimulation causes the heart to pump an excessive amount of blood, which in turn causes the blood vessels to constrict in order to reduce the elevated cardiac output. Thus, your heart and blood vessels are working at cross purposes. The constriction of the vessels causes the blood pressure to rise until you have hypertension.

Even if you don't have a hypertension problem, reducing the amount of salt in your diet is a good preventive measure. Unfortunately, this won't be as easy as you'd expect, given the high salt content of canned and packaged foods. There are strong commercial incentives for food manufacturers to use hidden salt additives, such as sodium nitrate or monosodium glutamate. They prolong shelf life.

The National Institute Task Force recommends the following strategies for achieving a low-salt diet: (1) check the labels on processed foods and avoid those with high salt or salt additives; (2) reduce the amount of salt you add to foods during cooking, possibly adding herbs, spices, or lemon instead; (3) never reach for the salt shaker at the table.

If you already have hypertension, no doubt your doctor has prescribed a low-salt diet in addition to medication. Studies have shown that moderate salt restriction enhances the effectiveness of drug therapy and sometimes significantly lowers the amount of medication needed. Reliance on less medication is all to the good, since drugs invariably have side effects.

Other methods for lowering blood pressure are to lose weight if you're overweight, stop smoking, cut down on the stress in your life, and exercise regularly. Alcohol consumption can contribute to elevated blood pressure, although this seems to apply only to heavy drinkers.

• **Cholesterol, triglycerides.** If anyone had any doubts about cholesterol's role in the promotion of heart disease, they were allayed in 1984 when researchers announced the results of an eight-year trial involving 3,800 middle-aged men. All had excessive levels of cholesterol. Over the course of the study, those volunteers who cut their levels the most, taking a drug and adhering to a low-fat diet, had a dramatic reduction in both fatal and nonfatal heart attacks, compared with those whose levels were trimmed only slightly or not at all.

A conclusion of the study: a 25 percent reduction in cholesterol levels can reduce the incidence of heart attacks by 50 percent.

What that 1984 study didn't explain is how or why cholesterol-lowering prevents heart attacks. A new study, released in June 1987, is the first firm evidence that the lowering of cholesterol can retard, even reverse, one of the prime causal agents of heart attacks—arteries clogged with fatty deposits.

This study involved 162 middle-aged men who had undergone bypass surgery and had confirmed arteriosclerosis. Researchers at the University of Southern California School of Medicine actually looked inside these men's coronary arteries before and after they went on a two-year diet/drug treatment program to lower cholesterol levels.

Results: While all the subjects went on low-fat diets, only the half who also took the cholesterol-lowering substances (niacin and colestipol) experienced significant drops in their cholesterol levels. Even more important, researchers discovered that some 62 percent of the drug-treated patients had fat deposits that had either stopped growing or had shrunk discernibly.

In chapter 12 we explained that cholesterol is made up of low-density lipoproteins (LDLs) and high-density lipoproteins (HDLs). LDLs promote a harmful buildup of plaque on arterial walls, while HDLs scour out those same passageways. Thus, you should aim to increase the ratio of HDL to LDL cholesterol in your body. Ideally, your HDL should comprise at least 25 percent of your total cholesterol count.

Triglycerides are also fats found in your blood. Researchers have discovered that when a person's triglycerides are high, usually their proportion of good HDLs is too low.

There are four recognized ways to maintain a good blood lipid balance—or to recover a good balance: (1) change your diet; (2) shed pounds if you're overweight; (3) exercise regularly; and (4) take the medications your doctor prescribes for you.

• **Diet rich in fats and cholesterol.** This is not only an indigestible diet, it's a dangerous one.

As we just mentioned, a change in your diet is one way to achieve blood lipid equilibrium. Eliminate the high-cholesterol foods and saturated fats—the all-American hamburger and french fries, for example—from your daily diet. Recommended substitutes are fish and poultry; and fish, olive, and vegetable oils. (See chapter 12.)

Fortunately, a new federally coordinated attack on cholesterol, called the National Cholesterol Education Program, should begin to show some results and make it easier for all of us to improve our diets. The program is expected to speed up the food industry's introduction of low-fat, low-cholesterol foods.

• **Obesity.** In chapter 13 we went to great lengths to drive home the message that obesity is not only unsightly. It can lead to an early death!

Studies show conclusively that obese people don't live as long as thin people. There are a variety of reasons for this. Excess weight is a contributing factor in high blood pressure and blood lipid imbalances. It's associated with gallbladder conditions, kidney disease, and various cancers. And it can trigger strokes and cardiovascular ailments.

But of all its heinous effects, obesity is the most strongly implicated in coronary disease. In and of itself, obesity raises your chances of having a heart attack even if none of the other 10 cardiac risk factors are present. That's highly unlikely, however. If you're overweight and have been for a significant period of time, it's probable that (1) you're inactive; (2) you're hypertensive; (3) you've got elevated blood lipids; and (4) you're a candidate for diabetes if you don't already have it. Note, these are all independent risk factors for heart disease.

• **Inactivity—sedentary living habits.** Among the many studies showing that exercise promotes cardiac health is one published in the December 17, 1982, issue of the *New England Journal of Medicine.* This University of Washington study focused on 163 men and women, ages 25 to 75, with no prior history of heart disease or any other major medical problems. Nevertheless, these people all suffered heart attacks and the majority died almost immediately.

The researchers interviewed the surviving spouses extensively on the subjects' prior exercise history, which they classified as either low-, medium-, or high-intensity. In addition, they identified a control sample of 163 people who had the same age, sex, marital status, residence (urban or suburban), and exercise profile as the original group.

To weed out any bias in the spouse reports, the 28 surviving members of the original group and nearly all of the control group were interviewed. No significant variation was noted.

The conclusion of the researchers was that the risk of primary cardiac arrest was 55 to 65 percent lower in people involved in high-intensity leisure-time activity—swimming, chopping wood, singles tennis, squash, or jogging—than in the low- to negligible-exercise group. This was just one more study supporting the hypothesis that regular, strenuous physical activity protects against primary cardiac arrest.

By what method does vigorous exercise promote cardiovascular health? In two predominant ways: by increasing the level of HDLs in your body and by lowering your blood pressure.

Studies show that while exercise does *not* reduce the level of total cholesterol, it *can* increase the level of good HDLs. One fifteen-month study of 19 women runners, a mean age of 29 years, is a case in point. While their total cholesterol and total body weight did not change, their HDL levels did. They went up significantly. The authors of the study speculated that this phenomenon was due either to the endurance training itself or to the associated decrease these women experienced in body fat content, or to both factors.

The kind of exercise you undertake also has some bearing on whether your HDL level rises. A study of 9 female runners versus 9 female weight trainers versus 9 sedentary controls came to this conclusion: there was no change in HDL levels among the latter two groups. Only the runners—the aerobic exercisers—showed significant HDL increases. And this reaction was the most pronounced in those runners who were nonsmokers, drank very little alcohol, and did not use oral contraceptives.

The cardio-protective effect of aerobics extends into the realm of hypertension too.

At the Cooper Clinic, we did a study of 3,552 healthy women, ages 18 to 75 years, to test the hypothesis that the greater a woman's physical fitness, the lower her likelihood of manifesting heart disease risk factors. This was an important study because few such inquiries target women, men being the primary focus of cardiovascular research. Second, our study used an objective measurement of physical fitness—a treadmill stress test—rather than the usual questionnaire or submaximal exercise tests from which researchers extrapolate estimates of subjects' maximum endurance.

As we expected, in general, the women in the higher fitness categories (superior or excellent) had the best risk factor profile. The results concerning blood pressure were particularly revealing: women with higher levels of fitness had heart rates and blood

**Maximum Heart Rates and Blood Pressures in Women by Physical Fitness Category and Age Group**

| | Low Fitness | | | Medium Fitness | | | High Fitness | | |
|---|---|---|---|---|---|---|---|---|---|
| Age (years) | HR (beats/min) | SBP (mm Hg) | DBP (mm Hg) | HR (beats/min) | SBP (mm Hg) | DBP (mm Hg) | HR (beats/min) | SBP (mm Hg) | DBP (mm Hg) |
| 18–24 | 191 | 157 | 75 | 191 | 155 | 71 | 191 | 154 | 66 |
| 25–29 | 187 | 147 | 74 | 189 | 151 | 70 | 188 | 163 | 67 |
| 30–34 | 182 | 149 | 74 | 184 | 151 | 71 | 185 | 160 | 69 |
| 35–39 | 181 | 151 | 76 | 184 | 155 | 73 | 185 | 160 | 70 |
| 40–44 | 175 | 156 | 77 | 180 | 155 | 73 | 182 | 158 | 71 |
| 45–49 | 171 | 157 | 79 | 175 | 160 | 74 | 178 | 165 | 71 |
| 50–54 | 167 | 169 | 80 | 170 | 167 | 80 | 176 | 172 | 75 |
| 55–59 | 162 | 161 | 79 | 168 | 167 | 78 | 172 | 174 | 71 |
| 60–64* | 160 | 186 | 77 | 161 | 176 | 79 | 166 | 158 | 65 |
| 65–75* | 146 | 191 | 85 | 153 | 170 | 76 | 158 | 178 | 73 |

*All cells in this age group contained less than 20 women.
HR = heart rate; SBP = systolic blood pressure; DBP = disatolic blood pressure.
Reproduced by permission of the *Journal of Cardiac Rehabilitation*, vol. 4, no. 11, November 1984.

pressure readings that showed a strong correlation with their aerobic performance on the treadmill, their age, and their body composition. The more physically fit women had higher maximum systolic blood pressures and lower maximum diastolic pressures as shown in the chart on page 269.

• **Cigarette smoking.** Hasn't the Surgeon General of the United States said it all? There has been enough written and debated on the subject of smoking that we need not go into great detail here.

One unhappy point must be made, though. Male smokers have heeded the Surgeon General's warning in greater numbers than have female smokers. According to the American Cancer Society, in 1964, 50 percent of all American men smoked, and 34 percent of all American women. By 1984, the figures were 33 percent for men and 28 percent for women, with the percentage even higher among black women. That's not much of a decrease on the distaff side.

This passivity on the part of female smokers is reflected in another statistic: in 1985, lung cancer overtook breast cancer as the leading malignant killer of American women. The trend is expected to continue unless women stop smoking in far greater numbers than they are now.

We hope things will change soon. A nationwide stop-smoking campaign was launched in 1986 by the 10,000-member American Medical Women's Association (AMWA). Among other things, AMWA wants to see more antismoking literature and media articles aimed directly at women, since, historically, men have been the focus.

Women are foolish to ignore the entreaties. A May 24, 1985, article in the *Journal of the American Medical Association* isolated cigarette smoking as responsible for as many as two-thirds of the heart attacks in women under age 50.

In the same issue of *JAMA*, another article offered hope to women who do muster the courage and self-control to quit. It suggests that even elderly people, who have smoked for three to four decades, can improve their health substantially and in a relatively short period of time by quitting. In as little as two weeks, their cerebral circulation and blood supply to the brain improved.

The agent of all of this bodily harm is a substance called nicotine, named after the French statesman Jean Nicot, in 1753. Nicotine is addictive and stimulates the central nervous system, the latter seemingly its great attraction for working women. (Women who work outside the home are more likely to smoke than housewives.) Its psychological effects are variously described as relaxing, arousing, and euphoriant. On the negative side, it increases heart rate by as much as 12 to 24 beats per minute, makes blood more likely to clot, and constricts blood vessels, which can increase systolic pressure by as much as 8 to 10 mm/Hg (millimeters/mercury).

A second culprit is the carbon monoxide in smoke. Like your automobile's exhaust, it diminishes your red blood cells' capacity to carry oxygen. As a result, your heart has to work harder. It has to pump more blood through your sooty, inefficient lungs to get the same amount of oxygen to your system.

If the causal relationship between smoking and heart attacks isn't sufficiently frightening for you smokers out there, there's one other piece of medical evidence you should know. A Harvard study released in 1986 made this statement: "Individuals who reported that they smoked more than one pack of cigarettes per day were 4.3 times as likely to have developed Alzheimer's disease as nonsmokers."

- **Oral contraceptives.** The birth control pill has many undesirable effects on the cardiovascular system.

First, it lowers HDL cholesterol. If you take the pill *and* smoke, the adverse effects can worsen. One study showed that women in their thirties who smoke and take oral contraceptives are nine times more likely to die of a heart attack than women their age who don't. The risk increases to fifty-five times more likely for women between 40 and 44 years of age.

Second, the pill decreases the level of a blood enzyme called plasmin. Its role is to keep blood from clotting. Without plasmin functioning in full force in your bloodstream, the chances of suffering a stroke increase.

You can stay on the pill and mitigate its negative effects somewhat, according to Duke University Medical School researchers. They found that women who are on the birth control pill have substantially lower plasmin levels, but if they exercise for 45 minutes, three times a week, they can increase those levels from 50 to 200 percent.

- **Glucose—diabetes.** Glucose is blood sugar. Significantly high levels may indicate a diabetic tendency or actual diabetes.

Diabetes is a condition in which the level of glucose in the blood rises abnormally because another organic substance—insulin—is low or is not doing its job properly. The job of insulin, a specialized hormone, is to control blood sugar levels. Symptoms of diabetes are increased thirst and hunger, frequent urination, unexplained weight change, dizziness, fatigue, and sweating.

There are two types of diabetes:

Type I is a genetic deficiency and manifests itself in childhood. The pancreas does not produce insulin, so the Type I diabetic requires daily injections of it. Type II diabetes seldom starts until the postmenopausal years and is often referred to as "adult onset diabetes." It is noninsulin-dependent in that the pancreas does produce insulin, but it either isn't sufficient or it's ineffective.

Type II diabetics are, typically, inactive and overweight. If they would lose weight and get in better condition, often they could control their problem *without* insulin or medications.

Controlling diabetes, even if the condition is mild, is important because the complications arising from untreated diabetes can be serious. They include problems with the kidneys, eyes, and heart. Diabetics are two times more likely to become heart attack victims than are nondiabetics. This risk is higher in younger diabetic women, who are even more prone to coronary artery disease than are diabetic men.

It's still unclear why heart disease is so common in diabetics. Researchers have a number of hypotheses, focusing on the greater prevalence of hypertension among sufferers (disputed) to obesity, high blood fats, and abnormally sticky blood composition (fibrinolysis). But no matter what the determinants, most physicians agree on the importance of a treatment regimen that emphasizes no smoking, reducing weight, control of elevated cholesterol levels, and strict monitoring and reduction of glucose levels.

Because diabetes is a chronic (meaning lifelong) condition, don't expect to cure it. But you can *control* it—and reduce the chances of developing complications. The means to that end are medication, diet, weight loss (if you are overweight), and exercise.

Exercise is a particularly useful therapy. Among other things, it burns calories, using up glucose. At the same time, it increases the body's sensitivity to insulin, which is frequently the Type II diabetic's problem. Even in the presence of insulin, this woman's body does not respond properly to it. Many diabetologists now claim that diabetics who participate in medically prescribed diet and exercise programs can nearly always reduce their insulin requirements and sometimes eliminate the need for medication entirely.

As an air force flight surgeon back in the 1960s, I saw firsthand the possibilities of exercise as treatment for diabetes. Air force medical regulations concerning pilots are very strict. In fact, there are few medications that active-duty pilots are allowed to take—and this includes oral medications to control adult onset diabetes, or Type II.

I discovered that in many cases, a pilot could control his diabetes without medication if he reduced to his ideal body weight and faithfully adhered to a regular physical activity program. These pilots found that not only their diabetes improved but other medical problems or conditions as well. The results were so good that I wrote about them in an article for pilots entitled, "Flying Status Insurance at No Cost."

## Your Coronary Risk Profile

We've discussed what you can do to avoid future heart trouble. Now we want to help you quantify your coronary risk profile. Are you at very low, low, moderate, high, or very high risk of developing heart disease?

The following charts will help you find out. Notice that each chart corresponds to a different age range. Select the one that applies to you. The next time you have a medical exam, bring that chart along and fill it in with your doctor's help.

Refer to the sample chart to see how to score yourself. Notice that the chart is divided according to coronary risk factors. Under each factor there are a series of numbers indicating the point value you should assign yourself under that risk factor. Write your point value in the box. Add up the numbers in all the little boxes and then place the total in the "Total Coronary Risk" box in the lower right-hand corner of the page.

# Coronary Risk Profile

**Cooper Clinic/Dallas, Texas**

**Name:** Jane Jogger | **Females: *40–49 Years of Age**

| Percentile Rankings | Balke Treadmill Time (min.) | Total Cholesterol/ HDL Ratio | Triglyceride (mg. %) | Glucose (mg. %) | % Body Fat | Resting Blood Pressure Systolic (mm HG) | Resting Blood Pressure Diastolic (mm HG) |
|---|---|---|---|---|---|---|---|
| Your Values | 11:00 [2] | 3.3 [0] | 100 [0] | 95 [0] | 28.9 [2] | 122 [0] | 80 [0] |
| 99 | 23:09 | 2.0 | 29.3 | 73.2 | 11.8 | 86.0 | 58.0 |
| 97 | 20:00 | 2.2 | 35.8 | 77.0 | 14.6 | 90.0 | 60.0 |
| 95 | 18:30 | 2.3 | 39.0 | 79.0 | 16.2 | 92.0 | 62.0 |
| 90 | 17:00 | 2.5 | 45.0 | 82.0 | 18.2 | 96.0 | 65.0 |
| 85 | 16:00 | 2.7 | 49.0 | 84.0 | 20.0 | 100.0 | 68.0 |
| 80 | 15:00 | 2.7 | 53.0 | 86.0 | 21.2 | 100.0 | 70.0 |
| 75 | 14:10 | 2.8 | 57.0 | 88.0 | 22.2 | 102.0 | 70.0 |
| 70 | 13:30 | 2.9 | 60.0 | 89.0 | 23.2 | 104.0 | 70.0 |
| 65 | [2] 13:00 | 3.0 | 63.0 | 90.0 | [1] 24.1 | 106.0 | 72.0 |
| 60 | 12:02 | 3.1 | 67.0 | 91.0 | 24.8 | 108.0 | 74.0 |
| 55 | 12:00 | 3.2 | 71.0 | 93.0 | 25.4 | 110.0 | 74.0 |
| 50 | 11:20 | 3.3 | 74.0 | 94.0 | [2] 26.3 | 110.0 | 76.0 |
| 45 | 11:00 | 3.4 | 79.0 | 95.0 | 27.2 | 112.0 | 78.0 |
| 40 | 10:22 | 3.5 | 84.0 | 96.0 | 27.9 | 114.0 | 80.0 |
| 35 | 10:00 [4] | 3.6 | 90.3 | 97.0 | 28.9 [3] | 116.0 | 80.0 |
| 30 | 9:30 | 3.8 | 98.0 | 99.0 | 29.9 | 118.0 | 80.0 |
| 25 | 9:00 | [1] 4.0 | 105.0 | 100.0 | 30.9 | 120.0 | 80.0 |
| 20 | 8:11 | 4.2 | [1] 115.0 | 102.0 | 32.0 | 122.0 | 82.0 |
| 15 | [5] 7:30 | [2] 4.4 | 128.0 | 104.0 | 33.3 | 126.0 | [1] 84.0 |
| 10 | 7:00 | [3] 4.8 | 146.0 | 108.0 | 35.0 | [1] 130.0 | [2] 88.0 |
| 5 | 6:00 | [4] 5.4 | [2] 181.8 | 111.0 | 37.7 | 138.8 | 92.0 |
| 3 | 5:00 | [5] 5.8 | 211.5 | [1] 115.0 | 39.1 | [2] 140.0 | [3] 96.0 |
| 1 | 4:00 | [10] 7.2 | 312.8 | [3] 125.5 | 41.0 | [4] 152.0 | [4] 102.0 |
| N | 1841 | 933 | 1524 | 1522 | 1412 | 1997 | 1997 |

**Personal History of Heart Attack or Bypass**

- 0 ☑ NONE
- 2 ☐ OVER 5 YEARS AGO
- 4 ☐ 2–5 YEARS AGO
- 5 ☐ 1–<2 YEARS AGO
- 8 ☐ 0–<1 YEAR AGO

[0]

**Family History of Coronary Heart Disease**

- 0 ☑ NONE OR OVER 65
- 2 ☐ YES, AGE 50–65
- 4 ☐ YES, UNDER AGE 50

[0]

**Known Coronary Heart Disease w/o Heart Attack or Bypass**

- 0 ☑ NONE
- 2 ☐ OVER 5 YEARS AGO
- 4 ☐ 2–5 YEARS AGO
- 5 ☐ 1–<2 YEARS AGO
- 6 ☐ 0–<1 YEAR AGO

[0]

**Smoking Habits**

- 0 ☐ NONE
- 0 ☐ PAST 1 YEAR OR MORE
- 1 ☑ PAST ONLY LESS THAN 1 YEAR
- 1 ☐ PIPE/CIGAR
- 2 ☐ 1–10 DAILY
- 3 ☐ 11–20 DAILY
- 4 ☐ 21–30 DAILY
- 5 ☐ 31–40 DAILY
- 6 ☐ MORE THAN 40 DAILY

[1]

**Tension—Anxiety**

- 0 ☐ NO TENSION, VERY RELAXED
- 0 ☐ SLIGHT TENSION
- 1 ☑ MODERATE TENSION
- 2 ☐ HIGH TENSION
- 3 ☐ VERY TENSE, "HIGH STRUNG"

[1]

- 3 ☐ DIABETES

[ ]

*Data based on first visit only

© Institute for Aerobics Research—1986

**Age Factor**

- 0 ☐ UNDER 30 YEARS OF AGE
- 1 ☐ 30–39 YEARS OF AGE
- 2 ☑ 40–49 YEARS OF AGE
- 3 ☐ 50–59 YEARS OF AGE
- 4 ☐ 60+ YEARS OF AGE

[2]

| Resting ECG | | Exercise ECG |
|---|---|---|
| 0 ☑ | NORMAL | 0 ☐ |
| 1 ☐ | EQUIVOCAL | 4 ☑ |
| 3 ☐ | ABNORMAL | 8 ☐ |

[4]

**Total Coronary Risk**

- ☐ VERY LOW ( 0– 4)
- ☑ LOW ( 5–12)
- ☐ MODERATE (13–21)
- ☐ HIGH (22–31)
- ☐ VERY HIGH (32+ )

[12]

Previous Total [ ]

## Coronary Risk Profile

**Cooper Clinic/Dallas, Texas**

**Name:** **Females: *<30 Years of Age**

| Percentile Rankings | Balke Treadmill Time (min.) | Total Cholesterol/ HDL Ratio | Triglyceride (mg. %) | Glucose (mg. %) | % Body Fat | Resting Blood Pressure Systolic (mm HG) | Resting Blood Pressure Diastolic (mm HG) |
|---|---|---|---|---|---|---|---|
| Your Values | | | | | | | |
| 99 | 27:00 | 1.9 | 28.1 | 67.1 | 5.7 | 84.0 | 54.0 |
| 97 | 24:44 | 2.1 | 33.0 | 73.0 | 9.3 | 90.0 | 58.0 |
| 95 | 23:02 | 2.2 | 36.0 | 76.0 | 10.9 | 90.0 | 60.0 |
| 90 | 21:00 | 2.4 | 42.0 | 79.0 | 14.2 | 92.0 | 60.0 |
| 85 | 20:00 | 2.5 | 45.0 | 80.7 | 15.6 | 96.0 | 62.0 |
| 80 | 18:14 | 2.7 | 48.0 | 82.0 | 16.8 | 98.0 | 64.0 |
| 75 | 18:00 | 2.8 | 50.0 | 84.0 | 17.8 | 100.0 | 66.0 |
| 70 | 17:00 | 2.8 | 54.0 | 85.0 | 18.7 | 100.0 | 68.0 |
| 65 | 16:00 | 2.9 | 57.0 | 86.0 | 19.5 | 102.0 | 68.0 |
| | [2] | | | | [1] | | |
| 62 | 15:20 | 3.1 | 60.0 | 87.0 | 20.4 | 104.0 | 70.0 |
| 55 | 15:00 | 3.1 | 64.0 | 89.0 | 21.1 | 106.0 | 70.0 |
| 50 | 14:30 | 3.2 | 68.0 | 90.0 | 21.7 | 108.0 | 70.0 |
| | | | | | [2] | | |
| 45 | 14:00 | 3.3 | 72.0 | 91.0 | 22.4 | 110.0 | 70.0 |
| 40 | 13:02 | 3.4 | 75.0 | 92.0 | 23.3 | 110.0 | 72.0 |
| 35 | 12:53 | 3.5 | 79.0 | 93.0 | 24.1 | 110.0 | 74.0 |
| | [4] | | | | [3] | | |
| 30 | 12:00 | 3.6 | 85.0 | 94.0 | 25.0 | 112.0 | 76.0 |
| 25 | 11:30 | 3.7 | 92.0 | 95.0 | 26.2 | 114.0 | 78.0 |
| 20 | 11:00 | 3.9 | 102.0 | 97.0 | 27.6 | 116.0 | 78.8 |
| | | [1] | | | | | |
| 15 | 10:10 | 4.1 | 112.0 | 99.0 | 29.4 | 119.5 | 80.0 |
| | [5] | | [1] | | | | |
| 10 | 9:32 | 4.3 | 130.0 | 101.0 | 31.8 | 120.0 | 80.0 |
| | | [2] | | | | | [1] |
| 5 | 7:46 | 5.0 | 162.5 | 105.0 | 35.4 | 126.0 | 85.3 |
| | | [3] | | | | | |
| 3 | 7:00 | 5.3 | 198.5 | 107.0 | 37.1 | 130.0 | 88.0 |
| | | [4] | [2] | | | [1] | [2] |
| 1 | 5:23 | 5.9 | 279.6 | 118.9 | 39.7 | 140.0 | 90.0 |
| | | [10] | | [3] | | [4] | [4] |
| N | 850 | 459 | 709 | 710 | 778 | 874 | 874 |

**Personal History of Heart Attack or Bypass**

- 0 ☐ NONE
- 2 ☐ OVER 5 YEARS AGO
- 4 ☐ 2–5 YEARS AGO
- 5 ☐ 1–<2 YEARS AGO
- 8 ☐ 0–<1 YEAR AGO

**Family History of Coronary Heart Disease**

- 0 ☐ NONE OR OVER 65
- 2 ☐ YES, AGE 50–65
- 4 ☐ YES, UNDER AGE 50

**Known Coronary Heart Disease w/o Heart Attack or Bypass**

- 0 ☐ NONE
- 2 ☐ OVER 5 YEARS AGO
- 4 ☐ 2–5 YEARS AGO
- 5 ☐ 1–<2 YEARS AGO
- 6 ☐ 0–<1 YEAR AGO

**Smoking Habits**

- 0 ☐ NONE
- 0 ☐ PAST 1 YEAR OR MORE
- 1 ☐ PAST ONLY LESS THAN 1 YEAR
- 1 ☐ PIPE/CIGAR
- 2 ☐ 1–10 DAILY
- 3 ☐ 11–20 DAILY
- 4 ☐ 21–30 DAILY
- 5 ☐ 31–40 DAILY
- 6 ☐ MORE THAN 40 DAILY

**Tension—Anxiety**

- 0 ☐ NO TENSION, VERY RELAXED
- 0 ☐ SLIGHT TENSION
- 1 ☐ MODERATE TENSION
- 2 ☐ HIGH TENSION
- 3 ☐ VERY TENSE, "HIGH STRUNG"

3 ☐ DIABETES

*Data based on first visit only



**Age Factor**

- 0 ☐ UNDER 30 YEARS OF AGE
- 1 ☐ 30–39 YEARS OF AGE
- 2 ☐ 40–49 YEARS OF AGE
- 3 ☐ 50–59 YEARS OF AGE
- 4 ☐ 60+ YEARS OF AGE

| Resting ECG | | Exercise ECG |
|---|---|---|
| 0 ☐ | NORMAL | 0 ☐ |
| 1 ☐ | EQUIVOCAL | 4 ☐ |
| 3 ☐ | ABNORMAL | 8 ☐ |

**Total Coronary Risk**

- ☐ VERY LOW ( 0– 4)
- ☐ LOW ( 5–12)
- ☐ MODERATE (13–21)
- ☐ HIGH (22–31)
- ☐ VERY HIGH (32+ )

Previous Total

# Coronary Risk Profile

## Cooper Clinic/Dallas, Texas

| Name: | | | | | Females: *30–39 Years of Age | | |
|---|---|---|---|---|---|---|---|
| Percentile Rankings | Balke Treadmill Time (min.) | Total Cholesterol/ HDL Ratio | Triglyceride (mg. %) | Glucose (mg. %) | % Body Fat | Resting Blood Pressure Systolic (mm HG) | Resting Blood Pressure Diastolic (mm HG) |
| Your Values | | | | | | | |
| 99 | 24:00 | 1.9 | 25.0 | 70.0 | 7.4 | 86.0 | 54.0 |
| 97 | 22:00 | 2.1 | 32.0 | 75.7 | 11.3 | 90.0 | 60.0 |
| 95 | 20:31 | 2.2 | 36.0 | 78.0 | 13.4 | 90.0 | 60.0 |
| 90 | 19:00 | 2.4 | 40.0 | 81.0 | 15.4 | 94.0 | 62.0 |
| 85 | 17:40 | 2.5 | 43.0 | 83.0 | 16.8 | 96.0 | 64.0 |
| 80 | 16:40 | 2.6 | 48.0 | 84.0 | 18.0 | 98.0 | 66.0 |
| 75 | 16:00 | 2.7 | 50.5 | 86.0 | 19.0 | 100.0 | 68.0 |
| 70 | 15:01 | 2.8 | 53.0 | 87.0 | 19.8 | 100.0 | 70.0 |
| 65 | [2] 15:00 | 2.9 | 56.0 | 88.0 | [1] 20.6 | 102.0 | 70.0 |
| 60 | 14:00 | 3.0 | 59.0 | 89.0 | 21.4 | 104.0 | 70.0 |
| 55 | 13:30 | 3.1 | 63.0 | 90.0 | 22.4 | 106.0 | 70.0 |
| 50 | 13:00 | 3.1 | 66.0 | 92.0 | [2] 23.1 | 108.0 | 72.0 |
| 45 | 12:30 | 3.2 | 69.0 | 93.0 | 23.9 | 110.0 | 74.0 |
| 40 | 12:00 | 3.3 | 73.0 | 94.0 | 24.9 | 110.0 | 75.0 |
| 35 | 11:30 | 3.4 | 78.0 | 95.0 | 26.0 | 112.0 | 76.0 |
| | [4] | | | | [3] | | |
| 30 | 11:00 | 3.5 | 82.0 | 96.0 | 27.0 | 114.0 | 78.0 |
| 25 | 10:25 | 3.6 | 87.0 | 98.0 | 28.2 | 116.0 | 80.0 |
| 20 | 10:00 | 3.8 | 93.0 | 100.0 | 29.4 | 118.0 | 80.0 |
| 15 | 9:00 | 4.0 | 101.0 | 101.0 | 31.0 | 120.0 | 80.0 |
| | [5] | [1] | | | | | |
| 10 | 8:00 | 4.4 | [1] 116.8 | 104.0 | 32.8 | 122.0 | [1] 84.0 |
| 5 | 7:00 | [2] 4.7 | 142.0 | 108.0 | 35.9 | 130.0 | [2] 90.0 |
| 3 | 6:15 | [3] 5.2 | 159.0 | 111.0 | 37.7 | 134.0 | 90.0 |
| 1 | 5:15 | [4] 6.2 | [2] 220.0 | 119.8 | 39.6 | [1] 144.0 | 98.0 |
| | | [10] | | [3] | | [4] | [4] |
| N | 2304 | 1029 | 1621 | 1623 | 1615 | 2373 | 2373 |

**Personal History of Heart Attack or Bypass**

0 ☐ NONE
2 ☐ OVER 5 YEARS AGO
4 ☐ 2–5 YEARS AGO
5 ☐ 1–<2 YEARS AGO
8 ☐ 0–<1 YEAR AGO

**Family History of Coronary Heart Disease**

0 ☐ NONE OR OVER 65
2 ☐ YES, AGE 50–65
4 ☐ YES, UNDER AGE 50

**Known Coronary Heart Disease w/o Heart Attack or Bypass**

0 ☐ NONE
2 ☐ OVER 5 YEARS AGO
4 ☐ 2–5 YEARS AGO
5 ☐ 1–<2 YEARS AGO
6 ☐ 0–<1 YEAR AGO

**Smoking Habits**

0 ☐ NONE
0 ☐ PAST 1 YEAR OR MORE
1 ☐ PAST ONLY LESS THAN 1 YEAR
1 ☐ PIPE/CIGAR
2 ☐ 1–10 DAILY
3 ☐ 11–20 DAILY
4 ☐ 21–30 DAILY
5 ☐ 31–40 DAILY
6 ☐ MORE THAN 40 DAILY

**Tension—Anxiety**

0 ☐ NO TENSION, VERY RELAXED
0 ☐ SLIGHT TENSION
1 ☐ MODERATE TENSION
2 ☐ HIGH TENSION
3 ☐ VERY TENSE, "HIGH STRUNG"

3 ☐ DIABETES

*Data based on first visit only



**Age Factor**

0 ☐ UNDER 30 YEARS OF AGE
1 ☐ 30–39 YEARS OF AGE
2 ☐ 40–49 YEARS OF AGE
3 ☐ 50–59 YEARS OF AGE
4 ☐ 60+ YEARS OF AGE

| Resting ECG | | Exercise ECG |
|---|---|---|
| 0 ☐ | NORMAL | 0 ☐ |
| 1 ☐ | EQUIVOCAL | 4 ☐ |
| 3 ☐ | ABNORMAL | 8 ☐ |

**Total Coronary Risk**

☐ VERY LOW ( 0– 4)
☐ LOW ( 5–12)
☐ MODERATE (13–21)
☐ HIGH (22–31)
☐ VERY HIGH (32+ )

Previous Total

## Coronary Risk Profile

**Cooper Clinic/Dallas, Texas**

**Name:** | **Females: *40–49 Years of Age**

| Percentile Rankings | Balke Treadmill Time (min.) | Total Cholesterol/ HDL Ratio | Triglyceride (mg. %) | Glucose (mg. %) | % Body Fat | Resting Blood Pressure Systolic (mm HG) | Resting Blood Pressure Diastolic (mm HG) |
|---|---|---|---|---|---|---|---|
| Your Values | | | | | | | |
| 99 | 23:09 | 2.0 | 29.3 | 73.2 | 11.8 | 86.0 | 58.0 |
| 97 | 20:00 | 2.2 | 35.8 | 77.0 | 14.6 | 90.0 | 60.0 |
| 95 | 18:30 | 2.3 | 39.0 | 79.0 | 16.2 | 92.0 | 62.0 |
| 90 | 17:00 | 2.5 | 45.0 | 82.0 | 18.2 | 96.0 | 65.0 |
| 85 | 16:00 | 2.7 | 49.0 | 84.0 | 20.0 | 100.0 | 68.0 |
| 80 | 15:00 | 2.7 | 53.0 | 86.0 | 21.2 | 100.0 | 70.0 |
| 75 | 14:10 | 2.8 | 57.0 | 88.0 | 22.2 | 102.0 | 70.0 |
| 70 | 13:30 | 2.9 | 60.0 | 89.0 | 23.2 | 104.0 | 70.0 |
| 65 | 13:00 | 3.0 | 63.0 | 90.0 | 24.1 | 106.0 | 72.0 |
| | [2] | | | | [1] | | |
| 60 | 12:02 | 3.1 | 67.0 | 91.0 | 24.8 | 108.0 | 74.0 |
| 55 | 12:00 | 3.2 | 71.0 | 93.0 | 25.4 | 110.0 | 74.0 |
| 50 | 11:20 | 3.3 | 74.0 | 94.0 | 26.3 | 110.0 | 76.0 |
| | | | | | [2] | | |
| 45 | 11:00 | 3.4 | 79.0 | 95.0 | 27.2 | 112.0 | 78.0 |
| 40 | 10:22 | 3.5 | 84.0 | 96.0 | 27.9 | 114.0 | 80.0 |
| 35 | 10:00 | 3.6 | 90.3 | 97.0 | 28.9 | 116.0 | 80.0 |
| | [4] | | | | [3] | | |
| 30 | 9:30 | 3.8 | 98.0 | 99.0 | 29.9 | 118.0 | 80.0 |
| 25 | 9:00 | 4.0 | 105.0 | 100.0 | 30.9 | 120.0 | 80.0 |
| | | [1] | | | | | |
| 20 | 8:11 | 4.2 | 115.0 | 102.0 | 32.0 | 122.0 | 82.0 |
| | | | [1] | | | | |
| 15 | 7:30 | 4.4 | 128.0 | 104.0 | 33.3 | 126.0 | 84.0 |
| | [5] | [2] | | | | | [1] |
| 10 | 7:00 | 4.8 | 146.0 | 108.0 | 35.0 | 130.0 | 88.0 |
| | | [3] | | | | [1] | [2] |
| 5 | 6:00 | 5.4 | 181.8 | 111.0 | 37.7 | 138.8 | 92.0 |
| | | [4] | [2] | | | | |
| 3 | 5:00 | 5.8 | 211.5 | 115.0 | 39.1 | 140.0 | 96.0 |
| | | [5] | | [1] | | [2] | [3] |
| 1 | 4:00 | 7.2 | 312.8 | 125.5 | 41.0 | 152.0 | 102.0 |
| | | [10] | | [3] | | [4] | [4] |
| N | 1841 | 933 | 1524 | 1522 | 1412 | 1997 | 1997 |

**Personal History of Heart Attack or Bypass**
- 0 ☐ NONE
- 2 ☐ OVER 5 YEARS AGO
- 4 ☐ 2–5 YEARS AGO
- 5 ☐ 1–<2 YEARS AGO
- 8 ☐ 0–<1 YEAR AGO

**Family History of Coronary Heart Disease**
- 0 ☐ NONE OR OVER 65
- 2 ☐ YES, AGE 50–65
- 4 ☐ YES, UNDER AGE 50

**Known Coronary Heart Disease w/o Heart Attack or Bypass**
- 0 ☐ NONE
- 2 ☐ OVER 5 YEARS AGO
- 4 ☐ 2–5 YEARS AGO
- 5 ☐ 1–<2 YEARS AGO
- 6 ☐ 0–<1 YEAR AGO

**Smoking Habits**
- 0 ☐ NONE
- 0 ☐ PAST 1 YEAR OR MORE
- 1 ☐ PAST ONLY LESS THAN 1 YEAR
- 1 ☐ PIPE/CIGAR
- 2 ☐ 1–10 DAILY
- 3 ☐ 11–20 DAILY
- 4 ☐ 21–30 DAILY
- 5 ☐ 31–40 DAILY
- 6 ☐ MORE THAN 40 DAILY

**Tension—Anxiety**
- 0 ☐ NO TENSION, VERY RELAXED
- 0 ☐ SLIGHT TENSION
- 1 ☐ MODERATE TENSION
- 2 ☐ HIGH TENSION
- 3 ☐ VERY TENSE, "HIGH STRUNG"

3 ☐ DIABETES

*Data based on first visit only



**Age Factor**
- 0 ☐ UNDER 30 YEARS OF AGE
- 1 ☐ 30–39 YEARS OF AGE
- 2 ☐ 40–49 YEARS OF AGE
- 3 ☐ 50–59 YEARS OF AGE
- 4 ☐ 60 + YEARS OF AGE

| Resting ECG | | Exercise ECG |
|---|---|---|
| 0 ☐ | NORMAL | 0 ☐ |
| 1 ☐ | EQUIVOCAL | 4 ☐ |
| 3 ☐ | ABNORMAL | 8 ☐ |

**Total Coronary Risk**
- ☐ VERY LOW ( 0– 4)
- ☐ LOW ( 5–12)
- ☐ MODERATE (13–21)
- ☐ HIGH (22–31)
- ☐ VERY HIGH (32 + )

Previous Total

## Coronary Risk Profile

**Cooper Clinic/Dallas, Texas**

| **Name:** | | | | | | **Females: *50–59 Years of Age** | |
|---|---|---|---|---|---|---|---|
| | | | | | | Resting Blood Pressure | |
| Percentile Rankings | Balke Treadmill Time (min.) | Total Cholesterol/ HDL Ratio | Triglyceride (mg. %) | Glucose (mg. %) | % Body Fat | Systolic (mm HG) | Diastolic (mm HG) |
| Your Values | | | | | | | |
| 99 | 20:57 | 2.0 | 37.0 | 73.2 | 11.4 | 90.0 | 60.0 |
| 97 | 17:00 | 2.4 | 42.0 | 79.0 | 16.2 | 94.0 | 62.0 |
| 95 | 15:56 | 2.5 | 47.0 | 81.0 | 18.5 | 98.0 | 64.0 |
| 90 | 15:00 | 2.7 | 55.0 | 85.0 | 20.7 | 100.0 | 68.0 |
| 85 | 13:15 | 2.8 | 61.2 | 87.0 | 22.7 | 104.0 | 70.0 |
| 80 | 12:09 | 2.9 | 66.0 | 89.0 | 24.3 | 106.0 | 70.0 |
| 75 | 12:00 | 3.1 | 71.0 | 91.0 | 25.4 | 110.0 | 72.0 |
| 70 | 11:07 | 3.2 | 76.0 | 92.0 | 26.2 | 110.0 | 74.0 |
| 65 | 10:39 | 3.4 | 81.0 | 94.0 | 27.1 | 112.0 | 76.0 |
| 60 | [2] 10:02 | 3.4 | 87.0 | 95.0 | [1] 27.9 | 114.8 | 78.0 |
| 55 | 10:00 | 3.5 | 92.0 | 96.0 | 28.9 | 118.0 | 80.0 |
| 50 | 9:30 | 3.7 | 99.0 | 97.0 | 29.9 | 120.0 | 80.0 |
| 45 | 9:00 | 3.8 | 105.0 | 99.0 | [2] 30.7 | 120.0 | 80.0 |
| 40 | 8:30 | 3.9 | 111.0 | 100.0 | 31.6 | 122.0 | 80.0 |
| 35 | 8:00 | [1] 4.1 | 120.0 | 101.0 | 32.6 | 125.0 | 82.0 |
| 30 | [4] 7:30 | 4.2 | [1] 126.0 | 103.0 | [3] 33.6 | 130.0 | 84.0 |
| 25 | 7:00 | 4.5 | 138.0 | 105.0 | 34.3 | 130.0 | [1] 86.0 |
| 20 | 6:30 | [2] 4.7 | 154.0 | 106.0 | 35.6 | 134.0 | 88.0 |
| 15 | 6:00 | 5.0 | 166.0 | 109.5 | 36.5 | [1] 140.0 | 90.0 |
| 10 | [5] 5:15 | [3] 5.4 | 188.0 | 113.0 | 37.9 | [2] 145.0 | [2] 93.6 |
| 5 | 4:22 | [4] 6.1 | [2] 225.0 | 120.0 | 39.7 | [3] 158.0 | 100.3 |
| 3 | 4:00 | [5] 6.7 | 252.0 | [1] 129.5 | 40.6 | 164.0 | [3] 100.0 |
| 1 | 2:40 | [6] 7.7 [10] | 364.9 | [2] 184.3 [3] | 49.6 | [4] 180.0 | 110.0 [4] |
| N | 1007 | 595 | 1020 | 1016 | 862 | 1231 | 1231 |

**Personal History of Heart Attack or Bypass**

- 0 ☐ NONE
- 2 ☐ OVER 5 YEARS AGO
- 4 ☐ 2–5 YEARS AGO
- 5 ☐ 1–<2 YEARS AGO
- 8 ☐ 0–<1 YEAR AGO

**Family History of Coronary Heart Disease**

- 0 ☐ NONE OR OVER 65
- 2 ☐ YES, AGE 50–65
- 4 ☐ YES, UNDER AGE 50

**Known Coronary Heart Disease w/o Heart Attack or Bypass**

- 0 ☐ NONE
- 2 ☐ OVER 5 YEARS AGO
- 4 ☐ 2–5 YEARS AGO
- 5 ☐ 1–<2 YEARS AGO
- 6 ☐ 0–<1 YEAR AGO

**Smoking Habits**

- 0 ☐ NONE
- 0 ☐ PAST 1 YEAR OR MORE
- 1 ☐ PAST ONLY LESS THAN 1 YEAR
- 1 ☐ PIPE/CIGAR
- 2 ☐ 1–10 DAILY
- 3 ☐ 11–20 DAILY
- 4 ☐ 21–30 DAILY
- 5 ☐ 31–40 DAILY
- 6 ☐ MORE THAN 40 DAILY

**Tension—Anxiety**

- 0 ☐ NO TENSION, VERY RELAXED
- 0 ☐ SLIGHT TENSION
- 1 ☐ MODERATE TENSION
- 2 ☐ HIGH TENSION
- 3 ☐ VERY TENSE, "HIGH STRUNG"

3 ☐ DIABETES

*Data based on first visit only



**Age Factor**

- 0 ☐ UNDER 30 YEARS OF AGE
- 1 ☐ 30–39 YEARS OF AGE
- 2 ☐ 40–49 YEARS OF AGE
- 3 ☐ 50–59 YEARS OF AGE
- 4 ☐ 60+ YEARS OF AGE

| Resting ECG | | Exercise ECG |
|---|---|---|
| 0 ☐ | NORMAL | 0 ☐ |
| 1 ☐ | EQUIVOCAL | 4 ☐ |
| 3 ☐ | ABNORMAL | 8 ☐ |

**Total Coronary Risk**

- ☐ VERY LOW ( 0– 4)
- ☐ LOW ( 5–12)
- ☐ MODERATE (13–21)
- ☐ HIGH (22–31)
- ☐ VERY HIGH (32+ )

**Previous Total**

# Coronary Risk Profile

**Cooper Clinic/Dallas, Texas**

| **Name:** | | | | | **Females: *≥60 Years of Age** | | |
|---|---|---|---|---|---|---|---|
| Percentile Rankings | Balke Treadmill Time (min.) | Total Cholesterol/ HDL Ratio | Triglyceride (mg. %) | Glucose (mg. %) | % Body Fat | Resting Blood Pressure Systolic (mm HG) | Resting Blood Pressure Diastolic (mm HG) |
| Your Values | | | | | | | |
| 99 | 19:26 | 2.0 | 35.2 | 75.2 | 5.1 | 90.0 | 59.7 |
| 97 | 16:18 | 2.4 | 44.6 | 80.0 | 14.8 | 94.1 | 60.0 |
| 95 | 15:34 | 2.6 | 49.9 | 84.0 | 17.4 | 100.0 | 64.0 |
| 90 | 13:54 | 2.8 | 59.9 | 86.0 | 20.5 | 106.0 | 70.0 |
| 85 | 12:00 | 2.9 | 65.9 | 88.0 | 22.9 | 110.0 | 70.0 |
| 80 | 11:21 | 3.1 | 73.0 | 90.0 | 24.6 | 114.0 | 72.0 |
| 75 | 11:00 | 3.2 | 79.8 | 91.0 | 26.1 | 118.0 | 74.0 |
| 70 | 10:00 | 3.4 | 85.0 | 92.7 | 27.0 | 120.0 | 76.0 |
| 65 | [2] 9:17 | 3.5 | 90.0 | 94.0 | 28.2 | 120.0 | 76.0 |
| 60 | 8:40 | 3.6 | 95.6 | 95.0 | [1] 29.1 | 122.0 | 78.0 |
| 55 | 8:10 | 3.8 | 103.0 | 97.0 | 29.8 | 126.0 | 80.0 |
| 50 | 8:00 | [1] 4.0 | 110.0 | 99.0 | [2] 30.4 | 128.0 | 80.0 |
| 45 | 7:05 | 4.1 | [1] 115.0 | 100.0 | 31.3 | 130.0 | 80.0 |
| 40 | 6:43 | 4.4 | 122.0 | 101.0 | 32.4 | 132.0 | 82.0 |
| 35 | [4] 6:30 | [2] 4.5 | 131.0 | 103.0 | 32.9 | 135.0 | 84.0 |
| 30 | 6:05 | 4.7 | 139.0 | 105.0 | [3] 33.9 | [1] 138.0 | [1] 86.0 |
| 25 | 6:00 | [3] 4.9 | 146.3 | 106.0 | 35.3 | [2] 140.0 | 88.0 |
| 20 | 5:34 | 5.1 | 164.2 | 109.0 | 36.4 | 142.4 | [2] 90.0 |
| 15 | [5] 5:00 | [4] 5.3 | [2] 178.3 | 112.0 | 37.7 | 148.0 | 90.0 |
| 10 | 4:11 | [5] 5.8 | 203.2 | 115.1 | 39.2 | [3] 154.0 | 94.0 |
| 5 | 3:15 | [6] 6.5 | 226.0 | [1] 128.0 | 40.4 | 163.6 | 100.0 |
| 3 | 3:00 | [7] 7.4 | 255.6 | [2] 139.4 | 41.3 | [4] 174.9 | [3] 101.0 |
| 1 | 2:12 | [10] 10.6 | 413.8 | [3] 199.6 | 45.1 | 182.0 | [4] 105.7 |
| N | 242 | 261 | 418 | 418 | 330 | 483 | 483 |

**Personal History of Heart Attack or Bypass**
- 0 ☐ NONE
- 2 ☐ OVER 5 YEARS AGO
- 4 ☐ 2–5 YEARS AGO
- 5 ☐ 1–<2 YEARS AGO
- 8 ☐ 0–<1 YEAR AGO

**Family History of Coronary Heart Disease**
- 0 ☐ NONE OR OVER 65
- 2 ☐ YES, AGE 50–65
- 4 ☐ YES, UNDER AGE 50

**Known Coronary Heart Disease w/o Heart Attack or Bypass**
- 0 ☐ NONE
- 2 ☐ OVER 5 YEARS AGO
- 4 ☐ 2–5 YEARS AGO
- 5 ☐ 1–<2 YEARS AGO
- 6 ☐ 0–<1 YEAR AGO

**Smoking Habits**
- 0 ☐ NONE
- 0 ☐ PAST 1 YEAR OR MORE
- 1 ☐ PAST ONLY LESS THAN 1 YEAR
- 1 ☐ PIPE/CIGAR
- 2 ☐ 1–10 DAILY
- 3 ☐ 11–20 DAILY
- 4 ☐ 21–30 DAILY
- 5 ☐ 31–40 DAILY
- 6 ☐ MORE THAN 40 DAILY

**Tension—Anxiety**
- 0 ☐ NO TENSION, VERY RELAXED
- 0 ☐ SLIGHT TENSION
- 1 ☐ MODERATE TENSION
- 2 ☐ HIGH TENSION
- 3 ☐ VERY TENSE, "HIGH STRUNG"

3 ☐ DIABETES

*Data based on first visit only



**Age Factor**
- 0 ☐ UNDER 30 YEARS OF AGE
- 1 ☐ 30–39 YEARS OF AGE
- 2 ☐ 40–49 YEARS OF AGE
- 3 ☐ 50–59 YEARS OF AGE
- 4 ☐ 60+ YEARS OF AGE

| Resting ECG | | Exercise ECG |
|---|---|---|
| 0 ☐ | NORMAL | 0 ☐ |
| 1 ☐ | EQUIVOCAL | 4 ☐ |
| 3 ☐ | ABNORMAL | 8 ☐ |

**Total Coronary Risk**
- ☐ VERY LOW ( 0– 4)
- ☐ LOW ( 5–12)
- ☐ MODERATE (13–21)
- ☐ HIGH (22–31)
- ☐ VERY HIGH (32+ )

Previous Total

## Barlows Syndrome—No Excuse for Inactivity

We see lots of women at the Cooper Clinic with Barlows Syndrome—otherwise known as "the Click Syndrome," "Click-Murmur Syndrome," "Ballooning Mitral Valve Syndrome," or "Mitral Valve Prolapse" (MVP). Most of these female patients have no idea they have MVP until one of our physicians diagnoses it. By and large, these women experience no symptoms and need have no hesitation about continuing their active lives and exercise programs.

MVP is found in 5 to 10 percent of the population and is far more common among women. Its incidence is the highest of all among women with such eating disorders as anorexia nervosa and bulimia.

Doctors detect MVP, in most cases, during routine chest exams with a stethoscope. The normal sound physicians hear listening to hearts is "lub-dub." When they also hear a swishing sound, caused by blood passing through the chambers and valves of the heart, they know the patient has a heart murmur. A clicking sound, on the other hand, indicates MVP. It's caused by the flopping of the mitral valve. It's not clear why this happens, but most physicians feel this inherited condition is simply a normal variant in heart structure, not a disease or serious abnormality as such.

In the vast majority of cases, MVP patients feel fine. They have no symptoms whatsoever. A minority of women have chest pain, but it's not the excruciating pain associated with angina, nor does it respond to nitroglycerin like angina. A few women with MVP experience heart palpitations. If they are serious arrhythmias, which most aren't, they may be controlled with medication. But there's still no cause for concern or resignation from aerobics.

A tiny number of MVP patients need special treatment because of complications associated with the condition. Progressive mitral regurgitation—or blackflow of blood into the heart atrium—is one. The heart wall enlarges to cope with the extra workload and the patient may feel tired, short of breath, or, in extreme instances, the symptoms of congestive heart failure. Mitral regurgitations can usually be treated medically, although surgery to replace the faulty valve with an artificial one is occasionally necessary.

A more common complication is infective endocarditis, or inflammation of the lining of the heart, which has an adverse effect on the valves in particular. If you've got MVP, be sure to tell your doctor or dentist *before* they perform any minor operations that might release harmful bacteria into your bloodstream. You should be sure to take an antibiotic *before* undergoing the procedure.

# 19

# Aerobics and Other Ailments

It takes a dozen or so research studies, all arriving at similar conclusions, before a watertight causal relationship can be established between a lifestyle issue, such as exercise, and a medical condition.

In this final chapter, we'll examine some physical ailments and diseases that may be amenable to aerobics treatment even though researchers haven't established the link through formal studies. In the case of cancer, we'll discuss whether there is any validity to the controversial claim that vigorous exercise can increase cancer risk.

## Arthritis and Exercise

While we can't say that exercise prevents arthritis, we can describe one case history after another of arthritic women at the Aerobics Center who have achieved excellent results through exercise therapy.

Lilly Dodson immediately springs to mind. Lilly is in her mid-sixties and joined the Aerobics Center in 1984 after years of inactivity. We should qualify that: Lilly was never athletic and had no exercise history. But for twenty-five years she's run an extremely popular women's specialty shop bearing her name. By nature, she's an active, involved woman who puts in twelve-hour work days five or six days a week.

We'll let her tell her own story:

> My introduction to the Aerobics Center was through the Cooper Clinic. I had chest pains that concerned me. What shocked me most during the visit, however, was the diagnosis about my weight. The doctor called me "obese." I really wasn't that overweight, but my body-fat ratio was high. Needless to say, the mere mention of the word motivated me, for the first time in my life, to start exercising.
>
> I eased into exercise by taking a 30-minute cardiac rehabilitation class every morning at seven. I didn't have a serious heart condition but the class was at the

right time and about the right level of challenge for a beginner like me. Soon I fell into the habit of arriving 45 minutes before the class so I could walk 3 miles around the track first.

After a couple of months, what surprised me most was how much more energetic I felt. There was something else too. Although my chronic arthritis was already under control through medication, exercise definitely helped eliminate any remaining stiffness and pain.

Things were fine until I started traveling a lot and stopped my regular exercise routine. During that period, I developed some swelling in my knees, a problem that runs in my family. A local knee doctor recommended arthroscopic surgery, but my doctor at the Cooper Clinic suggested I return to my former exercise regimen and see if that didn't help. It did, and I still haven't had that surgery. If I can continue to control the problem through exercise, I may *never* have that surgery!

## The Cancer Connection—Is There Any?

Women sometimes ask if vigorous exercise increases the risk of cancer.

To answer, we cite the current epidemiological research literature, which, taken in toto, does *not* support this contention. To the contrary, most studies indicate that being more physically active may actually protect you from cancer, particularly cancer of the colon.

In both sexes, cancer of the colon and rectum is one of the most common American malignancies, with an estimated 140,000 new cases this year and 60,000 deaths. For women, lung cancer is the next most frequent killer, followed by breast cancer. As you no doubt know, cancer, no matter where it is located in the body, is cell growth gone haywire. It is an uncontrolled, unpredictable, abnormal growth of cells.

While we've made important strides against heart disease over the last two decades, the same cannot be said about cancer, despite the many millions spent on research every year. Part of the problem is that these dollars are spent mostly on treatment research, with very little emphasis on prevention strategies.

To devise effective prevention strategies, more studies need to be conducted on cancer risk factors. For example, enough research has been done to support the contention that obesity and high dietary fat intake are associated with certain cancers. But, except to say that exercise helps people lose weight, we still cannot say definitively that exercise prevents cancer.

Because it's so common, cancer of the colon has been scrutinized the most, and a beneficial exercise effect seems well documented. In fact, Dr. Steven Blair, of our Institute for Aerobics Research, is studying the exercise–colon cancer link right now. His preliminary findings mirror those of other researchers. They hypothesize that active people are at less risk because exercise prevents constipation. By stimulating peristalsis, it shortens the time that any carcinogenic fecal matter remains in the intestine.

## Healthy Habits Are Key

With cancer, even more than with some other diseases, healthy lifestyle practices over an extended period seem to offer the most protection. That's because the disease has a latency period of twenty years or so. What you do in your thirties, when cancer risk in both men and women is low, can have a marked effect on whether you develop cancer in your postmenopausal years, when incidence shoots up dramatically.

The truth of this statement was underscored in a landmark study conducted by two medical researchers in Boston. It's one of the few longitudinal studies focusing solely on women.

In their Alumnae Health Survey, Drs. Rose E. Frisch and Isaac Schiff polled 5,398 women who graduated between 1925 and 1981 from eight colleges and two universities (Barnard, Bryn Mawr, Mount Holyoke, Radcliffe, Smith, Vassar, Wellesley, and Springfield colleges, and the universities of Wisconsin and Southern California). Their fourteen-page questionnaire gave a complete picture of the respondents' health and lifestyle habits over a lifetime. About half the sample were college athletes, most of whom had remained active over the years. The other half were more sedentary.

The major finding was that the lifetime prevalence of reproductive system cancers (uterus, ovary, cervix, and vagina) was distinctly lower among the athletic women than among their inactive classmates. The age-adjusted rates for such cancers was 3.7 cases for every 1,000 athletic women and 9.5 cases for every 1,000 inactive women. For breast cancer, the prevalence rate was 10.1 cases for every 1,000 athletes and 15.6 cases for every 1,000 nonathletes. Women who had never been pregnant had higher rates, although the rate was still lower among the athletes.

The authors summed up: "In whatever ways long-term athletic training achieves results, we conclude that it establishes a lifestyle that lowers the risk of cancers of the breast and reproductive system."

## Exercise and Asthma

Asthma is certainly a treatable illness, but you'd never know it from recent statistics. Between 1980 and 1985, the overall rate of deaths from asthma actually grew 23 percent to 1.6 deaths for every 100,000 people. Granted, that still amounted only to 3,760 deaths in the United States in 1985, but that's 3,760 too many, given what medical science knows about this ailment.

Some 10 million Americans currently suffer from asthma, a narrowing of the bronchial tubes that impedes breathing. Asthma is either inherited (intrinsic) or may be caused by infections or allergies to certain substances such as foods or airborne irritants (extrinsic). Asthma specialists, of course, try to remove the cause; but when that isn't possible, they settle for controlling the problem with oral or inhalable drugs that ease breathing.

Joyce Trygstad, a geologist and patient at the Cooper Clinic, developed chronic bronchial asthma twelve years ago as a young adult. Her asthma was so bad that she virtually lost a year of graduate school because she couldn't walk the five blocks to class much of the time. She was in and out of the local hospital emergency room more times than she cares to remember, and found significant relief only in the last three years thanks to an inhaled steroid. She also claims exercise has helped enormously:

> I've always liked sports, so it was instinctive for me to turn to exercise to keep up my strength, reduce stress, and maintain my musculature. But it wasn't until I came to the Cooper Clinic that I found a doctor who had the background to formally help me incorporate exercise into my medical care.
>
> I started out in the Aerobics Center's twelve-week cardiac rehabilitation course, followed by a stretching class. After combating my illness for so many years, I was very weak and actually had trouble keeping up with my classmates at first. But my strength and endurance improved dramatically in very short order.
>
> At the end of those initial twelve weeks, I went on a two-week hiking vacation in the Colorado Rockies. We spent all our time above 9,000 feet, averaging six hours a day of hiking most days. I was never tired or unusually short of breath. We even scaled Mount Sneffels (14,150 feet) and I felt *fantastic*!
>
> In the intervening year, I've remained faithful to a combination walking, swimming, and stretching program that adds up to approximately 30 aerobic points per week. Swimming is particularly good because breathing moist, warm air seems to help. I find I feel much better all over but especially in ease of breathing. My doctor tells me there's been a measurable increase in my lung function. I've had two episodes of colds or flu-like symptoms and neither has gone to my chest, which, for me, is critically important.
>
> Besides helping me to maintain my health and endurance, exercise helps my morale. It's fun, and I feel great afterwards. I may have asthma but I'm not suffering anymore.

## Miracles Do Happen!

Ko Green's story is even more remarkable.

Ko has been an amateur athlete and runner for twenty-five years. She never had hypertension or a weight problem and always ate sensibly—in all respects, a seemingly healthy woman.

Just before her fiftieth birthday, Ko was skiing in Colorado with her family. It was just after Christmas, which had been a particularly hectic time, and she remembers feeling tired. But she never expected what happened next:

> It was the third morning on the ski slopes. I got off the ski lift for my second downhill run and felt this horrible pain in the back of my neck and head. It was like the stabbing pain you feel when you eat very cold ice cream, only intensified a hundred times. I didn't want to cause a scene so I tried to ski back to the warming hut. But I couldn't make it. I got sick to my stomach and passed out on the way.
>
> I was semiconscious when they took me in an ambulance to a hospital in Durango. I remained there for several days. The doctors said I was either suffering from a form of meningitis or I'd had an aneurysm to rupture, a stroke.
>
> I was flown back to Dallas in an air ambulance. The doctors in Dallas diagnosed the problem as a ruptured blood vessel in the basilar artery at the base of my head. Apparently, I had a genetic defect that no one could have foreseen.
>
> The surgery they performed to save my life took almost nine hours. Later, the doctors explained that the location of my aneurysm made surgery extremely risky. I had a 20 to 1 chance of ever walking out the front door of the hospital. They also said my excellent cardiovascular conditioning was a prime factor in my survival.
>
> It's also what got me through the long, horrendous months of rehabilitation. After the surgery, my throat and right arm and leg were paralyzed. Not only that, but the left side of my face was paralyzed and one eyeball rolled back into my head so that you could only see the white part. I drooled all the time and could hardly speak. The whole experience seemed like a bad dream where my memory had gone fuzzy.
>
> My right leg wasn't as paralyzed as my arm, probably because of all those years of running. So the moment I was released from the hospital—I got out of my wheelchair and *walked* out the front door, by the way—I insisted on going for assisted walks around the neighborhood.
>
> The stroke occurred in January. For months I had regular at-home sessions with speech, physical, and occupational therapists. By May, I had improved enough—to my doctors' utter amazement—to visit the Aerobics Center.
>
> At first, I just went to the Bible study and a basic calisthenics and stretching class. I stayed in the back row and did what I could—mainly just lift my left leg. My nurse accompanied me. She frowned a lot because she felt I was doing too much. But I was so determined.
>
> The determination and love and prayers of my family and friends made all the difference. It made me well again. In October, I logged 137 miles walking and jogging around the outside paths. My speed was slow but I did it. Soon after, I regained the full use of my limbs, started to drive the car, and jog.
>
> Today, I come to the Aerobics Center every weekday morning. I run 3 to 5 miles and take an exercise class. As I did in the past, I also run 10K races again, especially the Turkey Trot on Thanksgiving Day, which is my favorite.

> You can't imagine how much I appreciate running now because, for a long while, I never thought I'd ever do it again. That's what makes it so special.
>
> How do I feel? I feel good. I feel normal, although I still have trouble with my memory sometimes.

Don't we all? What Ko didn't mention is that the Aerobics Center gave her the Comeback-of-the-Year Award in 1983, the year of her stroke. Seldom have any of the doctors at the Cooper Clinic seen a patient demonstrate the courage and physical resiliency that she has, not to mention the mental toughness.

## Dr. Kenneth Cooper's Testimonial

Since we're telling personal stories about the benefits of aerobics, I'd like to offer mine.

As hard as this may be to believe, I haven't missed a day of work because of illness in over thirty years. Millie says it's because I'm so disciplined, I go to work even if I do feel slightly under the weather. I attribute it to something else—the protection I've built up from running.

I did have one major bout with illness several years ago. I was stricken with a mild case of hepatitis, a viral infection, but I was on a trip to New Zealand at the time, so my opening statement stands. I feel that running has helped me guard against the usual, everyday illnesses—colds, flu, bronchitis, strep throat, and the like.

My theory is this:

The fact that I raise my core body temperature some 3 to 5 degrees every time I run is analogous to what happens when a person's body is invaded by an infectious agent. Here's the scenario:

When harmful bacteria enter your body, they immediately activate your defense system. Your white blood cells start proliferating and at some point release a substance called endogenous pyrogen (EP). EP goes to the hypothalamus, your body's thermostat located in the brain. The hypothalamus sends out signals to raise your body temperature and you develop a fever. But that fever is a weapon, a good thing. It creates a hostile environment for the invading bacteria and they can't reproduce.

Getting back to me . . . I run for 20 to 30 minutes, four or five days a week. During each session, my body temperature rises. Is it possible that I am pasteurizing my blood every time I go out on the track? And this process is cumulative and builds up my resistance to infectious disease?

My theory is conjecture, although at least one other researcher, Dr. Harvey B. Simon, is obviously thinking along the same lines. In an article in the *Journal of the American Medical Association,* he reviewed the immunology of exercise. He concludes that exercise does produce a transient increase in white blood cells and in the lymphocytes that are the body's main line of defense against infections. But he insists—and I agree—that further studies are needed before medical science can accept the premise that exercise provides clinically meaningful protection.

# Afterword
# I Have a Dream

In 1970, when I opened the Aerobics Center in Dallas, if you'd asked me to predict what I'd be doing seventeen years later, I would have missed it a thousandfold! I had no idea that the number of people working at the Aerobics Center would increase from two to more than two hundred. Or that the size of the facilities would increase from a two-room office to an estate of almost thirty acres. And if you'd told me that over thirty thousand patients would have been evaluated at the Cooper Clinic and almost thirteen hundred people exercising daily at the Aerobics Activity Center, I'd have questioned your sanity. And as for an annual operating budget for research of over $3 million? Impossible!

Yes, over $20 million have been spent on research during the past seven years by our nonprofit Institute for Aerobics Research. This investment has resulted in the publication of over 150 papers in the scientific literature. That is why this book is not based on theories, but is thoroughly documented with facts, many from our own research. Hopefully, we have "bridged that gap between fadism and scientific legitimacy in using exercise in the practice of medicine."

But what about the future?

We are steadily increasing the size and productivity of the Aerobics Center. I hope that we'll become more extensively involved in two areas: (1) aging, particularly the effect that exercise has on delaying the process of aging or, I hope, reducing its effects; (2) improving the health and fitness of American youth.

For years we've been taught that many of the physiological changes that occur with aging can't be prevented and are strictly the results of the normal processes that occur with aging. Yet, research has shown that many of those *physiological* responses are, in reality, not physiological but *adaptive*. In other words, our bodies deteriorate rapidly as we grow older—not so much because we are growing older, but because we are doing less physically as we grow older.

Remember, too, that to slow down the process of aging, three things must be eliminated, in this order: (1) cigarette smoking; (2) inactivity; and (3) obesity. I'm so convinced that great things can be done to slow down the aging process that we're increasing our research efforts in this field.

Over the past five years, in excess of 2.5 million students from kindergarten to the twelfth grade have been tested one or more times for level of fitness using our

Fitnessgram test. Testing their strength, flexibility, and endurance capacity, and then comparing the results with comparable studies performed in 1975, revealed some startling findings. In every category in which age-sex comparisons were made, the results were not better in 1985–86. In fact, in nearly all categories, they were considerably worse. The greatest deficiencies were in endurance performance and body weight.

Without question, our children in 1985–86 were not as fit aerobically as they were in 1975, and they were much fatter. Why? you might ask.

A decrease in the quality and quantity of physical education programs in our school systems is certainly one reason. Mechanization of our lifestyles, requiring considerably less physical activity, is another. Indoor, sedentary activities such as video games, TV, etc., promote lethargy. A change in the dietary habits of our youth—they're becoming more dependent upon high-calorie, low-nutrition fast foods as a major source of sustenance—is a problem. Finally, a government that seems less enthusiastic and more apathetic toward fitness than in previous years.

Unless these attitudes and habits change in the near future, the remarkable improvement in our longevity and decrease in deaths from cardiovascular disease that we have seen in the past two decades will start to reverse. After all, there is no way improvement in cardiovascular health can continue unless our children begin to follow the example of their more physically active, health-oriented parents.

So, I have many dreams. They all revolve around one thing: *improving the quality and quantity of life for people everywhere.* And remember this: It is much cheaper and more effective to maintain good health than it is to regain it once it is lost.

Even though I can't guarantee any woman who reads this book that she will prolong her life by even one day if she follows my guidelines, I can assure her that the life she lives will be healthier, happier, and more productive. That is my wish for all of you.

—Kenneth H. Cooper, M.D.

# Appendix

## The Point System

WALKING/RUNNING

| Time (hr:min:sec) | Point Value | Time (hr:min:sec) | Point Value | Time (hr:min:sec) | Point Value |
|---|---|---|---|---|---|
| **1.0 Mile** | | **1.1 Miles** | | **1.2 Miles** | |
| over 20:01 | 0 | over 33:01 | 0 | over 36:01 | 0 |
| 20:00–15:01 | 1.0 | 33:00–22:01 | 0.1 | 36:00–24:01 | 0.2 |
| 15:00–12:01 | 2.0 | 22:00–16:31 | 1.2 | 24:00–18:01 | 1.4 |
| 12:00–10:01 | 3.0 | 16:30–13:13 | 2.3 | 18:00–14:25 | 2.6 |
| 10:00– 8:01 | 4.0 | 13:12–11:01 | 3.4 | 14:24–12:01 | 3.8 |
| 8:00– 6:41 | 5.0 | 11:00– 8:49 | 4.5 | 12:00– 9:37 | 5.0 |
| 6:40– 5:44 | 6.0 | 8:48– 7:21 | 5.6 | 9:36– 8:01 | 6.2 |
| under 5:43 | 7.0 | 7:20– 6:19 | 6.7 | 8:00– 6:53 | 7.4 |
| | | under 6:18 | 7.8 | under 6:52 | 8.6 |
| **1.3 Miles** | | **1.4 Miles** | | **1.5 Miles** | |
| over 39:01 | 0 | over 42:01 | 0 | over 45:01 | 0 |
| 39:00–26:01 | 0.3 | 42:00–28:01 | 0.4 | 45:00–30:01 | 0.5 |
| 26:00–19:31 | 1.6 | 28:00–21:01 | 1.8 | 30:00–22:31 | 2.0 |
| 19:30–15:37 | 2.9 | 21:00–16:49 | 3.2 | 22:30–18:01 | 3.5 |
| 15:36–13:01 | 4.2 | 16:48–14:01 | 4.6 | 18:00–15:01 | 5.0 |
| 13:00–10:25 | 5.5 | 14:00–11:13 | 6.0 | 15:00–12:01 | 6.5 |
| 10:24– 8:41 | 6.8 | 11:12– 9:21 | 7.4 | 12:00–10:01 | 8.0 |
| 8:40– 7:27 | 8.1 | 9:20– 8:01 | 8.8 | 10:00– 8:35 | 9.5 |
| under 7:26 | 9.4 | under 8:00 | 10.2 | under 8:34 | 11.0 |

| Time (hr:min:sec) | Point Value | Time (hr:min:sec) | Point Value | Time (hr:min:sec) | Point Value |
|---|---|---|---|---|---|
| **1.6 Miles** | | **1.7 Miles** | | **1.8 Miles** | |
| over 48:01 | 0 | over 51:01 | 0 | over 54:01 | 0 |
| 48:00–32:01 | 0.6 | 51:00–34:01 | 0.7 | 54:00–36:01 | 0.8 |
| 32:00–24:01 | 2.2 | 34:00–25:31 | 2.4 | 36:00–27:01 | 2.6 |
| 24:00–19:13 | 3.8 | 25:30–20:25 | 4.1 | 27:00–21:37 | 4.4 |
| 19:12–16:01 | 5.4 | 20:24–17:01 | 5.8 | 21:36–18:01 | 6.2 |
| 16:00–12:49 | 7.0 | 17:00–13:37 | 7.5 | 18:00–14:25 | 8.0 |
| 12:48–10:41 | 8.6 | 13:36–11:21 | 9.2 | 14:24–12:01 | 9.8 |
| 10:40– 9:10 | 10.2 | 11:20– 9:44 | 10.9 | 12:00–10:19 | 11.6 |
| under 9:09 | 11.8 | under 9:43 | 12.6 | under 10:18 | 13.4 |
| **1.9 Miles** | | **2.0 Miles** | | **2.1 Miles** | |
| over 57:01 | 0 | over 40:01 | 1.0 | over 42:01 | 1.1 |
| 57:00–38:01 | 0.9 | 40:00–30:01 | 3.0 | 42:00–31:31 | 3.2 |
| 38:00–28:31 | 2.8 | 30:00–24:01 | 5.0 | 31:30–25:13 | 5.3 |
| 28:30–22:49 | 4.7 | 24:00–20:01 | 7.0 | 25:12–21:01 | 7.4 |
| 22:48–19:01 | 6.6 | 20:00–16:01 | 9.0 | 21:00–16:49 | 9.5 |
| 19:00–15:13 | 8.5 | 16:00–13:21 | 11.0 | 16:48–14:01 | 11.6 |
| 15:12–12:41 | 10.4 | 13:20–11:27 | 13.0 | 14:00–12:01 | 13.7 |
| 12:40–10:53 | 12.3 | under 11:26 | 15.0 | under 12:00 | 15.8 |
| under 10:52 | 14.2 | | | | |
| **2.2 Miles** | | **2.3 Miles** | | **2.4 Miles** | |
| over 44:01 | 1.2 | over 46:01 | 1.3 | over 48:01 | 1.4 |
| 44:00–33:01 | 3.4 | 46:00–34:31 | 3.6 | 48:00–36:01 | 3.8 |
| 33:00–26:25 | 5.6 | 34:30–27:37 | 5.9 | 36:00–28:49 | 6.2 |
| 26:24–22:01 | 7.8 | 27:36–23:01 | 8.2 | 28:48–24:01 | 8.6 |
| 22:00–17:37 | 10.0 | 23:00–18:25 | 10.5 | 24:00–19:13 | 11.0 |
| 17:36–14:41 | 12.2 | 18:24–15:21 | 12.8 | 19:12–16:01 | 13.4 |
| 14:40–12:35 | 14.4 | 15:20–13:10 | 15.1 | 16:00–13:44 | 15.8 |
| under 12:34 | 16.6 | under 13:09 | 17.4 | under 13:43 | 18.2 |

| Time (hr:min:sec) | Point Value | Time (hr:min:sec) | Point Value | Time (hr:min:sec) | Point Value |
|---|---|---|---|---|---|
| **2.5 Miles** | | **2.6 Miles** | | **2.7 Miles** | |
| over 50:01 | 1.5 | over 52:01 | 1.6 | over 54:01 | 1.7 |
| 50:00–37:31 | 4.0 | 52:00–39:01 | 4.2 | 54:00–40:31 | 4.4 |
| 37:30–30:01 | 6.5 | 39:00–31:13 | 6.8 | 40:30–32:25 | 7.1 |
| 30:00–25:01 | 9.0 | 31:12–26:01 | 9.4 | 32:24–27:01 | 9.8 |
| 25:00–20:01 | 11.5 | 26:00–20:49 | 12.0 | 27:00–21:37 | 12.5 |
| 20:00–16:41 | 14.0 | 20:48–17:21 | 14.6 | 21:36–18:01 | 15.2 |
| 16:40–14:19 | 16.5 | 17:20–14:53 | 17.2 | 18:00–15:27 | 17.9 |
| under 14:18 | 19.0 | under 14:52 | 19.8 | under 15:26 | 20.6 |
| **2.8 Miles** | | **2.9 Miles** | | **3.0 Miles** | |
| over 56:01 | 1.8 | over 58:01 | 1.9 | over 1:00:01 | 2.0 |
| 56:00–42:01 | 4.6 | 58:00–43:31 | 4.8 | 1:00:00– 45:01 | 5.0 |
| 42:00–33:37 | 7.4 | 43:30–34:49 | 7.7 | 45:00– 36:01 | 8.0 |
| 33:36–28:01 | 10.2 | 34:48–29:01 | 10.6 | 36:00– 30:01 | 11.0 |
| 28:00–22:25 | 13.0 | 29:00–23:13 | 13.5 | 30:00– 24:01 | 14.0 |
| 22:24–18:41 | 15.8 | 23:12–19:21 | 16.4 | 24:00– 20:01 | 17.0 |
| 18:40–16:01 | 18.6 | 19:20–16:35 | 19.3 | 20:00– 17:10 | 20.0 |
| under 16:00 | 21.4 | under 16:34 | 22.2 | under 17:09 | 23.0 |
| **3.1 Miles** | | **3.2 Miles** | | **3.3 Miles** | |
| over 1:02:01 | 2.1 | over 1:04:01 | 2.2 | over 1:06:01 | 2.3 |
| 1:02:00– 46:31 | 5.2 | 1:04:00– 48:01 | 5.4 | 1:06:00– 49:31 | 5.6 |
| 46:30– 37:13 | 8.3 | 48:00– 38:25 | 8.6 | 49:30– 39:37 | 8.9 |
| 37:12– 31:01 | 11.4 | 38:24– 32:01 | 11.8 | 39:36– 33:01 | 12.2 |
| 31:00– 24:49 | 14.5 | 32:00– 25:37 | 15.0 | 33:00– 26:25 | 15.5 |
| 24:48– 20:41 | 17.6 | 25:36– 21:21 | 18.2 | 26:24– 22:01 | 18.8 |
| 20:40– 17:44 | 20.7 | 21:20– 18:19 | 21.4 | 22:00– 18:53 | 22.1 |
| under 17:43 | 23.8 | under 18:18 | 24.6 | under 18:52 | 25.4 |
| **3.4 Miles** | | **3.5 Miles** | | **3.6 Miles** | |
| over 1:08:01 | 2.4 | over 1:10:01 | 2.5 | over 1:12:01 | 2.6 |
| 1:08:00– 51:01 | 5.8 | 1:10:00– 52:31 | 6.0 | 1:12:00– 54:01 | 6.2 |
| 51:00– 40:49 | 9.2 | 52:30– 42:01 | 9.5 | 54:00– 43:13 | 9.8 |
| 40:48– 34:01 | 12.6 | 42:00– 35:01 | 13.0 | 43:12– 36:01 | 13.4 |
| 34:00– 27:13 | 16.0 | 35:00– 28:01 | 16.5 | 36:00– 28:49 | 17.0 |
| 27:12– 22:41 | 19.4 | 28:00– 23:21 | 20.0 | 28:48– 24:01 | 20.6 |
| 22:40– 19:27 | 22.8 | 23:20– 20:01 | 23.5 | 24:00– 20:35 | 24.2 |
| under 19:26 | 26.2 | under 20:00 | 27.0 | under 20:34 | 27.8 |

| Time (hr:min:sec) | Point Value | Time (hr:min:sec) | Point Value | Time (hr:min:sec) | Point Value |
|---|---|---|---|---|---|
| **3.7 Miles** | | **3.8 Miles** | | **3.9 Miles** | |
| over 1:14:01 | 2.7 | over 1:16:01 | 2.8 | over 1:18:01 | 2.9 |
| 1:14:00– 55:31 | 6.4 | 1:16:00– 57:01 | 6.6 | 1:18:00– 58:31 | 6.8 |
| 55:30– 44:25 | 10.1 | 57:00– 45:37 | 10.4 | 58:30– 46:49 | 10.7 |
| 44:24– 37:01 | 13.8 | 45:36– 38:01 | 14.2 | 46:48– 39:01 | 14.6 |
| 37:00– 29:37 | 17.5 | 38:00– 30:25 | 18.0 | 39:00– 31:13 | 18.5 |
| 29:36– 24:41 | 21.2 | 30:24– 25:21 | 21.8 | 31:12– 26:01 | 22.4 |
| 24:40– 21:10 | 24.9 | 25:20– 21:44 | 25.6 | 26:00– 22:19 | 26.3 |
| under 21:09 | 28.6 | under 21:43 | 29.4 | under 22:18 | 30.2 |
| **4.0 Miles** | | **4.1 Miles** | | **4.2 Miles** | |
| over 1:20:01 | 3.0 | over 1:22:01 | 3.1 | over 1:24:01 | 3.2 |
| 1:20:00–1:00:01 | 7.0 | 1:22:00–1:01:31 | 7.2 | 1:24:00–1:03:01 | 7.4 |
| 1:00:00– 48:01 | 11.0 | 1:01:30– 49:13 | 11.3 | 1:03:00– 50:25 | 11.6 |
| 48:00– 40:01 | 15.0 | 49:12– 41:01 | 15.4 | 50:24– 42:01 | 15.8 |
| 40:00– 32:01 | 19.0 | 41:00– 32:49 | 19.5 | 42:00– 33:37 | 20.0 |
| 32:00– 26:41 | 23.0 | 32:48– 27:21 | 23.6 | 33:36– 28:01 | 24.2 |
| 26:40– 22:53 | 27.0 | 27:20– 23:27 | 27.7 | 28:00– 24:01 | 28.4 |
| under 22:52 | 31.0 | under 23:26 | 31.8 | under 24:00 | 32.6 |
| **4.3 Miles** | | **4.4 Miles** | | **4.5 Miles** | |
| over 1:26:01 | 3.3 | over 1:28:01 | 3.4 | over 1:30:01 | 3.5 |
| 1:26:00–1:04:31 | 7.6 | 1:28:00–1:06:01 | 7.8 | 1:30:00–1:07:31 | 8.0 |
| 1:04:30– 51:37 | 11.9 | 1:06:00– 52:49 | 12.2 | 1:07:30– 54:01 | 12.5 |
| 51:36– 43:01 | 16.2 | 52:48– 44:01 | 16.6 | 54:00– 45:01 | 17.0 |
| 43:00– 34:25 | 20.5 | 44:00– 35:13 | 21.0 | 45:00– 36:01 | 21.5 |
| 34:24– 28:41 | 24.8 | 35:12– 29:21 | 25.4 | 36:00– 30:01 | 26.0 |
| 28:40– 24:35 | 29.1 | 29:20– 25:10 | 29.8 | 30:00– 25:44 | 30.5 |
| under 24:34 | 33.4 | under 25:09 | 34.2 | under 25:43 | 35.0 |
| **4.6 Miles** | | **4.7 Miles** | | **4.8 Miles** | |
| over 1:32:01 | 3.6 | over 1:34:01 | 3.7 | over 1:36:01 | 3.8 |
| 1:32:00–1:09:01 | 8.2 | 1:34:00–1:10:31 | 8.4 | 1:36:00–1:12:01 | 8.6 |
| 1:09:00– 55:13 | 12.8 | 1:10:30– 56:25 | 13.1 | 1:12:00– 57:37 | 13.4 |
| 55:12– 46:01 | 17.4 | 56:24– 47:01 | 17.8 | 57:36– 48:01 | 18.2 |
| 46:00– 36:49 | 22.0 | 47:00– 37:37 | 22.5 | 48:00– 38:25 | 23.0 |
| 36:48– 30:41 | 26.6 | 37:36– 31:21 | 27.2 | 38:24– 32:01 | 27.8 |
| 30:40– 26:19 | 31.2 | 31:20– 26:53 | 31.9 | 32:00– 27:27 | 32.6 |
| under 26:18 | 35.8 | under 26:52 | 36.6 | under 27:26 | 37.4 |

| Time (hr:min:sec) | Point Value | Time (hr:min:sec) | Point Value | Time (hr:min:sec) | Point Value |
|---|---|---|---|---|---|
| **4.9 Miles** | | **5.0 Miles** | | **5.5 Miles** | |
| over 1:38:01 | 3.9 | over 1:40:01 | 4.0 | over 1:50:01 | 4.5 |
| 1:38:00–1:13:31 | 8.8 | 1:40:00–1:15:01 | 9.0 | 1:50:00–1:22:31 | 10.0 |
| 1:13:30– 58:49 | 13.7 | 1:15:00–1:00:01 | 14.0 | 1:22:30–1:06:01 | 15.5 |
| 58:48– 49:01 | 18.6 | 1:00:00– 50:01 | 19.0 | 1:06:00– 55:01 | 21.0 |
| 49:00– 39:13 | 23.5 | 50:00– 40:01 | 24.0 | 55:00– 44:01 | 26.5 |
| 39:12– 32:41 | 28.4 | 40:00– 33:21 | 29.0 | 44:00– 36:41 | 32.0 |
| 32:40– 28:01 | 33.3 | 33:20– 28:35 | 34.0 | 36:40– 31:27 | 37.5 |
| under 28:00 | 38.2 | under 28:34 | 39.0 | under 31:26 | 43.0 |
| **6.0 Miles** | | **6.5 Miles** | | **7.0 Miles** | |
| over 2:00:01 | 5.0 | over 2:10:01 | 5.5 | over 2:20:01 | 6.0 |
| 2:00:00–1:30:01 | 11.0 | 2:10:00–1:37:31 | 12.0 | 2:20:00–1:45:01 | 13.0 |
| 1:30:00–1:12:01 | 17.0 | 1:37:30–1:18:01 | 18.5 | 1:45:00–1:24:01 | 20.0 |
| 1:12:00–1:00:01 | 23.0 | 1:18:00–1:05:01 | 25.0 | 1:24:00–1:10:01 | 27.0 |
| 1:00:00– 48:01 | 29.0 | 1:05:00– 52:01 | 31.5 | 1:10:00– 56:01 | 34.0 |
| 48:00– 40:01 | 35.0 | 52:00– 43:21 | 38.0 | 56:00– 46:41 | 41.0 |
| 40:00– 34:19 | 41.0 | 43:20– 37:10 | 44.5 | 46:40– 40:01 | 48.0 |
| under 34:18 | 47.0 | under 37:09 | 51.0 | under 40:00 | 55.0 |
| **7.5 Miles** | | **8.0 Miles** | | **8.5 Miles** | |
| over 2:30:01 | 6.5 | over 2:40:01 | 7.0 | over 2:50:01 | 7.5 |
| 2:30:00–1:52:31 | 14.0 | 2:40:00–2:00:01 | 15.0 | 2:50:00–2:07:31 | 16.0 |
| 1:52:30–1:30:01 | 21.5 | 2:00:00–1:36:01 | 23.0 | 2:07:30–1:42:01 | 24.5 |
| 1:30:00–1:15:01 | 29.0 | 1:36:00–1:20:01 | 31.0 | 1:42:00–1:25:01 | 33.0 |
| 1:15:00–1:00:01 | 36.5 | 1:20:00–1:04:01 | 39.0 | 1:25:00–1:08:01 | 41.5 |
| 1:00:00– 50:01 | 44.0 | 1:04:00– 53:21 | 47.0 | 1:08:00– 56:41 | 50.0 |
| 50:00– 42:53 | 51.5 | 53:20– 45:44 | 55.0 | 56:40– 48:35 | 58.5 |
| under 42:52 | 59.0 | under 45:43 | 63.0 | under 48:34 | 67.0 |
| **9.0 Miles** | | **9.5 Miles** | | **10.0 Miles** | |
| over 3:00:01 | 8.0 | over 3:10:01 | 8.5 | over 3:20:01 | 9.0 |
| 3:00:00–2:15:01 | 17.0 | 3:10:00–2:22:31 | 18.0 | 3:20:00–2:30:01 | 19.0 |
| 2:15:00–1:48:01 | 26.0 | 2:22:30–1:54:01 | 27.5 | 2:30:00–2:00:01 | 29.0 |
| 1:48:00–1:30:01 | 35.0 | 1:54:00–1:35:01 | 37.0 | 2:00:00–1:40:01 | 39.0 |
| 1:30:00–1:12:01 | 44.0 | 1:35:00–1:16:01 | 46.5 | 1:40:00–1:20:01 | 49.0 |
| 1:12:00–1:00:01 | 53.0 | 1:16:00–1:03:21 | 56.0 | 1:20:00–1:06:41 | 59.0 |
| 1:00:00– 51:27 | 62.0 | 1:03:20– 54:19 | 65.5 | 1:06:40– 57:10 | 69.0 |
| under 51:26 | 71.0 | under 54:18 | 75.0 | under 57:09 | 79.0 |

| Time (hr:min:sec) | Point Value | Time (hr:min:sec) | Point Value | Time (hr:min:sec) | Point Value |
|---|---|---|---|---|---|
| **11.0 Miles** | | **12.0 Miles** | | **13.0 Miles** | |
| over 3:40:01 | 10.0 | over 4:00:01 | 11.0 | over 4:20:01 | 12.0 |
| 3:40:00–2:45:01 | 21.0 | 4:00:00–3:00:01 | 23.0 | 4:20:00–3:15:01 | 25.0 |
| 2:45:00–2:12:01 | 32.0 | 3:00:00–2:24:01 | 35.0 | 3:15:00–2:36:01 | 38.0 |
| 2:12:00–1:50:01 | 43.0 | 2:24:00–2:00:01 | 47.0 | 2:36:00–2:10:01 | 51.0 |
| 1:50:00–1:28:01 | 54.0 | 2:00:00–1:36:01 | 59.0 | 2:10:00–1:44:01 | 64.0 |
| 1:28:00–1:13:21 | 65.0 | 1:36:00–1:20:01 | 71.0 | 1:44:00–1:26:41 | 77.0 |
| 1:13:20–1:02:53 | 76.0 | 1:20:00–1:08:35 | 83.0 | 1:26:40–1:14:19 | 90.0 |
| under 1:02:52 | 87.0 | under 1:08:34 | 95.0 | under 1:14:18 | 103.0 |
| **14.0 Miles** | | **15.0 Miles** | | **16.0 Miles** | |
| over 4:40:01 | 13.0 | over 5:00:01 | 14.0 | over 5:20:01 | 15.0 |
| 4:40:00–3:30:01 | 27.0 | 5:00:00–3:45:01 | 29.0 | 5:20:00–4:00:01 | 31.0 |
| 3:30:00–2:48:01 | 41.0 | 3:45:00–3:00:01 | 44.0 | 4:00:00–3:12:01 | 47.0 |
| 2:48:00–2:20:01 | 55.0 | 3:00:00–2:30:01 | 59.0 | 3:12:00–2:40:01 | 63.0 |
| 2:20:00–1:52:01 | 69.0 | 2:30:00–2:00:01 | 74.0 | 2:40:00–2:08:01 | 79.0 |
| 1:52:00–1:33:21 | 83.0 | 2:00:00–1:40:01 | 89.0 | 2:08:00–1:46:41 | 95.0 |
| 1:33:20–1:20:01 | 97.0 | 1:40:00–1:25:44 | 104.0 | 1:46:40–1:31:27 | 111.0 |
| under 1:20:00 | 111.0 | under 1:25:43 | 119.0 | under 1:31:26 | 127.0 |
| **17.0 Miles** | | **18.0 Miles** | | **19.0 Miles** | |
| over 5:40:01 | 16.0 | over 6:00:01 | 17.0 | over 6:20:01 | 18.0 |
| 5:40:00–4:15:01 | 33.0 | 6:00:00–4:30:01 | 35.0 | 6:20:00–4:45:01 | 37.0 |
| 4:15:00–3:24:01 | 50.0 | 4:30:00–3:36:01 | 53.0 | 4:45:00–3:48:01 | 56.0 |
| 3:24:00–2:50:01 | 67.0 | 3:36:00–3:00:01 | 71.0 | 3:48:00–3:10:01 | 75.0 |
| 2:50:00–2:16:01 | 84.0 | 3:00:00–2:24:01 | 89.0 | 3:10:00–2:32:01 | 94.0 |
| 2:16:00–1:53:21 | 101.0 | 2:24:00–2:00:01 | 107.0 | 2:32:00–2:06:41 | 113.0 |
| 1:53:20–1:37:10 | 118.0 | 2:00:00–1:42:53 | 125.0 | 2:06:40–1:48:35 | 132.0 |
| under 1:37:09 | 135.0 | under 1:42:52 | 143.0 | under 1:48:34 | 151.0 |
| **20.0 Miles** | | **21.0 Miles** | | **22.0 Miles** | |
| over 6:40:01 | 19.0 | over 7:00:01 | 20.0 | over 7:20:01 | 21.0 |
| 6:40:00–5:00:01 | 39.0 | 7:00:00–5:15:01 | 41.0 | 7:20:00–5:30:01 | 43.0 |
| 5:00:00–4:00:01 | 59.0 | 5:15:00–4:12:01 | 62.0 | 5:30:00–4:24:01 | 65.0 |
| 4:00:00–3:20:01 | 79.0 | 4:12:00–3:30:01 | 83.0 | 4:24:00–3:40:01 | 87.0 |
| 3:20:00–2:40:01 | 99.0 | 3:30:00–2:48:01 | 104.0 | 3:40:00–2:56:01 | 109.0 |
| 2:40:00–2:13:21 | 119.0 | 2:48:00–2:20:01 | 125.0 | 2:56:00–2:26:41 | 131.0 |
| 2:13:20–1:54:19 | 139.0 | 2:20:00–2:00:01 | 146.0 | 2:26:40–2:05:44 | 153.0 |
| under 1:54:18 | 159.0 | under 2:00:00 | 167.0 | under 2:05:43 | 175.0 |

| Time (hr:min:sec) | Point Value | Time (hr:min:sec) | Point Value | Time (hr:min:sec) | Point Value |
|---|---|---|---|---|---|
| **23.0 Miles** | | **24.0 Miles** | | **25.0 Miles** | |
| over 7:40:01 | 22.0 | over 8:00:01 | 23.0 | over 8:20:01 | 24.0 |
| 7:40:00–5:45:01 | 45.0 | 8:00:00–6:00:01 | 47.0 | 8:20:00–6:15:01 | 49.0 |
| 5:45:00–4:36:01 | 68.0 | 6:00:00–4:48:01 | 71.0 | 6:15:00–5:00:01 | 74.0 |
| 4:36:00–3:50:01 | 91.0 | 4:48:00–4:00:01 | 95.0 | 5:00:00–4:10:01 | 99.0 |
| 3:50:00–3:04:01 | 114.0 | 4:00:00–3:12:01 | 119.0 | 4:10:00–3:20:01 | 124.0 |
| 3:04:00–2:33:21 | 137.0 | 3:12:00–2:40:01 | 143.0 | 3:20:00–2:46:41 | 149.0 |
| 2:33:20–2:11:27 | 160.0 | 2:40:00–2:17:10 | 167.0 | 2:46:40–2:22:53 | 174.0 |
| under 2:11:26 | 183.0 | under 2:17:09 | 191.0 | under 2:22:52 | 199.0 |
| **26.22 Miles** | | | | | |
| over 8:44:25 | 25.22 | | | | |
| 8:44:24–6:33:19 | 51.44 | | | | |
| 6:33:18–5:14:40 | 77.66 | | | | |
| 5:14:39–4:22:13 | 103.88 | | | | |
| 4:22:12–3:29:47 | 130.10 | | | | |
| 3:29:46–2:54:49 | 156.32 | | | | |
| 2:54:48–2:29:51 | 182.54 | | | | |
| under 2:29:50 | 208.76 | | | | |

## CYCLING

| Time (hr:min:sec) | Point Value | Time (hr:min:sec) | Point Value | Time (hr:min:sec) | Point Value |
|---|---|---|---|---|---|
| **2.0 Miles** | | **3.0 Miles** | | **4.0 Miles** | |
| over 12:01 | 0 | over 18:01 | 0 | over 24:01 | 0 |
| 12:00– 8:01 | 0.5 | 18:00–12:01 | 1.5 | 24:00–16:01 | 2.5 |
| 8:00– 6.01 | 1.5 | 12:00– 9:01 | 3.0 | 16:00–12:01 | 4.5 |
| under 6:00 | 2.5 | under 9:00 | 4.5 | under 12:00 | 6.5 |
| **5.0 Miles** | | **6.0 Miles** | | **7.0 Miles** | |
| over 30:01 | 2.0 | over 36:01 | 2.7 | over 42:01 | 3.4 |
| 30:00–20:01 | 3.5 | 36:00–24:01 | 4.5 | 42:00–28:01 | 5.5 |
| 20:00–15:01 | 6.0 | 24:00–18:01 | 7.5 | 28:00–21:01 | 9.0 |
| under 15:00 | 8.5 | under 18:00 | 10.5 | under 21:00 | 12.5 |

| Time (hr:min:sec) | Point Value | Time (hr:min:sec) | Point Value | Time (hr:min:sec) | Point Value |
|---|---|---|---|---|---|
| **8.0 Miles** | | **9.0 Miles** | | **10.0 Miles** | |
| over 48:01 | 4.1 | over 54:01 | 4.8 | over 1:00:01 | 5.5 |
| 48:00–32:01 | 6.5 | 54:00–36:01 | 7.5 | 1:00:00– 40:01 | 8.5 |
| 32:00–24:01 | 10.5 | 36:00–27:01 | 12.0 | 40:00– 30:01 | 13.5 |
| under 24:00 | 14.5 | under 27:00 | 16.5 | under 30:00 | 18.5 |
| **11.0 Miles** | | **12.0 Miles** | | **13.0 Miles** | |
| over 1:06:01 | 6.2 | over 1:12:01 | 6.9 | over 1:18:01 | 7.6 |
| 1:06:00– 44:01 | 9.5 | 1:12:00– 48:01 | 10.5 | 1:18:00– 52:01 | 11.5 |
| 44:00– 33:01 | 15.0 | 48:00– 36:01 | 16.5 | 52:00– 39:01 | 18.0 |
| under 33:00 | 20.5 | under 36:00 | 22.5 | under 39:00 | 24.5 |
| **14.0 Miles** | | **15.0 Miles** | | **16.0 Miles** | |
| over 1:24:01 | 8.3 | over 1:30:01 | 9.0 | over 1:36:01 | 9.7 |
| 1:24:00– 56:01 | 12.5 | 1:30:00–1:00:01 | 13.5 | 1:36:00–1:04:01 | 14.5 |
| 56:00– 42:01 | 19.5 | 1:00:00– 45:01 | 21.0 | 1:04:00– 48:01 | 22.5 |
| under 42:00 | 26.5 | under 45:00 | 28.5 | under 48:00 | 30.5 |
| **17.0 Miles** | | **18.0 Miles** | | **19.0 Miles** | |
| over 1:42:01 | 10.4 | over 1:48:01 | 11.1 | over 1:54:01 | 11.8 |
| 1:42:00–1:08:01 | 15.5 | 1:48:00–1:12:01 | 16.5 | 1:54:00–1:16:01 | 17.5 |
| 1:08:00– 51:01 | 24.0 | 1:12:00– 54:01 | 25.5 | 1:16:00– 57:01 | 27.0 |
| under 51:00 | 32.5 | under 54:00 | 34.5 | under 57:00 | 36.5 |
| **20.0 Miles** | | **21.0 Miles** | | **22.0 Miles** | |
| over 2:00:01 | 12.5 | over 2:06:01 | 13.2 | over 2:12:01 | 13.9 |
| 2:00:00–1:20:01 | 18.5 | 2:06:00–1:24:01 | 19.5 | 2:12:00–1:28:01 | 20.5 |
| 1:20:00–1:00:01 | 28.5 | 1:24:00–1:03:01 | 30.0 | 1:28:00–1:06:01 | 31.5 |
| under 1:00:00 | 38.5 | under 1:03:00 | 40.5 | under 1:06:00 | 42.5 |
| **23.0 Miles** | | **24.0 Miles** | | **25.0 Miles** | |
| over 2:18:01 | 14.6 | over 2:24:01 | 15.3 | over 2:30:01 | 16.0 |
| 2:18:00–1:32:01 | 21.5 | 2:24:00–1:36:01 | 22.5 | 2:30:00–1:40:01 | 23.5 |
| 1:32:00–1:09:01 | 33.0 | 1:36:00–1:12:01 | 34.5 | 1:40:00–1:15:01 | 36.0 |
| under 1:09:00 | 44.5 | under 1:12:00 | 46.5 | under 1:15:00 | 48.5 |

| Time (hr:min:sec) | Point Value | Time (hr:min:sec) | Point Value | Time (hr:min:sec) | Point Value |
|---|---|---|---|---|---|
| **26.0 Miles** | | **27.0 Miles** | | **28.0 Miles** | |
| over 2:36:01 | 16.7 | over 2:42:01 | 17.4 | over 2:48:01 | 18.1 |
| 2:36:00–1:44:01 | 24.5 | 2:42:00–1:48:01 | 25.5 | 2:48:00–1:52:01 | 26.5 |
| 1:44:00–1:18:01 | 37.5 | 1:48:00–1:21:01 | 39.0 | 1:52:00–1:24:01 | 40.5 |
| under 1:18:00 | 50.5 | under 1:21:00 | 52.5 | under 1:24:00 | 54.5 |
| **29.0 Miles** | | **30.0 Miles** | | **35.0 Miles** | |
| over 2:54:01 | 18.8 | over 3:00:01 | 19.5 | over 3:30:01 | 23.0 |
| 2:54:00–1:56:01 | 27.5 | 3:00:00–2:00:01 | 28.5 | 3:30:00–2:20:01 | 33.5 |
| 1:56:00–1:27:01 | 42.0 | 2:00:00–1:30:01 | 43.5 | 2:20:00–1:45:01 | 51.0 |
| under 1:27:00 | 56.5 | under 1:30:00 | 58.5 | under 1:45:00 | 68.5 |
| **40.0 Miles** | | **45.0 Miles** | | **50.0 Miles** | |
| over 4:00:01 | 26.5 | over 4:30:01 | 30.0 | over 5:00:01 | 33.5 |
| 4:00:00–2:40:01 | 38.5 | 4:30:00–3:00:01 | 43.5 | 5:00:00–3:20:01 | 48.5 |
| 2:40:00–2:00:01 | 58.5 | 3:00:00–2:15:01 | 66.0 | 3:20:00–2:30:01 | 73.5 |
| under 2:00:00 | 78.5 | under 2:15:00 | 88.5 | under 2:30:00 | 98.5 |
| **55.0 Miles** | | **60.0 Miles** | | **65.0 Miles** | |
| over 5:30:01 | 37.0 | over 6:00:01 | 40.5 | over 6:30:01 | 44.0 |
| 5:30:00–3:40:01 | 53.5 | 6:00:00–4:00:01 | 58.5 | 6:30:00–4:20:01 | 63.5 |
| 3:40:00–2:45:01 | 81.0 | 4:00:00–3:00:01 | 88.5 | 4:20:00–3:15:01 | 96.0 |
| under 2:45:00 | 108.5 | under 3:00:00 | 118.5 | under 3:15:00 | 128.5 |
| **70.0 Miles** | | **75.0 Miles** | | **80.0 Miles** | |
| over 7:00:01 | 47.5 | over 7:30:01 | 51.0 | over 8:00:01 | 54.5 |
| 7:00:00–4:40:01 | 68.5 | 7:30:00–5:00:01 | 73.5 | 8:00:00–5:20:01 | 78.5 |
| 4:40:00–3:30:01 | 103.5 | 5:00:00–3:45:01 | 111.0 | 5:20:00–4:00:01 | 118.5 |
| under 3:30:00 | 138.5 | under 3:45:00 | 148.5 | under 4:00:00 | 158.5 |
| **85.0 Miles** | | **90.0 Miles** | | **95.0 Miles** | |
| over 8:30:01 | 58.0 | over 9:00:01 | 61.5 | over 9:30:01 | 65.0 |
| 8:30:00–5:40:01 | 83.5 | 9:00:00–6:00:01 | 88.5 | 9:30:00–6:20:01 | 93.5 |
| 5:40:00–4:15:01 | 126.0 | 6:00:00–4:30:01 | 133.5 | 6:20:00–4:45:01 | 141.0 |
| under 4:15:00 | 168.5 | under 4:30:00 | 178.5 | under 4:45:00 | 188.5 |

| Time (hr:min:sec) | Point Value |
|---|---|
| **100.0 Miles** | |
| over 10:00:01 | 68.5 |
| 10:00:00– 6:40:01 | 98.5 |
| 6:40:00– 5:00:01 | 148.5 |
| under 5:00:00 | 198.5 |

Note: Points are determined considering an equal uphill and downhill course, and considering an equal time with and against the wind. For cycling a one-way course against a wind exceeding 5 mph, add ½ point per mile to the total point value.

## SWIMMING

| Time (hr:min:sec) | Point Value | Time (hr:min:sec) | Point Value | Time (hr:min:sec) | Point Value |
|---|---|---|---|---|---|
| **200 Yards** | | **250 Yards** | | **300 Yards** | |
| over 6:41 | 0 | over 8:21 | 0 | over 10:01 | 0 |
| 6:40–5:01 | 1.25 | 8:20–6:16 | 1.56 | 10:00– 7:31 | 1.88 |
| 5:00–3:21 | 1.67 | 6:15–4:11 | 2.08 | 7:30– 5:01 | 2.50 |
| under 3:20 | 2.50 | under 4:10 | 3.12 | under 5:00 | 3.75 |
| **350 Yards** | | **400 Yards** | | **450 Yards** | |
| over 11:41 | 0 | over 13:21 | 0 | over 15:01 | 0 |
| 11:40– 8:46 | 2.19 | 13:20–10:01 | 2.50 | 15:00–11:16 | 2.81 |
| 8:45– 5:51 | 2.92 | 10:00– 6:41 | 3.33 | 11:15– 7:31 | 3.75 |
| under 5:50 | 4.38 | under 6:40 | 5.00 | under 7:30 | 5.63 |
| **500 Yards** | | **550 Yards** | | **600 Yards** | |
| over 16:41 | 0 | over 18:21 | 0 | over 20:01 | 0 |
| 16:40–12:31 | 3.12 | 18:20–13:46 | 3.44 | 20:00–15:01 | 3.75 |
| 12:30– 8:21 | 4.17 | 13:45– 9:11 | 4.58 | 15:00–10:01 | 5.00 |
| under 8:20 | 6.25 | under 9:10 | 6.87 | under 10:00 | 7.50 |
| **650 Yards** | | **700 Yards** | | **750 Yards** | |
| over 21:41 | 0 | over 23:21 | 0 | over 25:01 | 0 |
| 21:40–16:16 | 4.31 | 23:20–17:31 | 4.88 | 25:00–18:46 | 5.44 |
| 16:15–10:51 | 5.67 | 17:30–11:41 | 6.33 | 18:45–12:31 | 7.00 |
| under 10:50 | 8.38 | under 11:40 | 9.25 | under 12:30 | 10.13 |

| Time (hr:min:sec) | Point Value | Time (hr:min:sec) | Point Value | Time (hr:min:sec) | Point Value |
|---|---|---|---|---|---|
| **800 Yards** | | **850 Yards** | | **900 Yards** | |
| over 26:41 | 0 | over 28:21 | 0 | over 30:01 | 0 |
| 26:40–20:01 | 6.00 | 28:20–21:16 | 6.56 | 30:00–22:31 | 7.13 |
| 20:00–13:21 | 7.67 | 21:15–14:11 | 8.33 | 22:30–15:01 | 9.00 |
| under 13:20 | 11.00 | under 14:10 | 11.87 | under 15:00 | 12.75 |
| **950 Yards** | | **1000 Yards** | | **1050 Yards** | |
| over 31:41 | 0 | over 33:21 | 0 | over 35:01 | 0 |
| 31:40–23:46 | 7.69 | 33:20–25:01 | 8.25 | 35:00–26:16 | 8:81 |
| 23:45–15:51 | 9.67 | 25:00–16:41 | 10.33 | 26:15–17:31 | 11.00 |
| under 15:50 | 13.63 | under 16:40 | 14.50 | under 17:30 | 15.38 |
| **1100 Yards** | | **1150 Yards** | | **1200 Yards** | |
| over 36:41 | 0 | over 38:21 | 0 | over 40:01 | 0 |
| 36:40–27:31 | 9:37 | 38:20–28:46 | 9.94 | 40:00–30:01 | 10.50 |
| 27:30–18:21 | 11.67 | 28:45–19:11 | 12.33 | 30:00–20:01 | 13.00 |
| under 18:20 | 16.25 | under 19:10 | 17.12 | under 20:00 | 18.00 |
| **1250 Yards** | | **1300 Yards** | | **1350 Yards** | |
| over 41:41 | 0 | over 43:21 | 0 | over 45:01 | 0 |
| 41:40–31:16 | 11.06 | 43:20–32:31 | 11.63 | 45:00–33:46 | 12.19 |
| 31:15–20:51 | 13.67 | 32:30–21:41 | 14.33 | 33:45–22:31 | 15.00 |
| under 20:50 | 18.88 | under 21:40 | 19.75 | under 22:30 | 20.63 |
| **1400 Yards** | | **1450 Yards** | | **1500 Yards** | |
| over 46:41 | 0 | over 48:21 | 0 | over 50:01 | 0 |
| 46:40–35:01 | 12.75 | 48.20–36:16 | 13.31 | 50:00–37:31 | 13.88 |
| 35:00–23:21 | 15.67 | 36:15–24:11 | 16.33 | 37:30–25:01 | 17.00 |
| under 23:20 | 21.50 | under 24:10 | 22.37 | under 25:00 | 23.25 |
| **1550 Yards** | | **1600 Yards** | | **1650 Yards** | |
| over 51:41 | 0 | over 53:21 | 0 | over 55:01 | 0 |
| 51:40–38:46 | 14.44 | 53:20–40:01 | 15.00 | 55:00–41:16 | 15.56 |
| 38:45–25:51 | 17.67 | 40:00–26:41 | 18.33 | 41:15–27:31 | 19.00 |
| under 25:50 | 24.13 | under 26:40 | 25.00 | under 27:30 | 25.88 |

| Time (hr:min:sec) | Point Value | Time (hr:min:sec) | Point Value | Time (hr:min:sec) | Point Value |
|---|---|---|---|---|---|
| **1700 Yards** | | **1750 Yards** | | **1800 Yards** | |
| over 56:41 | 0 | over 58:21 | 0 | over 1:00:01 | 0 |
| 56:40–42:31 | 16.12 | 58:20–43:46 | 16.69 | 1:00:00– 45:01 | 17.25 |
| 42:30–28:21 | 19.67 | 43:45–29:11 | 20.33 | 45:00– 30:01 | 21.00 |
| under 28:20 | 26.75 | under 29:10 | 27.62 | under 30:00 | 28.50 |
| **1850 Yards** | | **1900 Yards** | | **2000 Yards** | |
| over 1:01:41 | 0 | over 1:03:21 | 0 | over 1:06:41 | 0 |
| 1:01:40– 46:16 | 17.81 | 1:03:20– 47:31 | 18.38 | 1:06:40– 50:01 | 19.50 |
| 46:15– 30:51 | 21.67 | 47:30– 31.41 | 22.33 | 50:00– 33:21 | 23.67 |
| under 30:50 | 29.38 | under 31:40 | 30.25 | under 33:20 | 32.00 |
| **2100 Yards** | | **2200 Yards** | | **2300 Yards** | |
| over 1:10:01 | 0 | over 1:13:21 | 0 | over 1:16:41 | 0 |
| 1:10:00– 52:31 | 20.63 | 1:13:20– 55:01 | 21.75 | 1:16:40– 57:31 | 22.87 |
| 53:30– 35:01 | 25.00 | 55:00– 36:41 | 26.33 | 57:30– 38:21 | 27.67 |
| under 35:00 | 33.75 | under 36:40 | 35.50 | under 38:20 | 37.25 |
| **2400 Yards** | | **2500 Yards** | | **2600 Yards** | |
| over 1:20:01 | 0 | over 1:23:21 | 0 | over 1:26:41 | 0 |
| 1:20:00–1:00:01 | 24.00 | 1:23:20–1:02:31 | 25.13 | 1:26:40–1:05:01 | 26.25 |
| 1:00:00– 40:01 | 29.00 | 1:02:30– 41:41 | 30.33 | 1:05:00– 43:21 | 31.67 |
| under 40:00 | 39.00 | under 41:40 | 40.75 | under 43:20 | 42:50 |
| **2700 Yards** | | **2800 Yards** | | **2900 Yards** | |
| over 1:30:01 | 0 | over 1:33:21 | 0 | over 1:36:41 | 0 |
| 1:30:00–1:07:31 | 27.38 | 1:33:20–1:10:01 | 28.50 | 1:36:40–1:12:31 | 29.62 |
| 1:07:30– 45:01 | 33.00 | 1:10:00– 46:41 | 34.33 | 1:12:30– 48:21 | 35.67 |
| under 45:00 | 44.25 | under 46:40 | 46.00 | under 48:20 | 47.75 |
| **3000 Yards** | | | | | |
| over 1:40:01 | 0 | | | | |
| 1:40:00–1:15:01 | 30.75 | | | | |
| 1:15:00– 50:01 | 37.00 | | | | |
| under 50:00 | 49.50 | | | | |

Note: Points are calculated on overhand crawl, considering average skill in swimming, i.e., 9.0 kcal (kilo calories) per minute. Breaststroke is less demanding: 7.0 kcal per minute. Backstroke, a little more than breaststroke: 8.0 kcal per minute. Butterfly is the most demanding, i.e., 12.0 kcal per minute.

## HANDBALL/RACQUETBALL/SQUASH/ BASKETBALL/SOCCER/HOCKEY/LACROSSE*

| Time (hr:min:sec) | Point Value | Time (hr:min:sec) | Point Value |
|---|---|---|---|
| under 4:59 | 0 | 1:05:00 | 9.75 |
| 5:00 | 0.75 | 1:10:00 | 10.50 |
| 10:00 | 1.50 | 1:15:00 | 11.25 |
| 15:00 | 2.25 | 1:20:00 | 12.00 |
| 20:00 | 3.00 | 1:25:00 | 12.75 |
| 25:00 | 3.75 | 1:30:00 | 13.50 |
| 30:00 | 4.50 | 1:35:00 | 14.25 |
| 35:00 | 5.25 | 1:40:00 | 15:00 |
| 40:00 | 6.00 | 1:45:00 | 15.75 |
| 45:00 | 6.75 | 1:50:00 | 16.50 |
| 50:00 | 7.50 | 1:55:00 | 17.25 |
| 55:00 | 8.25 | over 2:00:00 | 18.00 |
| 1:00:00 | 9.00 | | |

*Continuous exercise. Do not count breaks, time-outs, etc.

## STATIONARY RUNNING

| Time (min:sec) | 60–70* Steps/Min | Point Value | 70–80* Steps/Min | Point Value | 80–90* Steps/Min | Point Value | 90–100* Steps/Min | Point Value | 100–110* Steps/Min | Point Value |
|---|---|---|---|---|---|---|---|---|---|---|
| 2:30 | | | 175–200 | .88 | 200–225 | 1.13 | 225–250 | 1.38 | 250–275 | 1.63 |
| 5:00 | 300–350 | 1.25 | 350–400 | 1.75 | 400–450 | 2.25 | 450–500 | 2.75 | 500–550 | 3.25 |
| 7:30 | | 1.88 | 525–600 | 2.63 | 600–675 | 3.38 | 675–750 | 4.13 | 750–825 | 4.88 |
| 10:00 | 600–700 | 2.50 | 700–800 | 3.50 | 800–900 | 4.50 | 900–1000 | 5.50 | 1000–1100 | 6.50 |
| 12:30 | | 3.63 | 875–1000 | 4.88 | 1000–1125 | 6.13 | 1125–1250 | 7.38 | 1250–1375 | 8.63 |
| 15:00 | 900–1050 | 4.75 | 1050–1200 | 6.25 | 1200–1350 | 7.75 | 1350–1500 | 9.25 | 1500–1650 | 10.75 |
| 17:30 | | 5.88 | 1225–1400 | 7.63 | 1400–1575 | 9.38 | 1575–1750 | 11.13 | 1750–1925 | 12.88 |
| 20:00 | 1200–1400 | 7.00 | 1400–1600 | 9.00 | 1600–1800 | 11.00 | 1800–2000 | 13.00 | 2000–2200 | 15.00 |
| 22:30 | | 8.13 | 1575–1800 | 10.38 | 1800–2025 | 12.63 | 2025–2250 | 14.88 | 2250–2475 | 17.13 |
| 25:00 | 1500–1750 | 9.25 | 1750–2000 | 11.75 | 2000–2250 | 14.25 | 2250–2500 | 16.75 | 2500–2750 | 19.25 |
| 27:30 | | 10.38 | 1925–2200 | 13.13 | 2200–2475 | 15.88 | 2475–2750 | 18.63 | 2750–3025 | 21.38 |
| 30:00 | 1800–2100 | 11.50 | 2100–2400 | 14.50 | 2400–2700 | 17.50 | 2700–3000 | 20.50 | 3000–3300 | 23.50 |

*Count only when the left foot hits the floor. Knees must be brought up in front, raising the feet at least 8 inches from the floor.

## STATIONARY CYCLING*
(Using a screw-down resistance)

| Time (min:sec) | Point Value 15 Mph/ 55 Rpm | 17.5 Mph/ 65 Rpm | 20 Mph/ 75 Rpm | 25 Mph/ 90 Rpm | 30 Mph/ 105 Rpm |
|---|---|---|---|---|---|
| 3:00 | — | — | — | — | 1 |
| 4:00 | .5 | — | 1 | — | — |
| 5:00 | — | — | 1.25 | 2 | 2.5 |
| 6:00 | .75 | — | 1.5 | 2.13 | 2.75 |
| 7:00 | — | 1 | 1.75 | 2.25 | 3 |
| 8:00 | 1 | 1.25 | 2 | 2.5 | 3.33 |
| 9:00 | — | 1.38 | 2.25 | 2.75 | 3.66 |
| 10:00 | 1.25 | — | 2.5 | 3 | 4 |
| 11:00 | — | 1.5 | 2.63 | 3.25 | 4.25 |
| 12:00 | 1.38 | 1.63 | 2.75 | 3.5 | 4.5 |
| 13:00 | 1.63 | 1.88 | 2.88 | 3.75 | 4.75 |
| 14:00 | 1.75 | 2 | 3 | 4 | 5 |
| 15:00 | 1.88 | 2.13 | 3.13 | 4.25 | 5.5 |
| 16:00 | 2 | 2.25 | 3.25 | 4.5 | 6 |
| 17:00 | 2.13 | 2.38 | 3.38 | 4.75 | 6.5 |
| 18:00 | 2.25 | 2.63 | 3.63 | 5 | 7 |
| 19:00 | 2.38 | 2.75 | 3.75 | 5.33 | 7.5 |
| 20:00 | 2.5 | 2.88 | 3.88 | 5.66 | 8 |
| 22:30 | 3 | 3.18 | 4.5 | 6.63 | 9 |
| 25:00 | 3.25 | 3.75 | 5 | 7.5 | 10 |
| 27:30 | 3.5 | 4.5 | 5.75 | 8.5 | 11.5 |
| 30:00 | 3.75 | 5 | 6.5 | 9.5 | 12.5 |
| 35:00 | 4.75 | 6 | 8 | 11 | 14.5 |
| 40:00 | 5.75 | 7.25 | 9.5 | 13 | 17 |
| 45:00 | 6.75 | 8.5 | 11 | 15 | 19.5 |
| 50:00 | 7.75 | 9.75 | 12.5 | 17 | 22.5 |
| 55:00 | 8.75 | 11 | 14 | 19 | 25 |
| 60:00 | 9.75 | 12.5 | 16 | 22 | 28 |

Note: Add enough resistance so that the pulse rate counted for 10 seconds immediately after exercise and multiplied by 6 equals or exceeds 140 beats per minute.

*Stationary cycling is awarded approximately half the points for regular cycling.

## STATIONARY CYCLING
(Adjusted for weight and resistance using the Schwinn Calibrated Resistance Ergometer)

| Load: Weight (lbs) | 1.0 | 2.0 | 3.0 | 4.0 |
|---|---|---|---|---|
| **15:00 Minutes** | | | | |
| | | Point Value | | |
| 100 | 3.20 | 8.72 | 18.79 | — |
| 120 | 2.18 | 5.60 | 12.03 | 20.44 |
| 140 | 1.48 | 4.09 | 8.18 | 14.39 |
| 160 | 1.13 | 3.20 | 5.94 | 8.37 |
| 180 | 0.77 | 2.58 | 4.54 | 7.05 |
| 200 | 0.37 | 2.01 | 3.76 | 6.13 |
| 220 | — | 1.56 | 3.19 | 4.91 |
| 240 | — | 1.30 | 2.67 | 4.12 |
| **30:00 Minutes** | | | | |
| | | Point Value | | |
| 100 | 6.40 | 17.44 | 37.58 | — |
| 120 | 4.35 | 11.19 | 24.05 | 40.88 |
| 140 | 2.96 | 8.18 | 16.36 | 28.79 |
| 160 | 2.27 | 6.40 | 11.87 | 16.74 |
| 180 | 1.53 | 5.15 | 9.09 | 14.09 |
| 200 | 0.73 | 4.01 | 7.57 | 12.26 |
| 220 | — | 3.13 | 6.38 | 9.82 |
| 240 | — | 2.60 | 5.34 | 8.24 |
| **45:00 Minutes** | | | | |
| | | Point Value | | |
| 100 | 9.60 | 26.16 | 56.36 | — |
| 120 | 6.53 | 16.79 | 36.08 | 61.31 |
| 140 | 4.43 | 12.26 | 24.54 | 43.18 |
| 160 | 3.40 | 9.60 | 17.81 | 25.10 |
| 180 | 2.30 | 7.73 | 13.63 | 21.14 |
| 200 | 1.10 | 6.02 | 11.27 | 18.38 |
| 220 | — | 4.69 | 9.56 | 14.72 |
| 240 | — | 3.89 | 8.01 | 12.36 |
| **60:00 Minutes** | | | | |
| | | Point Value | | |
| 100 | 12.80 | 34.88 | 75.15 | — |
| 120 | 8.70 | 22.38 | 48.10 | 81.75 |
| 140 | 5.91 | 16.35 | 32.72 | 57.57 |

| Load: Weight (lbs) | 1.0 | 2.0 | 3.0 | 4.0 |
|---|---|---|---|---|
| | | Point Value | | |
| 160 | 4.53 | 12.80 | 23.74 | 33.47 |
| 180 | 3.06 | 10.30 | 18.17 | 28.18 |
| 200 | 1.46 | 8.02 | 15.02 | 24.51 |
| 220 | — | 6.25 | 12.75 | 19.63 |
| 240 | — | 5.19 | 10.68 | 16.48 |

Note: Resistance is consistent, regardless of speed.

## STAIR CLIMBING

(10 steps; 6″–7″ in height; 25°–30° incline)

| | Round Trips—Average Number Per Minute | | | | | |
|---|---|---|---|---|---|---|
| Time (min:sec) | 5 | 6 | 7 | 8 | 9 | 10 |
| | | | Point Value | | | |
| 3:00 | .43 | .69 | 1.00 | 1.36 | 1.80 | 2.33 |
| 3:30 | .5 | .81 | 1.17 | 1.59 | 2.10 | 2.72 |
| 4:00 | .57 | .92 | 1.33 | 1.82 | 2.40 | 3.16 |
| 4:30 | .64 | 1.04 | 1.50 | 2.05 | 2.70 | 3.5 |
| 5:00 | .71 | 1.15 | 1.67 | 2.27 | 3.00 | 3.89 |
| 5:30 | .79 | 1.27 | 1.83 | 2.50 | 3.30 | 4.28 |
| 6:00 | .86 | 1.38 | 2.00 | 2.73 | 3.60 | 4.67 |
| 6:30 | .93 | 1.50 | 2.16 | 2.98 | 3.90 | 5.06 |
| 7:00 | 1.00 | 1.62 | 2.33 | 3.18 | 4.20 | 5.44 |
| 7:30 | 1.07 | 1.73 | 2.50 | 3.41 | 4.50 | 5.83 |
| 8:00 | 1.14 | 1.85 | 2.67 | 3.65 | 4.80 | 6.22 |
| 8:30 | 1.21 | 1.96 | 2.83 | 3.86 | 5.10 | 6.61 |
| 9:00 | 1.29 | 2.08 | 3.00 | 4.09 | 5.40 | 7.00 |
| 9:30 | 1.36 | 2.19 | 3.16 | 4.32 | 5.70 | 7.39 |
| 10:00 | 1.43 | 2.31 | 3.33 | 4.55 | 6.00 | 7.78 |
| 10:30 | 1.50 | 2.42 | 3.50 | 4.77 | 6.30 | 8.17 |
| 11:00 | 1.57 | 2.54 | 3.67 | 5.00 | 6.60 | 8.55 |
| 11:30 | 1.64 | 2.65 | 3.83 | 5.23 | 6.90 | 8.94 |
| 12:00 | 1.71 | 2.77 | 4.00 | 5.45 | 7.20 | 9.33 |
| 12:30 | 1.79 | 2.88 | 4.16 | 5.68 | 7.50 | 9.72 |
| 13:00 | 1.86 | 3.00 | 4.33 | 5.91 | 7.80 | 10.11 |
| 13:30 | 1.93 | 3.12 | 4.50 | 6.14 | 8.10 | 10.5 |
| 14:00 | 2.00 | 3.23 | 4.67 | 6.36 | 8.40 | 10.89 |
| 14:30 | 2.07 | 3.35 | 4.83 | 6.59 | 8.70 | 11.28 |
| 15:00 | 3.00 | 3.46 | 5.00 | 6.82 | 9.00 | 11.67 |

## Point Value for Using a Single Step (approximately 7 inches in height)

| Stepping Rate (per min) | Time (min:sec) | Point Value |
|---|---|---|
| 30 | 6:30 | 1.5 |
| | 9:45 | 2.25 |
| | 13:00 | 3.0 |
| 35 | 6:00 | 2.0 |
| | 9:00 | 3.0 |
| | 12:00 | 4.0 |
| 40 | 5:00 | 2.5 |
| | 7:30 | 3.75 |
| | 10:00 | 5.0 |

## ROPE SKIPPING

| Time (min: sec) | 70–90 Steps/Min | 90–110 Steps/Min | 110–130 Steps/Min |
|---|---|---|---|
| | | Point Value | |
| 5:00 | 1.5 | 2.0 | 2.5 |
| 7:30 | 2.25 | 3.0 | 3.75 |
| 10:00 | 3.0 | 4.0 | 5.0 |
| 12:30 | 4.25 | 5.5 | 6.75 |
| 15:00 | 5.5 | 7.0 | 8.5 |
| 17:30 | 6.75 | 8.5 | 10.25 |
| 20:00 | 8.0 | 10.0 | 12.0 |
| 22:30 | 9.25 | 11.5 | 13.75 |
| 25:00 | 10.5 | 13.0 | 15.5 |
| 27:30 | 11.75 | 14.5 | 17.25 |
| 30:00 | 13.0 | 16.0 | 19.0 |

Note: Skip with both feet together, or step over the rope, alternating feet.

## GOLF

| Holes | Point Value |
|---|---|
| under 4 | 0 |
| 4 | 0.6 |
| 6 | 1.0 |
| 9 | 1.5 |
| 12 | 2.0 |
| 15 | 2.5 |
| 18 | 3.0 |
| 21 | 3.5 |
| 24 | 4.0 |

GOLF, continued

| Holes | Point Value |
|---|---|
| 27 | 4.5 |
| 30 | 5.0 |
| 33 | 5.5 |
| 36 | 6.0 |

Note: No motorized carts!

## ROWING

| Time (min) | Point Value |
|---|---|
| 15:00 | 3.5 |
| 30:00 | 7.0 |
| 45:00 | 10.5 |
| 60:00 | 14.0 |

Note: 2 oars, 20 strokes a minute, continuous rowing.

## TENNIS/BADMINTON/AERIAL TENNIS (Doubles)

| Time (hr:min:sec) | Point Value |
|---|---|
| under 14:59 | 0 |
| 15:00 | 0.38 |
| 30:00 | 0.75 |
| 45:00 | 1.13 |
| 1:00:00 | 1.50 |
| 1:15:00 | 1.88 |
| 1:30:00 | 2.25 |
| 1:45:00 | 2.63 |
| 2:00:00 | 3.00 |

Note: Points are awarded to players of equal ability.

## (Singles)

| Time (min:sec) | Point Value |
|---|---|
| under 4:59 | 0 |
| 5:00 | 0.33 |
| 10:00 | 0.67 |
| 15:00 | 1.00 |
| 20:00 | 1.33 |

TENNIS/BADMINTON/AERIAL TENNIS
(Singles), continued

| Time (min:sec) | Point Value |
|---|---|
| 25:00 | 1.67 |
| 30:00 | 2.00 |
| 35:00 | 2.33 |
| 40:00 | 2.67 |
| 45:00 | 3.00 |
| 50:00 | 3.33 |
| 55:00 | 3.67 |
| 60:00 | 4.00 |

Note: Points are awarded to players of equal ability.

## WATER OR DOWNHILL SNOW SKIING

| Time (hr:min:sec) | Point Value |
|---|---|
| under 4:59 | 0 |
| 5:00 | 0.5 |
| 10:00 | 1.0 |
| 15:00 | 1.5 |
| 20:00 | 2.0 |
| 25:00 | 2.5 |
| 30:00 | 3.0 |
| 35:00 | 3.5 |
| 40:00 | 4.0 |
| 45:00 | 4.5 |
| 50:00 | 5.0 |
| 55:00 | 5.5 |
| 1:00:00 | 6.0 |
| 1:05:00 | 6.5 |
| 1:10:00 | 7.0 |
| 1:15:00 | 7.5 |
| 1:20:00 | 8.0 |
| 1:25:00 | 8.5 |
| 1:30:00 | 9.0 |
| 1:35:00 | 9.5 |
| 1:40:00 | 10.0 |
| 1:45:00 | 10.5 |
| 1:50:00 | 11.0 |
| 1:55:00 | 11.5 |
| 2:00:00 | 12.0 |

Remember, for downhill skiing, it requires 3 hours on the slopes to accumulate 1 hour of actual skiing.

## CROSS-COUNTRY SKIING

| Time (min:sec) | Point Value |
|---|---|
| 15:00 | 4.5 |
| 20:00 | 6.0 |
| 25:00 | 7.5 |
| 30:00 | 9.0 |
| 35:00 | 10.5 |
| 40:00 | 12.0 |
| 45:00 | 13.5 |
| 50:00 | 15.0 |
| 55:00 | 16.5 |
| 60:00 | 18.0 |

## ICE OR ROLLER SKATING

| Time (hr:min:sec) | Point Value |
|---|---|
| 15:00 | 1.13 |
| 30:00 | 2.25 |
| 45:00 | 3.38 |
| 1:00:00 | 4.50 |
| 1:15:00 | 5.63 |
| 1:30:00 | 6.75 |
| 1:45:00 | 7.88 |
| 2:00:00 | 9.00 |

Note: For speed skating, triple the point value.

## VOLLEYBALL

| Time (min:sec) | Point Value |
|---|---|
| under 4:59 | 0 |
| 5:00 | 0.33 |
| 10:00 | 0.67 |
| 15:00 | 1.00 |
| 20:00 | 1.33 |
| 25:00 | 1.67 |
| 30:00 | 2.00 |
| 35:00 | 2.33 |
| 40:00 | 2.67 |

VOLLEYBALL, continued

| Time (min:sec) | Point Value |
|---|---|
| 45:00 | 3.00 |
| 50:00 | 3.33 |
| 55:00 | 3.67 |
| 60:00 | 4.00 |

Note: For times greater than 1 hour, figure points at a rate of 1 point/15 minutes.

## FENCING

| Time (hr:min:sec) | Point Value |
|---|---|
| 10:00 | 1 |
| 20:00 | 2 |
| 30:00 | 3 |
| 40:00 | 4 |
| 50:00 | 5 |
| 1:00:00 | 6 |
| 1:10:00 | 7 |
| 1:20:00 | 8 |
| 1:30:00 | 9 |
| 1:40:00 | 10 |
| 1:50:00 | 11 |
| 2:00:00 | 12 |

Note: For times greater than 2 hours, figure points at a rate of 1 point/10 minutes.

## CALISTHENICS

| Time (min) | Point Value |
|---|---|
| 10:00 | 0.25 |
| 20:00 | 0.50 |
| 30:00 | 0.75 |
| 40:00 | 1.00 |
| 50:00 | 1.25 |
| 60:00 | 1.50 |

Note: These are continuous, repetitive calisthenics that are more stretching than muscle-strengthening.

## WALKING OR RUNNING ON A MOTORIZED TREADMILL SET AT VARIOUS SPEEDS AND INCLINES

| Speed (mph) | Time (Min) | 0% | 5% | 10% | 15% | 20% |
|---|---|---|---|---|---|---|
| 3 mph | 10:00 | 0.50 | 0.55 | 0.70 | 1.00 | 1.50 |
| | 15:00 | 0.75 | 0.82 | 1.05 | 1.50 | 2.25 |
| | 20:00 | 1.00 | 1.10 | 1.40 | 2.00 | 3.00 |
| | 25:00 | 1.50 | 1.65 | 2.10 | 3.00 | 4.50 |
| | 30:00 | 2.00 | 2.20 | 2.80 | 4.00 | 6.00 |
| | 45:00 | 3.50 | 3.85 | 4.90 | 7.00 | 10.50 |
| | 60:00 | 5.00 | 5.50 | 7.00 | 10.00 | 15.00 |
| 4 mph | 10:00 | 1.32 | 1.45 | 1.88 | 2.64 | 3.96 |
| | 15:00 | 2.00 | 2.20 | 2.80 | 4.00 | 6.00 |
| | 20:00 | 2.99 | 3.29 | 4.19 | 5.98 | 8.97 |
| | 25:00 | 3.98 | 4.38 | 5.57 | 7.96 | 11.94 |
| | 30:00 | 5.00 | 5.50 | 7.00 | 10.00 | 15.00 |
| | 45:00 | 8.00 | 8.80 | 11.20 | 16.00 | 24.00 |
| | 60:00 | 11.00 | 12.10 | 15.40 | 22.00 | 33.00 |
| 5 mph | 10:00 | 2.49 | 2.74 | 3.49 | 4.98 | 7.74 |
| | 15:00 | 4.00 | 4.40 | 5.60 | 8.00 | 12.00 |
| | 20:00 | 5.64 | 6.20 | 7.90 | 11.28 | 16.92 |
| | 25:00 | 7.32 | 8.05 | 10.25 | 14.64 | 21.96 |
| | 30:00 | 9.00 | 9.90 | 12.60 | 18.00 | 27.00 |
| | 45:00 | 14.00 | 15.40 | 19.60 | 28.00 | 42.00 |
| | 60:00 | 19.00 | 20.90 | 26.60 | 38.00 | 57.00 |
| 6 mph | 10:00 | 4.00 | 4.40 | 5.60 | 8.00 | |
| | 15:00 | 6.50 | 7.15 | 9.10 | 13.00 | |
| | 20:00 | 9.00 | 9.90 | 12.60 | 18.00 | |
| | 25:00 | 11.50 | 12.65 | 16.10 | 23.00 | |
| | 30:00 | 14.00 | 15.40 | 19.60 | 28.00 | |
| | 45:00 | 21.50 | 23.65 | 30.10 | 43.00 | |
| | 60:00 | 29.00 | 31.90 | 40.60 | 58.00 | |
| 7.5 mph | 10:00 | 6.50 | 7.15 | 9.10 | | |
| | 15:00 | 10.28 | 11.31 | 14.39 | | |
| | 20:00 | 14.00 | 15.40 | 19.60 | | |
| | 25:00 | 17.78 | 19.56 | 24.89 | | |
| | 30:00 | 21.50 | 23.65 | 30.10 | | |
| | 45:00 | 32.75 | 36.02 | 45.85 | | |
| | 60:00 | 44.00 | 48.40 | 61.60 | | |

## WALKING OR RUNNING ONE MILE AT VARIOUS ALTITUDES

| Time (min:sec) Standard | 5,000 Feet | Point Value | 8,000 Feet | 12,000 Feet | Point Value |
|---|---|---|---|---|---|
| 19:59–14:30 | 20:29–15:00 | 1 | 20:59–15:30 | 21:29–16:30 | 1 |
| 14:29–12:00 | 14:59–12:30 | 2 | 15:29–13:00 | 16:29–14:00 | 2 |
| 11:59–10:00 | 12:29–10:30 | 3 | 12:59–11:00 | 13:59–12:00 | 3 |
| 9:59– 8:00 | 10:29– 8:30 | 4 | 10:59– 9:00 | 11:59–10:00 | 4 |
| 7:59– 6:30 | 8:29– 7:00 | 5 | 8:59– 7:30 | 9:59– 8:30 | 5 |
| under 6:30 | under 7:00 | 6 | under 7:30 | under 8:30 | 6 |

## CIRCUIT WEIGHT TRAINING

| Time (min:sec) | Point Value |
|---|---|
| 5:00 | .84 |
| 10:00 | 1.68 |
| 15:00 | 2.52 |
| 20:00 | 3.36 |
| 25:00 | 4.20 |
| 30:00 | 5.04 |
| 35:00 | 5.88 |
| 40:00 | 6.72 |
| 45:00 | 7.56 |
| 50:00 | 8.40 |
| 55:00 | 9.23 |
| 60:00 | 10.07 |

## SUPER CIRCUIT WEIGHT TRAINING

| Time (min:sec) | Point Value |
|---|---|
| 5:00 | 1.30 |
| 10:00 | 2.60 |
| 15:00 | 3.90 |
| 20:00 | 5.21 |
| 25:00 | 6.51 |
| 30:00 | 7.82 |
| 35:00 | 9.12 |
| 40:00 | 10.42 |
| 45:00 | 11.72 |

## MINITRAMPOLINE

| Time (min:sec) | Point Value |
|---|---|
| 5:00 | 1.25 |
| 10:00 | 2.50 |
| 15:00 | 3.75 |
| 20:00 | 5.00 |
| 25:00 | 6.25 |
| 30:00 | 7.50 |
| 35:00 | 8.75 |
| 40:00 | 10.00 |
| 45:00 | 11.25 |
| 50:00 | 12.50 |
| 55:00 | 13.75 |
| 60:00 | 15.00 |

## AEROBIC DANCING AND OTHER EXERCISE PROGRAMS CONDUCTED TO MUSIC

| Time (min:sec) | Point Value |
|---|---|
| 5:00 | 1.0 |
| 10:00 | 2.0 |
| 15:00 | 3.0 |
| 20:00 | 4.0 |
| 25:00 | 5.0 |
| 30:00 | 6.0 |
| 35:00 | 7.0 |
| 40:00 | 8.0 |
| 45:00 | 9.0 |
| 50:00 | 10.0 |
| 55:00 | 11.0 |
| 60:00 | 12.0 |

# Index

## B



## C

## P

**Z**